COST ACCOUNTING

COST ACCOUNTING

Analysis and Control

W. ARMAND LAYNE
Lecturer in Accounting, Cave Hill Campus, University of the West Indies

with contributions from

COLIN RICKWOOD
Lecturer in Accounting, University of Birmingham, England

MACMILLAN

© Dr W. Armand Layne and Mr Colin Rickwood 1984

All rights reserved. No part of this publication may be reproduced or transmitted, in any form or by any means, without permission

First published 1984 by
Higher and Further Education Division
MACMILLAN PUBLISHERS LTD
Houndmills, Basingstoke,
Hampshire RG21 2XS
and London
Companies and representatives
throughout the world

British Library Cataloguing in Publication Data
Layne, W. Armand
Cost accounting.
1. Cost accounting
I. Title II. Rickwood, Colin
657'.42   HF 5686.C8
ISBN 978-0-333-36070-5   ISBN 978-1-349-17691-5 (eBook)
DOI 10.1007/978-1-349-17691-5

To Professor Trevor E. Gambling

Contents

Preface   xv

1 Introduction to Cost Accounting   1
1.1 Nature of cost accounting   1
1.2 Definition of a firm   1
1.3 Rationale for existence of the firm   2
1.4 The organisation chart   2
1.5 Purpose of cost accounting   3
1.6 Objectives of the firm   4
1.7 Cost terminology   5
1.8 Direct and indirect cost   6
1.9 Elements of cost   6
1.10 Historical cost and standard cost   6
1.11 Absorption costing and marginal costing   7
1.12 Scope of cost accounting   7
1.13 Tools of cost accounting   7
1.14 Summary   8
      Bibliography   8
      Discussion questions   9

2 Material Control and Costing Methods   10
2.1 Introduction   10
2.2 Material control   10
2.3 Pricing issues   13
2.4 Evaluation of issue pricing methods   17
2.5 Summary   18
     Bibliography   19
     Discussion questions   19
     Problems   19

2* Introduction to Matrices   21
2*.1 Introduction   21
2*.2 Matrix definition   21
2*.3 Vectors   22
2*.4 Arithmetic operations on vectors   23

2*.5 Subtraction of matrices 24
2*.6 Matrix multiplication 24
2*.7 Special features of multiplication 26
2*.8 Transpose of a matrix 26
2*.9 Identity matrix 27
2*.10 Determinant of a matrix 27
2*.11 Matrix inversion 28
2*.12 Equation system and inverse system compared 30
2*.13 Summary 31
Appendix 32
Bibliography 34
Problems 34

3 Direct Materials, Direct Labour, the Mechanics of Cost Allocation and Overhead Analysis 38

3.1 Introduction 38
3.2 Direct materials 38
3.3 Direct labour 39
3.4 Labour remuneration 40
3.5 Direct expenses 42
3.6 Overheads 42
3.7 Purpose of overhead rates 42
3.8 Process of accumulating overhead cost 43
3.9 Apportionment 44
3.10 Cost allocation 46
3.11 Purpose of cost allocation 47
3.12 Use of multiple overhead rates 47
3.13 Overhead absorption rate 48
3.14 Arguments for and against absorption bases 50
3.15 Predetermined overhead absorption rate (POHR) 51
3.16 Absorption costing and direct costing 52
3.17 Summary 53
Bibliography 53
Problems 54

4 Job Costing, Unit Costing, Process Costing and Joint Product Costing – 'The Quartet' 57

4.1 Introduction 57
4.2 Job costing 57
4.3 Job order cost system 58
4.4 Mechanics of job order system 58
4.5 Applying overhead to individual jobs 61
4.6 Use of direct, absorption or standard costing in job costing 61
4.7 Reports on completed jobs 64
4.8 Evaluation of job costing 64
4.9 Process costing 64
4.10 Functions of process costing 65
4.11 Procedures of process cost accounting 65
4.12 Concept of equivalent production 69

Contents

4.13 Concept of losses in production   73
4.14 Application of standards to process costing   76
4.15 Summary of job costing and process costing   78
4.16 Joint product costing   78
4.17 Reasons for costing joint products   79
4.18 Joint products and decision-making   82
4.19 By-products   83
4.20 By-product costing   84
4.21 Summary   85
     Appendix   86
     Bibliography   89
     Problems   89

5 Service Cost Allocation to Production Departments   97
5.1 Introduction   97
5.2 Methods of distributing service department expense   97
5.3 Extension of cost allocation via linear programming   103
5.4 Summary   105
    Bibliography   106
    Problems   106

6 Inventory Planning   109
6.1 Introduction   109
6.2 Inventory definitions   110
6.3 Cost associated with inventories   111
6.4 Derivation of EOQ model   111
6.5 EOQ and quantity discounts   114
6.6 Production runs   115
6.7 Inventory planning under probabilistic demand   117
6.8 Summary   119
    Bibliography   119
    Problems   119

7 Analysis of Cost Behaviour   124
7.1 Introduction   124
7.2 Patterns of typical cost functions   124
7.3 Step costs   126
7.4 Fixed costs   126
7.5 Semi-variable cost   127
7.6 The learning curve   129
7.7 Summary   133
    Bibliography   133
    Problems   133

8 Cost Estimation   136
8.1 Introduction   136
8.2 Total cost function of firm   136
8.3 Engineering approach   137
8.4 Account analysis method   137

8.5 Derivation of accountant's cost function   138
8.6 High–low method   138
8.7 Scatter charts   139
8.8 Regression analysis   140
8.9 Simple regression   141
8.10 Standard error   144
8.11 Further insights into regression theory   145
8.12 Derivation and use of variance/covariance matrix   146
8.13 Analysis of variance and the F test   147
8.14 Summary   147
    Bibliography   148
    Problems   148

9 Cost–Volume–Profit (C–V–P) Analysis   150
9.1 Introduction   150
9.2 Assumptions of accountant's break-even model   151
9.3 Marginal contribution to sales ratio (MCSR)   152
9.4 Variable cost ratio (VCR)   153
9.5 The multi-product case   153
9.6 Accountant's representation of break-even models   155
9.7 Utility of break-even analysis   156
9.8 Extension of break-even analysis   157
9.9 Short period economic model   159
9.10 Features of accountant's and economist's graph   160
9.11 Summary   162
    Bibliography   162
    Problems   162

10 Relevant Costs for Decisions   169
10.1 Introduction   169
10.2 Accept or reject decisions   169
10.3 Differential cost   169
10.4 Make or buy decisions   170
10.5 Mutually exclusive opportunities   170
10.6 Ranking decisions   170
10.7 Decisions with one scarce resource   173
10.8 Concept of internal opportunity cost   175
10.9 Relevant cost and book values   176
10.10 Relevance of fixed cost   180
10.11 Summary   180
    Bibliography   180
    Problems   181

11 Direct Costing and Absorption Costing   187
11.1 Introduction   187
11.2 Requirements of decision-maker   187
11.3 Report format   188
11.4 Contribution model   188
11.5 Report structures   188

Contents   xi

11.6   Further insights into contribution models   189
11.7   Inventory valuation   190
11.8   Inventory valuation problems   191
11.9   Direct costing model   192
11.10 Direct and absorption costing   193
11.11 Use of direct costing   194
11.12 Summary   195
       Bibliography   195
       Problems   195

12 Budgetary Planning   198

12.1   Introduction   198
12.2   The budget   198
12.3   Reasons for budgets   199
12.4   Preparation of budgets   199
12.5   Principal budget factor   199
12.6   Sales forecast   200
12.7   Sales budget   200
12.8   Selling and distribution cost budget   200
12.9   Production budget   200
12.10 Raw material purchasing budget   201
12.11 Labour budget   201
12.12 Factory expense budget   201
12.13 Inventory budgets   201
12.14 Capital expenditure budgets   201
12.15 Cash budget   202
12.16 Master budget   202
12.17 Summary   206
       Bibliography   207
       Problems   207

13 Budgetary Control   218

13.1   Introduction   218
13.2   Feedback information   218
13.3   Usefulness of feedback data   219
13.4   Usefulness of variance analysis   219
13.5   Report format of variance analysis   220
13.6   Controllable and uncontrollable cost   220
13.7   Management by exception   220
13.8   Variance analysis   220
13.9   Price and quantity variance   222
13.10 Nature of overhead variance   224
13.11 Variable overhead variance   224
13.12 Absorption of fixed overhead   225
13.13 Fixed overhead variance   225
13.14 Variance calculation by adjusting the budget   225
13.15 Marginal or direct costing method   226
13.16 Rationale of variance calculation   227
13.17 Causes of variance   228

13.18 Evaluation of performance 228
13.19 Human problems of budgetary control 228
13.20 Summary 229
 Bibliography 229
 Discussion questions 230
 Problems 230

14 Standard Costing 233
14.1 Introduction 233
14.2 Types of standard cost 233
14.3 Mechanics of standard costing 234
14.4 The standard hour 234
14.5 Reason for standard costing 234
14.6 Setting of standard cost 235
14.7 Standard direct material cost 235
14.8 Standard direct labour cost 236
14.9 Standard variable overhead cost 236
14.10 Causes of variance from standard 239
14.11 Nature of a flexible budget 240
14.12 Mechanics of a flexible budget 240
14.13 Measurement of activity 241
14.14 Fixed overhead analysis 241
14.15 Application of overhead in standard costing 243
14.16 Fixed overhead variance analysis 244
14.17 Control ratios 246
14.18 Variance analysis in technical firms 248
14.19 Variance analysis and 'blame laying' 250
14.20 Summary 251
 Bibliography 252
 Problems 252

15 Linear Programming and Cost Accounting 257
15.1 Introduction 257
15.2 Assumptions of linear programming 258
15.3 General form of linear programming model 258
15.4 Observations on linear programming solution 260
15.5 Simplex format 260
15.6 Procedures of simplex method 261
15.7 Insights into solution process 263
15.8 Algebraic method 263
15.9 The dual 264
15.10 The dual algorithm 265
15.11 Economic significance of the dual 267
15.12 Sensitivity analysis 267
15.13 Parametric programming 269
15.14 Summary 271
 Bibliography 271
 Problems 271

Contents xiii

16 Capital Budgeting 276
16.1 Introduction 276
16.2 Timing of capital projects 276
16.3 Compound interest 277
16.4 Future value of annuity 279
16.5 Sinking fund payments 280
16.6 Present value 280
16.7 Capital recovery 282
16.8 Summary 282
Bibliography 283
Problems 283

17 Project Financing and the Cost of Capital 284
17.1 Project financing 284
17.2 Cost of capital 284
17.3 The cost of equity 285
17.4 Retained earnings 286
17.5 The cost of debt 286
17.6 Calculating the marginal cost of capital 287
Bibliography 288
Problems 289

18 The Analysis of Capital Investment Decisions 290
18.1 Introduction 290
18.2 Pay-back 290
18.3 Accounting rate of return 293
18.4 Net present value (NPV) 294
18.5 Profitability index (PI) 296
18.6 Internal rate of return (IRR) 297
18.7 Unequal net cash flows 298
18.8 Multiple internal rates of return 299
18.9 Discounted pay-back 301
18.10 Summary 301
Bibliography 302
Problems 302

19 Risk and Uncertainty in Capital Budgeting 308
19.1 Introduction 308
19.2 Definition of risk and uncertainty 308
19.3 Expected value of probability distribution 308
19.4 Absolute measures of dispersion 309
19.5 Decision-maker's utility function 311
19.6 Summary 313
Bibliography 314
Problems 314

Appendix – Present Value Tables 317
Index 329

Preface

This book deals with cost accounting and control. In colleges and universities, the material can be used at the first- and second-year level in management accounting. The book is constructed not only for examination purposes but also to awaken curiosity in the reader for further research into this challenging area of accountancy. In this sense the book can be looked upon as a bridgehead to a broader and a deeper-oriented course.

The material in this book is concerned with quantitative decisionmaking, which involves the use of accounting data that decisionmakers will be called upon to analyse and use dynamically in the firm in resolving business problems. To resolve something, the decisionmaker must operate from a sensible framework and must have the requisite data and decision models from which to evaluate a decision. We therefore introduce the reader, for example, to the purpose of the firm; concepts of cost with its behavioural pattern under various operating conditions; service cost allocation; inventory planning; direct and absorption costing; capital budgeting; and analysis of capital investment decisions. We hope that the reader's analytical skill will be sharpened as he or she works through the examples in the text.

In the relevant chapters of this book can be found mathematical solutions which relate to the problems faced by the modern firm: (i) estimating the cost function; (ii) breakeven analysis; (iii) service cost allocation; (iv) stock control; (v) joint product allocation; (vi) budget construction; (vii) variance analysis; (viii) make or buy, add or drop a product, or replace equipment decisions; (ix) calculation of optimum product mix; (x) investment decisions.

We owe a particular debt to many accounting authors for the ideas contained in this book; the references at the end of each chapter attest to this fact. We must, however, express thanks to Professor T. E. Gambling, University of Birmingham, England, whose ideas were influential long before the book was ever dreamt of, and whose comments on the first draft of this work was encouraging. We also extend a hearty 'thank you' to an unknown professor who read the first draft, and whose comments were invaluable. Of course, for any mistakes which remain in the text, blame us.

We also appreciate the efforts of Monica Smith and Azena Louis, who typed the first draft of this work. The kind acts of Roy Daniel and Nigel Walrond were also appreciated.

In a very special way, Cynthia Layne is thanked for her patience and understanding.

The following accounting bodies, (i) the Association of Certified Accountants (ACA), (ii) the Institute of Cost and Management Accountants (ICMA), and (iii) the Institute of Chartered Accountants in England and Wales (ICA), who gave permission to reproduce their examination questions, are also thanked.

W ARMAND LAYNE
COLIN RICKWOOD

Acknowledgement

The authors and publishers are grateful to Van Nostrand Reinhold (UK) Co. Ltd for permission to reproduce tables from *Management of Company Finance* by J. M. Samuels and F. M. Wilkes.

Chapter 1
Introduction to Cost Accounting

The starting point for any field of study is to set forth its boundaries and determine its objectives.   (Hendriksen, 1970)

1.1 Nature of cost accounting

The phrase 'cost accounting', when used in isolation, is meaningless; the phrase when related to human effort in the firm is given substance. Cost accounting is a conscious and rational procedure by accountants for accumulating cost[1] and relating such costs to specific products or departments for effective management action. Such costs are used in balance sheets and income statements for the purposes of stock valuation and income determination.

1.2 Definition of a firm

A 'firm' is made up of human beings who are organised towards economic objectives. A firm acquires scarce resources from the environment, and utilises such resources for production. By 'production' is meant the transformation of inputs into an output (or outputs) of a distinct, different form; some value should be attached to this output (or outputs) by a particular society. For production to take place, there must also be availability of resources. The inputs into production will generally include raw materials and labour; finance and capital goods are further examples.

---

[1] 'Cost' is not easily defined. The following quotations highlight the meaning of cost: Alchian (1972) states that 'in economics, the cost of an event is the highest valued opportunity necessary forsaken. The usefulness of the concept is a logical implication of choice among available options. Only if no alternative were possible or if amounts of all resources were available beyond everyone's desires, so that all goods were free would the concept of cost and choice be irrelevant.' For accounting, Sprouse and Monnitz (1962) define cost as 'an exchange price, a forgoing, a sacrifice made to secure benefits'.

1.3 Rationale for existence of the firm

Coase (1937) states that a firm emerges because 'there is a cost of using the price mechanism and by forming an organisation and allowing some authority to an entrepreneur, to direct the resources, certain market costs are saved'. Alchian and Demsetz (1972) see the firm as existing because team output is higher than individual output, so that it is worth employing non-market means to control the work of individuals.

Coupled with existence is uncertainty. According to Knight (1921) 'the system under which the confident and venturesome assume the risk to ensure the doubtful and timid by guaranteeing to the latter a specified income in return for an assignment of the actual results . . . is the enterprise and wage system of industry'. Modern technology also makes the existence of the firm imperative. This also gives purpose to cost analysis, which has both control and planning features.

An important feature from an accounting viewpoint is the firm's measurement and allocation problem, which it must solve perennially in order to safeguard its existence. If the firm fails to cost its products correctly; if labour costs are negatively correlated with labour's productivity; then the firm will eventually cease to exist.

1.4 The organisation chart

The typical, static, organisation chart of a firm shows the principal management positions. The chart is made up of hierarchical structures, and helps to define authority, responsibility and accountability.

An organisational chart is essential to the development of a cost system and cost reports. The segmentation of the firm into cost units or cost centres draws top management's attention to the success (or failure) of the individuals who are in charge of such units. Figure 1.1 shows an organisation chart based on the line–staff concept. Two classes of functions are involved in the line–staff concept – the line and the staff function. The line function has direct responsibility for accomplishing the objectives of the firm; the staff function helps the line function in accomplishing those objectives. Production and sales are classified as line functions and at times it is also appropriate to include the finance function; purchasing, accounting, personnel, plant and quality control are classified as staff functions.

The chart is valuable when a firm's product lines are simple and not subject to frequent change. The philosophy underlying the chart is that all functional divisions can be classified into line and staff functions.[1] The line makes decisions; the staff gives advice, or performs any technical activities.

The completion of an organisation task depends on the effective, interrelated performances of the whole organisation, Figure 1.2 shows an organisation chart based on the functional teamwork concept of management. This concept places emphasis on the important functions of a firm, it shows that (i) business functions are grouped around resources, processes and human interrelations; (ii) the resources function involves the acquisition, disposal and the husbanding of tangible and (intangible) human (and physical) assets; (iii) the process function deals with activities – product design, advertising, purchasing, manufacturing, research and development and accounting; (iv) the human interrelations function directs the firm's efforts towards the behaviour of people inside and outside the organisation.

---

[1] See Fisch (1961), who argues that the line–staff relationship is obsolete.

Introduction to Cost Accounting 3

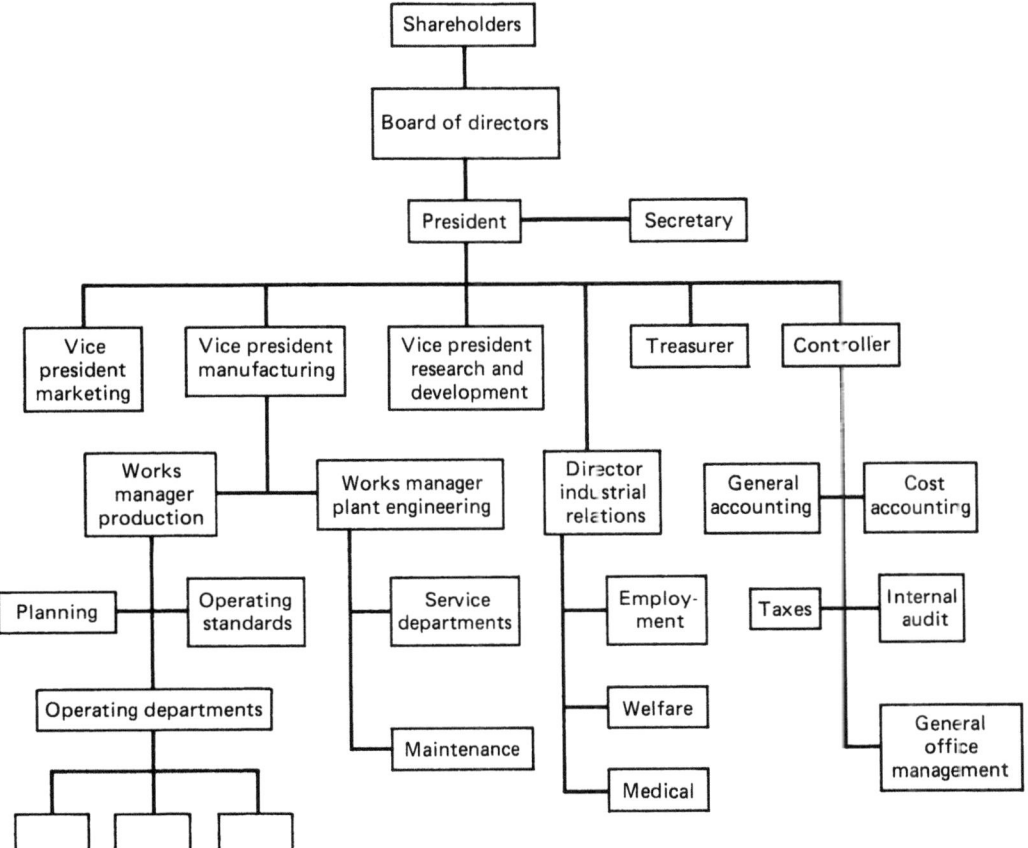

Figure 1.1 Organisation chart based on line–staff concept

1.5 Purpose of cost accounting

In providing data for management action, cost accounting considers three, major areas: (i) planning; (ii) decision accounting; (iii) control accounting.

'Planning' is the process of setting out programmes of activities which are desirable to the extent that they satisfy the objectives of the firm: planning provides the foundation upon which the control function operates. 'Control' involves those functions which direct and check to ensure that people's activities are satisfying the objectives of the firm, – and in particular that the activities are consistent with the budgets and plans. Effective planning, however, is based on collected and analysed facts. Planning is future oriented, it tries to ensure the firm's continuity.[1]

'Decision accounting' is concerned with the evaluation of alternative courses of action. The decision may entail commitments to long-term horizons (for example, to invest in new productive equipment) or affect only the short term (for example, to accept or to reject an order). Other types of decisions are: (i) whether to stop manufacturing a product; (ii) how to

---

[1] An important assumption of the accounting function.

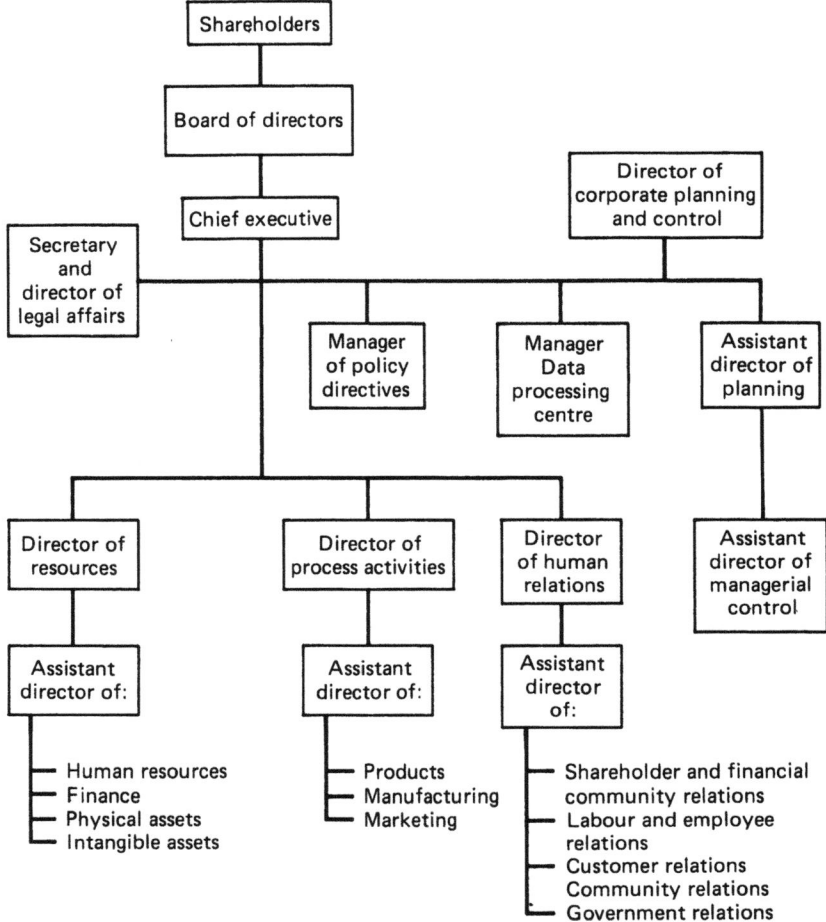

Figure 1.2 Organisation chart based on functional teamwork concept

determine the optimum output level of a product; (iii) the determination of a product's selling price.

Control accounting is concerned with analysing costs incurred, and hence with guiding the internal operations of the firm towards achievement of its plans and objectives; control is essential to planning. Control implies that the firm's budgeting plans[1] can be achieved by management through directing the human elements of the organisation towards effective coordination of effort. Control accounting also assumes that the predetermined plans of management are viable in the economic and political environment.

1.6 Objectives of the firm

A firm cannot function without manpower and money. These two factors are the operational and economic axes on which the organisation is founded. Such axes impose constraints on the

[1] Budgetary planning is the subject of Ch. 12.

Introduction to Cost Accounting 5

business objectives, and hence become instrumental in the determination of objectives.

An objective can be formulated only in relation to a purpose. What objective does the firm pursue? Neoclassical economic theory assumes profit maximisation, but that assumption is not the only objective of the modern firm. Modern behavioural theories of the firm (Baumol (1967), Marris (1964), Simon (1959), Williamson (1966)) posit that management may have other objectives:

(i) discretionary profits
(ii) long-run growth
(iii) maximisation of sales revenue, subject to a minimum profit constraint
(iv) satisficing

These theories are important in that they show the implications for the theory of the firm when the problems of decision making and of motivation are brought into the analysis. However, all such theories must be subjected to detailed empirical testing in order to command validity. We therefore posit that the management of a firm try simply to make shareholders 'happy', by showing adequate profit[1] in its published financial statements. This concept is bound up with a learning process, which involves two basic principles: (i) positive sensations are to be repeated; (ii) negative sensations are to be avoided by any means, if a repetition threatens to occur in the future. These principles are both linked to the budget. From the budget, the managers know what is expected and possible, and so can pursue policies that improve goal fulfilment over time. Another feature of importance is that the mathematical techniques and their solutions via the computer now available to managers will enable sound decisions to be made which in effect will create the opportunities for the maintenance of adequate profits.

It is a fact that the participants who make up the organisation may have different goals, which may conflict with the organisation's own aims. Conflict is inherent in instrumental organisations[2] such as manufacturing firms. Thus an important function of management – and the cost accountant in particular – is to harmonise as far as practical the goals of the participants and sub-units with those of the organisation as a whole.

1.7 Cost terminology

Variable and fixed costs

Accountants classify cost by behaviour. Variable and fixed cost is defined in terms of how a total cost changes in relation to fluctuations in the level of output. If the total cost changes directly in proportion to changes in the level of output, it is variable; a cost that remains unchanged in total, in spite of wide fluctuations in the level of output, is called a fixed cost.

Cost unit and cost centres

A cost unit is a unit of product to which costs can be related. The nature of the cost unit depends on the type of goods produced by the firm; cars and job contracts are examples of cost units.

---

[1] 'Adequate profit' can be defined as that profit figure, calculated before tax, which shows a reasonable return on capital employed, when compared with the returns of other firms in the same industry.

[2] A clear insight into this type of organisation is seen when it is compared with the normative organisation (for example, the church) or with the coercive organisation (for example, prison, slavery). Ch. 12 explains in greater detail what is meant by this type of organisation.

The costs which arise within a firm are not incurred by individual cost units, but by sections to which cost can be related. Typical cost centres are: (i) productive cost; (ii) service cost; (iii) administrative or selling cost.

1.8 Direct and indirect cost

A direct cost arises because of the capacity of that cost to be traced to a cost unit. Direct material and direct labour are two common classifications; they can be directly associated with the cost unit and in addition can be linked to a cost centre.

An indirect cost is one which does not arise because of the existence of a cost object. This means that the cost is shared by more than one cost unit or centre. A department's supervisory salary is a direct cost if the department is costed, but an indirect cost in terms of any particular unit of production.

1.9 Elements of cost

'Production creation' implies that production passes through stages. Accountants can therefore speak of the 'stages of production' and, hence, the elements of cost. The cost elements which go into the making and selling of a product are:

 (i) Direct materials
 (ii) Direct labour
 (iii) Direct expenses
 (iv) Indirect factory costs
 (v) Administration
 (vi) Selling
 (vii) Distribution

1.10 Historical cost and standard cost

'Historical cost' refers to the past monetary transactions engaged in by a firm and its business environment. The firm is generally engaged in transactions such as the acquisition of assets, goods or services. The moot point of historical cost, however, is that the cash receipts or cash payments entered in the firm's accounts are not adjusted for any change in the level of prices generally, or the specific price of the commodity in question. Historical cost, because it is a sunk cost, is not as important as standard cost in costing evaluations.

Modern business competition makes it imperative for the management of the firm to exercise cost control. To control cost involves the predetermination of cost, and the comparison of predetermined budgeted or standard cost with actual cost, i.e. the cost which has occurred within the firm. Standard cost, which is closely linked with the budget, is predetermined per unit cost, usually analysed into elements – direct material, direct labour, and factory overhead. Standard cost is established in many ways, the major data coming from that accumulated from past experience and from research studies. Standard cost is an effective aid to control, due to the

Introduction to Cost Accounting

link with budgets or plans, and to decisionmaking because it represents anticipated cost i.e. a cost which will exist in the future and is likely to be affected by decisions, made by management.

1.11 Absorption costing and marginal costing

Absorption costing is based on the premise that the normal costs of running a firm should be charged to the individual cost units in order to ascertain the total cost of each unit. By such an exercise, the cost units absorb the total costs. The product units are thus charged not only with direct cost, but also with a fair share of the overhead cost.

The marginal costing concept is based on the principle that each cost unit should be charged only with those costs which it exclusively caused to be incurred, this method is also known as direct costing or variable costing.

1.12 Scope of cost accounting

Cost accounting was once considered applicable only to manufacturing operations.[1] In today's economy, this idea is invalid. It is invalid because monetary values are the bases from which cost judgements are made. Cost accounting is therefore applicable to non-manufacturing activities of manufacturing firms, wholesale and retail businesses, banks, insurance companies, schools, colleges and universities, airlines, bus companies, shipping companies, governmental units, hospitals, churches, legal offices and households. Specific costing techniques may be required for the costing of non-manufacturing operations, but there is no doubt that cost accounting will aid the decision function in such organisations.

1.13 Tools of cost accounting

Economic decisions can be made from qualitative models. But for the management of a complex organisation to arrive at decisions without the aid of quantitative analysis, is to invite a problem. Questions such as: (i) what sales volume is required to produce a certain desired profit? (ii) what profit can be expected from a given level of sales? cannot be answered adequately except by quantitative analysis.

Cost accounting is a measurement process. By 'measurement' is meant the assignment of numbers to objects. The numbers assigned to objects are monetary values.[2] The monetary value is the unit of account which facilitates exchanges in a market economy.

The natural numbers, 1, 2, 3 . . . are abstract symbols for indicating how many objects there are in a set of discrete elements.[3] The laws by which the symbols are combined to yield other natural numbers are: (i) commutative laws; (ii) associative laws; (iii) distributive laws; and (iv) cancellation laws.

---

[1] The examples found in this book centre round manufacturing operations.
[2] The numbers can also be, e.g. lb, kg, tons, m or y. These can, however, be converted into monetary values simply by multiplying the amount by dollar values.
[3] Note also that the information coming into (and flowing out of) the firm is discrete in nature.

Within the set of natural numbers, inverse operations, subtractions and divisions are not always possible. To make those operations possible, the number 0 and negative integers are used. The totality of all those numbers is called the set of natural numbers; such numbers are obtained from unity by using the rational operations of calculation – addition, subtraction and division – except division by 0. The planning aspects of cost accounting utilise those concepts because the primitives of cost and management accounting analysis are recording, classification and evaluation.

The concepts of any measurement system are mathematical, thus mathematical tools[1] – calculi both finite and infinite, graph theory and network analysis, matrix algebra and statistics – are all useful to management decisionmaking. The choice of mathematical tool applicable to the solution process of the firm's activities depends upon (i) the state of management's current knowledge; (ii) management's search propensities; and (iii) the cost of using the tool in relation to the beneficial results of the activities being evaluated. Analytical tools, however, aid present and anticipatory management decisions. They also determine management's adaptive choices in the market economy.

1.14 Summary

In this chapter, it was stated that cost accounting data affect the firm's financial statements. Cost accounting is related to production, it is useful to managerial decisions in complex organisations. The organisation chart also aids the costing system. Cost accounting provides data to management for planning and control. It was posited that an objective of the firm is to make shareholders 'happy'. The terminology of cost accounting – variable and fixed cost, cost unit, cost centre and direct and indirect cost – was considered. The cost elements which go into production were demonstrated. Also historical cost and standard cost, absorption costing and marginal costing were defined and the scope of cost accounting considered. The concept of measurement in cost accounting was taken to include the employment of mathematical principles which facilitate managerial decisionmaking.

Bibliography

Alchian, A. A. (1968) 'Cost' in David L. Gill (ed.) *International Encyclopedia of the Social Sciences*, vol. 3, (Macmillan and Free Press) p. 404.
Alchian, A. A. and Demsetz, H. (1972) 'Production, Information Costs and Economic Organisation', *American Economic Review*, 62, December, pp. 777–95.
Baumol, W. J. (1967) *Business Behaviour, Value and Growth* (Harcourt, Brace & World).
Coase, R. H. (1937) 'The Nature of the Firm', *Economica*, vol. 4, November, pp. 386–405.
Fisch, G. G. (1961) 'Line Staff is Obsolete', *Harvard Business Review*, vol. 39, no. 5, pp. 67–79.
Hendriksen, E. S. (1970) *Accounting Theory* (Richard D. Irwin).
Knight, F. H. (1921) *Risk, Uncertainty and Profit* (Houghton Mifflin) pp. 269–71.
Marris, R. L. (1964) *Economic Theory of Managerial Capitalism* (Macmillan).
Simon, H. A. (1959) 'Theories of Decision Making in Economics and Behavioural Science', *American Economic Review*, 69, pp. 253–80.
Sprouse, R. T. and Moonitz, M. (1962) 'A Tentative Set of Broad Accounting Principles for Business Enterprises', *Accounting Research* Study, no. 3, (American Institute of Certified Public Accountants).
Williamson, J. H. (1966) 'Profits, Growth and Sales Maximisation', *Economica*, vol. 33, February, pp. 1–16.

---

[1] It could be stated also that any future mathematical discoveries will be beneficial to accounting, since it is a dynamic subject.

Introduction to Cost Accounting

Discussion questions

1.1 What do you understand by the term 'cost accounting'?

1.2 What are the reasons for the existence of the firm?

1.3 What is an organisational chart? How is it useful to the firm?

1.4 Explain the purposes of (i) planning, (ii) decision accounting, and (iii) control accounting in the firm.

1.5 Is profit maximisation the only theory of the firm?

1.6 Explain: (a) variable and fixed costs, (b) cost unit and cost centres, (c) direct and indirect cost.

1.7 List the cost elements which go into the making and selling of a product.

1.8 Briefly explain what is meant by 'historical cost' and 'standard cost', 'absorption costing' and 'marginal costing'.

1.9 Why is a measurement process of importance to cost accounting?

Chapter 2
Material Control and Costing Methods

The ascertainment of cost is therefore fundamental to inventory valuation except for those items which are capable of being disposed of outside the business with no effect on the continuity of operations. (Most, 1967)

2.1 Introduction

Costing methods are the ways by which certain managerial calculations are likely to be employed in the firm concerning material issues to the production process. That aspect is examined in 2.3 below. It is important, however, to show first how the raw materials used in the production process are controlled in the firm. That aspect is now examined.

2.2 Material control

Material control involves the following procedures:
 (i) Purchasing
 (ii) Reception
 (iii) Storage
 (iv) Stock control
 (v) Issue to production

Purchasing

The material procurement function is the responsibility of the central purchasing department. The department should have the records of the firm's suppliers, together with some knowledge about their reliability. It should also have a knowledge of the standards and prices of the raw materials which the firm wants to utilise.

Material Control and Costing Methods

For effective planning within the firm, the purchasing department's activities should be co-ordinated with the production plans of the firm. Production planning means not only decisions as to the effective mix of input factors which may produce the output at the least cost, but also decisions made about the supply of adequate quantities of the firm's raw materials from external sources. The timely supply and arrival of the firm's raw materials facilitates the production process.

Production planning can be a centralised or a decentralised way of doing things. Centralised production implies that all the production decisions of a firm and its subsidiaries are made at the firm's headquarters. Decentralised production implies that other departments of the firm, including its subsidiaries, have autonomy, which allows them to make input decisions regarding production. Investment decisions can also be made by the divisional departments of a decentralised firm. In a decentralised firm, a foreman can initiate a purchase order; such an act would not be allowed in a centralised firm.

In general, however, the routine purchasing stages are:

(i) purchasing department seeks out and selects a supplier and issues a purchase order, specifying quantity, quality, delivery date and price
(ii) purchasing department follows the progress of each order and when the occasion arises, asks the supplier to guarantee prompt delivery

Reception

The receipt of materials is recorded on a goods received note. The stores receives one copy with the materials; another copy goes to the accounts department for the purpose of verifying the invoice, when it is received.

The delivery note, when received, may be used to update the stores ledger. It is also sent to the wages office, where it acts as a verifier against the purchase order. In this sense, it also forms the basis for the payment for the goods by the firm.

Underlying the concept of reception is the concept of observation. To observe means to record, to note and to classify. The details of observation can thus be included on the goods received note.

Storage

Effective storage of materials is vital to the firm. It is also important that the stores be well planned and laid out. Bin cards are generally employed to enable the storekeepers to ascertain the stock levels, the bin cards showing quantities received, issued and the quantities on hand for each item in store. Figure 2.1 shows a typical layout of a bin card, which is concerned only with quantities.

Stock control

The management of any firm should devote adequate time and consideration to the stock levels which are to be maintained; this should be applied to:

(i) Bought in components
(ii) Finished goods

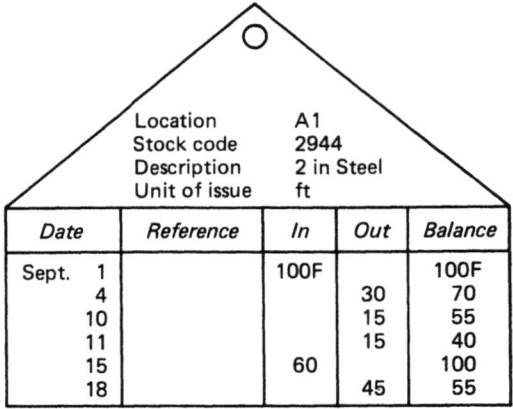

Figure 2.1 Bin card

(iii) Raw materials
(iv) Work-in-progress

Of crucial importance is the problem of over stocking. Over stocking will result in valuable working capital being tied up unnecessarily. But understocking will cause production stoppage, underrecovery of fixed overheads, and loss of current (as well as future) orders. Decisions on stock holding must be influenced by:

(i) cash availability and procurement cost
(ii) storage space availability
(iii) storage cost, premises costs, insurance of stocks and interest on capital invested in stocks
(iv) delivery delays
(v) risk of stock losses
(vi) minimum ordering quantities imposed by suppliers

The physical side of stock control is aided by the use of control levels, which show whether sufficient quantities of stocks are held. The levels below should be determined for each item of stock:

(i) Maximum
(ii) Minimum
(iii) Re-order

These levels are generally based on the normal rates of consumption, the anticipated delivery period, and the economic order quantity (EOQ).[1] Implicit in every level is a control aspect. (i) implies that a form of management control exists against excessive ordering of materials, and (ii) that a safety margin is in operation, i.e. a certain level beyond which stocks should not fall; (iii) takes account of usage during delivery delays. Associated with this is the perpetual inventory system.[2]

[1] See Ch. 6 for further details.
[2] A perpetual inventory system is one where the management function can determine the physical stock levels at any time from the perpetual inventory records. The computer is tailor made for this kind of operation – it can give a daily stock check which ensures that theoretical and physical values are in agreement. Periodic physical counts are necessary by management to discover (and to eliminate) discrepancies between the actual count and the balances on the material ledger cards. Discrepancies include mistakes in costing requisitions, errors in transferring invoice data to cards, spoilage and theft.

Material Control and Costing Methods 13

Issue to production

Materials used by the processing units of a firm are issued from the stores against a material requisition form, which specifies the material required and the use to which it may be put. In a similar way, the production planning section may issue a bill of materials which states the material requirements for a complete job (or batch of jobs).

The material requisition forms the basis for updating the stores ledger and the individual jobs. Figure 2.2 illustrates a typical material requisition form.

MATERIAL REQUISITION		Serial No. _____		
Charged to job overhead code				
Stock	Description	Quan-tity	Price	Amount
				$
Issued by:	Authorised by: Department:		Date:	

Figure 2.2 **Material requisition form**

2.3 Pricing issues

A problem which arises with issues to production is the price at which to charge individual issues.

The bases for pricing material issues include:

(i) FIFO, (i.e., First In, First Out)
(ii) LIFO (i.e., Last In, First Out)
(iii) Standard price
(iv) Weighted average cost

It is important to note that (i), (ii) and (iv) are actual costs.

The computational procedures for the pricing of issues by each of the four methods will be shown via matrices. For those students not acquainted with matrices, ch. 2* shows the basic principles of matrices and their application to some typical industrial problems.

EXAMPLE 2.1

Assume that the material stock movements of part A001 shown below took place in Andy Ltd during December 19X1.

Data	Reference	Units purchased	Price	Units issued	Market price
			$		$
1	GRN 125	400	25.00		15.00
5	GRN 171	200	15.50		15.50
7	MR 215			400	15.50
9	MR 227			10	15.75
12	GRN 185	300	15.80		15.80
14	MR 242			100	15.80
15	MR 249			75	15.80
24	GRN 189	400	15.90		15.90
26	MR 255			365	15.90

REQUIRED

Compute the prices at which the issues will be charged out using the four methods listed above. Assume that the standard price was $15.50. RN and MR are respectively goods received note and material received note. To solve the problem via matrices requires basic definitions:

Let a = receipt quantity vector
b = procurement price vector
c = issues quantity vector
d = issues price vector
d^* = market price vector
dl = Vector which contains LIFO dollar values
dl^* = Vector which contains LIFO price values for calculation of ending values
ds = Vector which contains standard prices
IU = Vector which contains split-up of ending balances
U = Unit vectors
V = Variance vector
W = Vector which contains the weighted average price per unit

SOLUTION

FIFO method
Units purchased are:

$$Ua' = e = [1,1,1,1] \begin{bmatrix} 400 \\ 200 \\ 300 \\ 400 \end{bmatrix} = 1300.$$

Physical quantity issues are:

$$Uc = f = [1,1,1,1,1,1] \begin{bmatrix} 400 \\ 100 \\ 100 \\ 75 \\ 225 \\ 140 \end{bmatrix} = 1\,040$$

Physical units on hand are:

$[e - f] = 260$

Units purchased in dollar values are:

$$da' = H = \$[5, 15.50, 15.80, 15.90] \begin{bmatrix} 400 \\ 200 \\ 300 \\ 400 \end{bmatrix} = \$20\,200$$

Material Control and Costing Methods

Issues in dollar values are:

$$d^*c' = k = \$[15, 15.50, 15.50, 15.80, 15.80, 15.90] \begin{bmatrix} 400 \\ 100 \\ 100 \\ 75 \\ 225 \\ 140 \end{bmatrix} = \$16\,066$$

Material dollar values on hand are:

$$[h-k] = \$[20\,200 - 16\,060] = \$4\,134$$

Check calculation:

$$260 \times \$15.90 = \$4\,134.$$

COMMENT

The FIFO method assumes that the materials are issued to production in the order in which they are received. The stock valuation is based on the historic cost of the most recently acquired item. The dollar values charged to production will therefore lag behind the current values when prices are rising.

SOLUTION

LIFO method

The units purchased, the physical quantities and the physical units on hand are:

$$e = 1\,300, f = 1\,040, \text{ and } [e-f] = 260$$

The issues to production are:

$$d/a' = p = \$[15.50, 15, 15, 15.80, 15.80, 15.90] \begin{bmatrix} 200 \\ 200 \\ 100 \\ 100 \\ 75 \\ 365 \end{bmatrix} = \$16\,168.5$$

The values of the materials on hand are:

$$d/^* M' = N = \$[15.90, 15.80, 15] \begin{array}{c} 35 \\ 125 \\ 100 \end{array} = \$4\,031.5$$

Check calculation

$$\$20\,200 = \$[16\,168.5 + 4\,031.5]$$

COMMENT

The LIFO method attempts to keep the values of issues to production close to current economic, monetary values. The stock valuation relates to the earliest units to be taken into stock, which results in a low stock valuation and an associated low profit figure. This example highlights overstocking, with the result that some issues are valued at out of date prices. The occurrence of this problem depends on the rate of stock turnover.

SOLUTION

Standard price method

The standard price was $15.50. The units purchased in dollar values are:

$$dsa' = q = \$[15.50, 15.50, 15.50, 15.50] \begin{bmatrix} 400 \\ 200 \\ 300 \\ 400 \end{bmatrix} = \$20\,150$$

The issued units in dollar values are:

$$dsIU = R = \$[15.50, 15.50, 15.50, 15.50, 15.50] \begin{bmatrix} 400 \\ 100 \\ 100 \\ 75 \\ 365 \end{bmatrix} = \$16\,120$$

The dollar values of the units on hand are:

$$[q - R] = \$[20\,150 - 16\,120] = \$4\,030$$

Check calculation:

$$260 \times \$15.50 = \$4\,030$$

The units purchased amounted to $H = \$20\,200$.

$H \neq q$. It follows that a material price variance[1] has occurred.

The difference between $[H - q]$, i.e. $\$[20\,200 - 20\,150] = \$50$ is the composite material price variance.[2] The finer parts of the material price variance can be derived as follows:

Let SP = Standard price
AP = Actual price
MPV = Material price variance

Then

$$\begin{matrix} SP & & AP & & MPV \\ \begin{bmatrix} 15.50 \\ 15.50 \\ 15.50 \\ 15.50 \end{bmatrix} & - & \begin{bmatrix} 15.00 \\ 15.50 \\ 15.80 \\ 15.90 \end{bmatrix} & = & \begin{bmatrix} 0.50 \\ 0.00 \\ -0.30 \\ -0.40 \end{bmatrix} \end{matrix}$$

and,

$$MPV' a = v = [0.50, 0.00, -0.30, -0.40] \begin{bmatrix} 400 & & & 0 \\ & 200 & & \\ & & 300 & \\ 0 & & & 400 \end{bmatrix}$$

where a_* is a diagonal matrix

$$v = [200, 0, -90, -160]$$

$[v]$ contains both positive and negative elements, which represent favourable and unfavourable variances. $[v]$ also shows the time occurrence of the variances. Summing the elements of $[v]$ gives also the composite, unfavourable variance of $\$50^{(U)}$.

COMMENT

The standard price method uses an expected purchase price as a standard. If the purchases are made at other than the standard price, the difference will be shown as a material price variance, which will be written off in the monthly profit and loss account.

SOLUTION

Weighted average method
The issue prices per unit are:

---

[1] Variance analysis is further discussed in Chs 13, 14.
[2] Moore and Jaedicke (1976) maintain that 'standard conditions can be built into the computer programme that controls the manufacturing process'.

Jan
1: $\dfrac{(400 \times \$15) + (200 \times \$15.50)}{600} = \$15.1667$ per unit

12: $\dfrac{(100 \times \$15.1667) + (300 \times \$15.80)}{400} = \$15.6417$

24: $\dfrac{(225 \times \$15.6417) + (400 \times \$15.90)}{625} = \$15.8070$

The issues in dollar values are:

$$wc' = w = \$[15.1667, 15.1667, 15.6417, 15.6417, 15.8070] \begin{bmatrix} 400 \\ 100 \\ 100 \\ 75 \\ 365 \end{bmatrix} = \$16\,090$$

The balance on hand is:

$[H - w] = \$[20\,200 - 16\,090] = \$4\,110$

Check calculation:

$260 \times \$15.8070 = \$4\,110$

The collected results are:

Method	Amount charged to production	Value of closing stock
	$	$
FIFO	16 066	4 134
LIFO	16 168.5	4 031.5
Standard price	16 120	4 030
Weighted average cost	16 090	4 110

2.4 Evaluation of issue pricing methods

It is important to note that the inventories in physical units can be divided into a part which is necessary for current production operations and a surplus part, which is not necessary to that operation. Inventory valuation thus serves periodic accounting. The methods used assume that the physical flows issued to production match cost flows. Advantages and disadvantages result from the use of the various methods.

FIFO's advantages are:

(i) valuation of the material remaining in stock is based on the most current purchases
(ii) the method is most compatible with the ideas of historic cost accounting, i.e. charging to the profit and loss account the historic cost of items acquired first

FIFO's disadvantages are:

(i) the method is problem-ridden if the purchases are made at different prices, and if several purchases are on hand simultaneously
(ii) costing difficulties also occur when returns to the vendors or to the stockroom are made

LIFO's advantages are:

(i) it provides a tax shelter for firms, if the method is allowed for tax purpose, and if stocks are rising
(ii) the tax deferral creates additional working capital
(iii) materials consumed are priced in a sensible way, i.e. the most recent cost is charged against current production

LIFO's disadvantages are:

(i) it results in lower reported earnings
(ii) inventories may be depleted due to the unavailability of materials (to the point of consuming inventories costed at old prices, which will create a mismatching of current revenue and cost).

The advantages of the standard price method are:

(i) stock records are maintained in units
(ii) the amount of clerical work in relation to stock accounting is reduced
(iii) all transactions are made at the standard price
(iv) calculation of the material price variance provides a check on the effectiveness of the purchasing department

The disadvantages are:

(i) it requires reasoned consideration before a standard is established
(ii) standard prices do not provide for trends in prices
(iii) production issues may therefore not be at current economic values

The advantages of the weighted average cost method are:

(i) each item taken from stock is made up of weighted quantities from each lot in stock at the date of issue
(ii) it minimises the effect of unusually high or low material prices, thus making possible more stable cost estimates for future work

The disadvantages are:

(i) the method is time consuming, i.e. every time a purchase is made, the previous calculation must be adjusted to take it into account
(ii) the method does not isolate specific price changes for purchases of materials

2.5 Summary

The material procurement function is the responsibility of the central purchasing department; this department plays a crucial role in ordering the firm's materials.

Production planning can be a centralised or a decentralised decision in the firm.

The receipt of the materials is recorded on a goods received note, a copy of which is sent to the accounts department. The accounts department's copy is then matched with the invoice.

Bin cards are used to enable management to ascertain the stock levels. A bin card shows the quantities of items on hand at a particular time.

The decision on the firm's stock holding is influenced by many factors. The physical side of stock control is aided by the use of control levels – maximum, minimum, and re-order level.

The material requisition forms the basis for updating the stores ledger and the individual job records.

Material Control and Costing Methods   19

The bases for pricing material issues include FIFO; LIFO; Standard price; (iv) Weighted average cost.

These methods have their own advantages and disadvantages. The standard costing method was shown to be superior because of its in built control mechanism. Such costing methods aid pricing decisions, which are central to income determination.

Bibliography

Copeland, R. M. and Shank, J. K. (1971) 'LIFO and the Diffusion of Information', *Empirical Research in Accounting: Selected Studies*, pp. 196–224.
Gambling, T. E. (1969) *A One-Year Accounting Course in Two Parts, Part II* (Pergamon Press) ch. 8.
Moore, C. L. and Jaedicke, R. K. (1976) *Managerial Accounting* (South-Western Publishing Co.) pp. 50–5.
Most, K. S. (1967) 'The Value of Inventories', *Journal of Accounting Research*, vol. 5. no, 1, Spring, p. 46.

Discussion questions

2.1 What do you understand by centralised and decentralised production planning decisions?

2.2 Describe the routine stages in a purchasing operation.

2.3 Describe the factors which influence the level of stockholding.

2.4 What are the advantages and disadvantages of the inventory methods used for valuing stock described in this chapter?

Problems

2.1 From the information shown below which relates to component ABC, prepare statements using each of the following methods of stock accounting:

(i) weighted average cost
(ii) standard cost

to show the following

(a) the amount to be charged to cost of production
(b) the value of the closing stock
(c) the difference, if any, between purchase cost and the aggregate of (a) and (b)

Indicate how (c) would be dealt with in the accounts.

	Receipts into stores	*Unit cost*	*Issues to production*	*Market unit price*
May	Units	$	Units	$
1	100	41		41
10	75	42		42
15			50	43
20			65	44
23	40	45		45
30			50	46

You may assume the company had no opening stock of component ABC and that in the case of method (ii) it is the company's practice to account for component ABC in terms of a standard unit cost of $40.

ACCA, FE[a], part B, Paper 6, Accounting 2, Costing June 1976.
[a] Foundation Examination.

2.2 S. Poynter PLC, an engineering company constructing special purpose equipment to customer specification, employs a system of job costing to determine the actual cost of products manufactured. Shown below is the incomplete stores account, for Month 11, of one component used in the construction of the equipment.

STORES ACCOUNT – COMPONENT XYZ

Date	Quantity	Price	Value	Date	Quantity	Price	Value
	Units	$	$		Units	$	$
1 Nov x1 Opening stock	35	2.00	70	1 Nov x1 Job 123	25		
5 Nov x1 Creditors	40	2.25	90	10 Nov x1 Job 147	38		
13 Nov x1 Creditors	30	2.50	75	24 Nov x1 Job 151	48		
23 Nov x1 Creditors	50	2.80	140	30 Nov x1 Closing stock	44		
	155		375		155		

Ten of the components issued on 24 November to Job 151 were to replace a unit which had been previously issued to that job, but had been damaged and scrapped as a result of incorrect installation.

REQUIRED

(a) Calculate the value of the closing stock of component XYZ using the following methods of pricing material issues:

   (i) FIFO
   (ii) LIFO

(b) Using the weighted average method of pricing, calculate the values of the components issued on 24 November.

ACCA, FE, Part B, Paper 6, Accounting 2, Costing 9 December 1981.

Chapter 2*
Introduction to Matrices[1]

> Objects are given to us by means of sensibility, and it alone yields us intuitions; they are thought through the understanding, and from the understanding arise concepts   (Kant, 1781)

2*.1 Introduction

From time immemorial, the concept of matrices must have existed, since man first saw things as signs. Signs are negative and positive. Those signs when converted to accounting conventions are debits and credits. The debits and credits even in the Paciolian[2] format can be expressed in matrix form. Nowadays, the complicated nature of the firm's production problem, coupled with the advancement in computer technology,[3] have made the acceptance of matrix concepts in industrial costing imperative. The adoption of matrices to cost analysis is simply an extension of the accounting function's development in harnessing mathematics to accounting problems, which eases computational effort and saves many manhours and associated dysfunctional aberrations.

To understand matrices and their structures, it is essential to commence with the basics.

2*.2 Matrix definition

A matrix is defined to be a rectangular array of numbers or elements:

$$A = \begin{bmatrix} a_{11} & a_{12}, \ldots, a_{1n} \\ a_{21} & a_{22}, \ldots, a_{2n} \\ a_{m1} & a_{m2}, \ldots, a_{mn} \end{bmatrix}$$

$$\begin{bmatrix} 1 & 2 \\ 3 & 4 \end{bmatrix}; \quad \begin{bmatrix} \frac{1}{2} & 1 & 2 \end{bmatrix}; \quad \begin{bmatrix} \sqrt{3} & i & 0 \\ 1 & \frac{4}{3} & 2 \end{bmatrix}$$

---

[1] Neophytes should consult, e.g. Hohn (1973), Lewis (1969) and Theodore (1975) for further insights into matrices.

[2] Luca Pacioli (?1445–1520) is considered to be 'the father of the balance sheet' (see Nakanishi, 1979).

[3] Many business problems of varying degrees of complexity are now solved by the computer. The solution process involves a computer program which instructs the machine to perform mathematical calculations.

These are all examples of matrices. If all of the entries of a matrix are 0, the matrix is called a null matrix and is denoted by 0. Italic letters are used here to distinguish matrices, small letters are used to distinguish scalars or vectors.

The matrix A, as given in the definition is made up of m rows and n columns. The subscript i of the entry a_{ij} designates the row in which the entry appears. The subscript j designates the column in which the entry appears. The subscripts (ij) are called the 'address' of the matrix. A matrix in which there are m rows and n columns of entries is said to be of order m by n. By convention, the number of rows is always stated first. A matrix is said to be square if $m = n$. Where $m \neq n$, the matrix is rectangular.

The matrix

$$A = \begin{bmatrix} 2 & 3 & 4 \\ 5 & 6 & 7 \\ 0 & 1 & 2 \end{bmatrix}$$

is a square matrix of order 3×3. The entry a_{31} is 0.

An m by n matrix A can succintly be expressed as:

$$A = [a_{ij}]_{m,n}$$

If some rows or columns of A are deleted, the remaining array is called a sub-matrix of A. For example, given

$$A = \begin{bmatrix} 1 & 2 & 3 \\ 4 & 5 & 6 \end{bmatrix}$$

the sub-matrices are:

$$\begin{bmatrix} 1 & 2 \\ 4 & 5 \end{bmatrix}, \begin{bmatrix} 1 & 3 \\ 4 & 6 \end{bmatrix}, \begin{bmatrix} 2 & 3 \\ 5 & 6 \end{bmatrix}$$

$$\begin{bmatrix} 1 \\ 4 \end{bmatrix}, \begin{bmatrix} 2 \\ 5 \end{bmatrix}, \begin{bmatrix} 3 \\ 6 \end{bmatrix}, \quad [1\ 2\ 3], [4\ 5\ 6]$$

$[1], [2], [3], [4], [5], [6], [1\ 2], [2\ 3], [1\ 3], [4\ 5], [4\ 6], [5\ 6]$

With large input–output and linear programming accounting models,[1] it is useful, for computational purposes to divide the system into sub-matrices, which makes the calculation easier.

Two matrices are said to be equal if they are of the same order, and if all their corresponding entries are equal, i.e.

$[a_{ij}]_{m,n} = [b_{ij}]_{m,n}$ for all $i = 1, 2 \ldots M$, and $j = 1, 2 \ldots N$

2*.3 Vectors

Matrices of order 1 by n are termed row matrices, or row vectors. Matrices of order n by 1 are called column matrices, or column vectors. A vector whose components are all 0 is called a null

---

[1] Input–output analysis was first applied to the American Economy by Leontief (1951). The input–output approach is now widely used to describe micro-accounting activity (see Farag (1968), Gambling (1970), and Ijiri (1968)).

Introduction to Matrices

vector. If the components are all real numbers, then the vector is a real vector. The following are examples of vectors:

$$b = \begin{bmatrix} 5 \\ 10 \\ 15 \end{bmatrix} \qquad c = \begin{bmatrix} 1 & 2 & 3 \end{bmatrix}$$

b is a three-element column vector (or a 3 × 1 matrix) and c is a three-element row vector (or a 1 × 3 matrix). In notation, b can be written as

$$b = \begin{bmatrix} b_{11} \\ b_{12} \\ b_{13} \end{bmatrix}, \qquad \text{or } b = \begin{bmatrix} b_1 \\ b_2 \\ b_3 \end{bmatrix}$$

Similarly c can be written as:

$$c = \begin{bmatrix} c_{11} \\ c_{12} \\ c_{13} \end{bmatrix}, \qquad \text{or} \qquad c = \begin{bmatrix} c_1 \\ c_2 \\ c_3 \end{bmatrix}$$

2*.4 Arithmetic operations on vectors

Two vectors of the same dimension are added by adding their corresponding components. A vector can be multiplied by an ordinary number (called a scalar), by multiplying each component of the vector by the specified scalar or number.

The examples below show the adding and multiplication procedures which can be carried out on vectors.

EXAMPLE 2*.1

Assume that a manufacturer produces the following chairs: mahogany, pine and iron. The cost of purchasing and transporting specific amounts of the three necessary raw materials to make the chairs from two different locations are given by the following matrices:

$$A = \begin{matrix} & \text{Purchase} & \text{Transportation} \\ & \text{cost} & \text{cost} \\ & \begin{bmatrix} 44 & 25 \\ 50 & 20 \\ 100 & 30 \end{bmatrix} & \begin{matrix} \text{Mahogany} \\ \text{Pine} \\ \text{Iron} \end{matrix} \end{matrix}$$

$$B = \begin{bmatrix} 40 & 18 \\ 35 & 20 \\ 90 & 35 \end{bmatrix} \begin{matrix} \text{Mahogany} \\ \text{Pine} \\ \text{Iron} \end{matrix}$$

The matrix representing the total purchase and transportation cost of each type of chair from both locations is given by

$$A + B = C = \begin{bmatrix} 44 & 25 \\ 50 & 20 \\ 100 & 30 \end{bmatrix} + \begin{bmatrix} 40 & 18 \\ 35 & 20 \\ 90 & 35 \end{bmatrix}$$

$$C = \begin{matrix} & \textit{Purchase} & \textit{Transportation} \\ & \textit{cost} & \textit{cost} \end{matrix} \\ \begin{bmatrix} 84 & 43 \\ 85 & 40 \\ 190 & 55 \end{bmatrix}$$

Assume that the manufacturer in Example 2*.1 asks you to calculate, from matrix C, the purchase and transportation cost of each chair for two accounting periods. Simple scalar multiplication gives:

$$2 \begin{bmatrix} 84 & 43 \\ 85 & 40 \\ 190 & 55 \end{bmatrix} = \begin{matrix} \textit{Purchase} & \textit{Transportation} \\ \textit{cost} & \textit{costs} \end{matrix} \\ \begin{bmatrix} 168 & 86 \\ 170 & 80 \\ 380 & 110 \end{bmatrix}$$

Another useful vector is the sum vector called sigma (σ) which contains 1s only. If a matrix is post-multiplied by σ, the result is a summation along the rows of the matrix to produce a column vector whose elements are the matrix row totals.

EXAMPLE 2*.2

Suppose the manufacturer in Example 2*.1 wants to know the sum totals respectively of the purchase and transportation cost. The calculation can be performed as follows:

$$\sigma C = \begin{bmatrix} 1 & 1 & 1 \end{bmatrix} \begin{bmatrix} 84 & 43 \\ 85 & 40 \\ 190 & 55 \end{bmatrix} = \begin{bmatrix} 359 & 138 \end{bmatrix}$$

2*.5 Subtraction of matrices

Given a matrix A and a matrix B of the same order, then the subtraction of matrices can be defined as:

$$A - B = A + (-1)B = C$$

EXAMPLE 2*.3

$$\begin{bmatrix} 5 & 3 \\ 1 & 6 \end{bmatrix} - \begin{bmatrix} 2 & 0 \\ 3 & 1 \end{bmatrix} = \begin{bmatrix} 5 & 3 \\ 1 & 6 \end{bmatrix} + \begin{bmatrix} -2 & 0 \\ -3 & -1 \end{bmatrix} = \begin{bmatrix} 3 & 3 \\ -2 & 5 \end{bmatrix}$$

The calculating procedures used above can be extended to matrix notation. Doing so enables us to generalise the calculating procedure to any problem that warrants such treatment. Below, we show the general nature of matrix multiplicatiion; we then apply the procedures to a numerical example.

2*.6 Matrix multiplication

The product of a row matrix of n coefficients by a column matrix of n variables is a 1 by n matrix. In general, such a system can be expressed as:

Introduction to Matrices

$$[a_{11} a_{12} \ldots a_{1n}] \begin{bmatrix} X_1 \\ X_2 \\ \vdots \\ X_n \end{bmatrix} = a_{11}x_1 + a_{12}X_2 + \ldots + a_{1n}X_n$$

Similarly, the product of an m by n matrix of coefficients by an n rowed column matrix of variables result in an m by n matrix:

$$\begin{bmatrix} a_{11} & a_{12} & \ldots & a_{1N} \\ a_{21} & a_{22} & & a_{2N} \\ \vdots & \vdots & & \vdots \\ a_{m1} & a_{m2} & & a_{mN} \end{bmatrix} \begin{bmatrix} X_1 \\ X_2 \\ \vdots \\ X_N \end{bmatrix} = \begin{bmatrix} a_{11}X_1 & a_{12}X_2 & +\ldots+ & a_{1N}X_N \\ a_{21}X_1 & a_{22}X_2 & & a_{2N}X_N \\ \vdots & \vdots & & \vdots \\ am_1 X_1 & a_{m2}X_2 & & a_{mN}X_N \end{bmatrix}$$

The procedures applied to matrix and vector multiplication can also be performed on two matrices, provided they are of the same dimension. It should be noted that the product of two matrices gives a third matrix. The order of the third matrix takes the rows of the first and the columns of the second matrix. Let A be an m by n matrix, and B be a q by r matrix. The product $C = AB$ which results is an m by r matrix, where each entry c_{ij} of C is obtained by multiplying corresponding entries of the ith row of A by those of the jth column of B and adding the results.

$$[A]_{m,n} \qquad \times \qquad [B]_{q,r}$$

$$\begin{bmatrix} a_{11} & a_{12} & \ldots & a_{1n} \\ a_{21} & a_{22} & \ldots & a_{2n} \\ \vdots & \vdots & & \vdots \\ a_{m1} & a_{m2} & & a_{mn} \end{bmatrix} \begin{bmatrix} b_{11} & b_{12} & \ldots & b_{1r} \\ b_{21} & b_{22} & \ldots & b_{2r} \\ \vdots & \vdots & \ldots & \vdots \\ b_{q1} & b_{q2} & \ldots & b_{qr} \end{bmatrix}$$

gives $[C]_{m,r}$

$$\begin{bmatrix} c_{11} & c_{12} & \ldots & c_{1r} \\ c_{21} & c_{22} & \ldots & c_{2r} \\ \vdots & \vdots & \ldots & \vdots \\ c_{m1} & c_{m2} & \ldots & c_{mr} \end{bmatrix}$$

The bracketed elements show that $c_{11} = a_{11}b_{11} + a_{12}b_{21} + \ldots + a_{1n}b_{q1}$. The other elements of matrix C are obtained in a similar way.

EXAMPLE 2*.4

Suppose that the chair manufacturer in Example 2*.1 enters the export market. He decides after drawing up contracts with the retailers in Jamaica, Trinidad and St Lucia, to export respectively 900 mahogany, 1000 pine and 1500 iron chairs to them. The prices per chair from the various countries are shown in the matrix below.

REQUIRED

Calculate the income that the manufacturer is respectively expected to receive from the three countries.

SOLUTION

```
                PRICE MATRIX              QUANTITY MATRIX
            Mahogany  Pine  Iron
Jamaica  ⎡  200      120   105 ⎤         ⎡ 900  ⎤
Trinidad ⎢  205      125   110 ⎥         ⎢ 1000 ⎥
St Lucia ⎣  210      135   120 ⎦         ⎣ 1500 ⎦
```

The income matrix is:

$$\begin{bmatrix} \$ \times \quad \$ \quad\quad \$ \\ 200 \times 900 + 120 \times 1000 + 105 \times 1500 \\ 205 \quad 900 \quad 125 \quad 1000 \quad 110 \quad 1500 \\ 210 \quad 900 \quad 135 \quad 1000 \quad 120 \quad 1500 \end{bmatrix} = \begin{bmatrix} \$ \\ 457\,500 \\ 474\,500 \\ 504\,000 \end{bmatrix}$$

2*.7 Special features of multiplication

Reconsider Example 2*.4. Call the price matrix A and the quantity matrix B. A close examination of the income matrix will reveal that AB will not give the same solution as BA. In fact, the multiplication of BA is impossible, because B has one column while A has three rows. Even if B had as many columns as A, the product BA would not be the same as AB. The product would have the same order only if A and B were symmetric, i.e. square. Even if they were square, corresponding terms would have different values. It is therefore apparent that matrices can be multiplied only when the number of columns of the left matrix is equal to the number of rows of the right matrix. In such cases, the matrices are conformable for multiplication.

2*.8 Transpose of a matrix

The transpose of a matrix results if the elements in row i and column j of a matrix are transferred to a position in row j and column i.

A prime or a small t (used in the same way as an exponent) is normally used to denote transposition:

$$A = \begin{bmatrix} a_{11} & a_{12} & a_{13} \\ a_{21} & a_{22} & a_{23} \end{bmatrix}$$

$$A^t = \begin{bmatrix} a_{11} & a_{21} \\ a_{12} & a_{22} \\ a_{13} & a_{23} \end{bmatrix}$$

Two useful results on transposition are:

(i) $[A+B]^t = A^t + B^t$
(ii) $[A-B]^t = B^t - A^t$

Introduction to Matrices

2*.9 Identity matrix

In matrix algebra, the matrix I plays the same role as the numeral 1 in scalar arithmetic. I is a square matrix which has unity elements on the main diagonal and 0s elsewhere. The multiplication of any matrix by matrix I of appropriate size leaves the original matrix unchanged:

$$\begin{bmatrix} 1 & 0 \\ 0 & 1 \end{bmatrix} \begin{bmatrix} 1 & 2 & 3 \\ 6 & 5 & 4 \end{bmatrix} = \begin{bmatrix} 1 & 2 & 3 \\ 6 & 5 & 4 \end{bmatrix}$$

It should be noted that an identity matrix plays an important role in matrix inversion (see 2*.11 below).

2*.10 Determinant of a matrix

This is a scalar function which is associated with any square matrix. It is related to inversion and latent roots, and is a useful aid in calculating integer values from some integer programming problems.

EXAMPLE 2*.5

The determinant of a square matrix A is written as $|a|$.
  For a matrix   of order
  1 by 1, $|a| = a$
  2 by 2, $|a| = a_{11} a_{22} - a_{12} a_{21}$

The determinant of the residual matrix left after deleting the ith row and jth column of A is called the minor, m_{ij} of a_{ij}, where a_{ij} is the element occurring in the ith row and the jth column.

REQUIRED

Given the matrix

$$A = \begin{bmatrix} 1 & 2 & 3 \\ 3 & 2 & 1 \\ 1 & 3 & 1 \end{bmatrix}$$

calculate its determinant.

SOLUTION

Expanding about the first row i.e. $i = 1$

$$|a| = 1 \begin{bmatrix} 2 & 1 \\ 3 & 1 \end{bmatrix} - 2 \begin{bmatrix} 3 & 1 \\ 1 & 1 \end{bmatrix} + 3 \begin{bmatrix} 3 & 2 \\ 1 & 3 \end{bmatrix}$$
$$= 1 \times (2-3) - 2(3-1) + 3(9-2)$$
$$= 16$$

Alternatively, expanding about the second row gives:

$$|a| = -3 \begin{bmatrix} 2 & 3 \\ 3 & 1 \end{bmatrix} + 2 \begin{bmatrix} 1 & 3 \\ 1 & 1 \end{bmatrix} - 1 \begin{bmatrix} 1 & 2 \\ 1 & 3 \end{bmatrix} = 16,$$

which shows that it is also permissible to expand about the columns. Note that the quantity $A_{ij} = (-1)^{i+j} M_{ij}$ is called the cofactor of a_{ij}. It is important to note also that matrix inversion, which is examined below, can also be calculated with the use of the determinant.

2*.11 Matrix inversion

In arithmetic, there is division. In matrix algebra, the corresponding operation is known as inversion. The inversion of a matrix A is defined to be the matrix A^{-1}, such that

$$A^{-1}A = AA^{-1} = 1$$

The equality of both the product A^{-1} and AA^{-1} to the identity matrix means that both products must have the same result, as well as the same order.

EXAMPLE 2*.6

Consider the composite matrix $[A \vdots 1]$. If row operations are carried out on A which convert it to an identity matrix, then in effect the identity matrix has bee pre-multiplied by A^{-1}. In the same way, if the same operations are carried out on the identity matrix, the result is A^{-1}, therefore:

$$A^{-1}[A \vdots 1] = [1 \vdots A^{-1}]$$

EXAMPLE 2*.7

Consider a production system with three cost points. Assume that cost point 1 transmits part (a) of its output to cost point 2 and part (b) to cost point 3. Cost point 3 transmits part (c) of its output to cost point 1. Figure 2*.1 show the flow of the data.

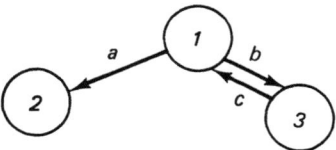

Figure 2*.1 Flow of data – Production system with three cost points

The matrix A captures the data in an input–output format:

$$A = \begin{matrix} \text{O} \\ \text{U} \\ \text{T} \\ \text{P} \\ \text{U} \\ \text{T} \end{matrix} \begin{matrix} & \text{INPUT} \\ & 1 \quad 2 \quad 3 \\ 1 \\ 2 \\ 3 \end{matrix} \begin{bmatrix} 0 & 0 & c \\ a & 0 & 0 \\ b & 0 & 0 \end{bmatrix}$$

In order to determine both the direct and indirect effects of the system, $I - A$ is required. It is:

$$I - A = \begin{matrix} 1 \\ 2 \\ 3 \end{matrix} \begin{bmatrix} 1 & 0 & -c \\ -a & 1 & 0 \\ -b & 0 & 1 \end{bmatrix}$$

from which row operations are carried out on $I - A$ to obtain the inverse. The pivot element is circled:

$$I - A^{-1} = \begin{vmatrix} \text{①} & 0 & -c & \vdots & 1 & 0 & 0 \\ -a & 1 & 0 & \vdots & 0 & 1 & 0 \\ -b & 0 & 1 & \vdots & 0 & 0 & 1 \end{vmatrix}$$

Introduction to Matrices 29

COMMENT

First row 1 is used to eliminate non-0 terms in column 1. Row 1 is divided by 1. The other operations are written alongside the matrix. The transformed matrix is:

$$\begin{vmatrix} 1 & 0 & -c & \vdots & 1 & 0 & 0 \\ 0 & ① & -ac & \vdots & a & 1 & 0 \\ 0 & 0 & 1-bc & \vdots & b & 0 & 1 \end{vmatrix} \begin{matrix} R_1 \div 1 \\ R_1 a + R_2 \\ R_1 b + R_3 \end{matrix}$$

Use row 2 to eliminate non 0 terms in column 2. The pivot is 1. The matrix remains the same, because of the 0s above and below it. This aspect also occurs in linear programming. Use row 3 to eliminate non-zero terms in column 3.   Divide row 3 by $1-bc$. The result is:

$$\begin{vmatrix} 1 & 0 & 0 & \vdots & \dfrac{1}{1-bc} & 0 & \dfrac{c}{1-bc} \\ 0 & 1 & 0 & \vdots & \dfrac{a}{1-bc} & 1 & \dfrac{ac}{1-bc} \\ 0 & 0 & 1 & \vdots & \dfrac{b}{1-bc} & 0 & \dfrac{1}{1-bc} \end{vmatrix} \begin{matrix} R_3 c + R_1 \\ R_2 ac + R_2 \\ R_3 \div 1-bc \end{matrix}$$

The inverse is given in the second half of the matrix.

COMMENT

An examination of the input/output matrix reveals (i) that some of its elements fall in the left hand triangle of the matrix,[1] (ii) an element appears above the diagonal. In general, these off-diagonal elements appear whenever reciprocal or feedback relationships exist. Chemical processes present examples of feedback. However, the inverse must show for the example presented, $1/1 - bc$ times an element, where $bc < 1$. For $bc > 1$, the Hawkins–Simon conditions are violated (See Rickwood, 1970).[2]

The inverse of partitioned matrices is similar to the inverse of ordinary matrices. Care must be taken, however, to ensure that the sub-matrices on the main diagonal are square.

Incidentally, if we assume that $K_i (i = 1, 2, 3)$ represents the cost from the processes $u_j (j = 1, 2, 3)$, it follows that:

$$K_1 = \frac{1}{1-bc} u_1 + O u_2 + \frac{c}{1-bc} u_3$$

$$K_2 = \frac{a}{1-bc} u_1 + u_2 + \frac{ac}{1-bc} u_3$$

$$K_3 = \frac{b}{1-bc} u_1 + O u_2 + \frac{1}{1-bc} u_3$$

which is a system of linear equations.

It is important for the reader to bear in mind that a system of linear equations can be solved by other methods. For cost accounting purposes, however, an inverse matrix (if one exists to a problem) gives better inights into cost analysis than the solution via other methods. We can show that this is so by comparing the two methods in 2*.12 below.

[1] A reverse format would show an upper, right hand triangle matrix see Appendix, Example A2*.1. A worked example of matrix inversion is also shown in Appendix 2*.2.
[2] The conditions are important, and should always be present in the minds of the model builders of the firm's production system. The condition not only guarantees non-negative coefficients in the inverse input–output, matrix, but non-negative outputs as well.

2*.12 Equation system and inverse system compared

This is best done via a simple input–output model. Figure 2*.2 shows the flow of materials (through a factory) which go into the manufacture of a product.

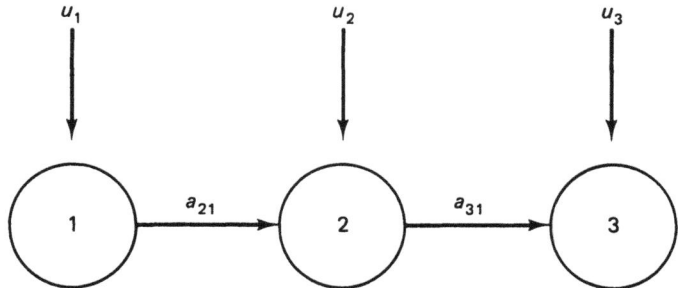

Figure 2*.2 Input–output model – Flow of materials through factory

The assumptions of Figure 2*.2 are:

(i) that cost point 1 transmit its entire output to cost point 2
(ii) that cost point 2 processes it, and passes the entire output to cost point 3

Since the entire output from cost point 1 goes to cost point 2, and cost point 2 sends it on to cost point 3, a_{21} and $a_{31} = 1$.
The other a_{ij}s $= 0$.
The input–output structure is:

$$A = \begin{array}{c} \text{OUTPUT} \\ \begin{array}{c} 1 \\ 2 \\ 3 \end{array} \end{array} \begin{array}{c} \text{INPUT} \\ \begin{array}{ccc} 1 & 2 & 3 \end{array} \\ \begin{bmatrix} 0 & 0 & 0 \\ 1 & 0 & 0 \\ 0 & 1 & 0 \end{bmatrix} \end{array}$$

$$A^{-1} = \begin{array}{c} 1 \\ 2 \\ 3 \end{array} \begin{array}{c} \begin{array}{ccc} 1 & 2 & 3 \end{array} \\ \begin{bmatrix} 1 & 0 & 0 \\ 1 & 1 & 0 \\ 1 & 1 & 1 \end{bmatrix} \end{array}$$

The equation system based on the model using $K_i (i = 1, 2, 3)$ to represent the cost points, is:

$K_1 = 1u_1 + 0u_2 + 0u_3 = u_1$
$K_2 = 1u_1 + 1u_2 + 0u_3 = u_1 + u_2$
$K_3 = 1u_1 + 1u_2 + 1u_3 = u_1 + u_2 + u_3$

Introduction to Matrices

Assume now that the exogenous cost for $u_1 u_2$ and u_3 are respectively $[50, 100, 50]$. The allocation of cost via the equatin system is:

	COST POINT		
	1	2	3
	$	$	$
Original cost u_1	50	100	50
Allocation of cost from cost point 1	–	50	–
Allocation of cost from cost point 2	–	–	150
Total cost of cost point Ki	50	150	200

The allocation of cost according to their origin via the reverse system is:

		COST POINT		
		1	2	3
		$	$	$
Total original cost		50	100	50
1[a]	50	50	0	0
2	150	50	100	0
3	200	50	100	50

[a] Total cost of points k_i divided according to cost point at which they arose.

COMMENT

The equation system gives a global picture of the firm's cost. Unlike reverse matrix, it cannot show the cost division based on origin, or the finer elements of such cost. A difference thus exists between cost calculation based on the equation system and that based on the reverse system. In the reverse system, the (ijs) show the proportion of the cost point u_j which is allotted to cost point i. It is those (ijs) which are of importance to managerial decisionmaking, since rationalisation measures can be applied to any of the cost points. Of more importance is that rule formulations for economic managerial decisions can be determined on the practical plane with the aid of the matrix concept.

It is important to note that the inverse can be (i) used as a control calculation, because $AA^{-1} = I$, and (ii) it is, like the break-even formula, a ready reckoner for quick calculations of output provided the production coefficients are stable.

2*.13 Summary

In this chapter, a matrix was defined to be a rectangular array of numbers or elements. It was also stated that when m the number or rows equals n the number of columns of a matrix, that it is square. By convention, italic letters are used to distinguish matrices, and small letters are used to distinguish scalars or vectors.

Arithmetic operations like addition, subtraction and multiplication can be performed on matrices. With matrix multiplication, it was stated that the two matrices must be conformable.

Examples were shown of the imput–output structure of a hypothetical production system of a firm. We showed how an inverse matrix can be calculated from such a system, and how use can be made of the inverse in calculating cost from the cost points of a production system. It was shown how calculations based on the inverse system give management better insights into cost analysis than those based on the equation system.

Appendix

A2*.1 Inverse of the upper triangular input–output matrices

The sequence of production in a manufacturing system generally has a 'tree-like' appearance. If the inputs as fractions of unity of the system are written in the columns and the outputs in the rows, an upper triangular matrix results.

EXAMPLE A2*1

Assume that the coefficient matrix A below shows the input–output structure of a manufacturing firm.

$$A = \begin{matrix} \text{INPUTS} \\ \begin{matrix} & & 1 & 2 & 3 & 4 & 5 \end{matrix} \\ \begin{matrix} 1 \\ 2 \\ 3 \\ 4 \\ 5 \end{matrix} \begin{bmatrix} 0.5 & & 0 & \\ & 0.4 & & \\ & & 0.7 & \\ 0 & & & 0.3 \\ & & & & \end{bmatrix} \end{matrix}$$

In order to derive the inverse, convert $[1-A]$ into $[1+A]$, then apply the formula:

$$A_{ij} = \begin{matrix} 0 * & i \leqslant j \\ 1 * & i = j \\ \sum_{}^{j-1} A_{ik}A^*_{kj} & \text{if } i < j \end{matrix}$$

Where A^*_{kj} is the updated matrix

The inverse is:

$$1-A^{*1} = \begin{matrix} \text{OUTPUTS} \\ \begin{matrix} & 1 & 2 & 3 & 4 & 5 \end{matrix} \\ \begin{matrix} 1 \\ 2 \\ 3 \\ 4 \\ 5 \end{matrix} \begin{bmatrix} 1 & 0.5 & 0.20 & 0.14 & 0.042 \\ & 1 & 0.4 & 0.28 & 0.084 \\ & & 1 & 0.7 & 0.21 \\ & & & 1 & 0.3 \\ & & & & 1 \end{bmatrix} \end{matrix}$$

Introduction to Matrices

EXAMPLE A2*.2

REQUIRED

Invert the matrix:

$$A = \begin{bmatrix} 1 & 2 & 3 \\ 3 & 1 & 4 \\ 4 & 2 & 1 \end{bmatrix}$$

SOLUTION

						CHECKSUM	OPERATIONS	
①	2	3	1	0	0	7		
3	1	4	0	1	0	9		
4	2	1	0	0	1	8		
1	2	3	1	0	0	7	(1) ÷ 1	*Updated*
0	−5	⊖5	−3	1	0	−12	(2) − 3 × (1)	*matrix*
0	−6	−11	−4	0	1	−20	(3) − 4 × (1)	
1	2	3	1	0	0	7		
0	1	1	$\frac{3}{5}$	$-\frac{1}{5}$	0	$\frac{12}{5}$	(2) ÷ −5	
0	−6	−11	−4	0	1	−20		
1	0	1	$-\frac{1}{5}$	$\frac{2}{5}$	0	$\frac{11}{5}$	(1) − 2 × (2)	*Updated*
0	1	1	$\frac{3}{5}$	$-\frac{1}{5}$	0	$\frac{12}{5}$		*matrix*
0	0	⊖5	$-\frac{2}{5}$	$-\frac{6}{5}$	1	$-\frac{28}{5}$	(3) + 6 × (2)	
1	0	1	$-\frac{1}{5}$	$\frac{2}{5}$	0	$\frac{11}{5}$		
0	1	1	$\frac{3}{5}$	$-\frac{1}{5}$	0	$\frac{12}{5}$		
0	0	1	$\frac{2}{25}$	$\frac{6}{25}$	$-\frac{1}{5}$	$\frac{28}{25}$	(3) ÷ −5	
1	0	0	$-\frac{7}{25}$	$\frac{4}{25}$	$\frac{1}{5}$	$\frac{27}{25}$	(1) − (3)	*Updated*
0	1	0	$\frac{13}{25}$	$-\frac{11}{15}$	$\frac{1}{5}$	$\frac{32}{25}$	(2) − (3)	*matrix*
0	0	1	$\frac{2}{25}$	$\frac{6}{25}$	$-\frac{1}{5}$	$\frac{28}{25}$		

Check or control calculation:

$$\begin{bmatrix} 1 & 2 & 3 \\ 3 & 1 & 4 \\ 4 & 2 & 1 \end{bmatrix} \begin{bmatrix} -\frac{7}{25} & -\frac{4}{25} & \frac{1}{5} \\ \frac{13}{25} & -\frac{11}{25} & \frac{1}{5} \\ \frac{2}{25} & \frac{6}{25} & -\frac{1}{5} \end{bmatrix} = \begin{bmatrix} 1 & 0 & 0 \\ 0 & 1 & 0 \\ 0 & 0 & 1 \end{bmatrix}$$

COMMENT

(i) The circled number is called the pivot
(ii) The bracket numbers in the operations' row are the equations

(iii) It is very easy to make arithmetical mistakes in calculating the inverse, so a column representing the sum of all the terms in a row is added. If the same operations are carried out on the check column as on the rest of the table, the checksum will always equal the sum of the terms in the row, yielding an easy check on arithmetic accuracy
(iv) The inverse is opposite the identify matrix, i.e. on the right of the last updated matrix
(v) The method is similar to the procedures of the simplex algorithm in linear programming.

Bibliography

Farag, S. M. (1968) 'A Planning Model for the Divisional Enterprise', *Accounting Review*, April, pp. 312–20.
Gambling, T. E. and Nour, A. (1970) 'A Note on Input–Output Analysis: Its Uses in Macro-Economics and Micro-Economics; *Accounting Review*, January, pp. 98–102.
Hohn, F. E. (1973) *Elementary Matrix Algebra*, 3rd edn (Macmillan).
Ijiri, Y. (1968) 'An Application of Input–Output Analysis to Some Problems in Cost Accounting', *Management Accounting*, April, pp. 49–61.
Kant, I. (1781) *Critique of Pure Reason*, N. K. Smith (trans. 1933) (Macmillan) p. 65.
Leontief, W. W. (1951) *The Structure of the American Economy*, 1919–1939 (Oxford University Press).
Lewis, J. P. (1969) *An Introduction to Mathematics for Students of Economics*, 2nd edn (Macmillan) ch. xxix.
Nakanishi, A. (1979) 'On the Life of Luca Pacioli', *Accounting Historians Journal*, vol. 6, no. 2, Fall, pp. 53–9.
Rickwood, C. P. (1970) 'Flows in Networks and the Hawkins–Simon Conditions', Faculty of Commerce and Social Science, Discussion Paper (University of Birmingham) Series B, no. 23.
Theodore, Chris A. (1975) *Applied Mathematics: An Introduction*, 3rd edn (Richard D. Irwin) ch. 9.

Problems

2*.1 The Trix Manufacturing Co. Ltd. produces four products – A, B, C and D. Each product is made from three raw materials – P, Q and R:

	PRODUCT					MATERIAL		
	A	B	C	D		P	Q	R
Production data To (per unit)	1				R	2	1	4
		1			E	5		3
			1		Q	5		3
				1	U	4	1	2
				1	I	4	1	2
					R			
					E			
					S			
	$	$	$	$		$	$	$
Raw material cost (per unit)						2	3	6
Direct production cost (per unit)	4	2	3	5				
Producer selling price	40	40	36	32				
Weekly demand (per unit)	400	500	600	200				

Introduction to Matrices

REQUIRED

(a) Prepare the following matrices:

   W – 4 × 3 matrix giving component requirements
   X – 1 × 4 matrix giving weekly demand for each product
   Y – 3 × 1 matrix giving unit raw material cost
   Z – 4 × 1 matrix giving direct production cost per unit for each product.

(b) Identify the matrices required to calculate the raw material cost per product and calculate them using matrix methods
(c) Using your result in (b), identify the other matrices you require to calculate the total weekly contribution, and determine the result
(d) Without making the calculations, what interpretation would you give to the matrix T where $T = XWY$?

ACA, PE, Section 2, Paper 12, Management Mathematics, June 1978

2*.2 Every day a shop purchases for $2 per unit a product which it sells for $4 per unit. For every unit of product sold, a wrapping cost of $0.20 is incurred. Since the product is perishable, units remaining unsold at the end of the day are returned, without wrapping, to the supplier, who refunds $1 for each returned item. The probability distribution for daily demand is as follows:

Possible no. of units demanded daily (X)	Probability that X units will be demanded daily $p(x)$
0	0.1
1	0.4
2	0.3
3	0.2

REQUIRED

(a) Draw up a table showing the profit earned for different order and demand levels
  Your table should be in the form:

PROFIT TABLE – ORDER LEVEL

	Q \ X	0	1	2	3
DEMAND LEVEL	0				
	1				
	2				
	3				

   Where Q is the order level
(b) Let the profit figures in your table be the elements of a matrix A
   If the probability vector P is given by (0.1 0.4 0.3 0.2) calculate the matrix PA
(c) Interpret the entries in the matrix PA and hence determine the optimal order level that the shop should place each day
(d) If the wrapping cost per unit increases dramatically to $1, write out the additional cost matrix, and determine the effect upon the order level policy

ACA, PE, Section 2, Paper 12, Management Mathematics, December 1976.

2*.3

REQUIRED

Prepare the matrix formulation to solve the following problems:

(a)

$40x + 70y + 7z - 300 = 0$
$22x + 35y + 12z - 525 = 0$
$y + z - 30 = 0$

in the form: $Ax = c$

(b) The total cost C of purchases from a supplier of four commodities each with a different price: in the form: $q'p = c$
(c) A matrix which shows the communication flow between four departments, A, B, C and D There is a two-way channel between A and B, A and C, B and D, C and D, but a one-way channel only from A to D
(d) A two-producer business makes chairs and table using wood and labour:

		Units of wood	Units of labour
Each chair (X_1)	REQUIRES	6	4
table (X_2)		12	3

There are only 90 units of wood and 40 units of labour available during the next period
Express the constraints in matrix form
(e) Following on from (d) above, if variable materials cost $4 per unit and variable labour cost $5 per unit, state the unit variable cost vector (V)
(f) Following on from (d) and (e) above, if the selling prices are $70 for each chair and $100 for each table, state the vector of contribution margins

ICMA, PS, Part 1, Quantitatives Techniques, November 1978.

2*.4 The chief materials used in the manufacture of three carpets designs called 'Floral Dance', 'Blue Danube' and 'Square Peg' are wool and acrilan.
The numbers in matrix below give the quantities of wool and acrilan, and the labour and machine times required, for each unit broadloom length of carpet type.

	Wool	Acrilan	Labour	Machine time
			hr	hr
Floral dance	1.0	2.0	0.7	1.0
Blue Danube	0.5	2.4	0.6	0.9
Square Peg	1.2	1.5	0.5	1.1

The quantities of wool and acrilan are given in 10 kg units. It has been proposed that the design of these three carpets be slightly changed, but the names retained. The extra amounts of wool, acrilan, and the times required, will be as follows:

	Wool	Acrilan	Labour	Machine time
			hr	hr
Floral Dance	+0.2	−0.2	+0.1	+0.1
Blue Danube	1	+0.01	+0.1	−0.2
Square Peg	+0.1	−0.2	+0.2	+0.2

Introduction to Matrices

The production and transportation cost per unit of each resource is:

	COST	
	Production	transport
	$	$
Wool	40	10
Acrilan	20	20
Labour	2	0
Machine time	10	0

REQUIRED:

(a) How would matrix addition and multiplication be used to find total production and total transportation costs for each of the new carpet types?
   Determine these costs from your matrix operations only
(b) Assume that the carpet manufacturers have decided to produce 200 new 'Floral Dance', 300 new 'Blue Danube' and 100 'New Square Peg' units of broadloom carpet length
   What matrix calculation(s) would produce the carpet manufacturer's total requirement for each of the inputs?
   Determine these requirements
(c) Matrices are use in input–output analysis

Give the relevant equation which relates the total output to the final demand. Describe briefly the constituent elements of each matrix used

ACA, PE, Section 2, Paper 12, Management Mathematics, June 1975.

Chapter 3

Direct Materials, Direct Labour, the Mechanics of Cost Allocation and Overhead Analysis

> All operating costs other than direct labour and direct material are usually classified as overhead by the accountant. This view differs somewhat from the Economist's definition of overhead, which includes only fixed cost.   (Bierman, 1976)

3.1 Introduction

This chapter examines the flow of direct materials in the manufacturing firm; it then looks at the role of direct labour and its relationship with direct materials, and draws attention to the mechanics of labour cost accounting.

The purpose of overhead expenses and how they are classified by an accountant are also examined; the reasons for cost allocation in the firm are demonstrated; and via a problem solution the final allocation of costs to the production departments of the firm is shown.

The many bases from which an overhead rate can be calculated are also illustrated, and the chapter ends by drawing attention to the difference in treatment of the overhead expenses in the direct and absorption costing statements.

3.2 Direct materials

Accounting for direct materials can best be illustrated by a diagram. Figure 3.1 shows the activities which occur in a manufacturing firm.

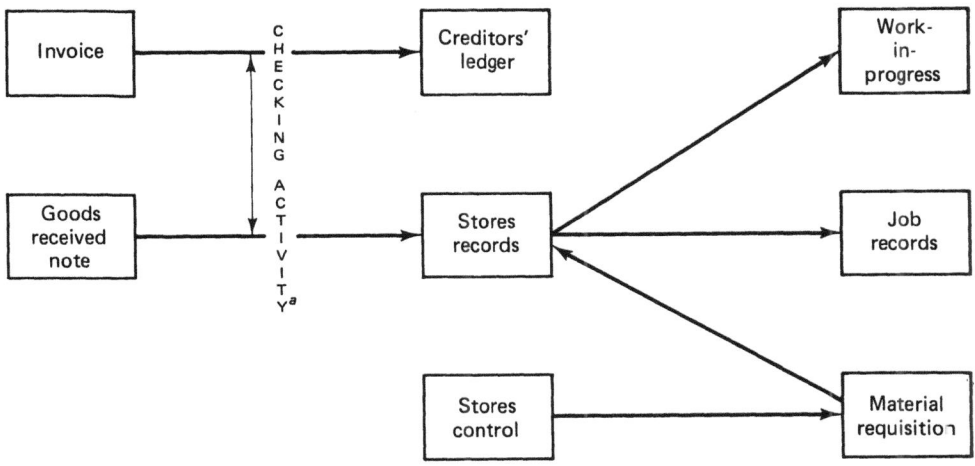

Figure 3.1 **Material cost accounting**

3.3. Direct labour

In the firm, top management determines the number of workers for each department but the hiring and dismissal functions are delegated to the personnel department.

The personnel department is the watchdog of the whole organisation. It explains the contract of employment to employees; it maintains records of past and present employees; it screens the employees who are employed in the production process. The employees engaged in production in a firm are then paid for their work by the wages department. Production, of course, has a time dimension, which is related to the work performance of the employees. Time, in relation to human work behaviour in the firm, implies a control aspect. The control aspects of timekeeping are:

(i) enforceable timekeeping by time clocks
(ii) time booking, which relates labour costs to individual jobs or processes for the accountant

Some common methods of timekeeping are:

(i) Daily timesheets
(ii) Weekly timesheets
(iii) Job tickets
(iv) Job cards attached to each job

COMMENT

The daily and weekly timesheets are prepared by the wages office, and should account for all working hours by production employees of the firm.

Job tickets may be completed by the employee or the cost department, and should relate to one activity which forms part of a job. When a job is being done, the ticket is submitted to the cost department, which summarises all the tickets which relate to a specific job in order to ascertain the total labour cost. This system involves a great deal of paperwork; it gives, however, a reliable figure of labour cost of work-in-process on the manufacturing floor.

Job cards circulate with the job. It is not therefore possible to ascertain the labour cost until the job is completed, and the card returned to the cost unit. In some manufacturing systems, the job card is returned to the cost department weekly for cost control, and is replaced by a 'balance card' for subsequent time records.

An analysis of labour is also required for costing purposes for the following categories of cost:

(i) production jobs, analysed by job no.
(ii) indirect labour, such as idle time or cleaning up
(iii) time taken setting up, the machines being analysed by job no.

3.4 Labour remuneration

There are three basic methods of labour remuneration:

(i) day rate, based on time
(ii) piecework, based on production
(iii) premium bonus, a combination of (i) and (ii)

COMMENT

(i) is the general system found in most organisations
(ii) piecework involves a rate per unit of production, and is suitable where the employee is able to control the level of production; the production output is based on quantity
(iii) implies that a time allowance is set for a job, and a premium is paid which relates to the time saved by the worker

EXAMPLE 3.1

Assume that an employee is paid a time rate of $6 per hour. In a particular week, the employee works 40 normal hours and 4 hours overtime. The overtime rate is at time and a half. During the 44 hours of work, the employee produced, 70 measured or standard hours of work. 50 per cent of the time saved is at the basic rate.

REQUIRED

Calculate the employee's gross pay for the week.

SOLUTION

The employee's pay for the week is:

(i) Pay based on attendance
    $40 + (4 \times 1.50)$ hr = 46 hr × $6 $276

(ii) Bonus
    Time saved = $(70 - 44)$ hr = 26 hr
    Bonus   = $0.50 \times 26 \times \$6$ $78

    Gross pay before deductions
                                     $354

The employee's gross pay for the week is $354.

Materials, Labour and Overhead Analysis

This illustrates a procedure for calculating labour costs. In general, the total cost of labour includes:

(i) gross wages
(ii) employer's national insurance contribution
(iii) employer's contributions to pension scheme
(iv) fringe benefits.

The total hours worked by the firm's employees is calculated as:

(i) weeks per year × hr per week *less*
(ii) statutory holiday allowance
(iii) allowance for sick leave
(iv) other non-productive time

The cost per hour to the firm is calculated as:

$$\text{Cost per hr} = \frac{\text{Total cost of employment}}{\text{Net productive hours}}$$

Obviously that measure can be used to apply labour costs to products for which the labour input in hours is known.

Figure 3.2 shows the mechanics of labour cost accounting.

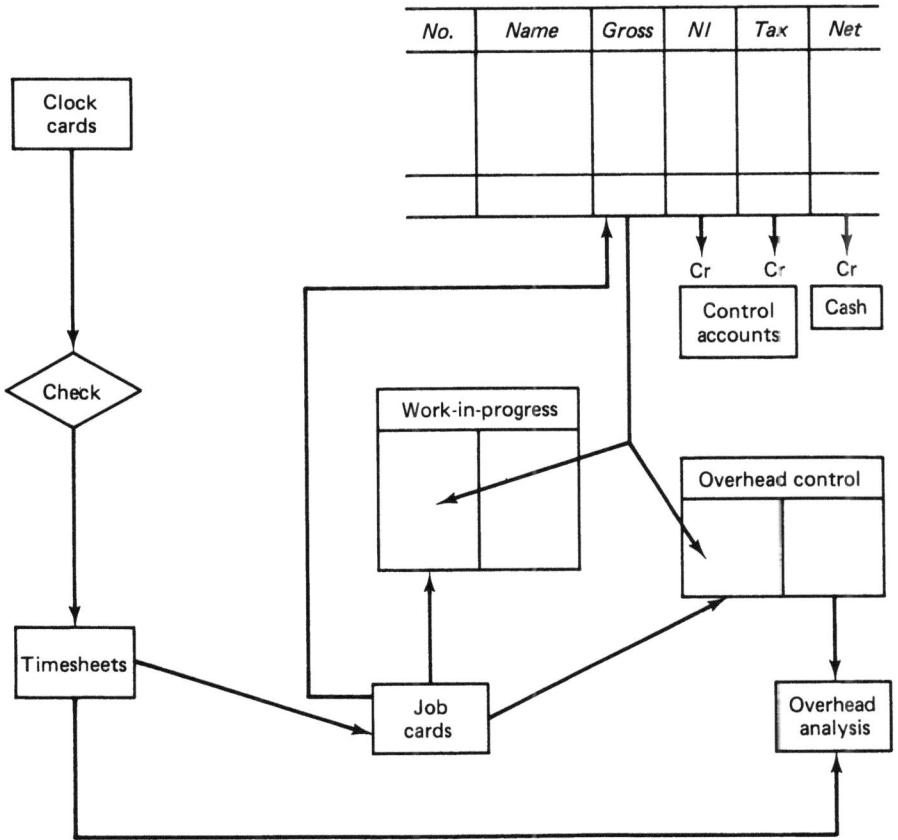

Figure 3.2 Labour cost accounting

COMMENT

(i) The clock cards are checked, and reconciled with the timesheets
(ii) The employee's gross pay is credited to the payroll control account, and debited either to a work-in-progress control account for the amount allocated to productive jobs, or to an overhead control account for total non-productive time
(iii) Each individual job will be charged with an amount attributable to it, or to an overhead analysis account
(iv) The national insurance and tax deductions from the gross pay will be debited to the payroll control account and credited to a control or suspense account pending disbursements to the state tax authority
(v) The net wages paid to the individual employees will be credited to the cash account and debited to the payroll control account; this transaction clears the payroll control account for the period

3.5 Direct expenses

Direct expenses are those costs other than material or labour which can be identified with a particular cost unit. Examples of direct expenses are sub-contracting expenses, e.g. cleaning or plating carried out by another company; royalties paid for manufacturing when based on output quantity.

3.6 Overheads

All costs which cannot be associated with an individual cost unit are overhead costs. Overheads are identified with:
(i) ledger classification
(ii) departments where they can be controlled

Overhead expense charges can arise from:

(i) material requisitions for small tools and insignificant items, which are not identified with production jobs
(ii) for services, such as telephone charges, material handling, foreman's salary, porterage/ maintenance services repairs and taxes

It is important to note that the incurral of overheads by the firm is a necessary adjunct to the creation of the social product.

Overhead rates, however, are applicable to job order and process costing systems, as well as to actual and standard costing systems.

3.7 Purpose of overhead rates

Overhead rates are used by the accounting function for the following reasons:

(i) to calculate the amount of the manufacturing overhead to be included in the cost of individual jobs, production lots, batches or processes
(ii) as a timely approximated rate, to be applied upon the completion of production

Materials, Labour and Overhead Analysis 43

(iii) to provide the basis for the formal accounting entries transferring costs from the manufacturing cost accounts to the work-in-process inventory accounts and
(iv) as an estimate of the manufacturing overhead costs which can be applied to a product in advance of the actual production

To be useful to managerial decisions, the overheads incurred by a manufacturing firm must be analysed and classified. The way an accountant may classify and accumulate the overheads for decision purposes is now examined.

3.8 Process of accumulating overhead cost

Overhead accumulation involves first the identification of the overheads, and secondly analysis by the accountant into their variable (V) and fixed (F) elements. The process is shown in Example 3.2

EXAMPLE 3.2

Assume that a firm in manufacturing a product incurred the overheads as shown below:

	$
Maintenance	50
Power & Light	30
Indirect labour	25
Supervision	40

REQUIRED

Show how a typical accountant will derive the fixed and variable overhead accounts

SOLUTION

As the cost is incurred, the accountant will assign it to an appropriate heading and will also classify the cost into fixed or variable overhead:

MAINTENANCE		POWER & LIGHT	
$	$	$	$
50	10 F	30	5 F
	40 V		25 V

INDIRECT LABOUR		SUPERVISION	
$	$	$	$
25	20 F	40	40 F
	5 V		

The cost now divided into a fixed and variable element will be charged to the fixed or variable overhead account:

FIXED OVERHEAD (OH) ACCOUNT	VARIABLE OVERHEAD (VO) ACCOUNT
$	$
10	40
5	25
20	5
40	
Actual $75	Actual $70

COMMENT

The two overhead accounts are debited for the actual cost incurred. The accounts are, however, credited periodically as work is performed, and, the offsetting debit is made to the work-in-process account.

Apportionment and allocation procedures also play an important role in the calculation of an overhead rate. It is therefore worthwhile to examine those procedures in more detail.

3.9 Apportionment

The word 'apportionment' means to distribute or to divide proportionally. In accounting, it is a simple arithmetical tool which the accountant utilises to split up the cost of indirect expenditures which are thereafter allotted to cost centres.

The accounting function usually bases its apportionment method on fairness and equity when apportioning indirect costs to the production and service departments. The apportionment calculations require the following historical data:[1] (i) floor space dimension; (ii) acquisition cost of the machinery; (iii) no of firm's, employees; (iv) physical output, i.e. in oz, lb, tons, gals, volume. (iv) naturally depends on the product being manufactured by the firm.

The solution to Example 3.3 shows how apportionment is carried out. The example assumes that the direct departmental overheads are traceable to production and service departments.

EXAMPLE 3.3

The Barney Co. has two production departments – P1 and P2 – and one service department – S – which the firm uses to manufacture its product.

Assume that the departmental cost data shown below were the actual costs incurred in the manufacturing of a product in an accounting period, which ended in June.

BARNEY MANUFACTURING CO. DEPARTMENTAL COST DATA – JUNE 19

	DEPARTMENTS			
	P1	P2	S	Total
	$	$	$	$
Direct departmental overhead:				
Indirect labour	500	500	1000	2000
Inspection	400	600		1000
Factory supplies	550	275	175	1000
Total direct departmental overhead	$1450	$1375	$1175	$4000
Indirect overhead:				
Factory rent	5000			
Machine depreciation	500			
Factory superintendence	6000			
	$11500			
Total overhead incurred	$12950			

[1] So called because such data can be readily obtained from the firm's records.

Materials, Labour and Overhead Analysis

Data from the firm's records were:

	DEPARTMENTS			
Historical data	P1	P2	S	Total
	$	$	$	$
Ft^2 of floor space	5000	4000	1000	10000
Acquisition cost of machinery	$50000	$40000	$10000	$100000
No. of employees	50	20	10	80
Maintenance manhours	600	200	—	800

REQUIRED:

(i) departmental distribution factors
(ii) how the indirect and service departmental cost is apportioned to the production department
(iii) the overhead rate for each production department, using direct labour hours as the base

SOLUTION

(i) Calculate the distribution factors:

BARNEY MANUFACTURING COMPANY: BASIS OF OVERHEAD DISTRIBUTION—JUNE 19

	DEPARTMENTS			
	P1	P2	S	Total
Ft^2	$\dfrac{5000 \times 100}{10000}$	$\dfrac{4000 \times 100}{10000}$	$\dfrac{1000 \times 100}{10000}$	
%	50	40	10	100
Machinery cost fraction	$\dfrac{50000}{100000}$	$\dfrac{40000}{100000}$	$\dfrac{10000}{100000}$	1
No. of Employees fraction	$\dfrac{50}{80}$	$\dfrac{20}{80}$	$\dfrac{10}{80}$	1
Maintenance manhours	$\dfrac{600 \times 100}{800}$	$\dfrac{200 \times 100}{800}$		
%	75	25		

(ii) Apply the distribution factor to the type of cost:

BARNEY MANUFACTURING CO.: DISTRIBUTION OF INDIRECT OVERHEAD AND SERVICE DEPARTMENTAL COST–JUNE 19X

Type of cost	Basis of distribution	P1	P2	S	Total
		$	$	$	$
Indirect labour	Direct	500	500	1000	2000
Inspection	Direct	400	600		1000
Factory supplies	Direct	550	275	175	1000
Factory rent	Ft²	2500	2000	500	5000
Machinery depreciation	Acquisition cost of machines	250	200	50	500
Factory superintendence	No. of Employees	3750	1500	750	6000
Total overhead cost incurred		$7950	$5075	$2475	$15500
Distribution of service maintenance Department cost	ManHours	1856.25	618.75	(2475)	
Total overhead in production department		$9806.25	$569.75	0	$15500
(iii) Divide each production Dept's dollar total by its DLH[b] Incurred overhead rate[b]		÷ 1060	÷ 1500		2560
		$9.2512	$3.7958		$6.0547

[a] Direct labour hour.
[b] $ per DLH.

COMMENT

Observe that two procedures are involved after the calculation of the distribution factors: (i) allocating the overheads to the production and service cost centre; (ii) apportioning the service cost overheads to the production cost centre. Procedure (iii) begs the question: why do the production centres have to bear such a penalty? This is to ensure that products and production centres bear their full costs. Allocation, however, must now be examined in depth.

3.10 Cost allocation

Cost allocation and cost apportionment have similar traits. A subtle difference in method between the two systems lies in the fact that the indirect overhead costs which can be identified with a cost centre or department are allocated, and not apportioned, to that cost centre or department.

The firm, viewed as an hierarchical systems demonstrates the concept of allocation. The top echelons of management allocate the production, sales and service functions to the managers of those departments. The managers, in turn, allocate specific duties to the various categories of personnel in their respective departments.

For cost allocation to be undertaken in a sensible way, the cost accountant must trace and link

Materials, Labour and Overhead Analysis 47

the cost to the product for classification and pooling purposes.[1] In one-product manufacturing firms, the task of tracing cost to products can be accomplished quite easily by the accountant. In multi-product firms, however, the tracing of all costs to products is a difficult task. What are the difficulties met by the cost accountant in such firms? The difficulties relate to cost identification. With direct cost, no difficulty arises. With indirect and common cost (for example, advertisement which relates to a group of products, research expenditure, and maintenance) the problem of traceability to products arises. The problem of traceability to products is also compounded by the fact that all costs have some 'jointness' about them in the multi-product firm. The implication of jointness is that the cost accountant's classification of cost in that sphere is unclear and arbitrary. As regards common cost, Marple (1967) says:[2] 'Cost allocation is an expedient – a device developed by accountants to convert common costs into direct charges based on assumptions and to make variable rates out of non-variable costs.'

As is obvious, the procedures followed in the solution to Example 3.3 are applicable to the allocation problem in a firm where there are not many interrelationships. Where there exist service and product department interrelationships, as in a multi-product firm, reasonable solutions to the allocation problem can be obtained from one of the following methods: (i) repeated distribution; (ii) simultaneous equations; (iii) matrix methods. These methods are examined in ch. 5.

There are, however, reasons for cost allocations in the firm.

3.11 Purpose of cost allocation

Cost allocation has a similar purpose to that which was outlined for overhead rates in 3.7 above. It should be noted that the overhead rate calculations are on a per unit basis, whereas allocations are made in lump sums.

Despite its arbitrary nature, a cost allocation will also be made: (i) as a means of motivating managers towards making realistic decisions; (ii) as a means of ascertaining an agreeable price between contracting parties.

COMMENT

In relation to (i), if the allocation of costs to departmental heads is seen as an imposed cost, which they have agreed to, then managers' resultant departmental acts must be in line with the cost allocation.

(ii) refers to the situation where no external market price exists for a product which the firm is asked to manufacture by an outside party. The firm's management, by revealing its allocation base (see 3.14) in the negotiating process will enable a price to be agreed upon.

The solution to Example 3.3 showed how the overhead rate is calculated, given the actual cost data of a manufacturing firm. The solution also provides an example of multiple overhead rates.

3.12 Use of multiple overhead rates

Instead of using one plantwide or blanket rate, the overhead rate can be divided into two (or more) parts. The logic behind the division of the overhead rate is to provide management with a

---

[1] Cost can be pooled by department, natural category, or behavioural pattern.
[2] Cited in Marple, R. P. (1967).

better per unit rate, which can be used for more accurate product costing. It should be noted, also, that overhead sub-divisions can be made:

(i) rate for each product department
(ii) rates for each cost centre
(iii) rates for applying the material-related and the facility-related part of overhead cost
(iv) rates for applying the fixed part of overhead and the variable part of overhead

Of course, the choice of any one of the rates for costing purposes must rest on the answer to this vital question: do the benefits to be received from the decision exceed the cost of implementing it?

3.13 Overhead absorption rate

To absorb the actual overhead into cost units requires the calculation of an overhead absorption rate (OHAR):

$$\text{OHAR} = \frac{\text{Total cost centre overheads}}{\text{Denominator}}$$

where the denominator base can be obtained from one of the following:

(i) Machine cost
(ii) Machine hour
(iii) Direct labour cost
(iv) Direct labour hour
(v) Direct material cost
(vi) Material unit
(vii) Total variable cost

How are the above rates calculated? The solution to Example 3.4 shows a way of making this computation.

EXAMPLE 3.4

Basil Ltd produces two products, B1 and B2. The actual data for the year were as follows:

	PRODUCT			
	B1		B2	
	$		$	
Variable cost per unit				
Material (6 lb × $2)	12.00	(4lb × $2.50)	10.00	
Labour (2 hr × $1.75)	3.50	(3hr × $2)	6.00	
Machine cost (1 hr × $3)	3.00	(2.5hr × $4)	10.00	
Total variable cost per unit	$18.50		$26.00	
Budgeted output (units)	10 000		8000	
Total actual overhead (TAH)	$185 000			

REQUIRED

Calculate the overhead absorbed by production according to each of the methods listed in 3.13 above.

Materials, Labour and Overhead Analysis

SOLUTION

Collect the terms of interest in matrix form, and perform simple matrix multiplication:

	UNIT DATA			UNITS					UNITS
Products				$B0$		B_1	B_2	$Total_i$	
MC	1	,	1	⎡10 000	0⎤	10 000	8 000	18 000	
MH	3	,	4	⎣	8000⎦	30 000	32 000	62 000	$
DLC	1	,	2.5			10 000	20 000	30 000	Hrs
DLH	3.50	,	6.0			35 000	48 000	83 000	$
DMC	2	,	3			20 000	24 000	44 000	$
MU	12	,	10			120 000	80 000	200 000	$
TVC	6	,	4			60 000	32 000	92 000	Lb
	18.50	,	26			185 000	208 000	393 000	$

Calculate $OHAR_i = TBOH \dfrac{1}{Total}$.

$OHAR_i \times$ each B_1 and B_2 gives the amount charged to each product.

The results are:

VALUES		OHAR$_i$		AMOUNT ABSORBED BY PRODUCTION	
				B_1 $	B_2 $
a	$\dfrac{1}{18\,000}$	$10.27778	Per unit	102 777.8	82 222.24
	$\dfrac{1}{62\,000}$	$ 2.98387[a]	Per $ of machine cost	89 516.1	95 583.04
	$\dfrac{1}{30\,000}$	$ 6.16667	Per machine hr	61 666.7	123 333.4
$185 000	$\dfrac{1}{83\,000}$	=$ 2.22892	Per $ of labour cost	78 012.0	106 988.24
	$\dfrac{1}{44\,000}$	$ 4.20455	Per labour hr	84 091	100 909
	$\dfrac{1}{200\,000}$	$ 0.925[a]	Per $ of material cost	111 000	74 000
	$\dfrac{1}{92\,000}$	$ 2.01087	Per lb of material used	120 652.2	64 347.84
	$\dfrac{1}{393\,000}$	$ 0.47074[a]	Per $ of TVC	87 086.9	97 913.92

[a] It is an accounting convention to express such figures in percentages. Line 2 would therefore be expressed as 298.387 per cent of the machine cost.

COMMENT

The rationale for charging overhead cost to products is to facilitate the calculation of accounting profit. The absorption method or the direct costing method can be used by the accountant to calculate profit; controversy surrounds both methods, and it is thus worthwhile to examine each briefly in relation to overhead cost (see 3.16 below).

The reader may ask; why are there so many bases, and which is the most suitable for product costing purposes? The answer lies in the fact, that cost accounting is not an exact science. There are arguments for and against the use of each of the common bases.

3.14 Arguments for and against absorption bases

MACHINE COST   The main justification for its use is in those cases where the labour and the equipment needed for the handling of materials forms a part of the overhead. The base, however, ignores the time factor, which is its major weakness.

MACHINE HOURS   This base can be used to apply overhead to the product in cases where machinery is the main factor in production, i.e. in automated factories. The base incorporates time. Against this, there is the measurement difficulty connected with: (i) the different vintages of machines, and hence with work performance on them; and (ii) the problem of calculating machine time on individual jobs.

DIRECT LABOUR COST   The base takes account of the time factor. If labour rates are even and if direct labour is the principal productive element, the base is a good one. The base can be justified on the grounds of its simplicity and low clerical cost.

When the overheads of a firm are a function of time and not cost, the direct labour costs figure is not representative of the overhead incurred.

DIRECT LABOUR HOURS   The base is a good one when labour operations constitute the central factor in production. The base incorporates the time factor but ignores the value added to the product by other factors of production.

DIRECT MATERIAL COST   The justification of this base is similar to that for machine cost. If the material used by the firm is controlled by machines so that output is related to time in an uniform way, the base is also useful. Against that view is the fact that the value of material used per time period is not uniform in manufacturing firms.

MATERIAL UNIT   The base is specially suited to situations where a uniform product is made and the work effort devoted to all the units is the same. The base is applicable only where a few closely related products are made.

TOTAL VARIABLE COST   The base includes the time factor, since labour is involved, which is indicative of time spent on manufacturing operations. If the elements, which make up total variable cost remain proportionate, the base for product costing purposes gives adequate results. Against this it can be argued that the inclusion of the material cost element in the total variable cost base dilutes it.

Any one of the these bases can be used by the accounting function for the actual calculation of the overhead rate. Most cost accounting decisions are future oriented; viewed from that perspective, it is clear that an actual overhead rate calculation can be beneficial to management only if it can be evaluated with another rate of a similar hue, but with a forward planning orientation. The predetermined overhead absorption (POHR) is such a rate.

Materials, Labour and Overhead Analysis

3.15 Predetermined overhead absorption rate (POHR)

This implies the determination of a decision rate before its actual ascertainment and verification. Why is such a rate required in relation to overhead analysis? Dynamic costing requires it for the following reasons: (i) for pricing and current costing of jobs, especially those completed during an accountancy period; (ii) to iron out month to month fluctuations in the incurred rate, thus permitting improved comparability of job costs. POHR is, of course, as estimate. It is calculated as follows:

$$\text{POHR} = \frac{\text{Budgeted overhead for the future period}}{\text{Budgeted denominator for the future period}}$$

Because of the uncertainties of estimates, it is an axiom that the actual overheads incurred will differ from the amount of overheads absorbed in an accounting period. The over-or under-absorption will be caused by two factors:

(i) the difference between the actual and the budgeted overheads and
(ii) the difference between the actual and the budgeted denominator base

The solution to Example 3.5 draws attention to those factors.

EXAMPLE 3.5

The management function of Bunny Ltd budgets that in an accountancy period the total overhead cost of the firm would be $60 000 and its labour hours 12 000.
The actual results at the end of the period were: overhead costs $65 000, labour hours worked 11 6000.

REQUIRED:

Calculate the deviation and show why it occurred.

SOLUTION

(i) Calculate the budgeted overhead absorption rate (BOAR)

$$\frac{\$60\,000}{12\,000} = \$5 \text{ per hr}$$

The amount charged to production is therefore

labour hr worked × BOAR = 11 600 hr × $5
= $58 000

which results in an underabsorption of $(65 000 − 58 000) = $7000.

(ii) The deviation occurred for two reasons:

(a) The difference between the actual and the budgeted overhead, i.e. $(65 000 − 60 000) = $5000 and
(b) the difference between the actual and the budgeted hours, i.e. (400 × $5) = $2000.

COMMENT:

The predetermined rate applied $7000 less overhead to the factory than was incurred during the period. Since in practice deviations (either under- or over-applied) will occur, the following question is appropriate: how are the deviations reflected in the firm's financial income statement at the end of an accounting period? The deviations will be adjusted to the cost of goods sold on the income statement. The journal entries which capture the events would appear thus:

	$	$
Under-applied overhead	7000	
Factory overhead applied	58 000	
Overhead control		65 000

To close overhead applied and overhead incurred, and to record the amount of overhead under-applied for the period:

	$	$
Cost of goods sold	7000	
Under-applied overhead		7000

To close under-applied overhead to cost of goods sold.

3.16 Absorption costing and direct costing

Absorption costing (the traditional approach) is a full costing system, where factory overhead is inventoried. In contrast, direct costing splits the factory overhead into its fixed and variable parts, and does not place the fixed part in inventory. Naturally the two systems, which utilise different format presentations, will give different profit figures. The solution to Example 3.6 shows why these differences occur.

EXAMPLE 3.6

Assume that Basil Ltd overhead (Example 3.4) was recovered on the basis of total variable cost, and that the selling prices of the products B_1 and B_2 were respectively $28 and $35.

REQUIRED

Compute the profit or loss of the two products, using respectively the absorption and the direct costing methods.

SOLUTION

Absorption costing

	PRODUCT			
	B_1		B_2	
Output (units)	10 000		8000	
Sales		$280 000		$280 000
Less TVC	$185 000		$208 000	
Overhead (0.47074 × TVC)	87 087	272 087	97 914	305 914
Profit (Loss)		$7913		$(25 914)

Materials, Labour and Overhead Analysis 53

Direct costing

	PRODUCT		
	B_1	B_2	Total
	$	$	$
Sales revenue	280 000	280 000	560 000
Less TVC	185 000	208 000	393 000
Contribution	$ 95 000	$ 72 000	$167 000
Fixed overhead cost			185 000
Profit (Loss)			$(18 000)

COMMENT

The absorption method shows that product B_2 is unprofitable and should on logical grounds be eliminated from the product line. The contribution line of the direct costing method, however, tells a different story.

The direct costing method separates the fixed cost from each product. The method also shows that both products make positive contributions to the firm. The total contribution, however, is insufficient to cover the fixed cost. If product line B_2 were eliminated, Basil Ltd will lose $72 000 (note that the contribution is simply the difference between the sales and the variable cost of each product).

3.17 Summary

The direct materials which the firm acquires from outside sources to produce goods can be accounted for through purchase invoices and requisitions. Purchase invoices can be classified according to type, and are used to update the creditors' ledger accounts. In a similar way, the purchase invoices can be used to update the stores record cards.

The employees of the firm are vital, and production employees are remunerated by three methods. The cost per hour to the firm can be calculated from the total cost of employment divided by net productive hours. This figure can be used by the firm to apply labour costs to products.

Costs which cannot be identified with a cost unit are overheads. Overheads are apportioned by many methods, and the choice of method depends on sound judgement.

Predetermined overhead absorption rates are necessary to the firm because of the dynamic, planning features of cost accounting; predetermined overheads are not accurate.

The rationale for absorbing overhead costs to products is to recover accounting profits, but care should be exercised when using the absorption costing method in decision analysis. The contribution method is better.

Bibliography

Bierman, H. and Dyckman, T. R. (1976) *Managerial Cost Accounting*, 2nd edn (Macmillan) p. 37.
Dearden, J. (1973) *Cost Accounting and Financial Control Systems* (Addison–Wesley) ch. 2.
Hart, H. (1973) *Overhead Costs: Analysis and Control* (Heinemann).
Marple, R. P. 'Management Accounting is Coming of Age', *Management Accounting*, 48, no. 11 (July 1967) pp. 3–16.
Schattke, R. W. and Jensen, H. G. (1978) *Managerial Accounting, Concept and Uses*, 2nd edn (Allyn & Baker) ch. 5.

Problems

3.1 The ABC Co. has two production departments, machining and finishing, and two service departments, maintenance and materials handling.

The overhead budgets per 4-week period are $9000 for the machining department, and $7500 for the finishing department. The machining department overhead is absorbed on a machine hour basis (300 per period) and finishing department overhead is absorbed on the basis of direct labour hours (3000 per period).

In estimating the overhead budgets of the production departments, service department costs have been dealt with as follows:

	%	
Maintenance	60	machining dept
	30	finishing dept, and
	10	materials handling
Materials	30	machine dept
handling	50	finishing dept, and
	20	maintenance dept

During period VI, the machining department was in operation for 292 hours, and the number of direct labour hours worked by finishing department personnel was 3100. Overhead incurred during period VI was as follows:

	Machining $	Finishing $	Maintenence $	Material handling
Materials	2000	3000	1000	200
Labour	3000	900	2000	3000
Other allocated costs	600	400	800	300

REQUIRED

(a) Write up the overhead account for each of the production departments for period VI, showing the disposition of any under- or over-absorption
(b) State the factors which gave rise to the under- or over-absorption and
(c) Analyse the under- or over-absorption under the headings you have stated in your answer to (b)

ACA, FE, Part B, Paper 6, Accounting 2, Costing, June 1975.

3.2 Shown below is next year's budget for a small engineering factory manufacturing two different products in two production departments, a machine shop and an assembly department. A canteen is also operated as a separate department:

Product	A	B
Selling price, per unit	$60	$70
Sales volume	1500 units	3000 units
Increase (Decrease) in finished stocks	500 units	(500) units
Material cost, per unit	$8	$5
Direct labour:	Hr per unit	Hr per unit
Machine shop ($3 per hr)	5	6
Assembly Dept ($2 per hr)	4	4
Machining:		
Machine shop	3	8
Assembly Dept	1	—

	Machine shop	Assembly dept	Canteen	Total
	$	$	$	$
Production overhead:				
Variable	26 000	9000	—	35 000
Fixed	42 000	30 000	16 000	88 000
	$68 000	$39 000	$16 000	$123 000
No of employees	15	9	1	
Floor area (ft²)	4000	1000	1000	

REQUIRED

(a) Establish an appropriate overhead absorption rate for each production department, and calculate the total budgeted cost per unit of each product. You must clearly state, and briefly justify, the methods of overhead absorption used
(b) Assuming the company operates a full absorption costing system, calculate the impact on budgeted profit if, next year, the actual results are as predicted except that sales and production of product A are 300 units higher than budget

ACA, FE, Part B, Paper 6, Accounting 2, Costing, December 1979.

3.3. B. Ilder commenced business on 1 May 1976, having obtained three orders for house extensions, the costs of which during his first month's trading were as follows:

	JOB		
	1	2	3
	$	$	$
Direct wages	528	451	308
Materials issued from stores	2752	2341	1473
Special materials bought in	215	—	46
Materials returned to stores	71	—	—

Ilder has estimated his overhead for the year ended 30 April 1977 at $10 500 and the direct labour hours at 17 500. Under a trade union agreement dated 1 May, all direct workers were paid 110p per hour from that date. For costing purposes, overhead is absorbed on a direct labour hour basis; the overhead incurred in May was $800.

Job No. 1 was completed on 31 May, and invoiced to the customer at the contracted amount of $4500.

REQUIRED

(i) cost accounts for each of the three jobs
(ii) control accounts for overhead and work in progress for May
(iii) profit and loss Account for May

3.4 Jonna Ltd manufactures two products, X_1 and X_2, to which the following details relate:

	PRODUCT	
	X_1	X_2
Direct material cost	$12	$18.50
Direct labour cost		
Machining $0.70 per h	5 hr	8 hr
Assembly $0.60 per h	3 hr	4 hr

The company plans to produce 40 000 of product X_1, and 50 000 of product X_2 during the forthcoming year, and estimates its overhead for that year at $200 000.

REQUIRED

(a) Calculate three overhead absorption rates:
   (i) percentage of prime cost
   (ii) direct labour hour
   (iii) machine hour

(b) Briefly state which of the three rates you consider most appropriate.

Chapter 4
Job Costing, Unit Costing, Process Costing and Joint Product Costing —'The Quartet'

An accounting system for a manufacturing concern would be inadequate if it did not provide for the determination of product costs. To begin with product costs are needed to arrive at inventory amounts for work-in-process and for finished goods. These amounts are required in the preparation of financial statements.   (Walgenbach *et al.*, 1977)

4.1 Introduction

Each element 'the quartet' — job costing, unit costing, process costing and joint product costing — has distinguishing features. Job costing deals with discrete systems. When products are made continuously, a process costing system emerges. Unit costing is applicable to both systems. Process manufacturing creates other products which are called joint products. Joint products give rise to by-products.

This chapter examines the costing tools applicable to 'the quartet'.

4.2 Job costing[1]

The word 'job' is generally applied to a piece of work done by an individual. In relation to the firm, job costing means the linking of work, activity, time, place, and money) to a specific item or batch of items. In relation to cost accounting, Kohler (1970) defines job costing as 'a method of

---

[1] The terms 'specific order', 'production order', 'job lot cost system' and 'job order costing' are also used.

cost accounting whereby costs are compiled for a specific quantity of products, equipment, repairs, or other services that move through the production process as a continuously identifiable unit'. With job costing, each individual job (or batch) is treated as if it were unique, and an attempt is made (see 4.4) to allocate the full cost of production to the job. Job costing[1] is usually employed by building contractors, furniture manufacturers, pottery and paper product industries and shipbuilders. It is particularly applicable when jobs are actually unique – when a specific item (or batch of items) is to be manufactured or modified according to a customer's specification.

4.3 Job order cost system

An important aspect of job costing is the cost sheet. This is a form on which charges for direct materials, direct labour and indirect manufacturing cost are accumulated as work on a job proceeds. Figure 4.1 shows a typical form.

Job no. _____   Date started _____
                    Date completed _____
Department _____
Manufactured for:
Stock _____
Customer _____   Units completed _____

MATERIALS		DIRECT LABOUR			MANUFACTURING OVERHEAD		
Req. no.	Amt	Card	Hr	Amt	Hr	Rate	Amount

COST SUMMARY		UNITS SHIPPED		
Materials		Date	No.	Balance
Direct labour				
Overhead				
Total cost				
Unit cost				

Figure 4.1 Job cost sheet form

4.4 Mechanics of job order system

When a production order is put in motion, a cost sheet – identified by a job number – is set up in the job ledger. The job sheet is prepared by the cost accounting department upon notification by

---

[1] The cost system outlined below does not apply to contractors who are handling large jobs that are expected to continue for long periods of time.

the production department that a production order has been issued for a particular job. The production order indicates that a contractual agreement has been made with the customer and the firm, in terms of quantities, price and shipment dates.

The production activity commences with the transfer of the direct raw materials from the storeroom to the production line. As materials are issued, the cost office or department makes entries directly on the job cost sheet,[1] thus charging the specific job in process. Of course, the charges — i.e., indirect labour that cannot be traced to the specific job — are treated as part of the manufacturing overheads.

The labour hours are accumulated by the employees on time tickets. The time tickets at the end of a day are each analysed by the cost office in terms of the number of hours assignable as direct labour to the specific job, and the number of hours assignable to manufacturing overheads as indirect labour. The cost summary section of Figure 4.1 shows the cost of the whole job.

The manufacturing overhead figure is an indirect cost to units of product. It includes a mixture of unlike items, e.g. variable and fixed costs. It is an estimated measure, since the actual overhead costs of the firm cannot be derived until after an accounting period is over. Chapter 3 showed its computation from several bases. However, in assigning the overhead cost to the job cost sheet, and thus to the units of product, the predetermined overhead rate is multiplied by the base activity for the job, and the total amount entered on the job cost sheet.

With the application of the manufacturing overhead to the job cost sheet, the total cost of the job is summarised in the cost summary. The cost of the individual units of the job is obtained by dividing the total cost by the units produced, which gives the unit cost.[2] The completed job cost sheet is then ready to be transferred to the finished goods inventory account, where it becomes an anchor measure for either costing unsold units in the ending inventory, or charging expense for units sold.

Figures 4.2 and 4.3 show respectively the flow documents and a general model of cost flows in a job order costing system; the solution to Example 4.1 shows how the technical aspects of job costing are handled.

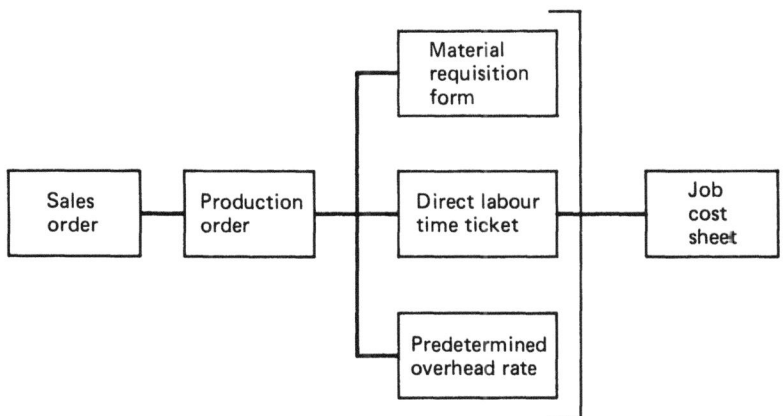

Figure 4.2 Flow of documents in a job order costing system

---

[1] Note that a centralised job cost system is envisaged here. A decentralised system is one where the cost sheets accompany job through the plant.

[2] See solution to Example 4.2, where unit cost calculations are shown.

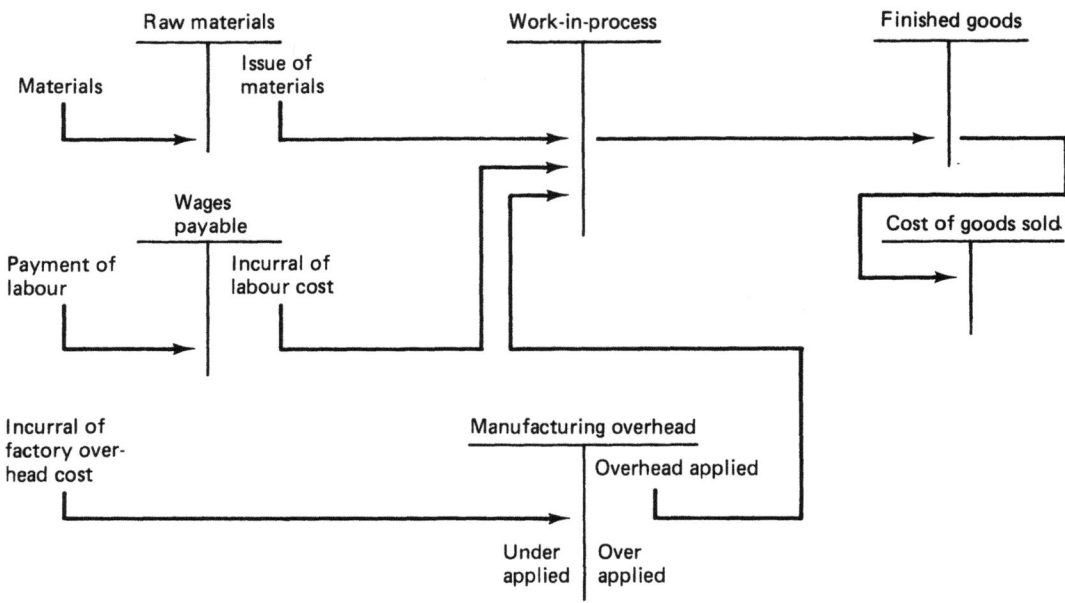

Figure 4.3 General model of cost flows in job order costing system

EXAMPLE 4.1

The Erlin firm contracted with one of its clients to make two products, called X_1 and X_2. The products were respectively given the job numbers 01 and 02. The data below relate to the making of the products:

		$
(i)	Purchased materials and supplies	4000
(ii)	Issues of materials	
	Direct materials:	
	Job Order no. 01	2000
	Job Order no. 02	700
		$2700
	Indirect materials	500
		$3200
(iii)	The payroll summary showed the following totals:	
	Direct labour:	
	Job no. 01-200hr @ $4.75	$950.00
	Job no. 02-105hr @ $4.75	498.75
		$1448.75
	Indirect labour	250.25
		$1699.00

'The Quartet' 61

(iv) Other indirect factory costs totalled $300
(v) Job order no. 01 was completed, and 200 units of product X_1 were transferred to the finished goods inventory. The indirect manufacturing costs were added to the cost sheet, using an application rate of $3.2789 per direct labour hour. The cost sheet was then totalled
(vi) 100 of the 200 units of product X_1 were sent to the customer
(vii) The indirect manufacturing cost (IMC) applied at the end of the period was 305 × $3.2789 = 1000 To bring the cost ledger up to date, indirect manufacturing costs of $105 × $3.2789 = $344 were added to the cost sheet for X_2, which was still in process

REQUIRED

Show the entries in the factory ledger, and the job ledger cost calculations.

SOLUTION

The entries in the factory ledger can be shown in two ways, either in the matrix format[1] or in the traditional T account format. Both methods are presented in Figures 4.4 and 4.5.

COMMENT

It can be seen that both methods give the same result. We aver, however, that the matrix format highlights the cost interrelationships of a production system. That factor is not so evident in the T account format. The matrix presentation enables one to perform easy arithmetical checks, since the sum of the rows − the sum of the columns = 0. It is important to note that the computer application to the problem would (with minor changes) be handled in a similar way.

So far, we have not examined the following topics in relation to job costing: (i) spoiled units, (ii) an appropriate base from which overhead can be applied to jobs; (iii) whether direct absorption or standard cost is applicable to job costing: (iv) the control aspects of job costing; and (v) an evaluation of job costing. Spoiled units are examined in 4.13 below. The other topics are now examined.

4.5 Applying overhead to individual jobs

The base through which overhead can be applied to individual jobs should be made up of parts that can be identified with individual jobs. Direct labour hours seem to be appropriate.

4.6 Use of direct, absorption or standard costing in job costing

Direct or absorption costing can be applied to job costing. When direct costing is employed, its impact is seen in the separation made of the manufacturing overhead cost into fixed and variable parts. The variable manufacturing costs are charged to the work-in-process and the appropriate charge sheets in relation to particular jobs.

Standard costing can be used in a job costing department.[2] Standard costing will always

---

[1] In the presentation, the credits are bracketed. The Number 1 . . . are inserted in the matrix so as to facilitate the tracing of entries. In essence, the system has an input/output structure. An appreciation of that fact helps one to trace the entries. As indicated earlier in, ch. 2* provides an introduction to matrices for the reader who is unfamiliar with this branch of mathematics.

[2] Standard costing techniques are applied in Example 4.5, see 4.13 below.

[3] ICMA (1974) defines conversion cost to be 'the sum of the production cost of converting purchased materials into finished products, i.e. Direct wages, Direct Expenses and Absorbed production overhead'.

DEBITS

	A Material & supplies	B Indirect manu-facturing cost	C Work-in-process	D Indirect manu-facturing cost applied	E Finished goods	F General ledger	G Cost of sales	CHECK FIGURES
A		(ii) 500	(ii) 2700			(i((4000)		(800)
B	(ii) (500)			(vii) 1000		(iii) (250.25) (iv) (300)		(50.25)
C	(ii) (2700)			(viii) (1000)	(v) 3606	(iii) (1,448.75)		(542.75)
CREDITS D		(vii) (1000)	(viii) (1000)					(1000)
E		(iii) 250.25 (iv) 300	(v) (3606)				(v9) 1803	(1803)
F	(i) 4000		(iii) 1 448.75		(vi) (1803)			5999
G					1803	(5999)	1803	(1803)
BALANCES $	800	50.25	1542.75	0				

Job ledger – Cost sheets

JOB ORDER NO. 01	$
Materials	2000
Direct labour	950
IMC applied:	
200 hrs × $3.2789	656
Completed ½	$3606
Cost of sales (100)	1803
Stock (100)	1803

JOB ORDER NO. 02	$
Materials	700.00
Direct labour	498.75
IMC applied:	
105 hrs × $3.2789	344.00
Cost of work-in-process	$1542.75

Figure 4.4 Factory ledger – Matrix format

Material supplies

		$			$
(i)	General ledger	4000	(ii)	Ind. manf. cost	500
			(ii)	Work-in-process	2700

General ledger

					$
			(i)	Material supp.	4000.00
			(iii)	Ind. manf. cost	250.25
			(iii)	Work-in-process	1448.75
			(iv)	Ind. manf. cost	300.00

Indirect manufacturing cost

		$			$
(ii)	Material supplies	500.00	(vii)	Cost applied	1000
(iii)	General ledger	250.25			
(iv)	General ledger	300.00			

Work-in-process

		$			$
(ii)	Material suppl.	2700.00	(v)	Finished goods	3606.00
(iii)	General ledger	1448.75			
(viii)	Indirect cost	1000.00			

Indirect manufacturing cost applied

		$			$
(vii)	Cost incurred	1000	(viii)	Work-in-process	1000

Cost of sales

		$			
(vi)	F. goods	1803.00			

Finished goods

		$			$
(v)	Work in process	3606.00	(vi)	Cost of sales	1803.00

Figure 4.5 Factory ledger – traditional 'T' A/c format

facilitate the preparation of job cost estimates on individual jobs, and will enable management comparisons and evaluations to be made.

4.7 Reports on completed jobs

A job costing system requires periodic review of operations. This is necessary for the calculation of profit or loss on individual jobs. It is therefore necessary that a monthly summary, which shows gross profit calculations by individual jobs, should be shown to management.

From a control viewpoint, the report on completed jobs should be submitted to a responsible officer of the firm, who is designated by top management to investigate any difference between the actual and the estimated cost of the jobs.

4.8 Evaluation of job costing

This is best illustrated by listing the advantages and disadvantages of job costing. A central advantage of a job costing system is that it compiles cost data in a manner that is useful to the administration of the business. A cost system must provide relevant cost data very soon after the expenditure is incurred, and in a usable form. The cost of obtaining that information must be compared with its worth, however. In the industries to which it is suited, job costing should enable management to detect which jobs are profitable, and which are not. Job costing should also help management to control operations, and to prevent fraud. Job costing combined with performance evaluation and review techniques (PERT) would be advantageous to many firms (PERT is not examined in this book).

The disadvantage of job costing is that it is expensive to operate, since it involves a great deal of clerical work. So direct labour workmen repairing a ship could each work on 10 different jobs in one week; the entries on the job cost sheets would require $50 \times 10 = 500$ separate postings. Another disadvantage of job costing is that it involves production employees in clerical, at the expense of productive, work.

4.9 Process costing

A dictionary definition of the word process is 'an act which continues and progresses'. In relation to cost accounting, process costing is a system through which costs are accumulated by processes or departments or cost centres in a manufacturing firm for a selected period of time — the time period for costing purposes usually lasts a month. During the cost period materials, labour and indirect manufacturing cost are charged to the different processes through which the product passes.

Process costing is applicable to those manufacturing situations where the output is homogeneous; the production process is continuous within each period; and production runs are repetitive and last for long periods of time. Example of process products can be found in the sugar, petroleum and cement industries.

4.10 Functions of process costing

The basic principle of process costing is to accumulate and allocate service department expenses; calculate the unit conversion cost for each process at the end of each cost period; transfer costs from process to process or from one department to another (in order to accomplish this, the transferred product must be priced, and a value must also be placed on any items which remain in process).

4.11 Procedures of process cost accounting

There are three major process cost systems: (i) sequential; (ii) parallel; (iii) selective. In illustrating the procedures of process cost accounting, we are concerned with sequential process cost. By 'sequential process cost', we mean the situation where the homogenous product goes through a series of processes in sequence. In this system, the costs are transferred from one process to another as the product is transferred, with the cost of the finished product being transferred from the last process account to the finished goods account. The T accounts in Figure 4.6 show the general flow of cost in a sequential process cost system.

It is important for the reader to note at this stage, that not all the units or materials which are put into production will pass through all the processing departments of the firm. Semi-finished products which are saleable will not reach the final processing stage, for example. Units will also be spoilt in processing. Note, too, that it is also possible that materials will not always be added by all the departments in a processing system.

Of importance to process costing is unit costing. Under a process cost system, unit costs are usually calculated monthly from cost data taken from the cost accounting records. Production data also come from the producing departments. In order to calculate unit costs, each department of the firm will make up a production record showing the number of units that were started in process during the period, the number of units that were spoiled or lost in the processing of the materials, the number of units that were completed, and the number of units that are still in process at the end of the period. If units (as is generally the case) are still in process, estimates of the stage of completion by cost element, material, labour and indirect manufacturing are estimated and included. Figure 4.7 shows what a typical production record looks like.

COMMENT

The control aspects of cost accounting must distinguish between normal and abnormal spoilage, not only for keeping management informed, but also for product costing prupuses. 'Normal spoilage' is a technical phenomenon; the management in process industries selects a spoilage rate that it regards as normal, after evaluating the human and mechanical aspects of man – machine efforts in processing materials. The cost of normal spoilage is accepted as part of the goods produced.

'Abnormal spoilage' is that which is not expected to arise under planned production operations.[1] The cost of abnormal spoilage is usually written off as a loss in the profit and loss

---

[1] See Appendix, p. 86 for an example demonstrating the treatment of a normal spoilage in process accounts.

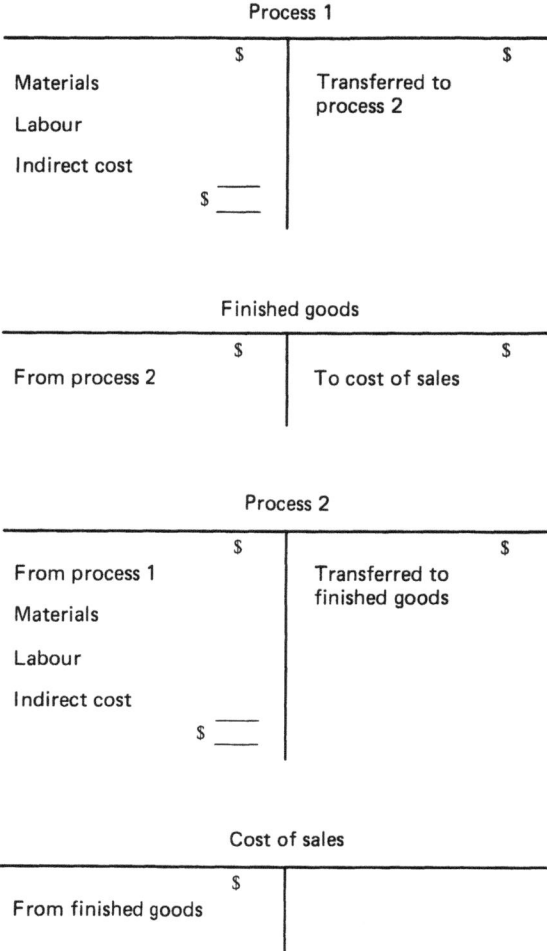

Figure 4.6   Flow of cost in sequential process cost system

account. For management information purposes, the loss from abnormal spoilage should be highlighted.

Let us, however, illustrate via the solution to Example 4.2 a typical set of postings that are required in a process cost system.

EXAMPLE 4.2

The Babe-Barrow Co. is engaged in making ceramic clay tiles. During a particular month, the transactions listed below occurred in the company.

1. materials and supplies purchased for factory use amounted to $50000
2. materials and supplies costing $30000 were issued; an analysis of the stores requisition showed the withdrawals by the department to be: assembly $13000; finishing $8600; building and maintenance $5400; factory office $3000
3. the factory payroll vouchered for payment total $30000; the payroll sheets showed the departmental breakdowns to be: assembly $8000; finishing $12000; building and maintenance $5000; factory office $5000

'The Quartet' 67

	DEPARTMENT	
MONTH January 19	Assembling	Finishing
Units started in dept or received from preceding dept		
Units lost in processing		
Units spoiled in processing:		
Normal		
Abnormal	——	——
Units completed	——	——
Disposition of completed production:		
Completed units retained in dept		
Completed units transferred out of dept	——	——
Total units completed	——	——

Figure 4.7 Manufacturing company production record

4. vouchers were prepared for the following invoices: rent $500; machinery repair $200, allocated 25 per cent to assembly, 75 per cent to finishing; electricity $300
5. depreciation of $4000 was estimated and recorded on machinery and equipment-Assembly $2000; finishing $2000
6. the building maintenance department costs were allocated to the factory office and the assembly and finishing departments in the ratios respectively of 0.2: 0.6: 0.2; the costs amounted to $800
7. the factory office costs were allocated to the two producing departments respectively 60 per cent and 40 per cent
8. all the production of 20000 units which was started in the assembly department was transferred to the finishing department; the costs accumulated in the former department was transferred to the finishing department.
9. all the production units started in the finishing department were completed during the period; the costs accumulated in the finishing department were transferred to finished goods inventory

REQUIRED

(a) Show the process accounting entries in the factory ledger for the particular month
(b) Show the unit cost data for the assembly, service and finishing departments

SOLUTION

The 'T' account headings which are shown in Figure 4.8 can be obtained from the question. The numbers alongside the postings facilitate the tracing of entries. The unit cost data can be shown as in Figure 4.9.

COMMENT

The essence of a process costing system is simply the transference of cost from one department to another, in order to calculate unit cost data for management decisionmaking.

The global formula for unit cost calculation in a process cost department is:

$$\text{Unit cost} = \frac{\text{Material} + \text{Labour} + \text{Manufacturing overhead}}{\text{Quantity produced}}$$

The finer calculations of unit cost facilitates comparisons by management between divisions of the firm. Note the segregation of the cost data in the statement, the significance of which is explained in ch. 9.

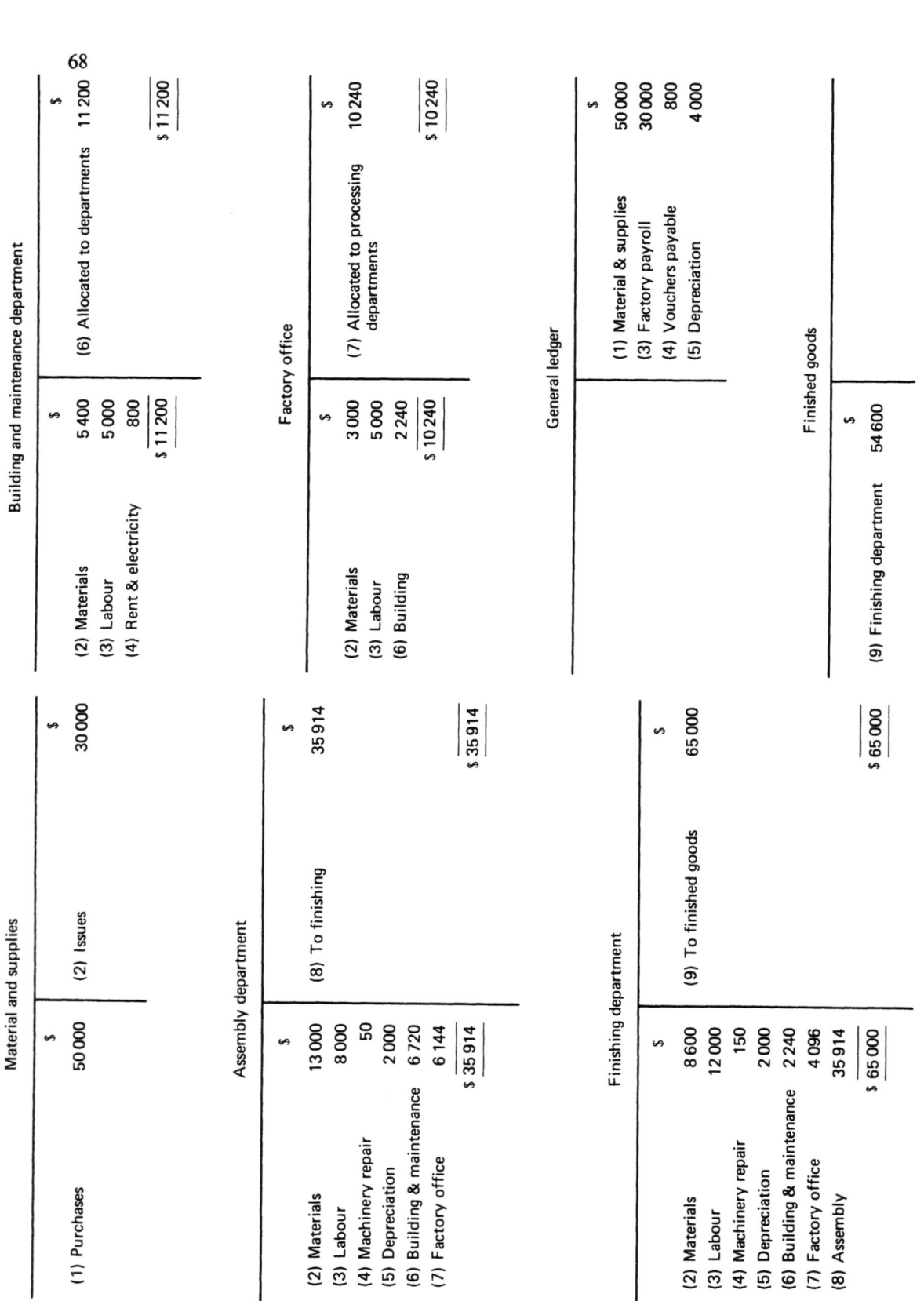

Figure 4.8 Factory ledger – Process accounting entries

MONTH................YEAR

Production 20 000 units

	ASSEMBLY DEPT		FINISHING DEPT	
Cost	Total cost	Unit cost[a]	Total cost	Unit cost[b]
Material	13 000	0.6500	8 600	0.4300
Labour	8 000	0.4000	12 000	0.6000
Indirect manufacturing cost	2 050	0.1025	2 150	0.1075
Direct department cost	$ 23 050	$ 1.1525	$ 22 750	$ 1.1375
Service department cost:				
Building & maintenance	6 720	0.3360	2 240	0.1120
Factory office	6 144	0.3072	4 096	0.2048
Cost from preceding dept	–	–	35 914	1.7957
Cumulative cost	$ 35 914	$ 1.7957	$ 65 000	$ 3.2500

[a] $\dfrac{13\,000}{20\,000} = 0.6500$. [b] $\dfrac{8\,600}{20\,000} = 0.4300$.

Figure 4.9 Babe-Barrow Manufacturing Co. – Unit cost data

The quantity produced can be expressed in any measure of production. The determination of the unit cost in a process costing system where there are large quantities of uncompleted units on hand at the beginning or end of a period present problems to accountants. How do accountants obtain a suitable unit cost figure by which to value completed and uncompleted units in such cases. Accountants, since they are practical people, express the work of a department in terms of a common denominator which is called equivalent production.[1] That concept is examined below.

4.12 Concept of equivalent production

'Equivalent production' represents the number of complete units that would have been produced if all the work performed during the period had been applied to units which were begun and finished during the period. Equivalent production therefore expresses partly completed goods in terms of completed units–500 units which are considered to be half completed are 'equivalent' to 250 completed units, for example.

To calculate a figure of equivalent production, the accountant must have quantitative data[2] as to the stage of completion of both opening and closing inventories, the units put into process, and the units completed. There are several ways of calculating equivalent production. The solution to Example 4.3 illustrates three methods.

---

[1] Note that if an accountant is asked to calculate the equivalent production of conversion, he must also be given data on materials, labour and overheads.

[2] The common denominator is also called 'effective production', 'effective effort', or equivalent effort'.

EXAMPLE 4.3

The Doreen firm, manufacturers of cloth caps, has collected the inventory and unit data shown below for an accounting period.

	Units	
Opening inventory	15000	2/5 complete
Put into process	20000	
Brought to completion	27000	
Ending inventory	8000	1/4 complete

REQUIRED

Calculate the equivalent production.

SOLUTION

The equivalent production can be calculated in three ways:

Method (i)

	Units
1. Units completed during period	27000
2. *Add* ending work-in-process inventory units started but not finished 8000 units × 1/4	2000
	29000
3. *Less* beginning work in process, i.e. work done in a previous period which is units brought to completion this period 15000 units × 2/5	6000
Equivalent production	23000 units

Method (ii)

1. % of work required to complete opening inventory 15000 units × 3/5	9000
2. *Add* no. of units started no. of units in ending inventory (20000–8000) units	12000
3. *Add* % of work done on ending inventory 8000 units × 1/4	2000
Equivalent production	23000 units

Method (iii)

1. % of work required to complete opening inventory 15000 units × 3/5	9000
2. *Add* units put into production	20000
	29000
3. *Less* % of work in units required to complete the ending inventory 8000 units × 3/4	6000
Equivalent production	23000 units

'The Quartet'

COMMENT

Any one of these methods will give the same solution; the reader can choose the method he or she prefers. The equivalent production calculation is a key measure. From it can be calculated a cost per equivalent unit and the cost allocation between transferred units and ending inventories. The solution to Example 4.4 illustrates the procedure.

EXAMPLE 4.4

The quantities and cost incurred by a process demartment of the Kip Asquith firm in an accounting period were as follows:

Cost information	$
Raw materials	54
Input from previous process	126
	180
Direct labour	50
Indirect cost	30
Total	$250

Output information	Units
Completed during period	25
Work-in-process at beginning of period	0
Work-in-process at end of period 15 units, 2/3 processed	10 equivalent production)

Assume that the input from the previous process entered at the beginning of this process, and that labour is expended throughout the process.

REQUIRED

Show Kip, the manager, how the equivalent production measure is used to divide the total cost between the work-in-process and the finished goods.

SOLUTION

1. Add up the material cost
   This amounts to $180
   This figure will be split between work-in-process and completed output (units).

Material cost: $180

Item	Completed	Equivalent production	Value of materials	1
	Units	%		
Work-in-process	15	100	15	67.50[a]
Completed cost	25	100	25	112.50
				1180.00

[a] $(\frac{15}{40}, \frac{25}{40})$ 1180 = 1 (67.50, 112.50)

2. Sum the conversion cost (labour and indirect cost)
   This amounts to 180
   Split that figure between work-in-process and completed output:

Conversion cost: 180

Item		Completed	Equivalent production	Value of materials
	Units	%		$
	15	2/3	10 (0.29)[a]	23.20[b]
Completed output	25	100	25 (0.71)	56.80
				80.00

[a] $(\frac{10}{35}, \frac{25}{35}) = (0.29, 0.71)$
[b] $(0.29, 0.71) \; 1180 = \$(23.20, 56.80)$

3. The total cost of production for the period is divided as follows:

	Raw material	Conversion cost	Total cost
	$	$	$
	67.50	23.20	90.70
Completed output	112.50	56.80	169.30
	$118.00	$80.00	$260.00

COMMENT

An assumption of the examples of this chapter has been that the inputs equal the output of the system (or, put differently, all the materials which were put in process were converted into work-in-process, inventories and saleable products – via human or machine effort, or by a combination of both – without losses, rejects or scrap[1] occurring in the process. That assumption is now relaxed. The realistic situation, where losses occur in the production process, is therefore examined below, together with their cost accounting treatment in process costing.

[1] Scrap is a waste from manufacturing operations which has measurable quantities. In some processing industries, scrap has no economic or monetary value, while in others scrap can produce revenue via sales. When scrap has no value, it can be ignored in process costing. When scrap can be sold or recycled to a process, it must be taken account of in the firm. Control procedures should be instituted by management in such cases, since the sale of scrap can add to the firm's revenue. The cost department should also receive notification of scrap recovery via a scrap report.

The revenues realised from the sale of scrap reduces the manufacturing cost of the product. The recoveries from scrap should be accounted for as follows in the general journal:

(i) If scrap is sold

	Dr	Cr.
General ledger (cash or debtor)	$**	
Scrap recovery		$**
To record the value of scrap recovery.		

(ii) If scrap is transferred to an inventory account

	Dr	Cr.
Scrap inventory	$**	
Indirect Manufacturing Costs: Scrap recovery		$**
To record the transfer of scrap to Inventory		

Note, that a scrap Inventory Account can only be carried in the Stores ledger if a market price exists for the scrap.

'The Quartet'

4.13 Concept of losses in production

Everyone knows that not all the materials which are put into the production process will end up as saleable products. Losses of material inevitably occur in the making of a product – in furniture making, part of the wood ends up as sawdust and scrap, and in industries where liquid products are made a portion of the inputs evaporates in the process. Such losses are called 'non-controllable losses', and are part of the normal cost of the product.

In addition to non-controllable losses, there are also losses that arise from human action, i.e. negligence and slips in judgement; these are called controllable losses. Controllable losses can be classified into two categories: (i) normal losses, where the amount does not exceed some predetermined limit set by management, and (ii) abnormal losses, where the amount exceeds the limit set by management.

The accounting treatment of recording lost or spoiled units on the cost statement depends on the nature of the loss. Normal losses are absorbed by good production, and abnormal losses are generally excluded from product costs.

To avoid complex calculations in process costing, the accountant assumes that spoilage occurs at a specific predetermined point in production, typically at a point when inspection takes place. Taking the two extreme possibilities we will consider that (i) normal losses or spoiled units occurred early in processing, and (ii) that spoiled units are discovered on final inspection after the processing is completed.

The cost accountant also works with a cost flow assumption in calculating the equivalent production when there exists a beginning and a closing inventory in the firm. There are many cost flow methods which can be used in process costing; the methods generally used are: (i) average method; (ii) FIFO method; (iii) standard method. The solution to Example 4.5 below (which illustrates the costing treatment of spoiled units) uses FIFO assumptions.

EXAMPLE 4.5

The Idalie Co. manufactures leather bags.

The firm has two process departments. In process department 1 the materials in units are assembled and partly made, and are then passed on to process department 2, where the finishing touches are applied to the product.

In a particular month, the process account of department 1 and its production data were as follows:

	PROCESS	ACCOUNT
	$	
Inventory	400	
Material	625	
Labour	1250	
Overheads	1520	

Production data	Units
Opening inventory, 25% complete	500
Put in process	1500
Transferred to process 2	1250
Closing inventory, 20% complete	550

It is also important for the reader to note, that expenses which are incurred by the firm for the disposal of its waste are added to the cost of goods manufactured through debits to the indirect manufacturing account. For example, if a company pays $X to a trucking firm to transport its waste to a 'dumping ground' the following entries would be made:

Indirect Manufacturing Cost-Waste disposal $**
General ledger (cash or creditor) $**
To record the payment for waste disposal.

Assume (i) that all the units were placed in process at the beginning, (ii) that 200 units were spoiled during the process, and that at the end of the process there was no salvage value for the spoiled units.

REQUIRED

1. Calculate the value of the closing inventory and of the transfer to process 2
2. Calculate the unit cost of the finished goods
3. Verify that the value of the transfer to process 2 is correct
   Separate calculations must be shown for assumptions (i) and (ii).)

SOLUTION

Assumption (i) Spoilage at the beginning

1. In this case there is no need separately to analyse the cost relating to the spoiled units, since under the assumption of spoilage at the beginning it is appropriate to include the cost relating to spoiled units in the cost per equivalent unit of good output
   Check the accuracy of the physical flow of the production data:

Inputs	Units	Outputs	Units
Opening inventory	500	Transferred to process 2	1250
Added to process	1500	Closing inventory	550
		Spoilt during processing	200
Total input in process	2000	Total outputs	2000

2. Use method (ii) to calculate the equivalent production
   The calculations are:

	Material	Labour	Overhead
Work completed on opening inventory	0	375	375
Units started and finished this period (1250–500) units	750	750	750
Work completed on closing Inventory	550	110	110
	1300	1235	1235

Check calculation via method (iii), and proceed as follows:

	Material	Labour	Overhead
Inventory (beginning) as above	0	375	375
Put in process (1500–200) units	1300	1300	1300
Total units handled	1300	1675	1675
Less: inventory ending	0	(440)	(440)
Equivalent production	1300	1235	1235
	$	$	$
3. Current process costs	625	1250	1520
4. Unit process costs (3./2.)	$0.4808	$1.0121	$1.2308

'The Quartet'

5. Work-in-process (ending):
   Material (550 × $0.4808 $264.4400
   Labour (550 × $1.0121) ×0.20) $111.3310
   Overhead (550 × $1.2308 ×0.20) $135.3880

6. Finished goods transfer
   (sum of process A/c – sum of work-in-
   process values as calculated about)
   $(3795.0000 – 511.1590) = $3283.8410

7. Unit cost of finished goods
   (6./1500 units) = $2.1892

   Verfication of cost of tranfers

	$
Inventory in process (process A/c 1)	400.0000
Work required to complete beginning inventory	
Labour (500 × $1.0121 ×0.75)	379.5375
Overhead (500 × $1.2308 ×0.75)	461.5500
	$1241.0875

   Standard and finished this period:

Material (750 × $0.4808)	360.6000
Labour (750 × $1.0121)	759.0750
Overhead (750 × $1.2308)	923.1000
Total value of transfers	$3283.8625[a]

[a] Due to rounding error.

Assumption (ii) Spoilage at end
Here it is necessary to identify the cost relating to spoilage
The cost of normal spoilage will be added to the costs of good output at the end of the calculation

	Material	Labour	Overhead
1. Work completed on opening inventory	0	375	375
Units started and finished this period (1250 + 200) units	1450	1450	1450
Work completed on ending inventory	550	110	110
Equivalent production	2000	1935	1935
2. Current process cost	$625	$1250	$1520
3. Unit process cost (2./1.)	$0.3125	$0.6460	$0.7855
4. Work-in process (ending):			
Material (550 × $0.3125)	$171.875		
Labour (550 ×0.6460 ×0.20)		$71060	
Overhead (550 × $0.7855 ×0.20)			$86.405

5. Finished goods transfer
   (Sum of process A/c sum of work-in-process values as calculated above)
   (3795.00 − 329.34) = 3,465.6600
   = $2.3104

6. Unit cost of finished goods
   (5./1500 units)
   Verification of cost of transfer
   Inventory in process (process A/c 1)   400.0000
   Work required to complete beginning inventory
   Labour (500 × $0.6460 × 0.75)   242.2500
   Overhead (500 × $0.7855 × 0.75)   294.5625
                                                                  ─────────
                                                                  $936.8125

   Started and finished this period
   (good units)
                                                      $
   Material (1250 × $0.3125)   390.6250
   Labour   (1250 × $0.6460)   807.5000
   Overhead (1250 × $0.7855)   981.8750
                                                  ─────────
                                                                  2180.000

   Value of spoiled units at end of process
   whose cost is absorbed by good units:
   Material (200 × $0.3125)   62.5000
   Labour (200 × $6460)   129.2000
   Overhead (200 × $0.7855)   157.1000
                                                  ─────────   348.8000

   Total value of Transfer $3 465.6125

ᵃ Due to rounding error.

COMMENT:

The two calculations show different unit costs, and hence different costs for the finished goods transfer. Method (ii) clearly shows the specific cost that must be recovered for the spoiled units.

4.14 Application of standards to process costing

The application of standard costing techniques to process manufacturing, according to Horngren (1977) 'eliminates the intricacies of weighted-average v. FIFO inventory methods; it also erases the need for burdensome computations of cost per equivalent unit. The standard cost is the cost per equivalent unit. In addition, a standard cost approach facilitates control.

In order to illustrate the techniques of standard costing to Example 4.5, we need standard cost data. Assume that the data shown below represents the standard cost data of the Idalie Co. for the processing of the product:

STANDARD COST DATA

	$
Material per unit at $0.50	0.50
Labour hr 0.5 h at $2	1.00
Overhead rate 1.20 at labour cost	1.20
	$2.70

'The Quartet'

The standard cost of goods completed can be calculated as follows:

	Units	Material	Labour	Overhead	Total
Finished goods[a]	1250	$625	$1250	1500	$3375
Closing inventory[b]	550	275	110	132	517
	1800	900	1360	1632	3892
Less opening inventory[c]		500	250	125	150	525
Standard units	1300				
Standard cost of work done		$650	$1235	$1482	$3367

Materials	Labour	Overhead
$ $	$ $	$ $
a 1250 × 0.5 = 625	1250 × 1 = 1250	1250 × 1 = 1250
b 550 × 0.5 = 275	550 × 1 × 0.20 = 110	550 × 1.20 × 0.20 = 132
c 500 × 0.5 = 275	500 × 1 × 0.25 = 125	500 × 1.20 × 0.25 = 150

The actual cost of the various cost elements − the standard cost of the same elements will show favourable or unfavourable variances.

The calculations are as follows:

	Actual costs		Standard Costs		Variances from standard
Material	$\begin{bmatrix} 625 \\ 1250 \\ 1520 \end{bmatrix}$	−	$\begin{bmatrix} 650 \\ 1235 \\ 1482 \end{bmatrix}$	=	$\begin{bmatrix} 25\ F \\ 15\ U \\ 38\ U \end{bmatrix}$
Labour					
Overhead					

The unfavourable variance is $28

VERIFICATION

	$
Standard costs of goods completed	3367
Actual outlay on goods	3395
Difference	$ 28 U

COMMENT

The variances calculated above can be analysed further into material cost variance, material quantity variance, labour rate variance and labour efficiency variance. In ch. 14, those variances are examined in detail.

It is worthwhile to end this section by summarising the essential characteristics of the job costing and the process costing systems.

4.15 Summary of job costing and process costing

Job costing is concerned with a job (or a batch of similar jobs). In job costing, each unit of output is treated as if it were unique. Costs are accumulated by job, or by production order, in this system. The costing of particular jobs requires detailed postings of material requisition and of direct labour time tickets to many separate cost sheets, and a distribution of indirect manufacturing cost over several jobs.

Process costing is concerned with the mass production of homogeneous units, which pass through a series of production steps called operations or processes. In this system, any one unit of output can be substituted for any other unit. There are problems associated with process costing in valuing the transfer of goods from one department or cost centre to another. A measure called 'equivalent production' facilitates such valuation; equivalent production is also a measure of the activity of a period.

Cost allocation and recovery procedures are common to both systems. With the job costing system, costs are allocated to (and recovered from) the various jobs undertaken by the firm. With process costing, costs are allocated to process departments or cost centres, and are recovered on the throughput of the department or cost centre for the period.

Standard costing is applicable to both systems. When standard costs are applied to process costing, many of the problems met by the accountant in using the usual cost flow assumption – for example, FIFO or the average method – are avoided.

4.16 Joint product costing

When more than one product is created simultaneously from a manufacturing operation, these are termed joint products. Joint products have economic meaning when each product has a significant sales value in relation to the other. The production of sugar provides an example of joint products – syrup, sugar, molasses and bagasse are created as a result of its production.

Joint production poses a problem for the cost accountant. With joint production, the accountant is forced to adopt arbitrary rules in apportioning the production cost in some way between the joint products. The extreme case of joint production is given by a process which necessarily produces more than one product in fixed proportions. In slaughtering a chicken, it is inevitable that the meat produced must comprise two legs, two wings, and a breast in those proportions. It is possible with some processes to vary the proportions, and even the selection of products produced (e.g. the cracking of crude oil). Where proportions can be varied the costing problem is eased, since marginal changes can be made and marginal costs established. This can best be illustrated with an example.

EXAMPLE 4.6

Products A and B can be produced by either of two methods:

Method	$	Units	Units
1 costs	228	to give 8 of A and	8 of B
2 costs	240	to give 10 of A	5 of B

REQUIRED

Calculate the value of A and B.

'The Quartet'

SOLUTION

These processes can be represented as a pair of simultaneous equations:

$8a + 8b = 228$
$10a + 5b = 240$

where a and b are the cost values of unit output of A and B respectively
The solution is:

$a = \$19.50, \quad b = \$9$

The case of fixed proportions does not lend itself to these marginal considerations.
Joint products have special characteristics. The joint products can be identified at a stage in the process known as the split-off point, and none of the products can be created without the creation of the other products. Costs can thus be distinguished. The costs incurred up to the split-off point are called joint product costs. The costs (if any) incurred on the products after the split-off point can be identified with specific products, and are dubbed 'separable' or 'additional processing' costs. Figure 4.10 attempts to show the primitives of joint production.

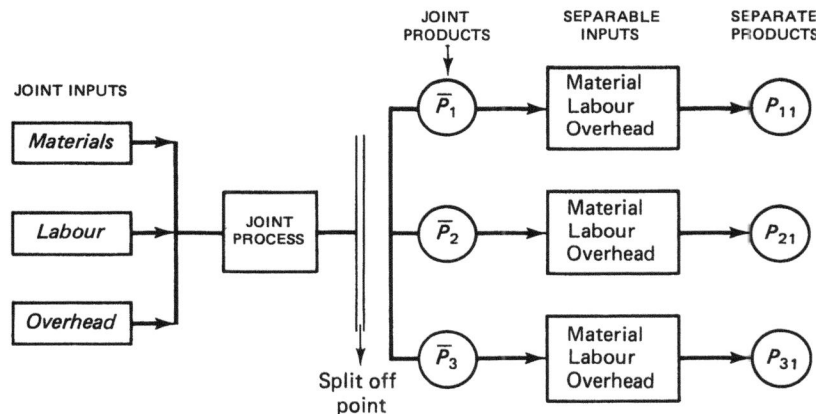

Figure 4.10 Primitives of joint production

4.17 Reasons for costing joint products

Joint products are costed for stock valuation and profit determination. Stock valuation implies that the costs for each product can be ascertained. The costs after split-off do not present problems, since such costs can be identified with specific products, but the joint product costs – i.e. the inputs to the joint process – do present problems.

The traditional methods of costing joint products are: (i) physical measures method (PMM); (ii) relative sales value method (RSVM).

EXAMPLE 4.7

A chemical plant produces two products, called P and $\bar{P}$. The joint costs of the process, which produces 50 lb of P and 30 lb of $\bar{P}$, are \$400. P and $\bar{P}$ are sold respectively for \$10 and \$12.

REQUIRED

(i) Draw the diagram of the system
(ii) Show how the joint cost is assigned, using the two methods and their profit statements

SOLUTION

(i) Figure 4.11 shows the system diagram; Figure 4.12 the assignment of cost.

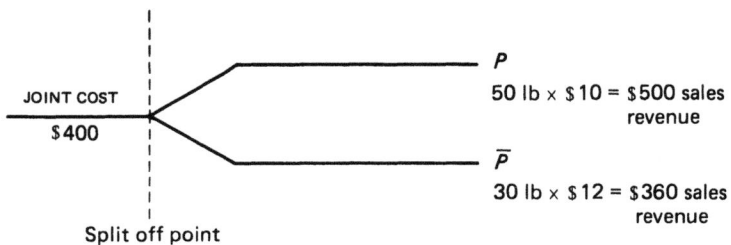

Figure 4.11 P and $\bar{P}$ – System diagram

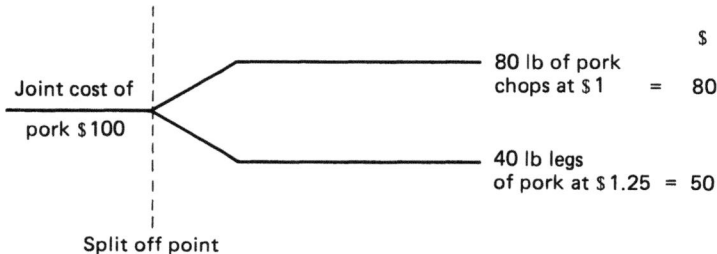

Figure 4.12 Assignment of cost

(ii) *PMM method*

Product	Production	Weights[a]	Joint cost assigned
	lb		$
P	50	0.6250 × $400	250
$\bar{P}$	30	0.3750 × $400	150
	80 lb		$400

[a] $\left(\dfrac{50}{80}, \dfrac{30}{80}\right) = 0.6250, 0.3750$.

The profit statement is:

	P	$\bar{P}$	Total
	$	$	$
Sales revenue	500	360	860
Joint cost assigned	(250)	(150)	(400)
Gross profit	$250	$210	$460
Gross profit as a % of sales	50	58.3	53.5

'The Quartet'

RSVM method

Product	Sales value of production	Weights[a]	Joint cost assigned
			$
P	500	0.5814 × $400	232.5
P̄	360	0.4187 × $400	167.5
	$860		$400

[a] $\left(\dfrac{500}{860}, \dfrac{300}{860}\right) = 0.5814, 0.4187$.

The profit statement is:

	P	P̄	Total
	$	$	$
Sales revenue	500.00	360.00	860
Joint cost assigned	(232.56)	(167.48)	(400)
Gross profit	$267.44	$192.52	$460
Gross profit as a % of sales	53.49	53.49	53.49

COMMENT

In some cases, the products which emerge from the joint process are not commercially viable, and are further processed for sale. Costs therefore cannot be assigned to the individual products according to the RSVM, when there is no sales value at the split-off point. For product costing purposes, a variation of RSVM dubbed the net relative sales value method (NRSVM), is used. The solution to Example 4.8 illustrates this.

EXAMPLE 4.8

Assume (i) that the additional costs of making P and P̄ in Example 4.7 are respectively $12 and $10, and (ii) their selling prices $11.50 and $12.50.

REQUIRED

Show how the joint cost is assigned by the NRSVM and the profit statement.

Product Type	Sales value of product	Separate process cost	NRSV	Weight[a]	Joint cost assigned
	$	$	$		$
P 11.50 × 50	575	12	563	0.6067 × 400	242.7
P̄ 12.50 × 30	375	10	365	0.3934 × 400	157.3
	$950	$22	$928		400.0

[a] $\left(\dfrac{563}{928}, \dfrac{365}{928}\right) = 0.6067, 0.3934$.

The profit statement is:

	P	P̄	Total
	$	$	$
Sales revenue	575.00	375.00	950
Cost of goods sold			
Joint costs assigned	(242.68)	(157.36)	(400)
Add processing costs	(12.00)	(10.00)	(22)
Gross profit	$320.32	$207.64	$528

4.18 Joint products and decision-making

The decision to process a joint product depends also on whether the additional revenue is greater than the additional cost. The techniques used for joint product costing must never be relied upon for delicate managerial decisions, as the solution to Example 4.9 illustrates.

EXAMPLE 4.9

A manager of a meat shop has a choice of selling pork chops and legs of pork as is shown in Figure 4.12, or of using the pork chops to make meatballs which will be packaged and frozen at an additional cost of $30 and sold for $2.40 per lb. 2 lb of pork chops produce 1 lb of meatballs.

SOLUTION

The joint costs can be allocated using either the PMM or the RSVM.
The procedures using both methods are as follows:

		PMM		RSVM		
	Weight^a		Joint cost	Sales value	Weight^b	Joint cost
	lb		$	$		$
Pork chops	80	0.6667 × $100	66.67	80	0.6154 × $100	61.54
Leg of Pork	40	0.3333 × $100	33.33	50	0.3846 × $100	38.46
	120		$100.00	$130		$100.00

^{a} $\left(\dfrac{80}{120}, \dfrac{40}{120}\right) = 0.6667, 0.3333.$

^{b} $\left(\dfrac{80}{130}, \dfrac{50}{130}\right) = 0.6154, 0.3846.$

If the allocated cost of pork shops is included in the calculation of the profitability of meat balls, the profit statement using PMN and RSVM is:

	$	$	$	$
Sales: 40 lb × $2.40		96.00		96.00
Cost of chops as above	67.67		61.54	
Add processing cost	30.00	(97.67)	30.00	91.54
Profit (Loss)		$(1.67)		$ 4.46

'The Quartet'   83

COMMENT

The result are conflicting. This is so because the inclusion of the joint costs (which includes arbitrarily allocated costs) distorts the calculations. The only approach which will give a reliable result is the incremental approach. This involves comparing the additional costs with the additional revenues, and ignoring the joint costs which are common to both chops and meatball production as irrelevant. Below is a solution based on the incremental approach.

SOLUTION

	$	$
Extra revenue from meatballs		96
Revenue lost from pork chops 80 × $1	80	
Additional processing cost	30	(110)
Additional Profit (Loss)		$(14)

VERIFICATION

Total profit figure.

	Sell as pork chops				Sell as meat balls	
	$	$		$		$
Sales: Chops	80		Meat balls	96		
Leg	50	130	Leg	50		146
Joint cost		(100)				(100)
Additional cost						(30)
Total profit		$30				$16

COMMENT

The question inherent in the Example 4.9 was whether meatballs were more profitable than pork chops. It is obvious that meatballs sell for a lower price than meat, and an extra cost is involved. The calculations showed that they were in fact a dead loss. The point was made, however, that it is profitable to incur additional costs on a product only so long as the additional revenues exceed the additional costs—if the meat balls are sold, the firm will give up $30 profit to make only $16 profit, losing $14 in the process.

4.19 By-products

By-products are those 'offshoot' items which result from the manufacturing of the main product. Their values are economically insignificant when compared with the saleable values of the main product. The cow provides an example of by-products in western economies – from it can be obtained (in addition to beef) bone, hair, hide and horn. In manufacturing firms, by-product definitions are not so simple, because the distinction between by-products and the main product is very fine. Observe, too, that scientific advancement alters a by-product classification – gasolene has now replaced kerosene as the main product in most modern industrial firms.

4.20 By-product costing

Economically significant by-products contribute to the firm's revenue. By-product revenues can be calculated in two ways: (i) in terms of the net sales revenue derived from the by-product actually sold; (ii) in terms of the net sales value of the by-product produced, sold or not sold. (i) places no value on the ending inventory; (ii) carries a by-product inventory. There are thus two methods of accounting for by-products: (i) net production cost method, where the by-product net revenue is shown as a deduction from the cost of production; (ii) cost of sales method, where the net realisable value of the by-product is shown as a deduction from the cost of sales.

EXAMPLE 4.10

The Charles Corp. produces a produt called X. A by-product $\bar{X}$ emerges at the end of the processing of X. During an accountancy period, the data below were collected for the product:

	Units	$
X Sales	2000	8000
Production	3000	6000

		$ per unit
$\bar{X}$ Sales	400	@1.25
Production	600	
Cost of disposal		0.25

REQUIRED

Compute the profit or loss for the period using, the two costing methods.

SOLUTION

(i) *Net production cost method*

	$	$
Sales of main product		8000
Cost of production		
Production cost	6000	
Less net revenue from sales of $\bar{X}$ – (400 × $1.00)	400	
Net production cost X	5600	
Closing stock (1/3)	1867	
Cost of sales		3733
Gross profit		$4267

(ii) *Net cost of sales method*

	$	$
Sales		8000
Cost of sales		
Production cost	6000	
Closing stock (1/3)	(2000)	
	4000	
NRV $\bar{X}$ produced 600 × ($1.25 – 0.25)	600	
Cost of sales		3400
Gross profit		$4600

'The Quartet' 85

COMMENT

The recording (or the ignoring) of the by-product inventories depends on their marketability and their realisation values. If the by-product values make significant contributions to revenue, it is sensible to record the inventory, particularly if the values are large enough to make significant changes to the unit cost associated with the major product.

4.21 Summary

The cost sheet plays an important role in recording cost items in job costing. The dollar values of those items are recorded in the firm's accounts. Job costing should be applied to those industries to which it is suited.

Not all the goods which are made in the firm will end up as saleable products; losses occur during processing. These losses are classified into two categories – non-controllable and controllable. The management function executes control procedures with normal losses. Abnormal losses are due to human error, and should be highlighted in the firm, not only for keeping management informed but also for product costing purposes.

Process costing is applicable to products which are made in sequence. The measure of equivalent production, which can be calculated by using any cost flow assumption, facilitates cost allocation between transferred, ending and lost output. In process costing, unit costing shows the average cost over a period of time of identical products which are made in a continuous sequence. When standard costing is applied to process costing, the need does not arise for cost assumptions on inventory; burdensome calculations are also avoided by its use.

Joint products mean that two or more products are created from one major product. Joint products are costed by two methods: (i) physical measures method (PMM); (ii) relative sales value method (RSVM). When a product emerges from the joint process that is uncommercial and further processing is required to make it saleable, the traditional methods of joint costing give conflicting results. Joint product problems of that nature are best analysed by incremental analysis.

By-products which are economically significant add to the firm's revenues. By-products are costed in a similar way (and for similar purposes) to the major product. If by-products make a large contribution to the firm's revenue and, as a result, affect the unit cost of the major product, the inventories should be recorded.

A4.1 Appendix: Abnormal spoilage

Identification

The identification of normal and abnormal spoilage is carried out mainly to determine accounting income for control purposes. Spoilage in excess of normal – i.e. abnormal spoilage – represents wastage which arises because of problems associated with the period in which it occurs, rather than with the usual operation of the production process. It is a period cost to be accounted for differently from the normal spoilage cost, since only the latter represents a normal production cost which can be included in stock valuation for accruals purposes. Further, since it indicates a deviation from planned activities, it provides a signal for control activities; if the normal spoilage cost is significant, its cause deserves investigation. The cause may be poor performance, inappropriate spoilage standards, or errors in the accounting measuring process.

There are two methods of dealing with the costs of abnormal spoilage: (i) decrease the gross profit immediately; (ii) assign the spoilage costs to an overhead account to be allocated to all the units produced over the financial period. The first method is similar to the accounting treatment of a loss. The second method implies that a worker will randomly cause a certain amount of wastage, which should not be identified with specific units of production but should be spread over all units; this treatment does not give proper recognition to the accruals principle for income measurement. Note that the separation of spoilage cost in process costing implies that it is a period loss. The term 'abnormal loss(es)' is thus used in the text in a similar way to 'abnormal spoiled units'.

Calculation of normal and abnormal usage

One calculation is required, and that is for normal spoilage. If the good units are known, and the normal spoilage is calculated, then the abnormal loss will be the balance of the input units. Note that the calculation should focus on the output quantity as the key factor, as is done in the standard costing system. In the case of spoilage, this is essential in ensuring that product costs associated with output include no more (or less) than the normal spoilage cost.

Let us now illustrate the calculation of the normal and abnormal usage. Assume that the normal loss of Karen Ltd manufacturers of car bodies, is 20 per cent of the input quantity. This means that

100 units = 80 good units (GU) + 20 normal spoilage units (NSU)

An extension of that statement implies that if Karen Ltd introduced 10000 units into its manufacturing process, then

10000 units = 8000 (GU) + 2000 (NSU)

Note that in both calculations the normal spoilage units can be expressed as 25 per cent of the good units. This, as the reader will soon discover, is a key calculation. We can now, utilising the

'The Quartet' 87

example of Karen Ltd, show the incorrect and correct methods for calculating the abnormal losses from the actual input data.

EXAMPLE 4.1

Assume that the 10000 units introduced into the manufacturing process of Karen Ltd produced 7000 units of output. Calculate the incorrect and correct figures for the normal spoiled units and the abnormal spoiled units.

INCORRECT CALCULATION

   10000 units = 7000 (GU) + 2000 (NSU) + 1000 abnormal spoiled units (ASU)

COMMENT

The incorrect method implies that the normal spoilage is independent of the output and that the loss, (abnormal spoiled units) for the period is also independent of output. This implication is of course nonsense; it would result in product costs for every seven output units which included the cost of two spoiled units, whereas the normal standard relationship is given as eight output units to include the cost of two spoiled units.

CORRECT CALCULATION

   10000 units = 7000 (GU) + 1750 (NSU) + 1250 (ASU)

COMMENT

The abnormal spoiled units can also be calculated as follows:

	Units
Actual input	10000
Normal input (7000 × 125%)	8750
Abnormal spoiled units	1250

Note that this method requires the input to be topped up by the standard percentage factor of the normal spoilage to the good units produced.

In the following examples, cost is introduced into the analysis, and we again show the incorrect and correct methods in calculating the cost per good units produced. The reader should note the importance of the inventoried cost in the calculations.

EXAMPLE A4.2

Assume that the 10000 units introduced into the production process of Karen Ltd produced 7000 good units, which cost $80000. Illustrate the incorrect and correct cost calculations for the good units produced.

INCORRECT CALCULATION

	$	$
Cost per unit	80000	8
	———	
	10000	
Good units (7000 × $8)		56000
Normal spoilage (2000 × $8)		16000
		———
		72000
Cost per good unit	72000	$10.29
	———	
	7000	

CORRECT CALCULATION

		$
Cost per unit	80000	8
Abnormal spoiled units		
1250 × $8		10000
Good units (7000 × $8)		56000
Normal spoilage 1750 × $8		14000
		———
Total cost inventoried		70000
Cost per good unit	$70000	$10.00

Note that had normal spoilage levels been achieved 10000 input units would have produced 8000 good units at a cost of $80 000; this would give a cost per good unit of $10.00, showing that the correct calculation has not distorted the cost because of abnormal performance in a particular period.

The discerning reader would, of course, ask about the calculation of abnormal gain. Abnormal gain is the opposite of abnormal spoiled units or abnormal loss. We can now illustrate the incorrect and correct method of calculating abnormal gain.

EXAMPLE A4.3

Assume that the 10000 units started in the production process of Karen Ltd produced 9500 units. The costs incurred were $80000. Calculate the abnormal gain, normal spoilage and the cost per good unit produced.

INCORRECT CALCULATION

	$
Abnormal gain 500 × $8	4000
Good units 8500 × $8	68000
Normal spoilage 2000 × $8	16000
Total cost inventoried	84000
Cost per good unit $84000	$9.88
8500	

CORRECT CALCULATION

	$
Abnormal gain (625 × $8)	5000
Good units (8500 × $8)	68000
Normal spoilage (2 125 × $8)	17000
	———
	85000
Cost per good unit $85000	$10
8500	

COMMENT

The incorrect calculations demonstrate erratic unit cost. By contrast, the correct calculations show a consistent pattern, with the cost per unit remaining constant throughout the calculation.

Bibliography

Amey, L. R. and Egginton, D. A. (1973) *Management Accounting* (Longman) ch. 14.
Horngren, C. T. (1977) *Cost Accounting: A Managerial Emphasis*, 4th edn (Prentice-Hall) p. 588.
ICMA (1974) *Terminology of Management and Financial Accountancy* (ICMA) p. 21.
Kohler, F. L. (1970) *A Dictionary for Accounts*, 4th edn (Prentice-Hall) p. 251.
Matz, A. and Usry, M. F. (1980) *Cost Accounting: Planning and Control*, 7th edn (South-Western Publishing Co.) ch. 5.
Walgenbach, P. H., Dittrich, N. E. and Hanson, E. I. (1977) *Financial Accounting: An Introduction*, 2nd edn (Harcourt, Brace Jovanovich) p. 544.

Problems

4.1

(a) Polimur Ltd operates a process which produces three joint products, all in an unrefined condition. The operating results of this process, for October 19X9, are shown below:

	Product	Kg
Output from process:	A	10000
	B	80000
	C	80000

The month's operating costs were $1300.00. The closing stocks were A 20000 kg, B 15000 kg, C 5000 kg. The value of the closing stock is calculated by apportioning costs according to weight of output. There were no opening stocks, and the balance of the output was sold to a refining company at the following prices:

Product		$ *Per* kg
A 5		5
B 4		4
C 9		9

REQUIRED

Prepare an operating statement showing the relevant trading results for October 19X9.

(b) The management of Polimur Ltd have been considering a proposal to establish their own refining operations.
The current market prices of the refined products are:

Product	$ *Per* kg
17	17.00
14	14.00
20.50	20.50

The estimated unit costs of the refining operations are:

Product	A	B	C
	$ per kg	$ per kg	$ per kg
Direct materials	0.50	0.75	2.50
Direct labour	2.00	3.00	4.00
Variable overhead	1.50	2.25	5.50

Prime costs would be variable. Fixed overheads, which would be $700000 monthly, would be direct to the refining operation. Special equipment is required for refining Product B, and this would be rented at a cost (not included in the above figures) of $360000 per month. It may be assumed that there would be no weight loss in the refining process, and that the quantity refined each month would be similar to October's output shown in (a) above.

REQUIRED

Prepare a statement which will assist management to evaluate the proposal to commence refining operations. Include in your answer any comment you consider relevant.

ACA, FE, Part B, Paper 6, Accounting 2, Costing, December 1979.

4.2 Everymans Foods PLC has recently acquired a factory which processes soya beans. The soya beans pass through a series of processes, including cleaning, roasting and grinding to a soya powder.

In the final process of the series, other ingredients are added to the powder, and four distinct products emerge. These are:

(i) soya flour, which is bagged and sold to the health food shops
(ii) soya broth soup, which is canned and sold to supermarkets
(iii) soya steak powder, which is passed through further operations to produce soya steak; the steak is then packed and sold to restaurants
(iv) a small quantity of liquid, which is sold to amateur gardeners as a liquid fertiliser

The management of Everymans Food PLC require a process costing system to be installed, using monthly actual costs, and have requested your advice.

REQUIRED

(a) Briefly explain the type of information which would be required in order to operate a process costing system in the above factory
(b) Outline the type of information which would be produced by the above system, and explain the uses and the limitations of that data

ACCA, FE, Part B, Paper 6, Accounting 2, Costing, December 1981.

4.3
(a) Distinguish between job costing and process costing
(b) Explain how you would treat the following items in the accounts of a process costing system:
   (i) Waste
   (ii) Scrap
(c) A chemical is produced by passing a basic ingredient through four processes, during each of which direct materials are added.

REQUIRED

From the information given below for the month of March, you are requested to prepare a statement in which each element of cost is analysed and the output evaluated, and to show the accounts of process 3 and abnormal loss

'The Quartet'

Data for Process 3 include:
Work-in-process:

STOCK

	Opening	Closing
Units	400	1000
Degree of completion:	%	%
Material		
X	80	50
Y	80	45
Labour	50	30
Overhead	40	25

Cost incurred during period:	Units	$
Transfer from process 2:	5400	6240
Material		
X		2862
Y		944
Labour		468
Overhead		1398

Transfer to process 4 during period:
4550 units rejections during the period:

	Units
Normal	200
Abnormal	50

Units rejected had reached the following stages:

	%
Material	
X	80
Y	80
Labour	60
Overhead	40

Rejected units are considered as waste
The cost per unit in February and March was the same

ICMA, PS[a], Part I, Cost Accounting 2, May 1982.
[a] Professional stage.

4.4 A company which manufactures industrial pumps has decided to computerise its stock control system. In doing so it is proposed to change the accounting procedures.
   The current system is to:

   (i) value all stock on a FIFO basis
   (ii) identify separately the cost of rejected material
   (iii) charge the cost of rejects to a scrap account, and credit this account with the value of scrap sold
   (iv) debit the balance on the scrap account to the finished goods account

   The proposed new system is to:

   (i) value all stock on an average cost basis
   (ii) average out the cost of defective material over the good production in each department
   (iii) credit the value of the scrap material to the department in which the rejection occurs

   The following data are given for component X.
   Component X is machined from a bought-out casting. There are three operations in the machining

department with direct wages in the proportion of 3:2:5. Direct expense is incurred equally by each operation.

Inventory at 1 October 19X9:

		$
Costs:	Direct material	16000
	Direct wages	1300
	Direct expense	500
Units:	600 not started	
	Operation	
	100 completed 1	
	200 completed 2	

During October 19X9:

		$
Costs incurred:	Direct material	108000
	Direct wages	59730
	Direct expenses	16500
Units:	5400 purchases	
	4800 transferred to finished goods	
	700 rejected from October castings at the end of:	

Operation	No.
1	200
2	200
3	300

Inventory at 31 October 19X9:

	Operation
Units:	500 completed 1
	300 completed 2

All scrapped material is sold, and has a net value equivalent to 20 of the original direct material cost.

REQUIRED

A. For component X, from the data given for the month of October 19X9, calculate:

(a) machining cost per unit of production during October showing the individual operations separately

(b) for the current system:

   (i) cost of material transferred from the machining department to the finished goods stores
   (ii) value of machining department inventory at 31 October

(c) for the proposed new system:

   (i) cost of material transferred from the machining department to the finished goods stores
   (ii) value of machining department inventory at 31 October

Unit costs should be calculated in $ to two decimal places, and any rounding differences should be included in the cost of materials transferred out.

B. Write brief notes on the effect of introducing the new system.

ICMA, PS, Part III, Management Accounting, November 1979.

4.5 A chemical company has a contract to supply annually 3600 tonnes of product A at $24 a tonne and 4000 tonnes of product B at $14.50 a tonne. The basic components for these products are obtained from a joint initial distillation process. From this joint distillation a residue is produced, which is processed to yield 380 tonnes of by-product Z. By-product Z is sold locally at $5 a tonne, and the net income is credited to the joint distillation process.

'The Quartet' 93

The budget for the year ended 30 June 19X1 includes the following data:

	Joint process $	SEPARABLE COSTS		
		A	B	Z
Variable cost per tonne of input,	5	11	2	1
Fixed cost per year	5000	4000	8000	500
Evaporation loss in process as % of input	6	10	20	5

Since the budget was compiled, it has been decided that an extensive 5-week overhaul of the joint distillation plant will be necessary during the year. This will cost an additional $17000 in repair costs, and reduce all production in the year by 10 per cent. Supplies of the products can be imported to meet the contract commitment at a cost of $25 a tonne for A, and $15 a tonne for B.

Experiments have also shown that the joint distillation plant operations could be changed during the year such that *either*:

(i) The output of distillate for product A would increase by 200 tonnes, with a corresponding reduction in product B distillate; this change would increase the joint distillation variable costs for the whole of that operation by 20 per cent

or

(ii) The residue for by-product Z could be mixed with distillate for products A and B proportionate to the present output of these products; by intensifying the subsequent processing for products A and B, acceptable quality could be obtained; the intensified operation would increase product A and B separable fixed costs by 5 per cent, and increase the evaporation loss for the whole operation respectively to 11 per cent and 21 per cent

REQUIRED

(a) calculate on the basis of the original budget

    (i) the unit costs of products A and B
    (ii) the total profit for the year

(b) Calculate the change in the unit costs of products A and B based on the reduced production
(c) Calculate the profit for the year if the shortfall of production is made up by imported products
(d) advise management whether either of the alternative distillation operations would improve the profitability calculated under (c), and whether you recommend the use of either.

ICMA, PS, Part III, Management Accounting 2, May 1980.

4.6 A chemical company produces amongst its product range two industrial cleaning fluids A and B. These products are manufactured jointly. In 19X9 total sales are expected to be restricted because home trade outlets for fluid B are limited to 54000 gals for the year. At this level, plant capacity will be underutilised by 25 per cent.

REQUIRED

From the information given below:

(a) draw a flow diagram of the operations
(b) calculate separately for fluids A and B for the year 19X9
    (i) total manufacturing cost
    (ii) manufacturing cost per gallon
    (iii) list price per gallon
    (iv) profit for the year

(c) calculate the break-even price per gal to manufacture an extra 3000 gals of fluid B for export, which would incur selling, distribution and administration costs of $1260
(d) state the price you would recommend the company should quote per gal for this export business, with a brief explanation for your decision

The following data are given:

1. Description of process

Process
1 Raw materials L and M are mixed together and filtered
  There is an evaporation loss of 10 per cent
2 The mixture from process 1 is boiled, and this reduces the volume by 20 per cent
  The remaining liquid distils into 50 per cent extract A, 25 per cent extract B, and 25 per cent by-product C
3 Two parts of extract A are blended with one part of raw material N, and one part of extract B with one part of raw material N, to form respectively fluids A and B
4 Fluid A is filled into 1-gal labelled bottles, and fluid B into 6-gal preprinted drums, and they are then both ready for sale
  1 per cent wastage in labels occurs in this process

2. Cost

Raw material	Cost per gal $
L	0.20
M	0.50
N	2.00

Containers	Cost $
1-gal bottles	0.27 each
6-gal drums	5.80
Bottle labels, per 1000	2.20

Direct wages

Process	Per gal of input processed $
1	0.11
2	0.15
3	0.20
4	0.30

Manufacturing overhead:

Process	Fixed per annum $	Variable, per gal of input processed $
1	6000	0.04
2	20250	0.20
3	19500	0.10
4	14250	0.10

Process cost is apportioned entirely to the two main products on the basis of their output from each process.

No inventories of part-finished materials are held at any time.

Fluid A is sold through agents on the basis of list price less 20 per cent, and fluid B at list price less $33\frac{1}{3}$.

Of the net selling price, profit amounts to 8 per cent, selling and distribution costs to 12 per cent, and administration costs to 50 per cent.

Taxation should be ignored

ICMA, PS, Part III, Management Accounting 2, November 1978.

'The Quartet' 95

4.7 A company manufactures a variety of liquids which pass through a number of processes. One of these products, P, passes through processes 1, 2 and 4 before being transferred to the finished goods warehouse.

REQUIRED

From the details given below, prepare accounts for the month of October 19X8 for:

(a) process 4
(b) abnormal loss/gain
(c) finished goods

Data for process 4, October 19X8:

	Cost $
Work-in-process, 1 October 19X8: 6000 units	19440
Degree of completion:	%
Direct materials added	60
Direct wages and production overhead	40

Transferred from process 2:

  48000 units at $2.30 per unit

Transferred to finished goods: 46500 units Incurred:	$
Direct materials added	27180
Direct wages	18240
Production overhead	36480

Work-in-process 31 Oct 1978: 4000 units Degree of completion:	%
Direct materials added	50
Direct wages and production overhead	30

Normal loss in process: 6 per cent of units
  in opening stock plus transfers from process 2
Less closing stock

At a certain stage in the process, it is convenient for the quality control inspector to examine the product, and where necessary reject it. Rejected products are then sold for $0.80 per unit. During October 19X8 an actual loss of 7 per cent was incurred, with Product P having reached the following stage of production:

	%
Direct materials added	80
Direct wages and production overhead	60

ICMA, PS, Part I, Cost Accounting 2, November 1978.

4.8 XY Copiers Ltd produces the Kwikflip Copier in batches of 1000. Each copier contains a special chemical unit plus various other chemicals and activating components. The assembly operations include the merging of the special unit with some of the other chemicals under prescribed humidity conditions, an operation which is not always successful. Experience indicates a success rate of 95 per cent which the company has accepted as standard performance.

On 1 May, production of Batch no. 47 was commenced and the necessary chemical units and other materials for the batch were issued from stores, the cost price thereof being $6175.

During May, wages amounting to $1788 were booked to Batch no. 47, and overhead at the rate of 75 per cent of labour cost was apportioned thereto.

At the end of May, 840 copies of Batch no. 47 had been completed, of which 60 had proved unsuccessful and, having no value, were scrapped. Production of the remainder of the batch had passed the critical chemical merging stage and were expected to pass final inspection; half of these were estimated to be 80 per cent complete so far as labour and overhead costs were concerned, and the remainder, 50 per cent complete.

REQUIRED

Write up the work-in-process account, showing full details of your workings

ACCA, PE,[a], Section IV, June 1972.

[a] Professional Examination.

4.9 Fancy Faucets Inc. make a single product, a decorative plumbing device which is made in two processes: forging and finishing. The forging process produces the basic component from molten metal at the start of the process in batches of 12. At the end of this process, the forgings are inspected, and on average two of the forgings are found to be defective and must be discarded. In the finishing department, the basic components are first cleaned and 'frazed'. At the half-way stage in this department, additional materials are introduced, and the product is completed by assembly and polishing. Conversion costs are incurred evenly throughout both processes.

The following data applies to April 19X0:

	FORGING Units	FINISHING Units
Work-in-process 1 April 19X0	15000 (2/3 complete)	20000 (3/4 complete)
Materials	$45000	$18000
Transferred in costs	–	$97000
Conversion costs	$20000	$30000
Cost incurred		
Materials	$270000	77000
Conversion costs	$163000	130000
	Units	Units
Units started	90000	72000
Work-in-process 30 April 19X0 (1/4 complete)	18000	16000
Completed output	72000 (transferred to finishing)	76000 (transferred to warehouse)

REQUIRED

Calculate the values of the work-in-process at 30 April 19X0 and of output transferred to the warehouse during April-19X0 using either the FIFO or weighted average method.

4.10 Curry Chemicals operate a joint process which produces two products, Flambex and Glycal. 50 lb of raw materials cost $100 in total, and are converted at a cost of $60 into 20 lb of Flambex and 30 lb of Glycal. The Flambex produced can be sold for $2 per lb but Glycal must be purified at a cost of $0.60 per lb before it can be sold for $1.40 per lb. At the end of January, 240 lb of Flambex and 80 lb of purified Glycal were in inventory.

REQUIRED

Calculate the value of the closing inventory for January using the net realisable value method (you should compute per unit costs for each product).

Chapter 5
Service Cost Allocation to Production Departments

Much of the accounting data used in management control and administrative decision making is a product of antecedent processes of cost allocation and expense distribution. Both of these operations assume the validity of cost divisibility and recombination.

(Williams and Griffin, 1964)

5.1 Introduction

Service departments provide beneficial services to the firm. They are not directly engaged in production, but give services to production departments. The types of service departments usually found in a manufacturing concern are catering, inspection, power plant, steam room and tool room.

The cost of a service department can be obtained in a similar way to the cost of a production department. The various ways for distributing service department expenses are now shown.

5.2 Methods of distributing service department expense

The traditional methods are: (i) to production departments only; (ii) by distributing a proportion of the service department expenses to other service departments before the final expense apportionments are made to the production departments.[1] The solution to Example 5.1 illustrates the procedure.

EXAMPLE 5.1

The Marion firm has three production units and two service departments. The overhead expenses allocated for a particular period to the departments are:

---
[1] Also called the 'step method'.

DEPARTMENTS

Production	$	Service	$
P_1	20	S_1	35
P_2	30	S_2	45
P_3	50		

The distribution factor calculations show that the percentage allocations[1] are as follows:

		ALLOCATIONS FROM				
	Department	P_1 %	P_2 %	P_3 %	S_1 %	S_2 %
Allocations to	S_1	40	20	30	—	10
	S_2	55	30	—	15	—

REQUIRED

Show how the total overhead expense is charged to the production departments via the two methods.

SOLUTION [2]

Method (i)

The apportionment[3] of S_1 is:

$$\$ [35] \begin{bmatrix} 0.4444 \\ 0.2222 \\ 0.3333 \end{bmatrix} \begin{bmatrix} P_1 \\ P_2 \\ P_3 \end{bmatrix} = \begin{matrix} \$ \\ 15.6 \\ 7.7 \\ 11.7 \\ \hline 35.0 \end{matrix}$$

Similarly, S_2's apportionment is:

$$\$ [45] \begin{bmatrix} 0.6471 \\ 0.3529 \\ 0.0000 \end{bmatrix} \begin{bmatrix} P_1 \\ P_2 \\ P_3 \end{bmatrix} = \begin{matrix} \$ \\ 29 \\ 16 \\ 0 \end{matrix}$$

The total overhead expense chargeable to the production units is:

OVERHEAD EXPENSE SUMMARY (OHES)

Department	P_1	P_2	P_3	S_1	S_2	Total
	$	$	$	$	$	$
Expense allocated	20	30	50	35	45	180
From S_1	16	7	12	(35)		
From S_2	29	16	—		(45)	
Total	$65	$53	$62	—	—	$180

[1] The solution to Example 3.3 shows how these percentages are calculated. Note that a reciprocal relationship exists between s_1 and s_2.
[2] The calculated figures are adjusted to integers, or allowed to float, to suit our convenience.
[3] The calculation of P_1 ratio is, e.g. 40/90 = 0.4444.

Service Cost Allocation to Production Departments

The advantages of this method are: (i) its simplicity; (ii) the accuracy of the product costs is not affected by a mixture of expenses from inter-department distribution. The disadvantages are: (i) the method fails to take account of service charges rendered by other departments, which can result in an under-statement of the cost of the operating department receiving the service; (ii) if reciprocity exists between the departments (and even between the service departments), the method is unsuitable.

Method (ii)

Method (ii) can be carried out by:

(a) continuous distribution
(b) simultaneous equation
(c) by matrix algebra.

SOLUTION

(a) Continuous distribution

The apportionment of S_1's expenses to the production departments and to S_2 is calculated as follows:

$$\$ 35 \begin{bmatrix} 0.40 \\ 0.20 \\ 0.30 \\ 0.10 \end{bmatrix} \begin{bmatrix} P_1 \\ P_2 \\ P_3 \\ S_2 \end{bmatrix} = \begin{array}{c} \$ \\ 14.0 \\ 7.0 \\ 10.5 \\ 3.5 \end{array}$$

The total overhead expense chargeable to the departments is:

OHES

	Department					Total
	P_1	P_2	P_3	S_1	S_2	
	$	$	$	$	$	$
Expense allocated	20	30	50.0	35	45.0	180
From S_1	14	7	10.5	(35)	3.5	—
Total	$34	$37	$60.5		$48.5	$180

S_2's total of $48.50 must now be apportioned to the production departments and to S_1, using the percentage from the question. The amounts are:

$$\$ [48.50] \begin{bmatrix} 0.55 \\ 0.30 \\ 0.00 \\ 0.15 \end{bmatrix} \begin{bmatrix} P_1 \\ P_2 \\ P_3 \\ S_1 \end{bmatrix} = \begin{array}{c} \$ \\ 26.675 \\ 14.550 \\ 0.000 \\ 7.2750 \end{array}$$

This step closes S_2's account, but re-opens S_1's account. The overhead expense charged to the departments now becomes:

OHES

	Department					Total
	P_1	P_2	P_3	S_1	S_2	
Expense allocated	$ 34.000	$ 37.00	$ 60.50	$ —	$ 48.50	$ 180
From S_2	26.675	14.55	0	7.275	(48.50)	
Total	$60.675	$51.55	$60.50	$7.275	—	$180

Since S_1's account is re-opened, further iterations must be performed to apportion S_1's total of $7.275 to the departments. The calculations are:

$$\$[7.275] \begin{bmatrix} 0.40 \\ 0.20 \\ 0.30 \\ 0.10 \end{bmatrix} \begin{bmatrix} P_1 \\ P_2 \\ P_3 \\ S_2 \end{bmatrix} = \begin{matrix} \$ \\ 2.910 \\ 1.4550 \\ 2.1825 \\ 0.7275 \end{matrix}$$

which gives:

OHES

	Department					Total
	P_1	P_2	P_3	S_1	S_2	
Expense allocated	$ 60.675	$ 51.550	$ 60.500	$ 7.275	$ —	180
From S_1	2.910	1.455	2.1825	(7.275)	0.7275	
Total	$63.585	$53.005	$62.6825	—	$0.7275	$180

This procedure re-opens S_2's account. It must be closed. Since the amount is small, the final apportionment is made to the production departments as follows:

$$\$[0.7275] \begin{bmatrix} 0.6471 \\ 0.3529 \end{bmatrix} \begin{bmatrix} P_1 \\ P_2 \end{bmatrix} = \begin{matrix} \$ \\ 0.4707 \\ 0.2568 \end{matrix}$$

The final distribution is:

OHES

	Department					Total
	P_1	P_2	P_3	S_1	S_2	
Expense allocated	$ 63.5850	$ 53.0050	$ 62.6825	$ —	$ 0.7275	$ 180
From S_2	0.4707	0.2568	—	—	(0.7275)	
Total	$64.0557	$53.2618	$62.6825	—	—	$180

Service Cost Allocation to Production Departments

COMMENT

The advantages of the method are:

(i) it charges each service department for the cost rendered to the other(s)
(ii) the procedure aids in the determination of the operating cost of the service departments

The disadvantages are:

(i) The method is time-consuming
(ii) It is not as accurate as the other methods

The method consists of closing and re-opening the service departments' accounts. Percentages are applied to the primary total of the department which serves the greatest number of production and service departments. That mechanism closes the account, and charges the apportioned amounts to other departments. The given percentages are again applied to the second service department, whose dollar total comprises the primary total plus an amount apportioned from the other service departments. The procedure is repeated until a service department's dollar total becomes insignificant. This enables a final apportionment to be made to the production departments.

(b) Simultaneous equation

This method utilises an equation system, where the percentages of the service departments are expressed as fractions, and set equal to the service dollar constants.

SOLUTION

Let S_1 represent the total cost of service department s_1
Let S_2 represent the total cost of service department s_2

The equation system is therefore:

$$s_1 - 0.15s_2 = 35 \tag{5.1}$$
$$-0.10s_1 + s_2 = 45 \tag{5.2}$$

The solution is:

$$[S_1, S_2] = \$\,[42.3858, 49.2387]$$

Observation reveals that the combined costs of $S_1 + S_2$ ($91.6245) $\neq$ $80
An adjustment must therefore be made as follows:

Department	Total cost	Inter-service cost		Charge to production
	$	%	$	$
S_1	42.3858	10 +	(4.2386)	38.1472
S_2	49.2387	15 +	(7.3859)	41.8528
	$91.6245		$(11.6245)	$80.0000

COMMENT

The advantages of the method are:

(i) the calculations are easily derived if the equation system is not too large
(ii) the actual cost of each service department can be compared with its budgeted cost, thus leading to variance analysis and the monitoring of the departments

A disadvantage of the method is that if there are more than three interdependent service departments, and if reciprocity exists between them, the method is cumbersome.
The equation system, however, provides the data for the matrix method.

(c) *Matrix method*[1]

Let A = Coefficient matrix
B = Percentage matrix
b = Vector of constants
c = Vector which contains the solutions respectively for S_1 and S_2
f = Vector which contains the final charges to the production departments

Then the system is:

$$As = b$$

where

$s = S_1, S_2$ respectively
$(I - A)s = b$

$$s = (I - A)^{-1} b$$

Inserting the relevant data, the system is:

$$[A] = \begin{bmatrix} 0 & 0.10 \\ 0.15 & 0 \end{bmatrix} \quad \begin{bmatrix} S_1 \\ S_2 \end{bmatrix} \quad b = \begin{bmatrix} 35 \\ 45 \end{bmatrix}$$

$$[I - A]^{-1} = \begin{bmatrix} 1.0148 & 0.0985 \\ 0.1478 & 0.9852 \end{bmatrix} \quad \begin{bmatrix} 35 \\ 45 \end{bmatrix} = \begin{bmatrix} 40 \\ 50 \end{bmatrix}$$

Simple matrix multiplication gives the final apportionment as follows:

$$\begin{matrix} [B] & & c & = & f \end{matrix}$$
$$\begin{bmatrix} 0.40 & 0.55 \\ 0.20 & 0.30 \\ 0.30 & 0.00 \end{bmatrix} \begin{bmatrix} 40 \\ 50 \end{bmatrix} \begin{matrix} 44 \\ 23 \\ 12 \end{matrix}$$

The total charge to the production departments is the sum of vector f. The OHES is:

OHES

	Department			Total[2]
	P_1	P_2	P_3	
	$	$	$	$
Expense allocated	20	30	50	100
From service depts	44	23	12	79
	$64	$53	$62	$179

COMMENT

Table 5.1 below shows the final results produced by each of these methods.

---

[1] There are two ways to express the reciprocal relationships by this method: (i) gross service method; (ii) net service method

[2] The difference is due to rounding.

Service Cost Allocation to Production Departments

Table 5.1 Allocation of overhead expense

Total service department costs			$180
Allotment method	Departments		
	P_1	P_2	P_3
Method (a)	65.0000	53.0000	62.0000
Method (b)	64.0557	53.2618	62.6825
Method (c)	64.0000	53.0000	62.0000

Table 5.1 reveals that methods (a) and (c) give similar results. Both methods differ slightly from method (b). Does this mean that method (a), for example, should be used exclusive of all other methods because of its simplicity? The correct answer to the question depends on the particular problem. In general, however, the matrix method, with its input–output orientation, is suited to large, interrelated, manufacturing cost systems. The solutions to the service cost allocation problems in such cases are obtained via the computer, and are better approximations than the solutions produced by the other two methods. Note that 'the better solutions' in such cases also depend on the measures through which the cost accountant captures the real system in figures.

5.3 Extension of cost allocation via linear programming

When overhead allocation decisions have to be made on, for example, managerial constraints on products, complementary products, or cases in which some of the overhead charges are avoidable if a product is not produced, the allocations can be ascertained via linear programming solutions (see Kaplan and Thompson, 1971). The solution technique of linear programming is now applied to an input–output example for cost allocation and external acquisition.

EXAMPLE 5.2

Assume that in an accountancy period the service relationships, the production requirements, and the internal and external unit costs were derived for the Marion firm as shown in Table 5.2. The direct cost of S_1 and S_2 is respectively $20 and $15. The output volume for the production departments are $U_1 = 200$, $U_2 = 100$.

Table 5.2 Cost allocation via linear programming

		Service departments	
		S_1	S_2
Units required			
Per unit of service	S_1	0	0.1
	S_2	0.2	0
Production	P_1	8	5
	P_2	4	3
		$	$
Unit production cost (internal)		33.47	17.35
External selling price per unit of product		30.47	20.45

REQUIRED

(i) Compute the flow through cost of the service departments
(ii) Allocate the cost to the production departments
(iii) Advise management on whether the external acquisition is worthwhile

SOLUTION

The problem formulation requires variable definition:

Let a_{ij} = No. of output units from service dept i required for one unit of output from dept j
b = No. of output units from service dept i directly required for the total production output
c_j = Unit cost of output from service dept j
M = No. of service depts
P_j = Unit price for service j when purchased externally
X_j = No. of output units from service dept j
V_j = Quantity of service j to be purchased externally
Y_i = Shadow prices or dual variables associated with the X_{ij}'s

For parts (i) and (ii) of the question, the model is:

$$\text{Minimise } Z = \sum_{j=1}^{M} c_j x_j$$

(5.3)

$$\text{Subject to } x_i - \sum_{j=1}^{M} a_{ij} x_j = b_i, \quad i = 1, 2$$

Inserting the data[1] into equation (5.3), the system is:

Minimise $Z = 33.47x_1 + 17.35x_2$
Subject to $x_1 - 0.10x_2 = 2\,000$
$-0.20x_1 + x_2 = 1\,300$
$x_1 \geqslant 0, x_2 \geqslant 0$

SOLUTION

Service dept output	Shadow prices[2]	Internal cost
$x_1 = 2173.47$	$Y_1 = 37.69$	$Z = \$102\,842.88$
$x_2 = 1734.69$	$Y_2 = 21.12$	

The allocation of the service costs requires the following calculations:

Flow through costs: $s_j = Y_j x_j$
$s_1 = \$37.69\,(2\,173.47) = \$81\,918.08$
$s_2 = \$21.12\,(1\,734.69) = \$36\,636.65$

The cost allocations:

$$P_j = u_j \sum_{i=1}^{M} b_{ij} Y_i$$

$$\begin{aligned} &&\$\\ P_1 &= 200\,[8(37.69) + 5(21.12)] = & 81\,424 \\ P_2 &= 100\,[4(37.69) + 3(21.12)] = & 21\,412 \\ \hline && \$102\,836 \end{aligned}$$

---

[1] Opportunity cost is the economist's term for the monetary benefits one must forgo if one rejects an alternative. If one has $200 000 and decides to use it to purchase a house, one forgoes the opportunity to invest it in fixed deposits (say) at 6 per cent. The $12 000 which is not an interest payment, is the sacrifice of income one accepts as a cost of rejecting the alternative investment in fixed deposits. The term 'opportunity cost' is referred to as 'shadow price' by the accountant.

[2] b, for example, is computed $(8 \times 200) + (4 \times 100) = 2000$.

Part (iii) of the question requires that the objective function and constraint equations (5.3) be augmented respectively by

$$\sum_{j=1}^{M} p_j v_j \text{ and } v_i$$

The model now becomes:

Minimise $Z = \sum_{j=1}^{M} c_j x_j + \sum_{j=1}^{M} p_j v_j$ (5.4)

Subject to $x_i - \sum_{j=1}^{M} a_{ij} x_j + v_i = b_i \quad i = 1, 2$

Substituting the figures into equation (5.4), the model is:

Minimize $Z = 33.47x_1 + 17.35x_2 + 30.47v_1 + 20.45v_2$
Subject to
$x_1 - 0.10x_2 + v_1 = 2000$
$-0.20x_1 + x_2 + v_2 = 1300$
$x_1 \geq 0, x_2 \geq 0, v_1 \geq 0, v_2 \geq 0$

SOLUTION

Internal quantities	External quantities	Shadow prices	Total cost
$x_1 = 0$	$v_1 = 2130$	$y_1 = 30.47$	$Z = \$87\,460$
$x_2 = 1300$	$v_2 = 0$	$y_2 = 20.45$	

$$\begin{array}{r}\$\end{array}$$

Flow-through costs: $S_1 = 64\,901$
$S_2 = 26\,520$
Cost allocations: $P_1 = 87\,460$
$P_2 = 22\,555$

From the analysis, it is clear that the firm should exploit the external service acquisition, since the total cost is reduced from $102 836 to $91 707.

COMMENT

The upper part of Table 5.2 utilised technological coefficients to show requirement per unit of service. The technological coefficients have advantages over the proportion of output coefficients. The latter coefficient matrix coupled with the linear programming techniques have advantages over the other methods. Also of importance is the fact that the method does not distort decisions requiring marginal cost data, since overheads are allocated in proportion to their marginal contributions.

5.4 Summary

The various methods of allocating service costs to production departments were demonstrated. The computational ease of the matrix method, coupled with its ease for handling reciprocity between departments, makes it superior to the other methods.

A linear programming model which utilised technological coefficients and dual solutions was applied to an internal and external service problem. The linear programming solution showed the desirability of acquiring one of the services externally.

Bibliography

Dopuch, N., Birnberg, J. G. and Demski, J. (1974) *Cost Accounting*, 2nd edn (Harcourt, Brace Jovanovich) pp. 579–98.
Kaplan, R. and Thompson, G. L. (1971) 'Overhead Allocation via Mathematical Programming Models', *Accounting Review*, vol. xlvi, no. 2, April, pp. 352–64.
Solomons, D. (1965) *Divisional Performance: Measurement and Control* (Richard D. Irwin) pp. 187–91.
Weingartner, H. M. (1974) *Mathematical Programming and the Analysis of Capital Budgeting Problems* (Kershaw Publishing Co.).
Williams, T. H. and Griffin, C. H. (1964) 'Matrix Theory and Cost Allocation', in L. S. Rosen (ed.) *Topics in Managerial Accounting* (McGraw-Hill) pp. 173–84.

Problems

5.1 The Suburbia Manufacturing Co. has two main products X and Y, each of which is produced in a separate department. In order to manufacture the products X and Y, the company has three major service departments, A, B and C.

An analysis of the work done by Departments A, B and C in a typical period is as follows:

Dept	USER DEPT					Total units of work done
	A	B	C	X	Y	
A	0	30	0	50	20	100
B	0	0	50	10	40	100
C	40	0	0	40	20	100

The costs of the service departments during a typical period are:

	A	B	C
	$	$	$
Variable labour & material cost	14 802	2 000	4000
Supervision	2000	2000	7000
Depreciation	4000	4000	5000
	20 800	8000	16 000

REQUIRED

1. Determine the allocation of the total costs of depts A, B and C to the products X and Y, using the reciprocal method of allocation
2. Given that dept A is a power plant generating 500 000 units, and that the company has the opportunity to obtain power from a third party supplier at a cost of $0.03 per unit, determine which source of supply is to be preferred

5.2

(a) A company has two operating departments A and B, which respectively produce pens and pencils, and one service department which supplies the required power for the whole company. Some

Service Cost Allocation to Production Departments

of the parts produced by B are required by A to be incorporated in the pen. The matrix Q' below shows the amount of each department's product required by the other.

Departmental provisions	Departmental requirements (per unit)		
	Pen	Pencil	Power
(A) Pen (units)	0	0	0
(B) Pencil (units)	0.3	0	0
Power (KW)	2.7	6.3	0.1

The three departments require three external resources – plastic, labour and oil – and the matrix D below gives the details for one gross unit of final product.

External resource	Departmental requirements per unit of finished product		
	Pen	Pencil	Power
Plastic (g)	2.0	1.0	0
Labour (hr)	0.3	0.1	0.5
Oil (l)	0	0	0.5

The required number of pens and pencils for sale for the month are respectively 200k and 100k.

REQUIRED

(i) Gross output for the month for each department
(ii) Total quantity of external resources needed for this level of output
 All calculations to the nearest k.
(b) The allocation of service costs to production departments has always been a problem for accountants. Two methods applying matrix algebra have been suggested as solutions.

REQUIRED

Briefly describe these methods, and how they differ from each other.
Which method is preferable, and why?

University of Birmingham, Degree of BCom(Accounting), Accounting G, June 1977.

5.3 Enterprising Limousines operate a fleet of cars in a large east coast city. Operations are organised in four regional areas, each the responsibility of a local manager. It has been decided to provide a central facility to provide for regular servicing of the vehicles. Major repairs are to be subcontracted. For internal control and costing purposes, all expenditures made by the central facility[a] are to be charged out to the four areas.
 Cost estimates for this facility at different annual levels of activity are available as follows:

---

[a] Assume that the costs of the central facility comprise a fixed element and a variable element with constant per unit costs.

Miles	$
500 000	176 000
400 000	152 000

The size of the central servicing facility is established following the submission of estimates of activity for the coming year by each local manager. During the year, the estimates were not met exactly. A comparison of results and estimates showed:

Region	Estimate miles	Actual miles
1	102 000	105 000
2	90 000	85 000
3	156 000	160 000
4	132 000	100 000

Total servicing expenditure amounted to $164 000.

REQUIRED

(a) Devise a scheme for allocating the servicing costs to regions which takes into account the behaviour of those costs, and show the resulting allocations for the year given
(b) How would your results have to be adjusted if total expenditure had been $159 000? Explain briefly

Chapter 6
Inventory Planning

Almost every business must stock goods to ensure smooth and efficient running of its operation.   (Taha, 1976)

6.1 Introduction

In ch. 2, inventory valuation methods and their impact on income measurement were considered. Now, inventory planning must be examined. Inventory planning, as envisaged here, is concerned with decisions on the optimal level of inventory which a firm should carry.

Inventories exist in the firm because they are needed to do business. Inventories are also important to the firm, because it wants (i) to provide and maintain good customer service; (ii) to smooth the flow of goods through the production process in order to avoid bottlenecks; (iii) to provide protection against the uncertainties of suppliers; (iv) to maintain a reasonable utilisation of equipment and man power.

The reason for this is that generally the cost to the firm of not having inventories in stocks are greater than the cost of having them. In addition, inventories provide management with a reserve that can be used when the opportunity arises. Horngren (1977) says that 'Inventories are cushions (a) to absorb planning errors and unforseen fluctuations in supply and demand, and (b) to facilitate smooth production and marketing operations. Further, inventories help to isolate or minimise the interdependence of all parts of the organisation for example, departments or functions so that each may work effectively.

The crucial importance of inventory planning is also seen in financial accounting. Three ratios are commonly used as guides for the effective management of inventories within the firm:

(i) $\dfrac{\text{Inventory}}{\text{Cost of sales}} \times \text{No. of days in year}$

(ii) $\dfrac{\text{Sales}}{\text{Inventory}}$

(iii) $\dfrac{\text{Inventory}}{\text{Total sales}} \times 100$

110 Cost Accounting

The use of any of the three ratios[1] helps to indicate to management whether the existing inventories are too high or too low, and leads to the correction of any imbalance that is discovered.

Inventory planning is not a simple matter, since it is concerned also with (i) logistic decisions; (ii) management risk level decisions; (iii) seasonality effects; (iv) production control decisions. The following topics are now examined: cost associated with inventories; derivation of the Economic Order Quantity model (EOQ); EOQ and quantity discounts; production runs; inventory planning under probabilistic demand.

Before examining those topics, a few inventory terms that are used in the discussion should be clarified.

6.2 Inventory definitions

LEAD TIME   An interval of time which elapses between the placing of an order for a good and the arrival of that good.

RE-ORDER LEVEL   When the inventory level falls to this point, the storeman notifies the purchasing department and a re-order is placed with the supplier. The re-order level is related to the expected demand during the lead time plus the safety stock.

SAFETY STOCK   The additional inventory held in excess of that needed to meet normal demand and which leads to the avoidance of stock outs.

STOCK OUT   This happens when a store or department runs out of a type of stock before the next order arrives.

Figure 6.1 further illustrates these concepts; it represents a typical inventory model where the re-order level is fixed.

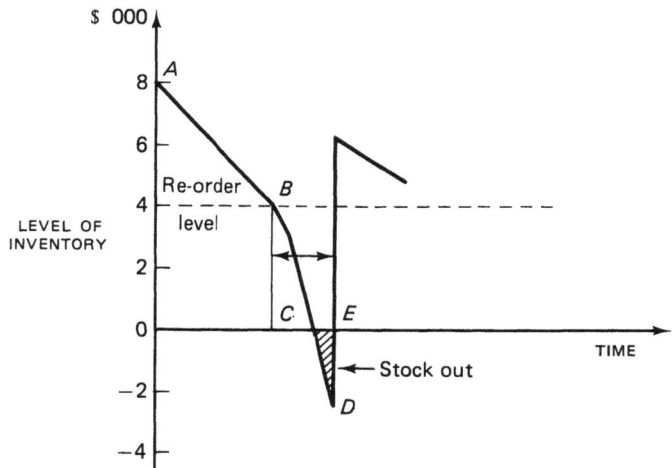

Figure 6.1   Inventory model – Fixed re-order level

---

[1] Financial textbooks usually stress the sanctity of ratio analysis, but ratio analysis *per se* can be misleading – see Lev (1974).

Inventory Planning   111

COMMENT

The model in Figure 6.1 begins with an inventory level of 8000 items at A. When the level of inventory falls to B, a fixed re-order is placed for 6000 items.

Now assume that demand increases more than was expected during the lead time; the best result is a stock out at C.

The area CDE represents the back orders during that period. Some of those orders will be lost because customers will switch to other sources. At time E, the order for 6000 items arrives. The inventory is above the re-order level once more, and the pattern is repeated (the distance between the arrows in Figure 6.1 represents the lead time).

6.3 Cost associated with inventories

There are three kinds of cost associated with inventory planning: (i) cost of ordering inventories; (ii) cost of carrying inventories; (iii) cost of not carrying sufficient inventories.

(i) is made up of clerical and transportation cost. (ii) is made up of handling cost, insurance, interest on capital invested in inventories, property taxes, obsolescence loss, and storage space cost. (iii) comprises added transportation charges, lost goodwill, ineffectiveness of production runs, and quantity discounts forgone.

The purpose of inventory planning is to minimise this cost. For the management function, the puzzle is of two kinds: how much inventory to order, and how often to do it. The EOQ model[1] partially helps management to resolve this.

The EOQ model is now derived. Thereafter we show how the model can be applied to decisionmaking under conditions of certainty and uncertainty.

6.4 Derivation of EOQ model

Consider the situation where the yearly known demand of a product of a firm is R units. The cost of setting up the production process is $\$S$, and the yearly cost of carrying the inventory is K dollars.

Assume (i) that the management function looks at a variety of lot sizes, ranging from one unit up to a large quantity lot; (ii) that the management function selects a lot size of some quantity (Q), which it thinks is economical to its manufacturing activities; and (iii) (for present purpose only) that stocks are delivered in a single lot so that the quantity in stocks falls until a delivery is received, and rises immediately to its maximum level when stocks are received.

Because the management function wants to avoid stock outs, it will consider an additional quantity, q, in addition to Q.

Now, the cost of not including q in the lot size will leave the number of orders required per year at R/Q with the yearly set up cost of $S(R)/(Q)$. If q is included, the number of set ups will decline to $(R/Q+q)$ with a cost of $S(R/Q+q)$.

---

[1] The reader should note that the EOQ, like other deterministic models, contains basic defects.

Clearly, the cost of having q will save the firm

$$\$\left(S\frac{(R)}{Q} - S\frac{R}{Q+q}\right).$$

Of course, under our assumption of a single delivery of each lot, the effect of having q in the lot size will increase the average size of the inventory by $q/2$, assuming an even usage rate. In turn, this increases the costs by $K\,q/2$. Management will thus include q only if the costs of not having it are greater than the cost of having it. Management will be indifferent if the costs are equal.

Equating the costs, we have:

$$S\left(\frac{R}{Q}\right) - S\left(\frac{R}{Q+q}\right) = K\left(\frac{q}{2}\right) \tag{6.1}$$

Simplifying:

$$\frac{SR(Q+q) - SR(Q)}{Q(Q+q)} = K\left(\frac{q}{2}\right)$$

Subtracting

Like terms in the numerator:

$$SR\left(\frac{q}{Q(Q+q)}\right) = K\left(\frac{q}{2}\right)$$

Dividing by q:

$$SR\left(\frac{1}{Q(Q+q)}\right) = \frac{K}{2}$$

Rearranging:

$$Q^2 + Qq = \frac{2RS}{K}$$

As q approaches 0, so does Qq. Thus, if $q = 0$, Q must be the optimal lot size, so

$$Q = \sqrt{\frac{2RS}{K}} \tag{6.2}$$

Where Q = Order size in units
R = Yearly quantity used in units
S = Cost of placing an order
K = Annual cost of carrying one unit in stock

The EOQ model is usually developed via calculus, but to work from basic principles shows directly that the EOQ is selected according to the principle of minimising inventory cost.

The inventory system depicted by equation (6.2) will incur two types of cost – ordering costs and carrying costs. Note that ordering costs are a function of the number of orders placed, while carrying costs are a function of time. Observe also that the model presents no difficulties to management, since the only problem is to decide n either the number of units to order at dates fixed in advance by the stores department, or the dates on which to order fixed amounts. How do management decide on how many orders to place during the year? The solution to Example 6.1 shows how. It is assumed in both methods that demand is constant throughout the year.

Inventory Planning

EXAMPLE 6.1

The data below relate to the only product of the Osford firm:

Annual demand	3750 units
	$
Order cost	200
Yearly carrying cost	1.50 per unit

REQUIRED

Determine (a) the EOQ, and (b) the replenishment periods by using (a) graphs, and (b) equation (6.2)

SOLUTION

(a) First, set up the facts for plotting purposes, as shown in Table 6.1 (see Figure 6.2 for details).

Table 6.1 No. of orders per year

	1	2	3	4	5	6
	$	$	$	$	$	$
(a) Value per order	3750	1875	1250	938	750	625
(b) Average inventory ($q/2$)	1875	938	625	469	375	313
(c) Carrying cost ($b \times \$1.50$)	2813	1407	938	704	563	470
(d) Ordering cost	200	400	600	800	1000	1200
(e) Total cost ($(c)+(d)$)	3013	1807	1538	1504	1563	1670

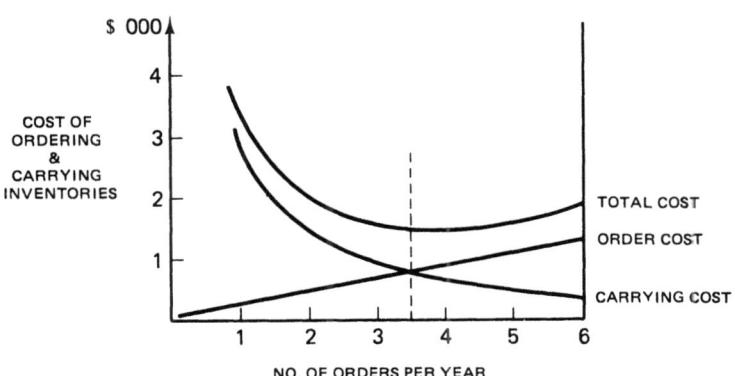

Figure 6.2 Determination of EOQ

COMMENT

Under conditions of certainty with constant demand, the EOQ is found at that point where the rising cost of ordering meets the falling cost of carrying the inventory.

Observe that the total cost curve is flat in the region of the optimal EOQ. This is the usual situation with this kind of model; it implies that the stores management of a firm can fix the EOQ around the theoretical optimum point without affecting the total cost in an adverse way.

(b) $\quad Q = \sqrt{\dfrac{2RS}{K}} = \sqrt{\dfrac{2(3750)(200)}{\$1.50}}$

$= 1000$ units

$3750 \div 1000 = 3.75$ yearly

The Osford firm should order the units in lots of 1000 3.75 times yearly.

6.5 EOQ and quantity discounts

Table 6.1 reveals, for example, that the ordering cost of inventory is proportionate to the quantity purchased. In the real world that situation is not so, since discounts which relate to the quantity of goods bought are usually given by the supplier of goods and are taken up by firms. The discount terms will affect the optimal EOQ, since the larger the order quantity the cheaper the order.

The solution to Example 6.2 below shows how discounts obtained by firms are included in the EOQ model.

EXAMPLE 6.2

The details regarding an item of inventory for the Osford firm is as follows:

Annual demand	4,000 units
Order cost	$60 per order
Carrying cost	20% of value of inventory
Unit cost	$10

The following discount terms are offered the company:

2% if the item of goods are bought in quantities of 500 or more
5% if the item of goods are bought in quantities of 1000 or more

REQUIRED

Advise the company if it would be cheaper to order the items for inventory five times per year, taking into consideration the discount option which minimises inventory costs.

SOLUTION

(i) The EOQ is found by adjusting the formula:

$$EOQ = \sqrt{\dfrac{2RS}{UK}}$$

where U = unit cost

$$= \sqrt{\dfrac{2(4,000)(60)}{}}$$

$$= \sqrt{\dfrac{480,000}{2}}$$

$EOQ = 490$ items

Ignoring the quantity discounts, the firm should order 490 items approximately eight times yearly.
(ii) Calculate the annual cost of buying the quantity allowed at each price break:
The cost of ordering four lots of 1000 at 5 % discount would be

	$
4000 × $10	40000
Less 5% × $40000	2000
	38000
Carrying cost 20% × ($10,000 − $500^a) × $\frac{1}{2}$	950
Ordering cost 4 × $60	240
	$39190

^{a} 1000 × $10 = $10000; 10000 × 0.05 = $500.

The cost of ordering five lots of 800 at 2% discount would be:

	A
4000 × $10	40000
Less: 2% × $40000	800
	39200
Carrying cost 20% × ($8000 − $160) × $\frac{1}{2}$	784
Ordering cost 5 × $60	300
	$40284

(iii) Compare the cost calculation of (i) with that of (ii). The conclusion is that the Osford firm should be advised to order the items for inventory four times yearly, and to accept the 5 per cent discount allowed, since it minimises its inventory cost.

The EOQ formula in a modified form is also applicable to production runs.

6.6 Production runs

A firm which produces a range of similar products, but do not keep all of them in continuous production, must resort to production runs. The duration of a production run can last a day, a week, or a month. A production run model takes the annual demand of the product into consideration. It follows that the decisions which a production run model determines are: (i) quantity of products to produce at each run; (ii) length of time that each run should last. Indeed, the purpose of the model to the firm is the minimisation of its annual costs, subject to the assumption that annual demand will be met. Here, we are considering a situation where there is no need to make the assumption made at the start of 6.4 above – that stocks are delivered in a single lot.

The production run model has similar features to the EOQ model. The notation listed below is applicable to its derivation:

Let D = demand
Hc = Holding cost
PR = Production rate

Q = Amount produced
s = Cost of setting up equipment
t = Time
u = Unit variable cost

When the firm's production rate is PR units per year, the time taken to produce those units will be given by

$$t = \frac{Q}{PR} \tag{6.3}$$

Multiplying equation (6.3) by D we get:

$$tD = \frac{QD}{PR}$$

which incorporates demand into the firm production rate analysis on a time basis.

The maximum inventory of the firm can be stated as the total amount produced, *less* the demand during the production run. The maximum inventory is given by:

$$Q - \frac{QD}{PR} = Q\left(1 - \frac{D}{PR}\right) \tag{6.4}$$

From the derivation of the EOQ model, we know that the average inventory will be half the maximum inventory given in equation (6.4):

$$\frac{1}{2}Q\left(1 - \frac{D}{PR}\right) \tag{6.5}$$

Incorporating the holding costs of the firm into equation (6.5), we get:

$$\frac{1}{2}QHc\left(1 - \frac{D}{PR}\right) \tag{6.6}$$

The replenishment cost per production run will be given by:

$$S + uQ \tag{6.7}$$

Multiplying equation (6.7) by D/Q gives the total replenishment cost per year:

$$(s + uQ)\frac{D}{Q} \tag{6.8}$$

Adding equations (6.6) and (6.8) gives the total cost, which is:

$$TK = \frac{1}{2}QHC\left(1 - \frac{D}{PR}\right) + (s + uQ)\frac{D}{Q}$$

Simplifying

$$TK = \frac{1}{2}QHc\left(1 - \frac{D}{PR}\right) + \frac{Ds}{Q} + Du$$

Using calculus

$$\frac{dTK}{dQ} = \frac{1}{2}Hc\left(1 - \frac{D}{PR}\right) - \frac{Ds}{Q^2}$$

Inventory Planning

Solving for Q gives:

$$0 = \frac{1}{2}Hc\left(1 - \frac{D}{PR}\right) - \frac{Ds}{Q^2}$$

$$2PRDs = Hc(Pr - D)Q^2$$

$$Q = \sqrt{\frac{2PRDS}{Hc(PR-D)}} \qquad (6.9)$$

Let us see how equation (6.9) can be applied to the case of determining the optimal size of a production run.

EXAMPLE 6.3

The Osford Co. has estimated that the production and cost data for one of its product line would be:

	$
Set up cost	700
Holding cost	4 for one item per year
	Units per year
Production cost	28000
Demand	18000

REQUIRED

Determine the number of production runs each year for the product line.

SOLUTION

Substitution into equation (6.9) gives:

$$Q = \sqrt{\frac{2 \times 28000 \times 18000 \times 700}{4(28000 - 18000)}} = 4200$$

The Osford Co. will minimise its costs by producing 4200 units approximately 4.3 times a year.

These examples have shown solutions for the situations where demand was known with certainty. We must now briefly examine the situation under probabilistic demand.

6.7 Inventory planning under probabilistic demand

When the demand for the firm's products are uncertain, probability evaluations can be useful to management.

The 'probability' of an event can be defined as the proportion of times it would occur in an infinite series of repeated trials of the same kind. The numerical limits of a probability measure is between 0 and 1. The sum of a series of probability measures = 1. A common way of estimating probabilities is on the basis of past experience.

The solution to Example 6.4 below shows the importance of probabilities to an inventory problem.

EXAMPLE 6.4

The weekly demand and probabilities for one of the products of the Osford Co. is as follows:

Demand	Probability
100	0.4
150	0.1
200	0.1
250	0.2
300	0.1
350	0.1

REQUIRED

(i) What is the expected value of the demand?
(ii) Assume that the cost[1] due to overstocking is $3 per unit and the cost of understocking is $2.50 per unit
If the listed demands only can occur, what is the optimum number of units to stock, if the company is to minimise the lost due to overstocking and to understocking?

SOLUTION

(i) Claculate the expected value of demand:

Demand	×	Probability	=	Expected value
100		0.4		40
150		0.1		15
200		0.1		20
250		0.2		50
300		0.1		30
350		0.1		35
		1.0		190

The expected value of demand is $190.

(ii) Determine the cumulative probability:

Demand	Probability
100	0.4
150	0.5
200	0.6
250	0.8
300	0.9
350	1.0

Order the first quantity for which the condition[2]

$$CUMP\ (D) > \frac{US}{US+OS}$$

---

[1] Overstocking cost can be obtained quite readily from the firm's records. Understocking cost will present some problems for firms because of the difficulty of measuring customers' lost goodwill.
[2] See Cocoran (1978) for a formal proof.

Inventory Planning 119

Where *US* = Understocking
OS = Overstocking

$$= \frac{2.50}{2.50\ 43.0}$$

$$= \frac{2.50}{5.50} = 0.5$$

The Osford Co. should order 150 units

The reader should note that the inventory models described in this chapter are static ones, and do not deal adequately with the complex inventory problems which beset the modern firm.

There are other models which try to capture and resolve real world inventory problems. A model which attempts to do so is a dynamic inventory one, the specifics of which are beyond the scope of this book.

6.8 Summary

Inventories are of vital importance to the firm. The simple, EOQ model can be used by management as a guide towards the minimisation of the cost of ordering inventories. When demand is uncertain, inventory planning requires probabilistic evaluations.

Bibliography

Cocoran, A. W. (1978) *Accounting, Analysis and Control* (John Wiley) ch. 14, p. 499.
Horngren, C. T. (1977) *Cost Accounting: A Managerial Emphasis*, 4th edn (Prentice-Hall) p. 463.
Lev, Baruch (1974) *Financial Statement Analysis: A New Approach* (Prentice-Hall) chs 1, 2.
Taha, H. A. (1976) *Operations Research: An Introduction*, 2nd edn (Macmillan) p. 389.
Vazsonyi, A. (1958) *Scientific Programming in Business and Industry* (John Wiley) ch. 10.

Problems

6.1

REQUIRED

(a)
 (i) explain the terms 're-order level' and 're-order quantity'
 (ii) list the factors which must be considered when determining the re-order level
 (iii) from the data given below, calculate for component 697:

   (a) re-order level
   (b) re-order quantity
   (c) minimum level
   (d) average stock level

DATA

Component 697 is one of thousands of items kept in the store of a manufacture

		Units
Max. stock level set at		17000
Expected consumption, (per month)	Max.	3000
	Min.	1600
	Months	
Estimated delivery period	Max. 4	
	Min. 2	

(b) On 31 March, one of the shops within a retailing group was destroyed by fire. For insurance claim purposes, it is necessary to establish the value of the stock on hand at the time.

REQUIRED

From the information given below, calculate the value of the stock. Present your answer in the form of statement showing how you have calculated the figure

DATA

Stock, at cost, 1 March $64200

During the period 1–31 March, the following transactions took place:

	$
Goods received by shop from central warehouse (at cost)	34000
Goods returned from shop to central warehouse (at cost)	4200
Sales	52000
Goods returned by customers and refunds given	2400

The retail group works on an average mark-up 33 1/3 on cost

ICMA, Fs[a], Section A, Cost Accounting 1, May 1982.
[a] Foundation Stage.

6.2 A small insurance company estimates that next year it will receive $5 million in premiums that will flow in a steady rate throughout the year. This income will be invested at 20 per cent per annum, but the cost to the company of making an investment is $200 for each investment made and, in addition 2 per cent of the sum invested.

REQUIRED

(a) Show that this situation is an inventory problem in structure, and that the EOQ model may be used to determine the optimum investment policy, i.e. the timing of making the company's investments
(b) Determine how many investments should be made during the year, and the total cost of the policy as given by the EOQ model
(c) A reorganisation of the company's investment department would cause investment costs to change to $450 for each investment made plus 1 1/2 of the sum invested. How would this affect the company's optimum investment policy according to the EOQ model?
(d) Instead of reorganising the investment department, the company decides to hold, as buffer stock, cash to the value of 2 per cent of the yearly premiums; what will be the maximum holding of cash at any one time?
(e) Comment on the practical inadequacies of the EOQ model in this situation.

ACCA, PE (adapted), Section 2, Paper 12, Management Mathematics, December 1981.

6.3 One representation of the EOQ inventory modes is:

$$Q = \sqrt{2\frac{CoA}{CH}}$$

Inventory Planning

Where Q = EOQ
Co = Cost of placing an order
A = Annual demand in units
CH = Cost of holding one unit in stock for one year

Data relevant to component K used by Engineering P1C in 22 different assemblies and to the company include:

Purchase price	$15 per 100
Annual wage	100 000 units
Cost of buying office:	
Fixed	$15 575 per annum
Variable	$12 per order

	$ per annum
Rent on component's store	3000
Heating	700
	% per annum
Interest	25.00
Insurance, based on total purchases	0.00
Deterioration, as % of all items purchased	1.00

REQUIRED

(a) Calculate the EOQ for component K
(b) Calculate the percentage change in total annual variable cost relating to component K if the annual usage was (i) 125000 units; (ii) 75000 units
(c) Use these figures to comment on the sensitivity of the EOQ to changes in annual usage

ICMA, PS, Part I, Quantitative Techniques, May 1982.

6.4 Pink Ltd is experiencing some slight problems concerning two stock items sold by the company.
The first of these items is product EXE, which is manufactured by Pink. The annual demand for EXE of 4000 units (which is evenly spread throughout the year) is usually met by production taking place four times per year in batches of 1000 units. One of the raw material inputs to product EXE is product DEE, which is also manufactured by Pink. Product DEE is the firm's major product and is produced in large quantities throughout the year. Production capacity is sufficient to meet in full all demands for the production of DEEs.
The standard cost of products EXE and DEE are:

STANDARD COST – PRE UNIT

	PRODUCT	
	EXE	DEE
	$	$
Raw materials–purchased from external supplies	13	8
–DEE standard cost	22	—
Labour–unskilled	7	4
–skilled	9	5
Variable overhead	5	3
Fixed overhead	4	2
	$60	$22

Included in the fixed overhead for EXE is the set up cost for each production run. The cost of each set up, which applies irrespectively of the size of the production run, is:

(i) Labour cost – skilled labour   66
(ii) Machine parts   70

Total $136

The 'machine parts' relate to the cost of parts required for modifications carried out to the machine on which EXE is produced. The parts can be used for one run only, irrespective of run length, and are destroyed by replacement on reinstatement of the machine. There are no set up costs associated with DEE.

The cost of financing stocks of EXE is 15 per cent per annum. Each unit of EXE in stock requires 0.40 m^2 of storage space and units cannot be stacked on top of each other to reduce costs. Warehouse rent is $20 per annum per m^2 and Pink is required to pay only for storage space actually used.

Pink is not working to full capacity, and idle time payments are being made to all grades of labour except unskilled workers. Unskilled labour is not guaranteed a minimum weekly wage, and is paid only for work carried out.

The second stock item causing concern is Product WYE. Product WYE is purchased by Pink for resale and the 10000 unit annual demand is again spread evenly throughout the year. Incremental ordering costs are $100 per order, and the normal unit cost is $20. However, the suppliers of WYE are now offering quantity discounts for large orders:

Quantity ordered	Unit price $
Up to 999	20.00
1000–1999	19.80
2000 and over	19.60

The purchasing manager feels that full advantage should be taken of discounts, and purchase should be made at $19.60 per unit using orders for 2000 units or more. Holding costs for WYE are calculated at $8.00 per unit per annum, and this figure will not be altered by any change in the purchase price per unit.

REQUIRED

(a) Show the optimum batch size for the production of EXEs. If this differs from the present policy, calculate the annual savings to be made by Pink Ltd from pursuing the optimal policy
Briefly explain the figures incorporated in your calculations (the time taken to carry out a production run may be ignored)
(b) Advise Pink Ltd on the correct size of order for the purchase of WYEs
(c) Briefly describe two major limitations or difficulties inherent in the practical application of the model used in (a) to determine the optimum batch size

ACAA, PE Section 2, Paper 14, Accounting 5, Management Accounting, June 1981.

6.5 The Singapore Stores imports dried milk from the UK, which it markets under its own brand name Klim.

Sales of the product show neglible seasonal variation, and run at 12 million packets per annum. To ensure that there are no stock outs the company always holds a base stock equal to 1 month's sales. The company's purchasing officer orders in amounts equal to 1 month's sales paying S $1.0 per packet. The lead time between placing an order and delivery of the consignment to the Singapore Stores' warehouse is 37 days.

The supplying exporter has offered to reduce the price of Klim by 10 per cent a packet if the Singapore Stores will treble the size of the orders that it places; however, it will also have to be prepared to accept twice the current lead time.

The purchasing officer discusses this with the company's management accountant. It is decided that if the change is made, the same base stock as before could be held, but the occupancy costs of the additional storage space associated with the increased stockholdings would cost S $72000 per annum, and that there would also be an increase in handling costs of 8c per packet sold.

The management accountant also requires an opportunity cost to be imputed for the company's cost of capital at a rate of 1 per cent per month on the value of average stocks, which is the same percentage as currently used.

REQUIRED

(a) Your opinion as to whether the exporter's offer should be accepted, based upon computations
(b) Your views on any qualitative information which should be brought into the decision analysis

ACCA, PE, Section 2, Paper 14, Accounting 5, Management Accounting, December 1976.

Chapter 7
Analysis of Cost Behaviour

All the characteristics of a production operation can affect its cost. (Alchian, 1959)

The learning-curve technique can be profitably used by many industries such as electronics ... and generally in cases where assembly or machining cost represent a large portion of the total manufactuirng costs. (Theodore, 1975)

7.1 Introduction

An understanding of cost behaviour by the accounting function contributes to effective and reliable managerial decisions. Failure to do so leads to bad cost planning, bad price settings, bad cash management and bad allocation of resources, the cumulative results of which lead inevitably to the demise of the firm.

The accounting function is faced continually with decisions of this nature. How many units should be made of a particular product? Should the selling price of a product be increased or decreased and if so, what will be the effect on the sales volume? To answer these questions, the accounting function must have an understanding of cost behaviour and cost–volume–profit (C–V–P) relationships.

7.2 Patterns of typical cost functions

The accounting function assumes that the cost pattern of a production system is either variable or fixed. Variable cost can be of two forms – linear or non-linear. Figures 7.1 and 7.2 show these two types of cost pattern.

In notation, the linear variable cost equation can be written as:

$y = bx$

Where y = Independent variable
x = Dependent variable
b = Constant, i.e. variable cost per unit

Analysis of Cost Behaviour 125

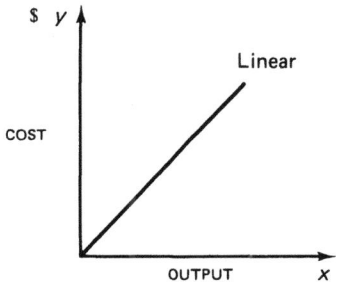

Figure 7.1 Linear variable cost

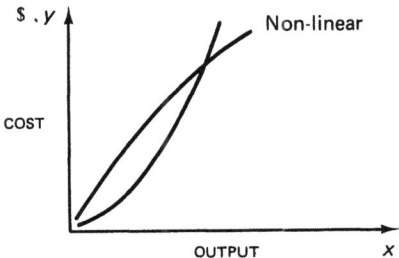

Figure 7.2 Non-linear variable cost

Of course, y and x also show respectively the cost and the level of output. Similarly, the non-linear variable cost can be written as:

$$y = ax + bx^2 + cx^3 + \ldots + kx^N$$

Where y and x are defined as before, and $a, b, c \ldots k$ are constants

Curvilinear or non-linear functions involve complex calculations. The accounting function therefore approximates such functions to linear forms. Where productive activity is involved, the linear approximations are done within the relevant range of output.

Figure 7.3 illustrates the procedure. The dashed line represents a linear approximation of the curve line within the relevant range of output.

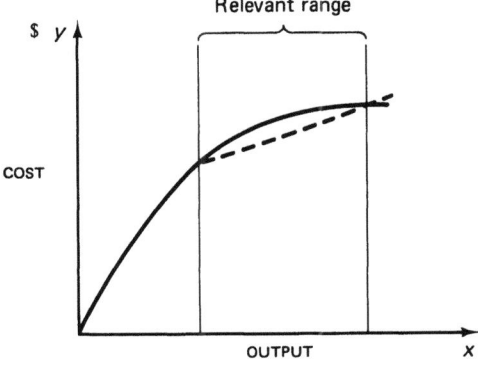

Figure 7.3 Linear approximation of non-linear function

To predict the measure of an item of linear variable cost, the equation $y = bx$ is utilised. If a firm manufactures doors and each door requires four nails which cost $0.14 each, the variable cost per door is $0.56. If 200 doors are to be made, the cost for the nails will be $112, i.e. $y = \$0.56\ (200)$.

7.3 Step costs

Step cost is a discontinuous function. It is the result of input factors that cannot be increased in very small portions. The appearance of step cost is similar to the stairs found in a house. Figure 7.4A shows the behaviour of step costs; the step function is usually shown as in Figure 7.4B.

Figure 7.4A also shows that the measured value of cost is constant at A_1 for the output level between 0 and 1. Above the output level 1, cost increases to A_2. It remains at A_2 up to output level 2, from whence it increases to A_3 with an output level of 3.

Step costs cannot be incorporated smoothly into the C–V–P model. To circumvent the problems created by step costs, the accountant again resorts to approximation. If the output levels in Figure 7.4A between 1 and 2 only are to be considered by management, the step cost will be treated as a fixed cost of A_2.

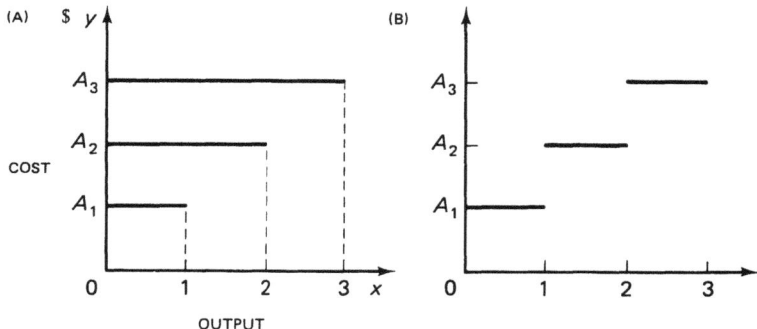

Figure 7.4 Two models of step cost – (A) Behaviour of step cost; (B) 7.4B The step function

7.4 Fixed costs

Fixed costs are those measured values of items which remain unchanged in the short term[1], i.e. an accounting period. Fixed costs are usually related to a given range of output. Seen in this way, fixed cost can be distinguished into costs which remain constant at the 0 output level, and costs which cannot be avoided at the 0 output level, but remain constant at all other output levels. Figures 7.5 and 7.6 shows the pattern.

---

[1] Baumol (1972) describes the short term as that situation 'where the firm has a minimum of free choice', a period so short that a firm 'will not be able to increase its output in response to increase customer demand, and can only supply increase demand out of inventory'. On the other hand, the long period can be described as 'a period of sufficient duration which enables the company to become completely free in its decisions from its present policies, possessions and commitments'.

Analysis of Cost Behaviour

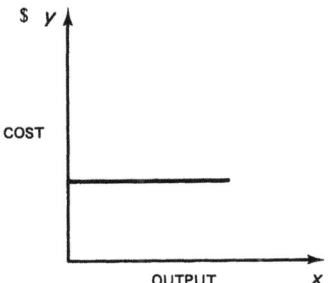

Figure 7.5 Fixed cost constant at 0 output

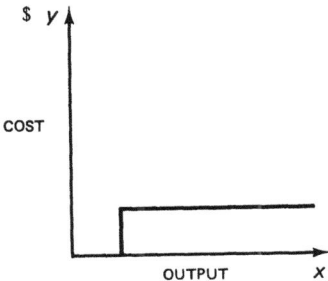

Figure 7.6 Fixed cost unavoidable at 0 output

7.5 Semi-variable cost

A cost which contains both a fixed and a variable part is called semi-variable. The variable part of a semi-variable function can be either linear or curvilinear. In mathematical notation, the linear semi-variable function can be written as

$y = a + b(x)$,

and the curvilinear function as

$y = a + b(x^2)$

Figures 7.7 and 7.8 show their forms.

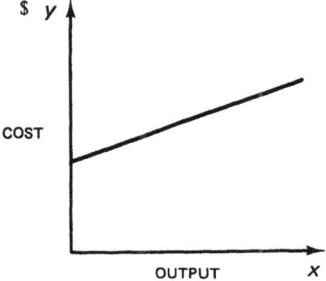

Figure 7.7 $y = a + b(x)$

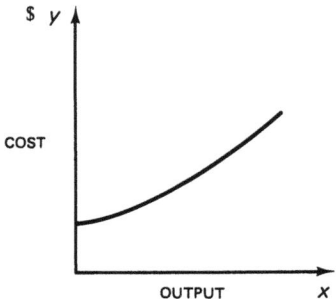

Figure 7.8 $y = a + b(x^2)$

There are some unusual costs patterns which do not fit any of the above models. These are now shown via examples and diagrammatic illustrations.

EXAMPLE 7.1

Consider an electricity corporation which calculates its rates as follows:

	KWH	$
First	10 000	500
Next	1000	0.50 per KWH
Next	1000	0.40
Next	1000	0.30

Figure 7.9 shows the cost patterns.

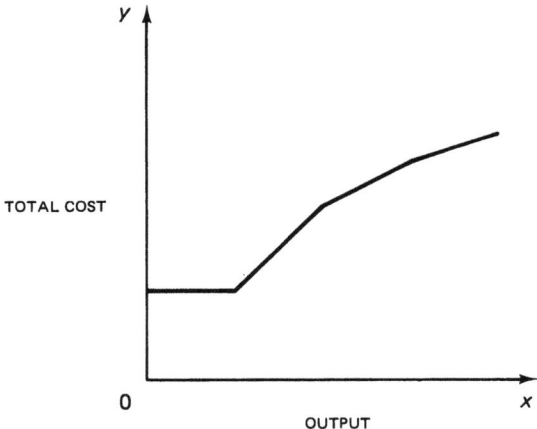

Figure 7.9 Electricity corporation – Cost pattern

EXAMPLE 7.2

Consider the purchase of materials at prices which fall as the volume increases: $2 per lb for an annual order of 1000 lb or less. $1.50 per lb for an annual order between 1001 and 2000 lb; $1 per lb for an annual order in excess of 2000 lb.
Figure 7.10 highlights this relationship.

Analysis of Cost Behaviour

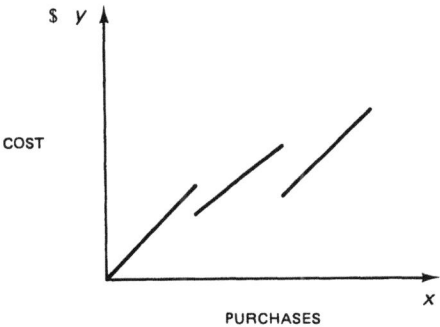

Figure 7.10 Model of falling price – increasing volume

EXAMPLE 7.3

Consider the remuneration of a salesman, who is paid by commission at a rate which decreases as volume increases 10 per cent is paid on the first $15000 of sales; 7 per cent on the next $15000; 5 per cent on any sales beyond $30000 per year.

Figure 7.11 shows this relationship.

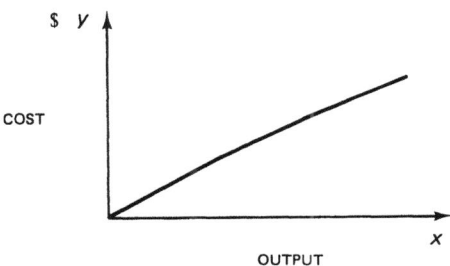

Figure 7.11 Model of decreasing commission – increasing volume

An advantage for management purposes of drawing a cost graph is its immediate visibility. From it, the management function can discern its general behaviour. Relevant information can be obtained directly from it, though in an imprecise manner. These statements are also applicable to the learning curve.

7.6 The learning curve

Dopuch *et al.* (1974) says that the 'The learning curve phenomenon is relevant to business decisions when the reduction in production time per unit leads to a reduction in unit cost'. The meaning of the 'learning effect' is that employees gain proficiency from repetitions of a manufacturing operation. Indeed, the learning effect may be inhibited where automated machines limit the speed of the employees, or where the pace of working is preset externally for an assembly line. The learning effect was first discerned during the Second World War, where aircraft companies found that an 80 per cent learning curve was applicable.[1] A firm can obtain a learning curve by espionage from a similar concern by assuming the rate of its own industry, or by deriving its own curve via regression analysis[2] from observed pilot study results.

Table 7.1 shows how an 80 per cent learning rate is calculated for production units using 60 hours as the average time.

Table 7.1 Calculation of learning rate

Unit		Average hr	Total hr
1		= 60.00	$1 \times 60 = 60$
2	0.80×60	= 48.00	$2 \times 48 = 96$
4	0.80×48	= 38.40	$4 \times 38.40 = 153.60$
8	0.80×38.40	= 30.72	$8 \times 30.72 = 245.76$

The mathematical formula is:

$$Y = ax^b$$

Where a = Time taken for first unit
b = Exponent
x = Cumulative no. of units produced
y = Average time per unit

Equation (7.1) is a power function; its graph is shown in Figure 7.12.

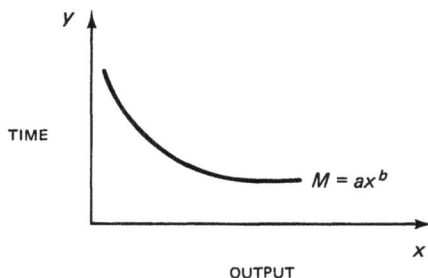

Figure 7.12 Graph of equation (7.1)

How does the management function utilise equation (7.1) to estimate the marginal time needed to make X units? This is done by solving equation (7.1) with the aid of logarithms,[3] or by using calculus.

Now, Table 7.1 reveals that as output doubles from 1 to 2 units, the average time falls to 80 per cent of the time taken for the first unit. Numerically, the average time is 60×80 per cent. Using equation (7.1), since the cumulative number of units in this case is 2, we can write:

$$60 \times 80 = 60 \times 2^b$$

[1] It is doubtful whether such a high rate holds in the dynamic countries today. In undynamic countries, the learning effect has never been tested, to the author's knowledge.

[2] Regression analysis is discussed in the following chapter (see particularly 8.8, 8.9 and 8.11).

[3] The logarithm is to the base 10. This is called a common logarithm. When the logarithm is to the base e, it is called a natural or Naperian logarithm. For those not acquainted with logarithms, see Theodore (1975).

Analysis of Cost Behaviour

Dividing by 60 we get

$0.80 = 2^b$

Taking Logs of both sides

$\text{Log } 0.80 = b \text{ Log } 2$

$b = \dfrac{\log 0.80}{\log 2} = \dfrac{0.9031 - 1}{0.3010}$

$b = -0.322$, the exponent

Assuming that the management function wants to know the number of hours it will take to make five units, the solution is:

$$Y(5) = 60(5)^{-0.322}$$
$$-0.322 \text{ Log } 5 = 0.322 \,(0.6990)$$
$$= -0.2251$$
$$\text{Log}^{-1}(\text{Antilog}) -0.2251 = 0.7749 - 1 = 0.5955$$
$$\therefore Y(5) \qquad\qquad = 60(0.5955) = 35.73 \text{ hr}$$

The marginal calculation[1] is as follows:

	hr
	$= 35.73 \text{ hr} \times 5 = 178.65$
(see Table 7.1)	$= 153.60$
Marginal time (difference)	$= 25.05 \text{ hr}$

Equation (7.1) can be used in standard costing and in contract bidding – for example, for setting standards – and for profit calculations. The equation is not the only function which can be used by management for decisionmaking purposes; an example and its solution is now shown, based on the function e^{-x}.

EXAMPLE 7.4

Dodson Ltd has just recruited a number of employees to work on a special product for the export market. The recruits are trained for 6 weeks (of 5 working days each) in assembling a product. Experience has shown that the learning rate is:

$X = 50(1 - e^{-dk})$

---

[1] Applying calculus to the example, the marginal time it will take to make one extra unit can be found as follows:

Total hr $\qquad = y \times x = ax^b$
$\qquad\qquad\quad = ax^{b+1}$

Differentiating $\dfrac{dT \text{ hr}}{ax}\qquad$ = marginal hr = $a(b+1)x^b$

When $x = 5$, the marginal time is 24.23 hr
The answer is found by substituting the values of a, b and x in $a(b+1)x^b$.

[1] Note that the answer differs slightly from that which is obtained via logarithms. When $x = 4.5$, the correct answer is obtained.

Where d = No. of days the employee has attended the practice sessions
k = Constant
x = Skill achieved by the employee in assembling a number of units per hour

REQUIRED

If after 3 weeks of the sessions, the assembly rate is 30 units per hour, what is the rate after 4 weeks and upon completion?

SOLUTION

Compute d.

$d = 3 \times 5 = 15$
x given $= 30$

Put the values of d and x into the formula:

$30 = 50(1 - e^{-15k})$

$(1 - e^{-15k}) = 0.6$
$e^{-15k} = 0.4$

Take Log_e of both sides:

$15k = 0.91629$
$k = 0.0611$
$\therefore x = 50(1 - e^{-0.0611})$

$d = 20$ for 4 weeks:

$x = 50(1 - e^{1.22})$
$= 50(1 - 0.295230)$
$= 35$ units per hr, and

upon completion:

$x = 50(1 - e^{-(30 \times 0.0611)})$
$= 50(1 - e^{-1.83})$

COMMENT

The values of x, e^x and e^{-x} for Example 7.4 are shown in Table 7.2.

Table 7.2 Values of x, e^x and e^x

x	e^x	e^{-x}
0.06	1.0618	0.941765
⋮	⋮	⋮
1.83	6.2339	0.160414

The learning curve model can be applied in many ways:
(i) preparation of cost estimates
(ii) setting standards and budget allowances
(iii) evaluating performances by comparing progress reports with the anticipated goals made by management from the learning model
(iv) setting of incentives wage rates

It is important to note, that Morse (1972) argues that 'A cost allocation model based on the learning curve phenomenon will better disclose the relationship between effort and accomplishment.'

Analysis of Cost Behaviour

7.7 Summary

Accountants classify costs as either variable or fixed. Accountants also work from linear cost functions, although some costs functions are non-linear.

The cost patterns of the firm, though imprecise, portray the cost bounds of the firm's operations.

The learning curve is a power function. It can be used for the determination of a learning rate and the setting of standards.

Bibliography

Alchian, A. A. (1959) 'Cost and Output', in W, Breit and H. M. Hochman (eds), *Reading in Microeconomics*, 2nd edn (Holt, Rinehart & Winston) p. 159.
Baumol, W. J. (1972) *Economic Theory and Operations Analysis*, 3rd edn (Prentice-Hall) pp. 287–8.
Dopuch, N. et al. (1974) *Cost Accounting*, 2nd edn (Harcourt, Brace Jovanovich) p. 81.
Morse, W. J. (1972) 'Reporting Production Costs that follow the Learning Curve Phenomenon', *Accounting Review*, vol. xlvii, no. 4 , October p. 761–73.
Summers, E. L. and Welsch, G. A. (1970) 'How Learning Curve Models can be Applied to Profit Planning', *Management Services*, March–April, pp. 45–50.
Theodore, Chris A. (1975) *Applied Mathematics: An Introduction*, 3rd edn (Robert D. Irwin) p. 177.

Problems

7.1
REQUIRED

(a) Graph the following curve:

$Y = 120x^{-0.322}$

General form: $y = ax^{-b}$
For values of $x = 1, 2, 4, 25, 100, 200$

(b) Given that:

y = average no. of direct labour hr per unit
a = no. of direct labour hr for first unit
x = the cumulative no. of units produced

Comment on the graph, and suggest circumstances in which the use of such a graph would assist in management accounting (assume for example, that an order for additional units has been received).

ICMA, PS, Part I, Quantitative Techniques, May 1979.

7.2 Your company has been asked to quote for a new product. Although you were not involved in the manufacture of the prototypes, similar products have been made by the existing labour force and machinery.

The production records for two similar products, K and L, have been examined and the direct labour cost is summarised below:

Cost of unit	Product K $	Product L $
First	250	520
Second	200	380
3 and 4	360	760
5, 6, 7 and 8	648	1280
9–16 (incl.)	1166	2400

It has been estimated that the direct labour cost of the first unit of the new product will cost $400. Regression analysis must be employed.
Formulate which may be useful include:

$$Y = aX^{-b}$$

where Y = Cumulative average cost
a = Cost of first unit
X = Cumulative units completed
b = Learning rate

and, in the standard regression equation

$$y = a + bx$$
$$a = \frac{(\Sigma y)(\Sigma x^2) - (\Sigma x)(\Sigma xy)}{n(\Sigma x^2) - (\Sigma x)^2}$$
$$b = \frac{n(\Sigma xy) - (\Sigma x)(\Sigma y)}{n(\Sigma x^2) - (\Sigma x)^2}$$

Based on the information given above, the learning rate for product K is 0·1522.

REQUIRED

(a) Determine the relationship between the cumulative no. of units completed and the cumulative average direct labour cost for product L
(b) Estimate a relationship for the new product
(c) Using this relationship, estimate the direct labour cost for a subsequent quantity of 7, i.e. units 2–8 (inclusive) of the new product.

ICMA, PS, Part I, Quantitative Techniques, November 1979.

7.3 AB Ltd, which has a fairly full order book, is approached by a customer with the offer of a contract for a model that is a variant, in terms of dimensions and materials used, of one of its existing products.

Though the customer expects to pay a normal price for the model, he wants AB Ltd to take account of an 80 per cent learning curve in its price calculations; this level has been shown to be reasonable in AB Ltd's industry for relevant work.

The prospective contract is for a total of 464 units, made up of an initial order of 160 units, two subsequent orders of 80 units each, and three subsequent orders of 48 units each.

AB Ltd estimates the following costs for the initial order:

Direct materials:

		$
P	8 mm	3.50 per m
Q	12 kg	1.00 per kg

Direct wages:

Dept	hr	$ per hr
1	4	1.25
2	50	1.50
3	15	1.00

Variable overhead: 20% of direct wages
Fixed overhead rates, per hour

Dept	$
1	2.00
2	1.00
3	0.80

Analysis of Cost Behaviour

The nature of the work in the three production departments is as follows:

Dept 1
Uses highly automatic machines
Although the operators on these machines need to be fairly skilled, their efficiency affects only the quality of the work but can have little impact on the quantity of this department's output which is largely machine controlled

Dept 2
Partially mechanised

Dept 3
An assembly department.

In both depts 2 and 3, the skill of operators is a major determinant of the volume of output. The terms of the contract price allow for:

	% profit margin
Direct materials cost plus	2½
Conversion cost plus	12½

REQUIRED

(a) Calculate the price per unit for:

    (i) initial order of 160 units
    (ii) second, third and fourth orders, if given successively but without guarantee of further orders
    (iii) whole contract of six orders if given from the start, but on the same basis of production and delivery

(b) Discuss what factors should be considered in deciding whether the learning curve should be taken into account when setting standards for a standard costing system

Note that an 80 per cent learning curve on ordinary graph paper would show the following relationship between the x axis (volume) and y axis (cumulative average price of elements subject to the learning curve):

x	y %	x	y %
1.0	100	2.1	78.9
1.1	96.9	2.2	77.8
1.2	93.3	2.3	76.8
1.3	91.7	2.4	76.0
1.4	89.5	2.5	74.9
1.5	87.6	2.6	74.0
1.6	86.1	3.7	73.2
1.7	84.4	2.8	72.3
1.8	83.0	2.9	71.5
1.9	81.5	3.0	70.0
2.0	80.0	3.1	70.0

ICMA, PS, Part III, Management Accounting 2, May 1977.

Chapter 8
Cost Estimation

Effective budgeting and control depend upon the ability of management to estimate cost accurately under different circumstances.   (Moore and Jaedicke, 1976)

There is no way to attain certain information for the future. What can be achieved is only to state degrees of likelihood, credibility, reasonableness, or acceptability of prognoses.   (Kosiol, 1969)

8.1 Introduction

Cost estimation is used by the management function for prediction purposes. Prediction premises a course of action; prediction has an aura of prophecy about it; cost prediction can be accurate or inaccurate. The moot point underlying cost prediction, however, is that the management function can make use of the data via statistical analysis as guidelines for budgeting, choice of action in markets, and performance evaluation.

8.2 Total cost function of firm

The total cost function of a firm is constructed to explain the determination of individual items of cost – for example, labour cost or the determination of total costs.

The total cost function of a firm might be expressed as:

$$TK = a + b(x) \tag{8.1}$$

Where TK = total cost

a, b = parameters which seek to explain the causal relationships between total cost and output (x).

Two questions can be asked which cast doubt on the general applicability of equation (8.1): (i) Does a simple linear function like this capture the isomorphism of a firm's production system?

(ii) Is it good practice to treat the firm's total cost as being determined by a single independent variable? The answer to both questions is 'yes', only where the firm's production system is not complex. Where the production system is complex, the answer is 'no'. The engineering approach provides a working model for complex production systems.

8.3 Engineering approach

A reasonably valid production function on which a total cost function is based should describe the consumption of all types of production factors. This is what the engineering approach attempts to do.

The engineering approach builds up a complete specification of the input needed to produce a particular level of output. Its specification indicates the input which should be used. The material input is based on the material content of the product's specification, and the labour input is based on time and motion studies.

The total cost function of the engineering approach tries to capture the technical specification of the products, and the operating efficiency of the factory's machines, and so determine the consumption of input factors. In this way, the cost function relates output to time, in terms of cost and throughput per hour. This implies that the total output required to satisfy the production schedule is also a base for the determination of the rate of production activity. Required output and rate of activity thus act as a surrogate for the cost function.

To predict the total production cost, the engineering method uses expected price for each input. The measured value of each input implies a partial and transient production function, as well as a partial and transient cost function. The engineering approach thus builds up piecemeal systems from a firm's production and operating characteristics. This forms the base for the aggregate cost function on which cost predictions are made.

8.4 Account analysis method

The accountant, however, has other tools in his kit for the determination of the firm's cost function. One such tool is the account analysis method.

This method requires an examination of the firm's accounting records, arranging each element of cost into a fixed and variable category.

The procedure is simply this. The accounting records of a recent period are selected. The management accountant classifies each cost category in a subjective way–the cost of material may be treated as variable, and administrative overheads may be treated as fixed, for example. Other items may be treated as semi-variable cost, and an estimate will be made of the fixed element of the cost from available evidence.

The total of the variable cost of the period will be divided by the output of that period. This calculation gives an estimate of the variable cost per unit of output. The derived figure, plus the total costs for the same period, will be used as variables for the cost function. A measure of output must be established to carry out this calculation. In the simple case of a single product, the number of units produced may be sufficient. Where there are a number of products, output must be expressed so that the production of different products can be aggregated. Each type of product must be attributed an output 'value', expressed in common terms for all products. Standard labour hours are a common measure, and a full discussion of standard costs is to be found in ch. 14.

8.5 Derivation of accountant's cost function

Table 8.1 shows the production cost statement for an accounting period. Column (1) shows the actual costs incurred on the production of 300 units of output; the classification of the costs into fixed and variable elements is shown in columns (2) and (3).

Table 8.1 Production cost statement for accounting period

	Total (1)	Fixed (2)	Variable (3)
	$	$	$
Material used	5000		5000
Direct labour	6000		6000
Supervisory labour	400	400	
Factory rent & rates	500	500	
Fuel & power	2500		2500
Maintenance	220		220
Depreciation	3000	3000	
Accounts office	3500	3500	
Miscellaneous	1000	1000	
	$22120	$8400	$13720

Using the account analysis method, the variable cost per unit is:

$$\frac{\$13720}{300} = \$45.73$$

$$\therefore TK = 8400 + 45.73x$$

The account analysis method has advantages and disadvantages. The advantages are that it is simple, inexpensive, and can be revised easily. The disadvantage is that it is highly subjective, relying on the assumed nature (i.e. fixed or variable) of the costs collected. The method is also insensitive to the apportionment of indirect costs which are fixed for the firm as a whole, but variable for the departments. Dopuch et al. (1974) say that 'the account classification method should be used only when a crude approximation of cost behaviour is sufficient for making decisions'.

8.6 High–low method

Another approach used by accountants to estimate the cost function is the high–low method.

This approach uses the cost for two levels of output of a recent period to determine the distinction between the fixed and variable cost. The cost data for two levels of output are the highest and the lowest from the sample.

EXAMPLE 8.1

The Frank firm has made a number of observations of its cost at different levels of operating output. The largest recorded output in any accounting period was 3000 units, which were produced at a cost of $60000; the lowest output was 2000 units, produced at a cost of $50000.

Cost Estimation

REQUIRED

Determine the firm's total cost function by the high–low method.

SOLUTION

Highest output gives:	$60000 = a + 3000X$	(8.2)
Lowest output gives:	$50000 = a + 2000X$	(8.3)
Solving the equations give:	$(a, x) = 30000, 10$	
	$\therefore TK = 30000 + 10X$	

COMMENT

An advantage of the high–low method is that it is inexpensive, and determines a seeming relationship between costs and output. However, because the method uses two extreme values, it ignores all the data which lie between the extreme cost items. The method is therefore unreliable, except in the most simple cases. Another disadvantage is that the method leads to ambiguities (see Nurnberg, 1977).

8.7 Scatter charts

Another valuable accounting tool is the scatter chart. This procedure is best illustrated by an example and comment.

EXAMPLE 8.2

The total costs and output for the first 6 months of the year for the Frank firm were as follows:

Month	Output 000	Total cost $000
1	70	100
2	80	105
3	90	110
4	70	104
5	100	115
6	110	112

COMMENT

The six observations are plotted on a graph; this representation is called a scatter chart. Figure 8.1 shows the plotted observations and the line of best fit, drawn on a purely subjective basis to pass through the scattered observations. The line of best fit is shown in Figure 8.1 as AB.

Figure 8.1 also shows that if the line is extended backwards until it meets the vertical axis, it intersects when the cost is $80000. It may appear that this represents the fixed costs which will be incurred by the firm irrespective of the production level.[1] However, since there are no observations of cost at any output level below 70000, it may be unwise to assume that the relationship given by AB applies at a 0 output level.

It is usual to assume that the relationship holds only for levels of output near those for which we have observations. This is known as the 'relevant range'. What might be said is that within the range from output of 70000–110000, cost behaves as represented by the line AB. But does a visual inspection of the cost function and the scatter of observations establish the true behaviour of cost? If

---

[1] The line is, in fact, the total cost line which is examined in break-even analysis.

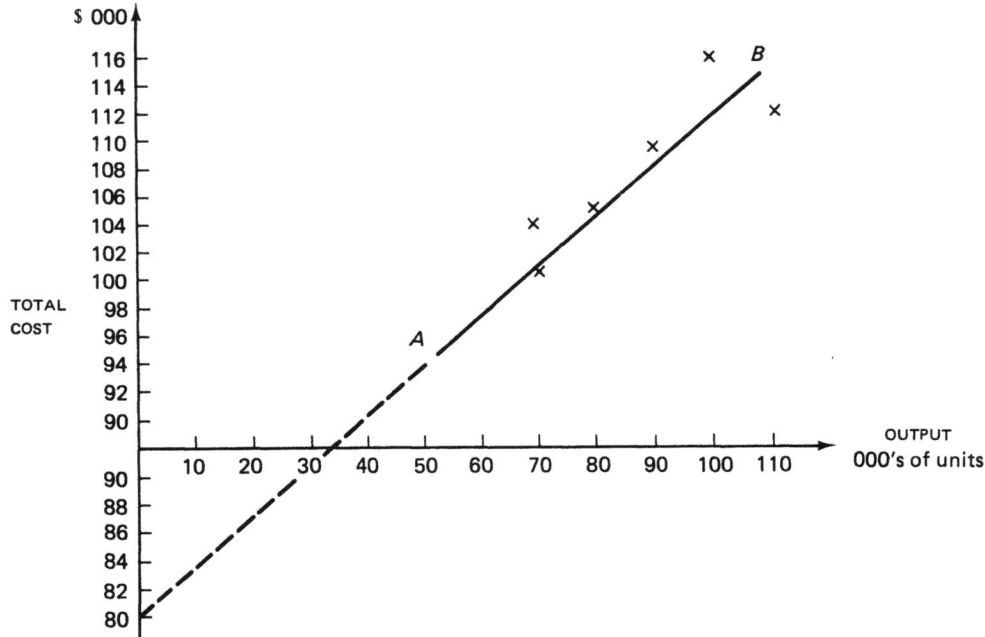

Figure 8.1 Frank firm – Total cost and output

the observations are scattered about the chart, and are not consistently close to the estimated line, the independent variable does not provide a reasonable explanation of the determination of total cost; determination of best fit has been described as purely subjective. It may be useful to examine more technical methods of establishing the position of the line.

8.8 Regression analysis

Statistical methods can be used to remove the subjective bias of the visual approach, and these take the form of regression analysis. When regression is used to fit a straight line to a scatter of observations, this is known as linear regression analysis.

One of the assumptions of linear regression analysis is that the relationship between the variables X and Y can be described adequately by a straight line. Regression analysis refers to the measurement of the average amount of change in one variable that is associated with the unit increase in the amounts of one or more variables. When two variables are studied together, the analysis is called simple regression. When more than two variables are studied together, the analysis is called multiple regression.[1]

---

[1] Multiple regression is not examined here. It is, however, an extension of simple regression, so an understanding of simple regression leads to an understanding of multiple regression. Multiple regression is facilitated by the computer. Other related topics to regression analysis – for example, heteroscedasticity and multicollinearity – are not examined either. The accountant should make himself aware of those factors when undertaking a regression exercise.

Cost Estimation

8.9 Simple regression

The object of simple regression is to determine an equation of the form $\hat{Y} = a + b(x)$ which will give the best explanation of the relationship of the observed data. In this context, 'best explanation' is taken to mean that the sum of the squares of differences from the line to each corresponding cost observation is minimised.[1] This is known as the least squares method, and the values of the parameters 'a' and 'b' for the line can be found from the data using the normal equations. The normal equations are:

$$na + b\Sigma X = \Sigma Y$$
$$a\Sigma X + b\Sigma X^2 = \Sigma XY$$

Where n = No of observations
ΣX = Sum of the observations of the independent variable (X = output or volume level)
ΣY = Sum of the observations of the dependent variable (Y = total cost)
ΣX^2 = Sum of the squares of the X observation
ΣXY = Sum of the product of each pair of observations

How are the normal equations used by the management function for cost prediction? A numerical example makes explicit the computational procedures.

EXAMPLE 8.3

Assume that a firm has experienced the cost and output volumes (in thousands) for the past 12 months as is shown in the Y and X columns of Table 8.2.

Table 8.2 Cost and output volume

Month	Cost Y	Volume X	X^2	XY	Total $(\bar{Y}-Y)^2$	VARIANCE INFORMATION Explained $(\bar{Y}-\hat{Y})^2$	Unexplained $(\hat{Y}-Y)^2$
	000	000					
1	58	8	64	464	20.25	10.5411	1.5908
2	71	11	121	781	72.25	54.4408	1.2580
3	53	6	36	318	90.25	106.7110	0.6891
4	67	9	81	603	20.25	0.0870	17.6820
5	55	7	49	385	56.25	46.0824	0.5064
6	64	8	64	512	2.25	10.5411	22.5312
7	70	10	100	700	56.25	14.7203	13.4698
8	57	9	81	513	30.25	0.0870	33.5820
9	56	8	64	448	42.25	10.5411	10.5840
10	51	6	36	306	132.25	106.7110	1.3687
11	76	13	169	988	182.25	209.1437	0.9251
12	72	12	144	864	90.25	119.2486	2.0167
Σ	750	107	1009	6882	795.00	688.8551	106.1338

[1] See Wonnacott and Wonnacott (1979) for the justification of this method.

Table 8.2 also contains other relevant data which will be used and explained in due course. Since there are 12 observations, $n = 12$ and the normal equations can be seen to be:

$12a + 107b = 750$

$107a + 1009b = 6882$

'a' and 'b' could be found either by solving these simultaneous equations, or by the use of matrix algebra. The results give $a = 30.92$ and $b = 3.54$, which could be checked by substituting back in both the above equations. In this case, the use of simultaneous equations is simple enough. However, in more advanced work it is useful to put the normal equations into matrix form. This is done as follows:

$$\begin{bmatrix} N & \Sigma X \\ \Sigma X & \Sigma X^2 \end{bmatrix} \begin{bmatrix} a \\ b \end{bmatrix} = \begin{bmatrix} \Sigma Y \\ \Sigma XY \end{bmatrix}$$

Applying the standard statistical symbols to the problem set, which will become evident soon, we have:

$$[X^T X]B = [X^T Y]$$
Solving for B, $[X^T X]^{-1}[X^T X]B = [X^T X]^{-1}[X^T Y]$
$$IB = [X^T X]^{-1}[X^T Y]$$
$$B = [X^T X]^{-1}[X^T Y]$$

COMMENT

$[X]$ contains the observed X data. It also contains a column of 1s to allow for an intercept. $[B]$ contains the regression coefficient estimates. It also provides for the elements of a and b. This formula is widely used in mathematical statistics, and though it appears to be formidable, its manipulations are quite simple.

The data in Table 8.2 are related to matrices as follows:

$$\overset{X^T}{\begin{bmatrix} 1 & 1 & \ldots & 1 \\ X_1 & X_2 & \ldots & X_{12} \end{bmatrix}} \overset{X}{\begin{bmatrix} 1 & X_1 \\ 1 & X_2 \\ \vdots & \vdots \\ 1 & X_{12} \end{bmatrix}} = \overset{X^T X}{\begin{bmatrix} N & \Sigma X \\ \Sigma X & \Sigma X^2 \end{bmatrix}}$$

$$\overset{X^T}{\begin{bmatrix} 1 & 1 & \ldots & 1 \\ X_1 & X_2 & \ldots & X_{12} \end{bmatrix}} \begin{bmatrix} Y_1 \\ Y_2 \\ \vdots \\ Y_{12} \end{bmatrix} = \overset{X^T Y}{\begin{bmatrix} \Sigma Y \\ \Sigma XY \end{bmatrix}}$$

$$\overset{B}{\begin{bmatrix} a \\ b \end{bmatrix}} = \overset{(X^T X)^{-1}}{\begin{bmatrix} \Sigma X^2 & -\Sigma X \\ -\Sigma X & N \end{bmatrix}} \overset{X^T Y}{\begin{bmatrix} \Sigma Y \\ \Sigma XY \end{bmatrix}} = \begin{bmatrix} \Sigma X^2 \Sigma Y - \Sigma X \Sigma XY \\ N\Sigma XY - \Sigma X \Sigma Y \end{bmatrix}$$

Observe that the 2×2 matrix can be solved by utilising the difference from:

$N\Sigma X^2 - (\Sigma X)^2$

as a divisor. This will become clear from the numerical calculation which follows:
Inserting the data for the cost and volume shown in Table 8.2, we get:

$$\overset{X^T}{\begin{bmatrix} 1 & 1 & \ldots & 1 \\ 8 & 11 & \ldots & 12 \end{bmatrix}} \overset{X}{\begin{bmatrix} 1 & 8 \\ 1 & 11 \\ \vdots & \vdots \\ 1 & 12 \end{bmatrix}} = \overset{X^T X}{\begin{bmatrix} 12 & 107 \\ 107 & 1009 \end{bmatrix}}$$

Cost Estimation

$$X^T \quad Y \quad X^T Y$$

$$\begin{bmatrix} 1 & 1 & \ldots & 1 \\ 8 & 11 & \ldots & 12 \end{bmatrix} \begin{bmatrix} 58 \\ 71 \\ \vdots \\ 72 \end{bmatrix} = \begin{bmatrix} 750 \\ 6882 \end{bmatrix}$$

$$B = \quad [X^T X]^{-1} \quad X^T Y$$

$$\begin{bmatrix} 1009 & -107 \\ -107 & 12 \end{bmatrix} \begin{bmatrix} 750 \\ 6882 \end{bmatrix}$$

$$\overline{12(1009) - 107^2}$$

$$= \begin{bmatrix} \dfrac{1009}{659} & -\dfrac{107}{659} \\ -\dfrac{107}{659} & \dfrac{12}{659} \end{bmatrix} \begin{bmatrix} 750 \\ 6882 \end{bmatrix} = \begin{bmatrix} 1.5311077 & -0.1623672 \\ -0.1623672 & 0.0182094 \end{bmatrix} \begin{bmatrix} 750 \\ 6882 \end{bmatrix}$$

Approximating to four decimal places, the equation for estimating cost is:

$\hat{Y} = 30919.7 + 3541.7X$ (000s restored)

This equation can now be used to calculate the last three columns of Table 8.2. The procedure is shown below for the last three values of the first row.
The mean of Y is given by $\overline{Y}$

$\overline{Y} = \Sigma Y/N = 750/12 = 62.50$

Let us take a particular pair of observed values:

$Y = 58, X = 8$

The expected value of Y, given by $\hat{Y}$, can be found to be

$\hat{Y} = 30.9197 + 3.5417(8) = 59.2533$

Hence $(\overline{Y} - Y)^2 = (62.50 - 58)^2 = 20.25$
$(\overline{Y} - \hat{Y})^2 = (62.50 - 59.2533)^2 = 10.5411$
$(\hat{Y} - Y)^2 = (59.2533 - 58)^2 = 1.5708$

The variations from the mean explained by the equation is $\overline{Y} - \hat{Y}$, leaving $\hat{Y} - Y$ unexplained. In a least squares regression, it is useful to consider the sums of the squares of these values which are known as the explained variation and the unexplained variation.
Observe that:

Explained variation	688.8551
+	
Unexplained variation	106.1338
=	
Total variation	794.9889

How good is the estimating equation for management purposes? In regression analysis, the goodness of fit is measured by the coefficient of determination τ^2 which is the ratio of explained variation divided by the total variation. From Table 8.2,

$$\tau^2 = \frac{\Sigma(\overline{Y} - \hat{Y})^2}{\Sigma(\overline{Y} - Y)^2} = \frac{688.8551}{795.000} = 0.8665$$

τ^2 can be interpreted to mean that from the observed data which were used in calculating the regression line, 86.65 per cent of the variation from the mean value of Y can be explained by the regression line.

Another statistic which emerges from τ^2 is

$$\tau = \sqrt{\tau^2}$$

which is known as the coefficient of correlation. The statistic shows whether there exists a linear relationship between the variables X and Y. If τ is close to 0, statisticians say the fit is poor; if τ is close to ± 1, they say a strong correlation exists between the variables. In Example 8.3, $\tau = 0.93$.

8.10 Standard error

This statistic is a measure of the standard deviation of regression. It is used to establish confidence bands around estimates. The statistic is designated by Syx (this is an estimate made from the data of the true standard deviation σyx). It equals the square root of the unexplained variance. It is expressed as:

$$Syx = \sqrt{\frac{\Sigma(\hat{Y}-Y)^2}{N}}$$

$$= \sqrt{\frac{106.1338}{12}} = 2.97$$

Statisticians generally adjust the estimates for the degrees of freedom loss. For Syx, two degrees of freedom were lost in estimating the parameters a and b, therefore the above equation must be modified as follows:

$$\hat{S}yx = Syx \sqrt{\frac{N}{N-2}}$$

$$= 2.97 \sqrt{\frac{12}{10}} = 3.25$$

$\hat{S}yx$ aids the calculation of confidence limits. 'Confidence limits' mean that upper and lower bounds can be calculated for estimates, with the result that the estimates can be stated with some degree of reliability. How are confidence limits calculated? They are calculated from the formula:

$$\hat{Y} \pm t_{N-2}, \beta \hat{S}yx \frac{1}{N} + \sqrt{\frac{(X-\bar{X})^2}{\Sigma(X-\bar{X})^2}}$$

Where β = the confidence level required
t = reading from abridged t distribution shown in Table 8.3.

Assume now, that the cost accountant of the firm wishes to establish a 95 per cent confidence band for the equation: then

$$t_{N-2}, \beta = t_{10}, 0.95$$

Cost Estimation

Table 8.3 Confidence levels β

	N	0.60	0.75	0.90	0.95	0.975
Degree	10	0.260	0.700	1.372	1.812	2.228
of	11	0.260	0.697	1.363	1.796	2.201
freedom	12	0.259	0.695	1.356	1.782	2.179

The calculation for $X = 8$ is:

$$30.9197 + 3.5417(8) \pm 2.228(3.25)\sqrt{\frac{1}{12} + \frac{(8-8.9167)^2}{54.9162}}$$

59.2533 ± 2.2737 giving 61.53, 56.92
                          Upper Lower
                          limit limit

Table 8.4 shows the other calculated values.

Table 8.4 95% Confidence Limits

X	Upper	Lower
8	61.53	56.98
11	71.05	68.70
6	55.70	48.64
9	64.89	60.70
7	58.52	52.91
8	61.53	56.98
10	68.68	63.99
9	64.89	60.70
8	61.53	56.98
6	55.70	48.64
13	81.47	72.46
12	77.09	69.75

[a] 000s omitted.

8.11 Further insights into regression theory

Regression theory makes use of sampling techniques, so assumptions must be made by the decisionmaker about the population from which the data is taken. These assumptions are: (i) that the independent variable Y and the error term e associated with it are random variables, while the independent variable X (which is selected by the decisionmaker) is not random; (ii) the value of each X has an accompanying set of Y values; (iii) the set of Y values and its associated error terms are normally distributed; (iv) the error term e is independent of the chosen X values and has a mean of 0 (i.e., $E(e) = 0$), as well as an unknown variance $V(e)$; (v) that the variance of each sub-set of Y values is equal to the variance of the error term; (vi) that the variation about the line $Y = E(Y/X) + e$ holds for its entire length, so that within the range of past observations there is a set of Y values such that the point on the line is the expected value of that set and the standard deviation σ is the deviation of the set of observed data; (vii) the variance of the error term is σ^2; (viii) that since the actual value of σ^2 is not known, the sampling variance $\hat{S}yx$ is used as a surrogate for σ^2.

Assumptions (vii) and (viii) enable the decisionmaker to calculate the variance covariance matrix V.

8.12 Derivation and use of variance/covariance matrix

The matrix V is derived as follows:

$$V = \hat{S}^2 yx [X^T X]^{-1}$$

Inserting the relevant data Example 8.3 into the matrix, we have:

$$V = 10.61 \begin{bmatrix} 1.5311077 & -0.1623672 \\ -0.1623672 & 0.0182094 \end{bmatrix}$$

$$= \begin{bmatrix} 16.2451 & -1.7227 \\ -1.7227 & 0.1930 \end{bmatrix}$$

The standard error of the fixed and the variable cost can be obtained by squaring each diagonal element $\sqrt{V_{ii}}$

The standard error of the fixed cost and variable cost is thus:

$$\sqrt{16.2451}, \sqrt{0.1930} = \$(4.03, 0.44) \text{ respectively}$$

Assume now that the accountant desires to know the marginal cost of a change in volume. This is done by differentiating the function

$$\hat{Y} = 30.9197 + 3.541.7X$$

with respect to X as follows:

$$\frac{d\hat{Y}}{dX} = 3.5417$$

If the accountant wishes to work with a 95 per cent confidence range of marginal cost, the limits are:

$$3.5417 \pm 2.228(0.44) = \$(4.5220, 2.5614)$$

V can also be used for the testing of regression results and hypothesis testing, for example, H_0: $B_0 = 0$ and the alternative $H_1 : B \neq 0$. How are these determined? Using a 95 per cent confidence level, with $t = 2.228$, the testing statistic for the marginal cost is

$$t = \frac{b - B}{\sqrt{V_{22}}} = \frac{3.5417}{0.44} - 0 = 8.05$$

The t value exceeds the critical value of 2.228, so the statistician would conclude that the alternative hypothesis cannot be rejected and hence the regression line should be retained.

Cost Estimation

8.13 Analysis of variance and the F test

The F test is a composite measure. It tests the whole estimating equation, and not just one β-coefficient at a time. It is important to note that if regression does not pertain in the population, there will be no slope. If regression pertains, the explained variation will be large, while the unexplained variation will be small. When these variations are divided by their respective degrees of freedom, the results are estimates of the population variance, and are called the mean square estimates. The division of the mean square estimates results in the F ratio. The calculation of F can be determined from Table 8.5.

Table 8.5 Analysis of variance table

Source of variation	Degrees of freedom	Sum of squares	Mean squares
Regression	1	688.8551 ÷ 1	688.8551
Error	10	106.1338 ÷ 10	10.6134
Total	11	795.0000 ÷ 11	72.2727

$$F = \frac{688.8551}{10.6134} = 64.90$$

Note that when the F test is combined with the null hypothesis, the decisionmaker can also determine the acceptance or rejection region. The F statistic also provides a measure from which the decisionmaker can form probabilistic judgements. In this sense, the F statistic is superior to the coefficient of determination.

Clearly, regression analysis is of value to the accountant. Let us recall the equation

$$\hat{Y} = 30.9197 + 3.5417X$$

to see how it can be used for cost planning purposes.

Assume that the firm plans to produce 14.5(000) in the first month of the following year. The total cost of the firm for that month will be estimated, to be:

$\hat{Y} = 30.9197 + 3.5417(14.5)$

$\quad = 30.9197 + 51.3547$

$\quad = \$82274.35$ (000s restored)

8.14 Summary

Cost prediction is of importance to the firm for planning purposes. The total cost function of the firm is separated into a fixed and a variable part. This separation is vital to cost analysis.

The accountant has many tools for estimating the cost function of a firm–the engineering approach, the account analysis method, the high–low method, the scatter chart, and regression analysis.

The engineering approach tries to use a scientific approach to the construction of the firm's total cost function. The account analysis method, the high–low method, and the scatter chart (which is used for the visual determination of the cost function), are applicable only to simple cases. These methods are subjective, and will give misleading results if applied to complex situations.

The use of regression analysis in estimating the cost function of the firm removes some of the subjectivity from the data. Regression analysis is based on sampling theory.

An important feature of regression analysis is to determine a line of best fit. Regression analysis provides the accountant not only with the estimating equation, but with other important data as well, which can be utilised for making intelligent judgements on cost planning.

Bibliography

Benston, G. (1966) 'Multiple Regression Analysis of Cost Behaviour', *Accounting Review*, vol. xli, no. 4, October, pp. 657–672.
Dopuch *et al.* (1974) *Cost Accounting* (Harcourt, Brace Jovanovich) ch. 3.
Draper, N. and Smith, H. (1966) *Applied Regression Analysis* (John Wiley) chs 1–4.
Kosiol, E. E. (1969) 'Accounting Models as Bases for Managerial Decisions', *International Journal of Accounting, Education and Research*, vol. 5, no. 1, Fall, p. 58.
Moore, C. L. and Jaedicke, R. K. (1976) *Managerial Accounting*, 4th edn (South-Western Publishing Co.) p. 61.
Nurnberg, H. (1977) 'An Unrecognised Ambiguity of the High–Low Method', *Journal of Business Finance and Accounting*, vol. 4, no. 4, Winter, pp. 427–42.
Wonnacott, R. J. and Wonnacott, T. H. (1979) *Econometrics* 2nd edn (John Wiley) chs 1–4.

Problems

8.1 The following data were collected from the Industrial Products Manufacturing Co. Ltd.

Month	Total overhead y	Direct labour Hr (DLH) x	Plant Hr (PH)
Jan	15000	736	184
Feb	14500	800	160
Mar	15750	1008	168
Apr	15250	880	176
May	16250	1056	176
Jun	15000	840	168
	$\Sigma y = 91750$	$\Sigma x = 5320$	

$\bar{y} = 15291.7 \quad \bar{x} = 886.7$

REQUIRED

(a) Compute a least squares cost equation based on direct labour hours
(b) Compute the coefficient of determination (r^2) for (a)
(c) Compare and discuss the relationship of your solution in (a) to the equation of

Total overheads $= 5{,}758 + 4.7\,DLH + 31\,PH$

obtained by a regression using *DLH* and *PH* as variables and coefficient of determination $R^2 = 0.9873$
(d) Estimate the total overhead for a month with 1000 *DLH* and 168 *PH*, using the equation in (c).

ICMA, PS, Part I, Quantitative Techniques, May 1979.

8.2 A sample of eight employees is taken from the production department of a light engineering factory. The data below relate to the number of weeks' experience in the wiring of components, and the number of components which were rejected as unsatisfactory last week.

Employee	A	B	C	D	E	F	G	H
Weeks' experience (*X*)	4	5	7	9	10	11	12	14
No. of rejects (*Y*)	21	22	15	18	14	14	11	13

$\Sigma x = 72 \quad \Sigma y = 128 \quad \Sigma xy = 1069 \quad \Sigma x^2 = 732 \quad \Sigma y^2 = 2156$

Cost Estimation

REQUIRED

(a) Draw a scatter diagram of the data.
(b) Calculate a coefficient of correlation for these data and interpret its value.
(c) Find the least squares regression equation of rejects on experience
    Predict the number of rejects you would expect from an employee with 1 week of experience

ICMA, FS, [a], *Section B, Mathematics and Statistics, May 1982.*
[a] Foundation Stage

8.3 A sample of 11 observations on the variables X and Y yielded the following sample calculations:

$\bar{Y} = 22 \quad \Sigma x_i y_i = 569 \quad \Sigma y_i^2 = 176$

$\bar{X} = 52 \quad \Sigma x_i^2 = 1695$

Here $\bar{Y} = n^{-1} \Sigma Y_i$, $\bar{X} = n^{-1} \Sigma X_i$, $x_i = X_i - \bar{X}$, $y_i = Y_i - \bar{Y}$, and all sums are over the n sample observations.

REQUIRED

(a) Estimate a and b in $Y = a + bX$, assuming that the observed X values are constant in repeated sampling
(b) Calculate the sample correlation coefficient, r, between Y and X
(c) What is minimised in least squares regression?

University of Birmingham, Degree of B.Soc.Sc. (Economics, Politics and Sociology), Final Examination, Economic Statistics (A and B), June 1970.

Chapter 9
Cost–Volume–Profit (C–V–P) Analysis

The analysis of industrial volume–profit experience and planning requires a more sensitive segmentised approach. Account should be taken of changes in the levels and shapes of the operative functions over as fine a variation of output ranges, on variations of interval of time, as is administratively possible for budget and accounting purposes.   (Vickers, 1960)

9.1 Introduction

An understanding of the 'trilogy'–cost, volume and profit – by the management function results from the solutions of simple algebraic equations. The data for cost–volume–profit (C–V–P) analysis can be obtained by arranging information about the firm's activities in the manner shown in Figure 9.1 utilising the direct costing format. The presentation in the form of graphs, and the reporting of C–V–P analysis to top management highlight the essentials of economic forecasting decisions which are important to their executive decisions. Those decisions are fundamental in the achievement of the firm's objectives.

Sales

Less variable expense:

Manufacturing
Selling
Administration   _____

Less fixed expense:

Manufacturing
Selling
Administrative   _____   _____

Net profit $ _____

Figure 9.1 Direct costing format

Cost–Volume–Profit Analysis

The use of this data in carrying out C–V–P analysis requires recognition of the assumptions of break-even models.

9.2 Assumptions of accountant's break-even model

(i) Cost and revenue behaves in a linear way over the relevant range of output – (a) variable cost varies directly and proportionately with the level of output, increases in output having effects on cost which are identical in size per unit but opposite in sign to decreases in output; (b) the cost identified as fixed cost is constant within the range of output level considered; (c) the selling price of the product remains unchanged regardless of the level of sales.
(ii) The analysis relates to one product or to a constant mix of products in a multi-product firm.
(iii) Stock levels are 0.
(iv) Volume is the only factor which affects costs.

These assumptions show that the accountant's break-even model deals with static conditions. The model is quantitative, and so mathematical symbols can be used as aids to C–V–P analysis. The notation shown below is used in the examples which follow:

B_s = Break-even locus[1] (total sales $)
B_u = Break-even locus (units)
c = Contribution per unit = $SP - V$
SP = Selling price (per unit)
V = Variable cost (per unit of output)
Fk = Fixed cost
π = Required profit
u = Units produced

EXAMPLE 9.1

The Erine firm produces a single product. The selling price is $6 per unit. The fixed costs are $1000 per year and the variable costs are expected to be $4 per unit.

REQUIRED

(i) Calculate the break-even locus
(ii) Calculate the number of units to be sold which would result in a profit of $8000

SOLUTION

(i) $B_u = \dfrac{Fk}{c} = \dfrac{\$(1000)}{2} = 500$ units

(ii) Sales units which will result in the required profit:

$$= \dfrac{Fk + \pi}{c} = \dfrac{1000 + 8000}{2} = 4500 \text{ units}$$

---

[1] Most accounting writers used the word 'point'. This is misleading, since the word 'point' implies exactness. The word 'locus', as used here, refers to the area which bounds the point determined by the equation. However, when exact relationships are assumed for cost, price and volume, a specific point will be calculated.

EXAMPLE 9.2

REQUIRED

From the data of Example 9.1, calculate the sales revenue from:

(i) The break-even locus
(ii) The level of sales which will result in a profit of $8000

SOLUTION

(i) $B_s = \dfrac{Fk}{c} \times Sp = \$\dfrac{(1000 \times 6)}{2} = \$3000$

(ii) Level of sales which will result in the required profit:

$= \dfrac{Fk + \pi}{c} \times Sp = \dfrac{\$(1000 + 8000 \times 6)}{2} = \$27000$

9.3 Marginal contribution to sales ratio (MCSR)

This ratio expresses the relationship between contribution and sales as a percentage. It is the complement of the variable cost ratio (VCR) (see 9.4 below). It is computed by subtracting the variable cost percentage from 100. For management purposes, MCSR permits a quick determination of the increase (or decrease) in profits with every change in sales volume, holding other factors constant.

EXAMPLE 9.3

The revenue statement of the Erick firm is:

	$	$
Sales		
Less variable cost:	30	
Fixed cost	20	
Total cost		50
Profit (Loss)		(10)

REQUIRED

Use the MCSR to calculate:

(i) the break-even locus
(ii) Level of sales required to earn a profit of $25
(iii) Break-even level of sales, if the fixed costs increase by $10

SOLUTION

Calculate (i)

$C = SP - V = \$(40 - 30)$
$ = \$10$

$MCSR = \dfrac{C}{S} \times 100 = \dfrac{10}{40} \times 100 = 25\%$

$B_s = \dfrac{Fk}{MCSR} = \$\left(\dfrac{20}{0.25}\right) = \$80$

Cost–Volume–Profit Analysis

(ii) Level of sales which will result in the required profit

$$= \frac{Fk + \pi}{MCSR}$$

$$= \$\frac{(20+10)}{0.25} = \$180$$

(iii) $B_s = \dfrac{Fk}{MCSR} = \$\dfrac{(20+10)}{0.25} = \$120$

9.4 Variable cost ratio (VCR)

This ratio can also be calculated as a percentage:

$$VCR = \frac{V}{S} \times 100$$

Using the data of Example 9.3, VCR = 75 per cent. Observe that VCR + MSCR = 100 per cent; therefore, $S - V = C$, or $V + C = S$ is a truism.

9.5 The multi-product case[1]

An important factor which must be taken into account with multi-production is the sales mix. If the sales mix changes, the C–V–P relationship changes also. In notation, the break-even sales and the profit calculations for the multi-product situation are:

(i) $$B_s = \frac{FK}{\sum_{j=1}^{N} [u_j(SP_j - V_j)] | \sum_{j=1}^{N} SP_j u_j}$$

(ii) $$\pi = \sum_{j=1}^{N} [u_j(SP_j - V_j)] - FK$$

EXAMPLE 9.4

The Erskin firm manufactures three products, X_1, X_2 and X_3. Table 9.1 shows the plant's requirement per unit of product and the production demand, together with the selling price and the variable cost of the products. The fixed cost of the firm is $730.

---

[1] 'Multi-production' refers to the situation where many products are manufactured in the firm.

Table 9.1 Production data

	Plant Requirement				Product Demand		
	X_1	X_2	X_3				
	2	3	7			150	
	1	1	0			200	
	5	3	0			150	
Product	1	0	0				
	0	1	0		Selling price	40	30	35
	0	0	1		Variable cost	15	12	10

The advertising manager makes an assumption that 25, 10 and 25 units of the products X X_2 and X_3 can be sold in the current period.

REQUIRED

Determine the break-even sales, and the profits.

SOLUTION

	PRODUCT		
	X_1	X_2	X_3
	$	$	$
SP	40	30	35
V	15	12	10
$c = SP_i - V_i$	25	18	25
MCSR = VPR_i	$\frac{25 \times 100}{40}$	$\frac{18 \times 100}{30}$	$\frac{25 \times 100}{35}$
= %	62.5	60	71.43

Total variable profit = $[25(25) + 10(18) + 25(25)] = 1430$

Total sales = $[25(40) + 10(30) + 25(35)] = 2175$

$VPR = \dfrac{1430}{2175} \times 100 = 65.75\%$

$B_s = \dfrac{FK}{VPR} = \dfrac{730}{0.6575} = 1110$

$\pi = (1430 - 730) = 700$

This profit can also be found by calculating the contribution from sales in excess of the break-even level

$$\pi = \$(2175 - 1110) \times 65.75\% = \$700.$$

COMMENT:

The change in the product mix is important to the analysis. The variable profit ratio indicates that the product X_3 is the most profitable. If the management function decides to produce all of X_3, the net profit will be $824-$(2175 \times 0.7143 - 730)$. Although a profit of $824 exceeds the model's profit of $700, observe that 62.14 units of X_3–i.e., $(2175/35)$–is greater than the output constraint 21.43, i.e.

Cost–Volume–Profit Analysis

150/7. The model is thus unsuitable for the multi-product case, which is best resolved via linear programming[1] on input–output analysis.

9.6 Accountant's representation of break-even models

The graphic representation of the C–V–P relationship by the management function is an attempt in diagrammatic form to help top management understand these relationship, and enable them to decide on some near-optimum level of output.

There are different ways of presenting C–V–P relationships via graphs (i) traditional approach, where total cost equals total revenue; (ii) contribution approach, where fixed cost equals total contribution; (iii) profit–volume graph.

EXAMPLE 9.5

The Essen Co. manufactures a single product. The selling price and the variable cost of the product is respectively $0.75 and $0.35 per unit. The fixed cost is $4000.

REQUIRED

Show the break-even charts according to the above three methods. Figures 9.2–9.4 show their form.

COMMENT

It can be seen by looking at the contribution graph (Figure 9.3) that at output levels below the break-even locus, the contribution representing the excess of sales revenue over variable cost is insufficient to cover the fixed cost, which is a loss to the firm. At output levels above the break-even locus, the contribution is sufficient to cover the fixed cost. The result is a profit to the firm.

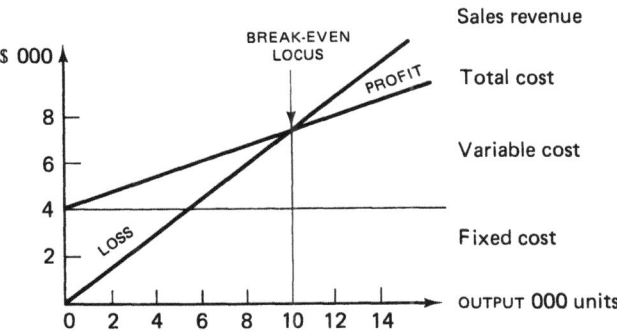

Figure 9.2 Traditional break-even graph

---

[1] Linear programming is examined in ch. 16. The linear formulation of the problem is:

$$\text{Max } Z = 15X_1 + 18X_2 + 25X_3$$
$$\text{St } 2X_1 + 3X_2 + 7X_3 \leqslant 150$$
$$X_1 + X_2 \leqslant 200$$
$$5X_3 + 3X_2 \leqslant 150$$
$$X_1, X_2, X_3 \geqslant 0$$

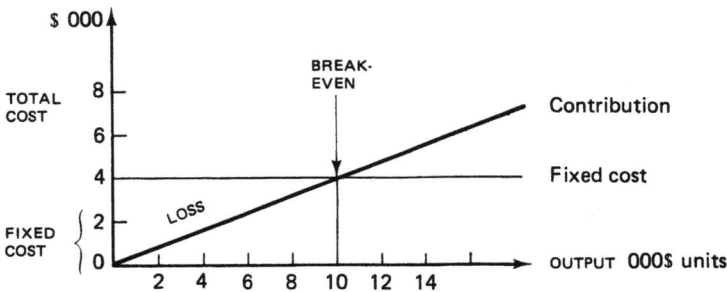

Figure 9.3 Contribution graph

The profit–volume graph (Figure 9.4) shows that where no output occurs the maximum loss is $4000, which is the fixed cost. The break-even locus is still at 10000 units. Beyond that area, profits will accrue to the firm at the rate of $0.40 per unit.

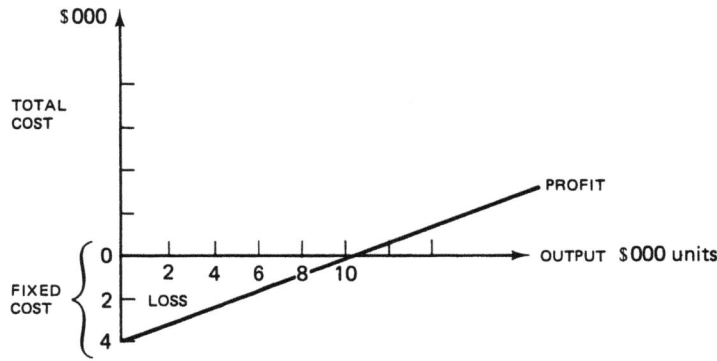

Figure 9.4 Profit–volume graph

9.7 Utility of break-even analysis

Break-even analysis is not a powerful analytical tool, but it is a useful ready-reckoner for determining output levels. Output levels can be regarded by management as a minimum level, below which losses will be incurred by the firm. They are a working tool by which the management function can assess the possibility of making profit, given the contribution from the product and the fixed cost of the factory operations.

The observations from such graphs should provide top management with insights into profit determination, since the sensitivity of profits to deviations from various output levels can be assessed.

9.8 Extension of break-even analysis[1]

The traditional C–V–P model assumed away risk and uncertainty, although these two factors are inherent in real world business decisions. Jaedicke and Robichek (1968) remarked: 'The fact that the traditional C–V–P analysis does not include adjustment for risk may, in any given circumstances, severely limit its usefulness'.

To incorporate risk and uncertainty into the C–V–P model requires probabilities. The profit–volume graph also aids the analysis. Statistical data which reflect an aspect of risk can be introduced into the analysis if the forecast output volume is described in terms of a distribution of possible volumes rather than a single figure. In this analysis it is assumed that possible output volumes can be described by a normal probability distribution curve. The single forecast now becomes the mean or expected value; the way possible outcomes are distributed is another aspect of forecasting but for ease of exposition the normal distribution is assumed to be appropriate. In addition to the mean, one other parameter, the variance, will be needed to determine the particular distribution fully. The variance is a measure of the dispersion of outcomes i.e., how much the volume might vary with a given likelihood. The graph, linked with the normal probability distribution curve and with the associated subjective expectations about risk, can be used by the decisionmaker for evaluation purposes.

The model is shown in Figure 9.5.

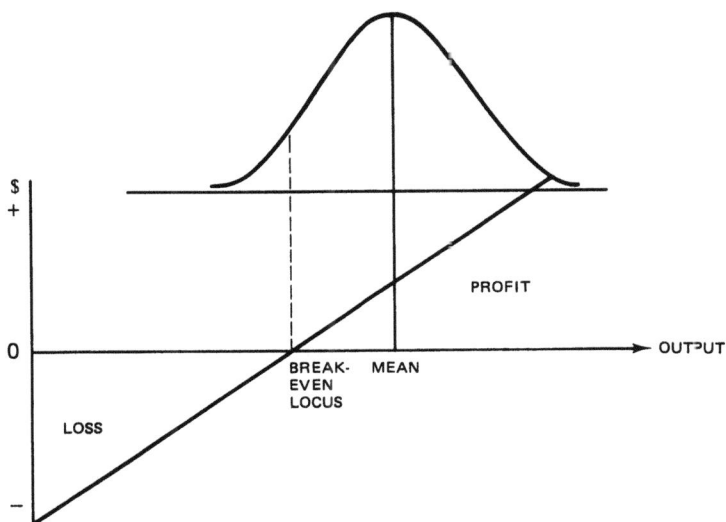

Figure 9.5 Extension of break-even analysis

The curve of Figure 9.5 is symmetrical. The expected profit can be obtained by calculating the profit for the mean of the range. In our notation, it is:

$$E(\pi) = E(u)(SP - V) - FK$$

---

[1] We draw on Jaedicke and Robichek (1968) for this analysis. See also Charnes et al. (1963), Manes (1968) and Morrison and Kaczka (1969) for further extensions of break-even analysis.

Once the mean and the variance is known, the answers to the question below can be determined by the decisionmaker, with the aid of standard probability tables–what is the probability of:

(i) at least breaking even?
(ii) not achieving the break-even sales volume?
(iii) incurring a loss?
(iv) profits greater than the mean?

Let us illustrate this numerically by extending example 9.1. Suppose that a particular product has a variable cost of $4 per unit, and its selling price is $6 per unit. Suppose the expected number of units of output for a given period has a mean of 600 units, and is normally distributed with a standard deviation of 50 units. If fixed cost is given as $1 000 for the given period, the break-even point can be calculated in the same manner as shown earlier in example (9.1):

$$\text{Break-even quantity} = \frac{1\,000}{\$(6-4)} = 500 \text{ units}$$

The expected quantity of 600 units is 100 units more than that required to break-even. For statistical purposes, it is useful to express this quantity in terms of standard deviations. In this case, 100 units equals 100/50, or 2 standard deviations. From statistical tables, we can find the probability of an output of at least 500 units, i.e. no more than two standard deviations less than the mean (or the expected) value of 600 units. Tables typically show the proportion of the area under the normal curve within the limits of a number of standard deviations, as in Figure 9.6.

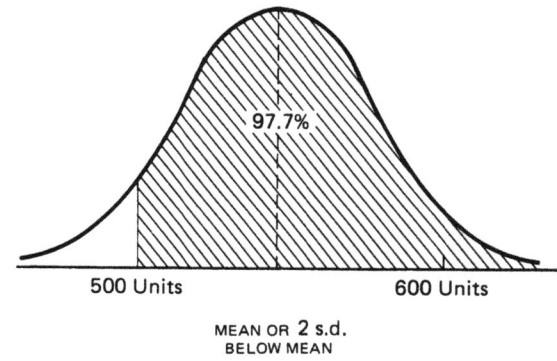

Figure 9.6 **Area under normal curve**

With the values in this extended Example 9.1, this proportion is 97.7 per cent, and indicates that the probability of at least breaking even is 97.7 per cent. The probability of not achieving the break-even sales volume is obviously 100 per cent -97 per cent $= 2.3\%$, which is identical to the probability of incurring a loss. The mean level of profit is that given by an output of 600 units. This level is 100 above the break-even level and represents profits of $\$100 \times (6-4) = \$200$. The chances of having sales greater than 600 units are identical to those of sales less than 600, since the distribution of expected sales volumes is symmetrical about 600 units. It follows that the probability of profits greater than the mean = the probability of profits less than the mean = 50 per cent.

Considerations of variations in data used in break-even analysis can be extended from the

Cost–Volume–Profit Analysis 159

expected output to considering fluctuations in selling price, variable cost and fixed cost. In our notation, the expected profit would become:

$$E\pi = E(u)[E(SP) - E(v)] - E(FK)$$

Not surprisingly, combining the statistical effects for all these variables will lead to more complex calculations.

The analysis which is determined from the above is valuable to the firm, since the sales function will know the sales profile which offers the largest expected gain. This extension of C–V–P is valuable to the firm, since it incorporates risk. It also adds a new dimension to the traditional approach, which calculates only a crude, single-valued figure.

The C–V–P model of the accountant differs from the C–V–P model of the economist. It is appropriate now to examine the latter's model.

9.9 Short period economic model

An assumption of the economist's C–V–P model is that the firm possesses a fixed set of resources, which commit it to a certain level of fixed cost for at least a short period. How does the economist determine output and price for the single-product case? Example 9.6 and its solution clarifies the concepts involved.

EXAMPLE 9.6

Assume that a firm manufactures a single product (X), which is also the quantity that the firm expects to sell during the short term. Assume also that the demand and price for the product is as given in Figure 9.5, and that the total cost function of the firm is quadratic[1] of the form

$$\frac{1}{5}X^2 + 2.4x + 2000$$

REQUIRED

Determine the output level and selling price of the product.

SOLUTION

Figure 9.7 shows that for each increase in output of 50 units, the price the firm will be able to charge is $20/50 on $0.40. The equation of the price line is thus:

$$SP = 120 - 0.40X \tag{9.1}$$

The total revenue will be the product of the price and the quantity of the units to be produced and sold:

$$TR = SP(X) = 120X - 0.4X^2 \tag{9.2}$$

$$TK = \tfrac{1}{5}(x^2) + 2.4X + 2000 \tag{9.3}$$

---

[1] Note that the curve can take other forms, which must be determined empirically.

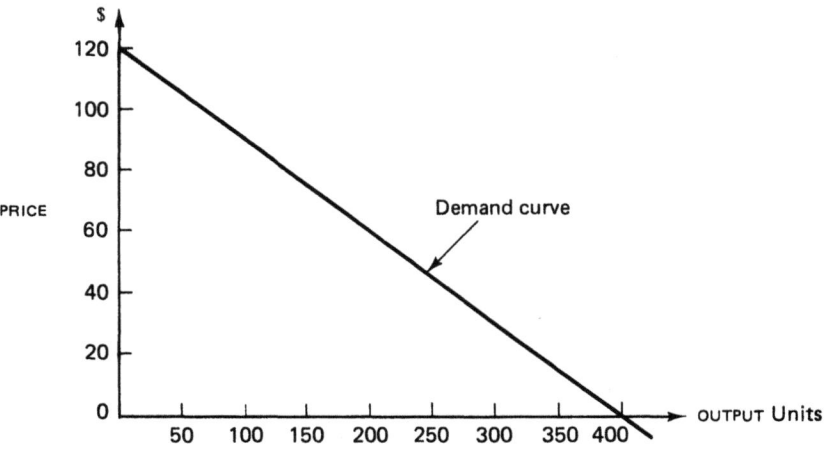

Figure 9.7 Output level and selling price

The economist draws on differential calculus to obtain the optimal solution as follows:

$$\text{Marginal revenue} = \frac{dTR}{dx} = 120 - 0.8X \tag{9.4}$$

$$\text{Marginal cost} = \frac{dTK}{dx} = 0.40X + 2.4 \tag{9.5}$$

Equating equations (9.4) and (9.5), and solving for the optimal output level, subject to $X > 0$, the solution is:

$$120 - 0.8x = 0.40X - 2.4$$
$$X = 98 \text{ units}$$

By substituting for X in equation (9.2), the price can be found at which the firm will be able to sell its output:

$$SP = \$[120 - 0.40\,(98)]$$
$$= \$80.8$$

The total revenue will be \$ (80.8 × 98) = \$7918.40. The total cost will be \$4156. The profit is therefore \$(7918.40 − 4156) = \$3762.40.

COMMENT

The above analysis provides a contrast with the accountant's methods. Do the various methods have common features? These features are now examined.

9.10 Features of accountant's and economist's graph

Table 9.2 contains[1] the data for plotting the economist's graph. In order to show the accountant's and economist's graphs together, we will consider the range of output between 10 and 125 units which is required for the accountant's graph. From Figure 9.8, the features of both methods can be seen.

[1] Observe that the table also shows an alternative way of deriving a solution to the problem.

Cost−Volume−Profit Analysis

Table 9.2 Data for economist's graph

Output	TR	− TK	= π (Loss)
x	$120x - 0.40x^2)$	$0.20x^2 + 2.4x + 2000$	$(117.6x - 0.6x^2 - 2000)$
0	0	2000	(2000)
50	5000	2620	2380
98	7918.4	4156	3762.4
100	8000	4240	3760
150	9000	6860	2140
200	8000	10480	(2480)

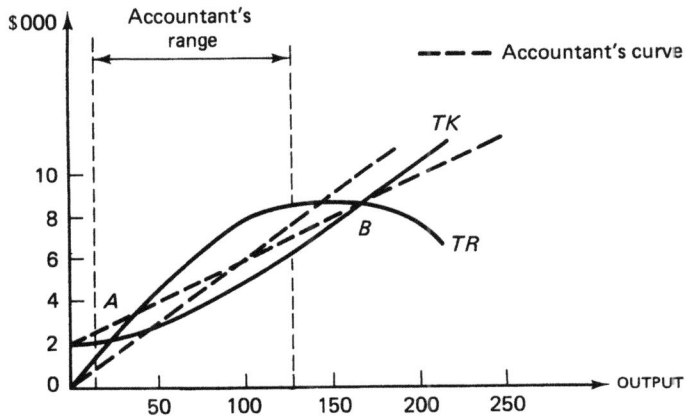

Figure 9.8 Accountant's and economist's graph

It is important to note that the economist's graph depicts profit maximisation. Its purpose is not to calculate the break-even locus, though it does show two such loci, but the output at which profit will be maximised.

Note also that the cost and revenue curves are curvilinear. The revenue curve takes that form because in order to sell an increasing number of units the unit selling price would have to be reduced. The curve, in fact, depicts an imperfect market situation.

There are two break-even loci. The first, shown at A, is equivalent to the break-even locus of the accountant, it shows the minimum level before profit can be made. The second, shown at B, is not even recognised in the accountant's graph. It shows that level of output beyond which losses will be made. Neither of these loci is important to the economist. The economist's interest lies in the profit area which falls between them.

The locus of maximum profit is where the vertical distance between the total revenue and the total cost curve is greatest. This, of course, is where marginal revenue = marginal cost.

The two graphs show similarities and differences:

(i) within the relevant range, the two graphs do not deviate from each other markedly
(ii) the accountant's graph implies that profit will increase with any increase output within the limits of the relevant range

(iii) the economist's graph takes into account the effect on per unit cost and selling price of increased output; it shows the effects of the cumulative price reduction that may be necessary to achieve increased sales and the resulting diminishing returns – the identification of demand behaviour is crucial to the analysis.

9.11 Summary

The solution of simple algebraic equations which represent the C–V–P relationship of the firm gives insights both to management and top management. C–V–P analysis utilises the direct costing format.

The marginal contribution to sales ratio (MCSR), which is the complement of the variable cost ratio (VCR), facilitates quick decisions about an increase (or decrease) in profits with every change in sales volume.

The traditional tools of C–V–P analysis are not suited to the multi-product case.

A seeming understanding of the C–V–P model is facilitated by graph representation.

The C–V–P model can incorporate risks via probability concepts; the inclusion of probability concepts in the model gives it substance.

The economist's model differs markedly from the accountant's C–V–P model; the former is more realistic than the latter.

Bibliography

Charnes, A., Cooper, W. and Ijiri, Y. (1963) 'Breakeven Budgeting and Programming to Goals', in H. R. Anton and P. A. Firmin (eds), *Contemporary Issues in Cost Accounting*, 2nd edn (Houghton Mifflin).

Jaedicke, R. K. and Robichek, A. A. (1968) 'Cost–Volume–Profit Analysis Under Conditions of Uncertainty', in D. Solomon (ed.), *Studies in Cost Analysis*, 2nd edn (Sweet & Maxwell) pp. 106–274.

Manes, R. (1968) 'A New Dimension to Break-even Analysis', in D. Solomon (ed.), *Studies in Cost Analysis*, 2nd edn (Sweet & Maxwell) pp. 275–89.

Morrison, T. A. and Kaczka, E. (1969) 'A New Application of Calculus and Risk Analysis to Cost–volume–profit Changes', in A. Rappaport (ed.), 2nd edn (Prentice-Hall) pp. 116–29.

Vickers, D. (1960) 'On the Economics of Breakeven', in H. R. Anton and P. A. Firmin (eds) *Contemporary Issues in Cost Accounting* (Houghton Mifflin) pp. 284–94.

Problems

9.1 A company has the following demand and cost function for a particular item:

Demand function: $p = 600 - 2q^2$
   Cost function: $c = 100 + 216q$

   Where p = Price of the item ($)
      q = Quantity produced and sold
      c = Total cost of producing the item ($)

REQUIRED

Determine:
   (i) price and quantity for maximum sales revenue, and find the maximum revenue
   (ii) price and quantity for maximum profit, and find the maximum profit.

ACA, PE[a]. Section 2, Paper 12, Management Mathematics, June 1981.
   [a] Professional Examination.

Cost–Volume–Profit Analysis

9.2 A manufacturer has fixed costs of $5000 per week and variable cost of $\frac{1}{2}X^2 + 10X$, where X is the number of tons produced; research has shown that, within the range of practicable prices, the relationship between price, P, and quantity X, is approximately

$$P = 160 - \tfrac{1}{2}X$$

All production can be sold.

REQUIRED

By examining the break-even position (or otherwise), advise the company of the production level at which it would be rational to operate.

ICMA, FS, Section B, Mathematics and Statistics, May 1982.

9.3
(a) Next year's forecasted trading results for Caribee Ltd, a small company manufacturing three different types of product, are shown below:

Product	A	B	C	Total
	$	$	$	
Selling price (per unit)	10	$12	$8	
	$000	$000	$000	$000
Sales	100	96	32	228
Variable cost of sales				
Prime cost	40	38	13	91
Variable overhead	20	18	11	49
Share of general fixed overhead	30	27	10	67
Profit (Loss)	10	13	(2)	21

REQUIRED

(i) Explain how the company's forecasted profit would be affected if product C were discontinued It should be assumed that sales of the remaining products would not be affected
(ii) Additional advertising for product B would cost $8000 next year, this amount is not included in the forecast shown above. Calculate the minimum extra sales, in units, of product B required to cover this additional cost
(iii) Calculate the increase in sales volume of product A necessary to compensate for a 10 per cent reduction in the selling price of the product. Carefully explain why the increase in volume is proportionately greater than the reduction in selling price

(b) The production director of Caribee Ltd has just been informed that next year's suppliers of a material used in the manufacture of each of the three products will be restricted to 92000 kg, no substitute material is available, and the estimated consumption of this restricted material is available and the estimated consumption of this restricted material, per product, is:

Product	Kg per unit
A	8
B	4
C	1

The sales director estimates that the maximum demand for each product is that which is shown in the original forecast in (a) above; also he decides that advertising or adjustments to selling price are not possible. Assume that stocks of materials, work-in-progress or finished goods cannot be carried.

REQUIRED

Calculate the optimum quantities of product A, B and C which should be manufactured next year in order to maximise company profit.

ACCA, FE, Part B, Paper 6, Accounting 2, Costing, June 1981.

9.4 A company manufactures plastic-covered steel fencing in two qualities: standard and heavy gauge. Both products pass through the same processes involving steel-forming and plastic-bonding.

The standard gauge sells at $15 a roll, the heavy gauge at $20 a roll. There is an unlimited market for the standard gauge, but outlets for the heavy gauge are limited to 13000 rolls per year. However, the factory operations of each process are limited to 2400 hours each per year.

Other relevant data are given below:

Variance costs per roll:

Gauge	Direct material	Direct wages	Direct expense
	$	$	$
Standard	5	7	1
Heavy	7	8	2

Processing h per 100 rolls:

Gauge	Steel-forming	Plastic-bonding
Standard	6	4
Heavy	8	12

Agreement has been reached on revised working methods that will increase output of all processes by 10 per cent. This could be achieved without additional manpower or longer working hours.

REQUIRED

Calculate:

(a) production mix which will maximise total contribution:

   (i) at present output levels
   (ii) assuming the 10 per cent production improvement is achieved

(b) the total amount of productivity bonus which will be paid to employees under (a) (ii) on the basis of their receiving 40 per cent of the additional contribution

ICMA, PS, Part III, Management Accounting, November 1979.

9.5 As the first management accountant employed by a manufacturer of power tools, you have been asked to supply financial results by product line to help in marketing decisionmaking.

The following account was produced for the year ended 30 September 1981

	$000	$000
Sales		1200
Cost of goods sold:		
Materials	500	
Wages	300	
Production expense	150	
Marketing cost	100	1050
Net profit		150

A statistical analysis of the figures shows the following variable element in the costs:

	%
Materials	90
Wages	80
Production expense	60
Marketing cost	70

Below is given, as percentages, the apportionment of the sales and the variable elements of the costs among the five products manufactured.

	PRODUCT					
	A	B	C	D	E	Total
Sales	30	15	7	28	20	100
Materials	40	20	10	20	10	100
Wages	15	25	10	25	25	100
Production expense	30	10	10	30	20	100
Marketing cost	10	30	20	30	10	100

REQUIRED

From the information given:
(a)
  (i) prepare a statement for the year showing contribution by product
  (ii) comment on these contributions

(b) calculate the following
  (i) break-even sales level
  (ii) order of sales preference for additional orders to maximise contribution as a percentage of sales
  (iii) a revised mix of the $1 200 000 sales to maximise contribution, assuming that existing sales by products can be varied only 10 per cent either up or down
  (iv) a product mix to maximise contribution, if manpower availability were reduced by 10 per cent but the product mix could be varied by up to 20 per cent
  (v) the percentage commission which could be offered to an overseas agent on an order of $30 000 worth each of products A, C and E, and obtain a 20 per cent contribution on the total sales value.

ICMA, PS, Part III, Management Accounting 2, November 1981.

9.6 The accountant of XYZ Ltd has produced the following statement of cost and profit for his company's product, the annual production/sales level of which is 50 000 units:

	$
Direct material	25
Direct labour	3
Variable overhead	2
Fixed overhead	5
Profit	15
Selling Price	50

REQUIRED

(i)
  (a) Prepare a chart from which the contribution and profit at levels of activity up to 50 000 units per annum may be read
  (b) Show on your chart any adjustment(s) necessary to reflect an increase of 5 per cent in direct material cost

(ii) Calculate the additional production/sales which would be necessary to maintain the company's annual profit, taking into account the additional cost referred to in (b) above, assuming there are no other changes in costs, or in selling price
(iii) State and comment upon the assumptions inherent in charts of the type required in (i) above

ACCA, FE, Part B, Paper 6, Accounting 2, Costing June 1976.

9.7 A company has decided that its profit on turnover is insufficient and after investigation, has concluded that it must attempt to change its mix of sales.

REQUIRED

(a) Present on graph paper a profit–volume (P/V) graph to show:

(i) results of the budgeted sales mix for the year
(ii) expected results if the sales mix were changed to that recommended by the sales director

(b) Comment on the results shown on your graph

	$
Budgeted data for year:	000
Total budgeted sales value	5000
Total fixed overhead	800
Sales of individual products	

Product	Mix %	Total variable cost
		$000
W	40	1500
X	10	600
Y	30	1200
Z	20	600

Proposed budget for the year – the sales director is faced with severe competition in his market, so does not believe that he can increase total sales. However, he believes that if he discontinues product X, he can increase sales of the remaining products, so that the original total budgeted sales value would be unchanged. His recommendation is based on an estimate that the sales mix should be:

Product	%
W	40
Y	20
Z	40

ICMA, PS, Part I, Cost Accounting 2, November 1978.

9.8 The Norman Co. produces a product which sells at $20. Sales amounting to $5 million represent 75 per cent of capacity of the factory, and that percentage is regarded as the normal level of activity which cost as follows:

Cost–Volume–Profit Analysis

	$	Including variable cost $
Prime cost per unit	5	
Factory indirect cost	255000	75000
Selling cost	105000	63000
Distribution cost	90000	40000
Administrative cost	840000	

The commission payable for the promotion of the product averages 2 per cent of the sales value.

REQUIRED:

1. Calculate the break-even activity level respectively at the maximum and normal capacity levels:
2. Prepare statements showing sales income, cost and profit:
   (a) at the normal level of activity
   (b) if the unit selling price is reduced by 12 per cent, thereby increasing the sales volume by 20 per cent of the normal level
   (c) if the unit selling price is reduced by 20 per cent, thereby increasing the sales volume by 60 per cent of the normal activity level
3. Calculate the P/V ratio at the three levels of activity referred to in 2 above

9.9 A company selling an air conditioner has estimated the market capacity as 50000 units a year. The directors have set the company a sales objective of between 50 per cent and 80 per cent of this potential. The sales force is divided into five equal areas, and the objective is expected to be achieved by using the salesmen in the following manner:

Salesmen used per area	Market penetration expected
No.	%
5	50
6	58
7	65
8	71
9	76
10	78
11	80

All the products are manufactured at one location at an ex-factory cost of $80 each, and are sold at a standardised price of $100. The transport and installation cost varies in relation to the distance from the factory as under:

Sales area	Variable distribution cost per unit
	$
1	10
2	8
3	6
4	4
5	2

At present 35 salesmen are employed at an average cost of $8000 each per annum. In 19X5, they were divided evenly among the five areas. In 19X6, the sales manager decided to use 25 salesmen to meet the basic 50 per cent penetration in all areas, and to concentrate the other 10 salesmen equally in the two areas nearest the factory where the unit contribution is the highest.

The calculations shown below indicate that this year's profit will be nearly 6 per cent lower than that in 19X5.

	19X5		19X6	
	$000	$000	$000	$000
Income from sales		3250		3060
Cost:				
Ex-factory	2600		2448	
Distribution	195		167	
Salesmen	280		280	
		3075		2895
Total contribution		$175		$165

For the purpose of this question, inflation should be disregarded.

REQUIRED

As the company's management accountant:

(a) analyse the total contribution by areas for both 19X5 and 19X6
(b) explain briefly why concentrating on the highest contribution areas has not increased profit
(c) calculate the highest total contribution possible using the 35 salesmen
(d) advise whether increasing the sales force would improve the total contribution.

ICMA, PS, Part III, Management Accounting 2, November 1976.

Chapter 10
Relevant Costs for Decisions

The effectiveness and efficiency of a decision are largely dependent on the relevance, timeliness and adequacy of the underlying information. (Qureshi, 1980)

10.1 Introduction

The dictionary defines the word 'relevant' to mean, 'bearing upon, connected with, pertinent to, the matter in hand'. The definition clarifies the concept, but what is needed is an operational statement for accounting purposes. Horngren (1977) provides such a statement: 'For a cost or revenue to be relevant to a particular decision, it must meet two criteria: (i) It must be an expected future cost; and (ii) it must be an element of difference between alternatives.

In this chapter, the concept of relevant costs for managerial decisions is explained in a systematic manner. However, the concepts which impinge on such decisions themselves require clarification. These concepts are: (i) accept or reject decisions; (ii) differential costs; (iii) make or buy decisions; (iv) mutual exclusive opportunities; and (v) ranking decisions.

10.2 Accept or reject decisions

This is an isolated particular decision, which will not affect the firm's ability to accept other projects that are expected to become available. The criterion of acceptance or rejection rests on the particular opportunity's suitability or unsuitability, since it cannot be compared with other opportunities.

10.3 Differential cost

'Differential cost' is the cost and income difference between alternative courses of action. The courses of action must have some bearing on the future – the management function cannot make present decisions that will alter its past; decisions can be made only about alternatives that affect its future.

10.4 Make or buy decisions

The management function is often faced with the choice between buying a component from a producer, or causing it to be produced within the firm. The evaluation of this problem depends on whether production capacity is scarce in the economic unit which makes the product. If production capacity exists, it will be beneficial to the firm to buy the component if the marginal cost of production is greater than the purchase cost. If no spare capacity exists within the firm, the manufacturing of the component will mean the displacement of other work. When this situation prevails, the purchase cost is compared with the marginal cost of production plus the contribution lost because of work displacement.

10.5 Mutually exclusive opportunities

Two or more opportunities are said to be mutually exclusive when the acceptance of one of them precludes the acceptance of the others, for reasons other than a shortage of resources.

10.6 Ranking decisions

This type of decision requires the management function to make a choice between many competing opportunities. The need to rank the opportunities cardinally is created because financial constraints exist which prevent the management function from accepting all the opportunities that seem to be profitable.

Relevant cost decisions require simple cash flow calculations. The solutions followed by comments to the examples below clarify the issues.

EXAMPLE 10.1

The Frankel firm has 200 lb of material in stock which it is considering using on a project. The firm uses the material regularly. The replacement cost of the material is $4 per lb.

REQUIRED

The firm wants to find the cost of using the materials on the project.

SOLUTION

To solve this problem, we must compare the cash budgets under each proposal, ensuring that we are comparing like with like. In this way, we establish the differential cost. In the case of the material, if we do not accept the project the material will remain in stock; if we do accept the project, the material will be used. To make the positions comparable, since we are regularly using the material and would want to replace that which is used, our budgets should allow for this replacement.

In calculating the cost of the material the relevant part of the cash budgets would show:

Relevant Costs for Decisions

	(i) Accept project $	(ii) Reject project $	(iii) Difference (i)−(ii) $
Material	−800	0	−800

COMMENT

The relevant cost of using materials depends on whether or not the materials are owned by the firm. If the firm owns the materials, two decisions are present: (i) use the material on other projects; (ii) sell the materials.

In (i), the relevant cost is the current replacement cost of the materials. In (ii), the relevant cost is equal to the sale proceeds, *less* any cost involved in selling them. Example 10.1 indicated that (i) was relevant, since the materials were in regular use.

A − sign indicates a cash outflow. A + sign indicates a cash inflow. If the firm accepts the projects, $800 must be spent on replacing the material used. If the project is rejected, no cash flow arises. The difference of $800 is the net cash outflow, i.e. cost resulting from the acceptance of the project. It is equal to the current replacement material cost.

EXAMPLE 10.2

The Frankel firm has 50 ton of materials in stock which it is considering using on a contract. The material is infrequently used by the firm. If it is not used on the contract, it can be sold for $1000 per ton. The selling cost will be $1000, and the replacement cost is $1500 per ton.

SOLUTION

In this case, the Frankel firm will not be interested in replacing the material, if it is rarely used and could be sold for only $1000 per ton *less* selling expenses. To compare like with like, the budgets should show the alternative ways of using the stock of materials.

(i) Accept $	(ii) Reject $	(iii) Difference $
0	50000 −1000	−50000 1000
$0	$49000	$−49000

COMMENTS

If the firm rejects the contract, it will receive $49000 net from selling the materials. If it accepts the contract, it receives nothing. The relevant cost of acceptance is $49000, which is the net realisable value.

EXAMPLE 10.3

The Frankel firm is considering a project that would need five employees to work on it full time. If the project is rejected, the employees will be dismissed with a redundancy 'handshake' of $500 each. If the contract is accepted, the firm will pay a total of $5,000 in respect of wages and national insurance contributions.

SOLUTION

(i)	(ii)	(iii)
Accept	Reject	Difference
$	$	$
−5000	−2500	−2500

COMMENT

The relevant cost to the firm of using the employees on the project is $2500. To calculate the relevant cost of labour, a distinction must be made between the firm's long-term and short-term contracted employees. The latter are hired for specific jobs. The relevant costs for such labour is the hiring cost. For the former, the relevant costs depend on the alternative uses to which such labour can be put.

Relevant cost concepts also apply to (i) depreciation, (ii) fixed overhead, and (iii) variable overhead. These are now examined.

EXAMPLE 10.4

The Frankel firm wants to use a machine on a new project. The current value of the machine is $140000, and its value after the completion of the project is estimated to be $80000. If the machine is not used during the project's period, its value at the end of the period is estimated to be $120000.

SOLUTION

	(i) Accept $	(ii) Reject $	(iii) Difference $
Machine value now	−140000	−140000	0
Machine value after Project	80000	120000	−40000
	$ −60000	$ 20000	$ −40000

COMMENT

First, a distinction must be made between time depreciation and use depreciation. Unlike time depreciation, use depreciation results from using the machine in the production of goods.

Note that the dollar figures are not cash flows, but are relevant costs since the firm forgoes the sums involved in order to own the machine. Column (i) shows the depreciation if the machine is used–$60000. Column (ii) shows the deprciation if the machine is not used. Column (ii) also shows the time depreciation. Column (iii) shows just the use cost which is relevant.

EXAMPLE 10.5

The Frankel firm contracts to manufacture 100 beds. Assume (i) that its management expects to incur $3 variable overhead for each bed, made, and (ii) that those costs would not be incurred if the contract were rejected.

SOLUTION

(i)	(ii)	(iii)
Accept	Reject	Difference
$	$	$
−300	0	−300

Relevant Costs for Decisions

COMMENT

The relevant variable overhead is $300.

The principle underlying the solutions to these examples is consistent with the economic concept of 'opportunity cost'. The opportunity cost of using a specific resource on a specific project is the value of the best opportunity forgone by not using the resource in another way

An assumption underlying Example 10.1 was that the Frankel firm could buy all the required input factors at current, procurement prices. This assumption is now relaxed, and the case is examined where one of the firm's input factors is scarce.

10.7 Decisions with one scarce resource

Nearly all the tangible resources that a firm uses are scarce. Observe that nothing is scarce by itself — a thing is scarce only in the light of wants and purposes. A resource is scarce, however, if a firm has insufficient supplies of it. Where resources are scarce in the firm, the factors competing for the scarce resource must be ranked numerically to highlight choice priorities for management purposes. Where one resource is scarce, the principle is to select the factors according to the contribution produced per unit of the scarce resource, the factors producing the greatest contribution per unit are chosen. Since the availability of the resource is limited, this will produce the greatest total contribution, i.e. fixed quantity of the resource available × largest contribution per unit available. This approach is highlighted in Example 10.6.

EXAMPLE 10.6

The Frankel firm is considering its production plan for the coming period. Products, X_1, X_2, X_3 and X_4 are available. Each product needs the same type of raw material, and the same kind of labour.

The details of the products' selling prices and the external opportunity costs, together with the inputs requirement and maximum demand data, are shown in Table 10.1. Assume (i) that there is no production for inventories; (ii) that only 5000 hours are expected to be available in the coming month.

REQUIRED

Determine the production plan.

Table 10.1 Selling price and external opportunity cost

	X_1	X_2	X_3	X_4
	$	$	$	$
Selling price	20	30	40	25
External opportunity cost:				
Labour ($2 per hr)	(6)	(8)	(10)	(12)
Materials (1 per lb)	(8)	(9)	(7)	(6)
Contribution per unit	6	13	23	7
Inputs required per unit:				
Labour (hr)	3	4	5	6
Materials (lb)	8	9	7	6
Maximum demand:				
Expected units	1000	400	600	1500

SOLUTION:

(i) Determine the total labour hours required. Labour hr per unit × demand = Labour hr required per product

$X_1\ X_2\ X_3\ X_4$

$[3, 4, 5, 6] \begin{bmatrix} 1000 & & & 0 \\ & 400 & & \\ & & 600 & \\ 0 & & & 1500 \end{bmatrix} = 3000, 1600, 30000, 9000$

(ii) Rank the products according to the contribution they produce per unit of the scarce resource (i.e., labour hours) as follows:

Units Per labour hr	Contribution Per unit	Contribution Per labour hr
$\left[\frac{1}{3}, \frac{1}{4}, \frac{1}{6}\right]$	$\begin{bmatrix} 6 & & & 0 \\ & 13 & & \\ & & 23 & \\ 0 & & & 7 \end{bmatrix}$	$= 2.00, 3.25, 4.6, 1.17$
	Product	Ranking
	X_3	1
	X_2	2
	X_1	3
	X_4	4

(iii) Determine the demand limits for the products. Product X_3 should be produced to its demand limits. X_2 is the next best, and should also be produced to its demand limit. Between them X_2 and X_3 require 4600 labour hours, which leaves 400 hours available.

(iv) Determine the demand limits for the next best product (i.e., X_1) as follows:

$400 \div 3 = 133.33$ units

No labour hours remain to manufacture product X_4

(v) Determine (i) the optimal production plan, and (ii) the contribution per products:

Product	Ranking	Units to be produced	Labour hr required		Contribution
X_3	1	600	3000	23 × 600	= 13800.00
X_2	2	400	1600	13 × 400	= 5200.00
X_1	3	133.33	400	6 × 133.33 =	799.98
X_4	4	0	0	0	—
		1333.33	3000		19799.98

(vi) Test for optimality. The production plan is optimal if no substitution of a rejected product for an accepted one is possible that will increase the total contribution from its present position.

The test for optimality can be made as follows. As can be seen, the only products for which some demand remain unsatisfied are X_1 and X_4.

Relevant Costs for Decisions

If we wished to make 10 units of X_4 we must use 60 hours of labour. In the solution above all the labour is being used, so this can be achieved only by reducing the production of one of the other products. Since X_3 requires 5 labour hours per unit, we would have to cut back X_3 production by 12 units to allow for the 10 units of X_4. The contribution lost by this cutback would be 12 × $23, i.e. $276. But the contribution from the extra X_4 is only 10 × $7, i.e. $70, and the substitution is not worthwhile.

Other alternatives are:

(i) Make 10 X_4 by reducing output by 15X_2
Contribution lost 15 × $13 or $195; contribution gained only $70
(ii) Make 10X_4 by reducing output by 20X_1
Contribution lost 20 × $6 or $120; contribution gained only $70

Similarly, if we substitute some X_1 (say, 20 units) for X_2 or X_3, the contribution would fall:

(i) Make 20X_1 by reducing output by 15X_2
Contribution lost 15 × $13 or $195; contribution gained only 20 × $6 or $120
(ii) Make 20X_1 by reducing output by 12X_2
Contribution lost 12 × $23 or $276; contribution gained only $120

We can see that no substitution possibility exists which will increase the contribution given in the plan. We therefore conclude that the plan calculated above is optimal.

10.8 Concept of internal opportunity cost

To estimate the worth of production opportunities, the internal opportunity cost of labour can be added to its external opportunity cost to find the total opportunity cost of labour. This procedure ensures an effective allocation of scarce labour time. The solution to Example 10.6 again highlights the calculations.

If the Frankel firm is deprived of 1 labour hour, the production of X_1 (the marginal product) will have to be reduced by 1/3 unit. The effect on total contribution is:

	$
Reduction in sales revenue (0.33 × $20)	= 6.66
Less savings on materials (0.33 × $8)	= 2.66
Reduction in total contribution (excluding labour costs)	4.00

These calculations show that it is worthwhile for the firm to pay up to $4.00 to avoid losing 1 labour hour. To be worthwhile also, a new product must return at least $4.00 on each labour hour it requires. The total opportunity cost of 1 marginal labour hour is made up of an external opportunity cost of $2.00 (i.e., the payment made to the resource) and an internal opportunity cost of $2.00.

Such calculations are an integral part of such models, and are of value to management. Of course, the management function is also involved with make or buy decisions in the firm, as Example 10.7 illustrates.

EXAMPLE 10.7

The production manager of the Sobers firm estimated the cost of manufacturing a component as follows:

	$
Direct materials	15
Direct labour (4 h)	5
Variable overhead	4
Fixed overhead	6
	30

Assume (i) that the component can be bought from an outside supplier for $26; (ii) that there is spare production capacity; (iii) that there is no spare production capacity.

REQUIRED

Advise the manager as to whether the firm should make or buy the component.

SOLUTION

For condition (ii), it is worthwhile for the firm to make the component because the firm's marginal costs of $24 is less than the buying out price.

For condition (iii) more information is required.

Suppose the additional information shown below was given to you concerning the production of the existing product. Production of the new component would use labour currently engaged on the existing product:

	$	$
Selling price		15.00
Direct materials	3.50	
Direct labour (2 hr)	2.50	
Variable overhead	1.50	7.50
Standard contribution per hour of production		7.50

(i) Determine the contribution that will be earned per hour on standard production:

$$\frac{\$4}{2} = \$2$$

(ii) Determine the total costs of manufacturing one component as follows:

	$
Direct materials	15
Direct labour	5
Variable overhead	4
Contribution loss from displaced production, i.e. 4 hr × $2	8
	32

(iii) Evaluate the alternative and make conclusions.

The conclusion is that the costs to the firm when it has no spare capacity is $32. The firm should buy the component from the supplier.

10.9 Relevant cost and book values

We often hear discussion of a decision, focussing on the effects it may have on the accounting or book values of a business. In general, 'book values' refer to the past, representing an expense

Relevant Costs for Decisions

that has already been made. As was stated in 10.3 above, management decisions can be made only about alternatives that affect its future – the relevant data is future data. The solution to Example 10.8 shows how the book and scrap values of an asset are evaluated in relevant decisionmaking.

EXAMPLE 10.8

The Fields Co. have just purchased 1000 bolts for $100. They have re-examined the production methods for the job on which they were to use the bolts, and found that if they purchase another type of bolt for $120, they can save $0.15 per bolt in labour cost. However, if they do this, they are unable to use the bolts already purchased, and they must be scrapped for only $20.

The management are concerned that the decision to change to the new bolts will mean writing off the old bolts to give a book loss of $80. What should they do?

SOLUTION

We should consider how the alternatives affect *future* cash flows:

	Old bolts	New bolts	Difference
Labour saving	—	150	150
Sale of old bolts	—	20	20
		170	170
Less cost of new bolts	—	120	120
Saving		50	+50

It is unfortunate that the company have already purchased the old bolts, but it is better for the company to scrap the old bolts than to use them. The price paid for the old bolts is an irrelevant sunk cost. A further example illustrating the irrelevance of sunk costs is given in ch. 17.

The scrap or salvage value of the old bolts was relevant, as it represented a future cash flow under the alternative to use the new bolts, but not under the other alternative. It should also be noted that in general, where a decision must be made regarding the economic advantage of replacing a piece of equipment, the undepreciated book value of the old equipment is irrelevant, but the salvage value is a relevant factor in the calculations.

The management of companies at times wish to know whether a particular department or division of a firm should be closed down because of apparent losses. Relevant cost decisions are applicable to those situations. The solution to Example 10.9 shows how such relevant decisions can be arrived at.

EXAMPLE 10.9

Two sisters and a brother rent a city department store which has three departments. The budgeted profit and loss statement of the store is:

BUDGETED PROFIT AND LOSS STATEMENT

Departments	1	2	3	Total
	$	$	$	$
Sales	240	160	80	480
Direct cost:				
Purchases	131	116	53	300
Labour	132	20	11	63
Fixed expense:				
Avoidable if dept. is closed	11	8	9	27
Bent (apportioned by space)	12	6	9	27
Management expenditure (apportioned by sales)	24	16	8	48
Total cost	$210	$166	$84	$460
Budgeted profit (Loss)	$30	($6)	($4)	$20

REQUIRED

As a consultant, you are asked to advise them as to whether the departments which are making losses should be closed.

SOLUTION

Recast the statement as shown below:

BUDGETED PROFIT AND LOSS STATEMENT

Departments	1	2	3	Total
	$	$	$	$
Sales	240	160	80	480
Direct cost				
Purchases	131	116	53	300
Labour	32	20	11	63
Department's contribution	$77	$24	$16	$117
Department's fixed expense	11	8	3	22
Contribution to fixed cost and profit	$66	$16	$13	$95
Fixed cost				
Rent			27	
Management expenditure			48	75
Budgeted profit				$20

COMMENT

Observe that rent and the management expenditure are not affected by any decision regarding a particular department. The departments make a positive contribution to fixed costs of the store; the team should therefore be advised not to close the departments which are seemingly making losses.

Relevant Costs for Decisions 179

Example 10.10 below deals with the making of a product, and the selling of a product below manufacturing cost.

EXAMPLE 10.10

The Gwendolyn firm makes shirts. At present, the firm is operating below capacity of 100 shirts. The firm's projected profit statement, together with the per unit information is shown below:

PROJECTED PROFIT STATEMENT

	$	Per unit information $
Sales (50 shirts ×12.50 each)	625	2.50
Cost of goods sold[a]	300	6.00
Gross profit	325	6.50
Selling expense[b]	200	4.00
Net profit	$125	$2.50

[a] Figure includes fixed manufacturing cost $75.
[b] Figure includes fixed selling cost $50.
   The remaining $150 consists of transportation expenses ($3 per shirt).

A Trinidadian firm offers to buy 25 shirts at $5 each. The firm will pay for the transportation expense. The manager thinks that the order should be rejected because the offered price is not sufficient to cover the manufacturing cost of $6 per shirt.

REQUIRED

Advise the manager as to what should be done.

SOLUTION

Step 1 redraft the statement using the contribution model
Step 2 calculate the profit or loss from the order

The procedures are:

	Without the order 50 shirts		With the order 75 shirts	Difference
	$		$	$
Sales	625.00		750.00	125.00
Variable costs				
Manufacturing $(300–75)	225.00	$(225/50) ×75	337.50	112.50
Selling	150.00		150.00	—
Total variable cost	375.00		487.50	112.50
Contribution	250.00		262.50	12.50
Fixed cost				
Manufacturing	75.00		75.00	—[a]
Selling	50.00		50.00	—[a]
Total fixed cost	125.00		125.00	—[a]
Profit	125.00		137.50	12.50[b]

a Since these costs do not change under either alternative, they are not relevant to the selection of one of these alternatives.

b An alternative solution is:

Sales price		5.00
Less manufacturing cost		4.50
Variable selling cost		
Transport		0
25 shirts	×	$3.50
	=	$12.50

COMMENT

The additional sales revenue is $125. The additional manufacturing cost is $112.50. The contribution from the order is $12.50. The manager should be advised to accept the order.

In Example 10.10, the relevant cost was the variable cost. This does not mean that all the fixed cost in decisions of this nature is not relevant.

10.10 Relevance of fixed cost

In making decisions, the decisionmaker must examine the fixed cost to see if it will be affected by the outcome of a decision, if not – as will often be the case – it is irrelevant. With some special orders, the activity level may change to such a degree that additional plant equipment is required by the firm. In such cases, the fixed cost will become relevant.

Reconsider Example 10.10. If the firm was operating at full capacity, and in order to accommodate the Trinidadian firm a piece of machinery costing $10 would be needed, then the fixed cost would be affected. The profit would be reduced to $127.50, but this is still an improvement on the initial position.

10.11 Summary

Relevant cost is pertinent to managerial decisions. Relevant cost decisions are future oriented. Relevant cost must be different between alternatives.

When resources are scarce in the firm, the management function should utilise a ranking procedure, which should be based on the contribution approach. For some decisions, the internal opportunity cost from the model provides calculations which help the management function to make sensible decisions. A statement which shows the contribution of departments helps the management function to appraise economic units also.

The fixed cost of the firm must be examined to see whether it will be changed by certain decisions. If the decision variables cause a change in the fixed cost, then the fixed cost is relevant to the analysis.

Bibliography

Dillon, R. D. and Nash, J. F. (1978) 'The True Relevance of Relevant Costs', *Accounting Review*, vol. liii, no. 1, January, pp. 11–18.

Garrison, R. H. (1978) *Managerial Accounting, Concepts for Planning, Control, Decision Making*, revised edn (Business Publications) ch. 11.

Horngren, C. T. (1962) 'Choosing Accounting Practices for Reporting to Management', in H. R. Anton and P. A. Firmin (eds), *Contemporary Issues in Cost Accounting* (Houghton Mifflin) pp. 3–20.

Horngren, C. T. (1977) *Cost Accounting: A Managerial Emphasis*, 4th edn (Prentice-Hall) p. 353.

Qureshi, M. (1980) 'The Nature and Identity of Management Accounting', *Journal of the Institute of Cost and Management Accountants*, p. 40.

Problems

10.1 MNO Ltd. produces and sells for $25 an office machine for which there is a heavy demand which the company is prevented from meeting because of a shortage of skilled labour. The direct material and labour cost of the machine is $10 and $5 respectively. The labour force is paid $1.25 per hour. All other cost may be regarded as fixed.

The company's foreign representative has been invited by one of his customers to supply, for $2000, a batch of machines of modified design and capacity which the customer wishes to incorporate into his own product, a large multi-purpose machine. MNO's estimator has calculated that to execute the order 200 direct labour hours would be required, and the cost of material would be $850 (excluding the cost of special switches which could be brought in for $100 or, alternatively, made by the company for a material cost of $40 and labour time of 20 hours).

REQUIRED

Advise the management of MNO Ltd whether to accept the foreign offer.

ACCA, FE, Part B, Paper 6, Accounting 2, Costing, December 1975.

10.2 Following a fire at the factory of Elgar Ltd, the management team met to review the proposed operations for the next quarter. The fire had destroyed all the finished good stock, some of the raw materials, and about half of the machines in the forming shop.

At the meeting of the management team, the following additional information was provided:

(i) Only 27000 machine hours of forming capacity will be available in the forthcoming quarter Although previously it was thought that sales demand would be the only bidding limitation on production, it has now become apparent that for the forthcoming quarter the forming capacity will be a limiting factor
(ii) It will take about 3 months to reinstate the forming shop to its previous operational capacity; the restriction on forming capacity is thus for the next quarter only
(iii) Some details of the product range manufactured by Elgar are provided in the following table:

ELGAR LTD

	Per unit detail product range of Product				
	A	B	C	D	E
	$	$	$	$	$
Sales price	50	60	40	50	80
Units of special material required for production					
W or X	2	2	2	1	3
Y	—	—	—	—	6
Z	1	2	1	1	—
Other direct material cost	6	12	6	5	13
Other variable production cost	8	4	8	4	4
Fixed production cost (Based on standard cost)	6	3	6	3	3
Forming hr required	5	6	2	10	6

(iv) The forecast of demand, in units, for the coming quarter is:

Product	A	B	C	D	E
Units demanded	2000	2000	4000	3000	4000

It was originally intended that the number of units produced would equal the units demanded for each product
(v) Due to a purchasing error, there is an excess of material W in stock; this has a book value of $6 per unit which is also its current replacement cost; this could be sold to realise $4 per unit after sales and transport costs

Material X could be used instead of Material W; Material X is not in stock, and has a current replacement cost of $5 per unit

(vi) Material Y was in stock at a book value of $2 per unit, which is its normal cost if ordered 3 months in advance, but the stocks of this material were entirely destroyed by the fire; in order to obtain the material quickly, a price of $3 per unit will have to be paid for the first 3000 units obtained in the quarter, and any additional units required will cost $6 per unit; these special prices will apply only to this quarter's purchases

(vii) Some of the stock of material Z was destroyed by the fire; the remaining stocks of 2000 units have a book value of $7 per unit; the replacement price for Z is currently $8 per unit

(viii) As a result of the fire, it is estimated that the fixed production cost will be $42000 for the next quarter, and the administration and office overhead will amount to $11500

(ix) The demand figure shown in (iv) includes a regular order from a single customer for 3000 units of C and 3000 units of E; this order is usually placed quarterly, and the customer always specifies that the order be fulfilled is total, or not at all

REQUIRED

(a) Ignoring the information contained in (ix) for this section of the question, determine the optimum production plan for the forthcoming quarter, and prepare a statement which indicates to the management of Elgar Ltd the estimated financial results of their planned production, in terms of total contribution, net current operating profit and financial accounting profit

(b) Prepare a statement which clearly shows the management of Elgar Ltd the financial consequences of both acceptance and rejection of the order mentioned in (ix)
Advise Elgar Ltd on the desirability of acceptance of the order in total
Indicate what further information would be useful in arriving at a decision whether to accept or reject the order

ACCA, PE, Section 2, Paper 14, Accounting 5, Management Accounting, December 1981.

10.3 Ayeco Ltd, with a central organisation in Ayetown, has three manufacturing units, one is Beetown, the second in Ceetown and the third in Deetown. The company manufactures and sells an air conditioner under the brandname of Ayecool at a price of $200. It is unable to utilise fully its manufacturing capacity.

Summarised profit and loss statements for the year are shown below:

	Beetown	Ceetown	Deetown	Total
	$000	$000	$000	$000
Cost				
Direct materials	200	800	400	1400
Direct wages	200	900	350	1450
Production overhead				
Variable	50	300	150	500
Fixed	200	600	300	1100
Sub-total	650	2600	1200	4450
Selling overhead				
Variable	25	200	100	325
Fixed	75	250	150	475
Administration overhead	100	450	200	750
Sub-total	850	3500	1650	6000
Central organisation cost	50	200	100	350
Total	900	3700	1750	6350
Profit	100	300	250	650
Sales	1000	4000	2000	7000

Relevant Costs for Decisions

The management of the company has to decide whether or not to renew the lease of the property at Beetown, which expires next year. The company has been offered an extension to the lease at an additional cost of $50000 per annum. This situation concerning the lease has been known for some time, so the accountant has collected relevant information to aid the decision. It is estimated that the cost of closing down Beetown would be offset by the surplus obtained by the sale of plant, machinery and stocks.

If Ayeco Ltd does not renew the lease of Beetown property it can:

(i) accept an offer from Zeeco Ltd, a competitor, to take over the manufacture and sales in the Beetown area and pay to Ayeco Ltd a commission of $3 for each unit sold
(ii) transfer the output at present made in Beetown to either Ceetown or Deetown; each of these units has sufficient plant capacity to undertake the Beetown output, but additional costs in supervision, salaries, storage and maintenance would be incurred; these additional costs are estimated as amounting yearly to $250000 at Ceetown and $200000 at Deetown

If the Beetown sales connections are transferred to either Ceetown or Deetown, it is estimated that additional transport costs would be incurred in delivering to customers in the region of Beetown, and that these would amount respectively to $15 and $20 per unit.

REQUIRED

(a) Present a statement to the board of directors of Ayeco Ltd to show the estimated annual profit which would arise from:

 (i) continuing production at all three sites
 (ii) closing down production at Beetown, and accepting the offer of the sales commission from Zeeco Ltd
 (iii) transferring Beetown sales to Ceetown
 (iv) transferring Beetown sales to Deetown

(b) Comment on your statement, indicating any problems which may arise from the various decisions which the board may decide to take

ICMA, PS, Part I, Cost Accounting 2, November 1978.

10.4 The original budget for the K department of Hilton Ltd for the forthcoming year was as follows:

Budget for forthcoming year – K dept
Budgeted sales and production – 30000 units

	Per unit of output	Total for 30000 units
	$	$000
Sales revenue	10.0	300
Manufacturing cost: *Material per unit*		
Material A–1 l	2.0	60
Material B–1 kg	1.5	45
Production labour	2.0	60
Variable overhead	1.0	30
Fixed manufacturing overhead	2.0	60
	8.5	255
Non-manufacturing cost	1.0	30
Total cost	9.5	285
Budgeted net profit for year	0.5	15

As part of Hilton's long-term strategic plan, the K department was due to be closed at the end of the forthcoming year. However, rumours of the closure have resulted in the majority of K's labour force leaving the firm, and this has forced the abandonment of the original budget for the department.

The managing director has suggested that the department could be closed down immediately or, by employing contract labour, could be operated to produce 10000 or 20000 units in the year. With the exception of the foreman (see (v) below), the few remaining members of K's production labour force would then be redeployed within the firm.

The following further information is available:

(i) Each hour of contract labour will cost $3.00, and will produce one unit of the product; contract labour would have to be trained at a fixed cost of $20000
(ii) There are 30000 litres of material A in stock; this material has no other use, and any of it not used in department K will have to be disposed of; cost of disposal will be $2000 plus $0.50 per l disposed of
(iii) There are 15000 kg of material B in stock; if the material is not used in department K, then up to 10000 kg could be used in another department to substitute for an equivalent weight of a material which currently costs $1.8 per kg; material B originally cost $1.5 per kg, and its current market price (buying or selling) is $2.0 per kg; cost to Hilton of selling any surplus material B will amount to $1.00 per kg sold
(iv) Variable overhead will be 30 per cent higher, per unit produced, than originally budgeted
(v) Included in Fixed manufacturing overheads are:

(a) $6000 salary of the departmental foreman
(b) $7000 depreciation of the machine used in the department

If the department is closed immediately the foreman, who will otherwise return at the end of the year, will be asked to retire early and paid $2000 compensation for agreeing to this; the only machine used in the department originally cost $70000 and could currently be sold for $43000; this sales value will reduce to $40000 at the end of the year and, if used for any production during the year, will decrease by a further $500 per 1000 units produced
(vi) All other cost included in Fixed manufacturing overhead and all Non-manufacturing costs is apportionment of general overhead, none of which will be altered by any decision concerning the K department
(vii) The sales manager suggests that a sales volume of 10000 units could be achieved if the unit sales price were $9.00; a sales volume of 20000 units would be achieved if the sales price per unit were reduced to $8, and an advertising campaign costing $15000 were undertaken

REQUIRED

(a) Advise Hilton Ltd of its best course of action regarding department K, presenting data in tabular form
(b) For each of the following separate circumstances, show how the advice given in (a) above is altered:
  (i) immediate closure of department K would enable its factory space to be rented out for 1 year at a rental of $8000
  (ii) the quoted level of efficiency of the contract labour is the average for production of the first 5000 units, and any additional production would reflect the effect of the 90 per cent learning curve which will be experienced
  Show also the revised labour cost

Ignore taxation, and the time value of money.

ACCA, PE, Section 2, Paper 14, Accounting 5, Management Accounting, June 1981.

10.5 MC Ltd operates four departments, in which three products are manufactured. The company is currently experiencing a critical shortage of labour in department 3, and there are no immediate prospects of an improvement in this situation.

REQUIRED

(a) Show the contribution which each product can make towards company profit

Relevant Costs for Decisions

(b) Suggest the product on which the company should concentrate its resources, giving brief reasons
(c) Indicate the steps necessary to achieve the production you have recommended in answer to (b) above
(d) Calculate the amount of profit per annum that could be expected if the company were to adopt your suggestion

Product	Price per unit	X Units	Y Units	Z Units
Cost:				
Direct material:	A = 3.0	3	5	3
	B = 5.0	4	6	7
	Rate per hr	hr	hr	hr
Direct wages:				
Dept: 1	1.50	4	8	10
2	1.75	12	4	8
3	2.00	3	2	4
4	2.25	8	12	4
		$	$	$
Variable overhead		20	25	35
Selling price		136	140	165
Budgeted data for year:				
Direct wages:				
Dept: 1				495000
2				1225000
3				360000
4				1175000
Fixed overhead				1000000

ICAA, PS, Part I, Cost Accounting 2, May 1979.

10.6 A company is asked to quote for a special order to be delivered ex works.
Direct material costs per unit of output are:

For total of	$ each	% discount
100	18	
200	18	less 10
400	18	less 20

The work would be done in two departments:

Dept
  F Employs highly skilled operators paid at $2.50 per hour
      Each unit of output requires 6 direct labour hours of work for the first 100 units
      However, experience has shown that an 80 per cent learning curve can be expected to operate
  G Employs skilled operators paid at $2.00 per hour
      Each unit of output requires 3 direct labour hours of work for the first 100 units
      Here, too, an 80 per cent learning curve is expected

Overtime in either department is paid at time and a half. No premium for overtime is included in standard manufacturing overhead.

Standard manufacturing overhead per direct labour hour is:

	DEPT F	DEPT G
	$	$
Variable	1.00	1.00
Fixed	3.50[a]	2.00[b]

		Budgeted DLH per period
a	Based on	3000
b	Based on	2000

The special order will require special tooling of $300, which is chargeable to the customer.

If the order received is for 100 or 200 units, the work will have to be done in period no. 8, which, for dept F, is already loaded with 2200 direct labour hours of work. Dept G, however, will be working at only around 55 per cent of capacity.

On special orders of this type, it is the company's practice to add the following margins on cost in arriving at selling prices:

Dept	%
F	20
G	10
Direct materials	2
Sub-contractor's work (when used)	2

An outside sub-contractor has offered, irrespective of the size of the order, to do the work of dept G on this order for a price of $8 per unit, including collection from and delivery to the works.

REQUIRED

Calculate

(a) price per unit for an order of 100 units if made entirely in the company
(b) price per unit for an order of 200 units if made entirely in the company
(c) separate price per unit for an extra 200 units subsequent to the order for 200 in (b) above, thus bringing the total order to 400 units–you are to assume that:

   (i) This additional order for the extra 200 units could be done when there are no capacity limitations in either dept
   (ii) the materials supplier would give the full discount for the 400 units

(d) change in unit selling price that would result from using the outside sub-contractor instead of department G for an order of:

	Units
(i)	100
(ii)	200
(iii)	400

ICMA, PS, Part III, Management Accounting 1, November 1979.

Chapter 11
Direct Costing and Absorption Costing

Decision making in business depends in part on a knowledge of costs and their structure and behaviour.   (Yamey, 1975)

11.1 Introduction

Direct costing and absorption costing are two quantitative accounting models that are used by the decisionmakers of the firm for two different purposes – for internal and for external reporting. The two models show the administration of the firm's economic resources, but from different perspectives. Horngren (1977) emphasised that 'when an accounting system is designed, managers and accountants must choose an inventory valuation method. This decision is vital for many reasons, including its effects on reported income in any given year, on the evaluation of a manager's performance, and on pricing decisions'. The choice between direct and absorption costing is thus crucial to the firm's control function. Hendriksen (1970) stated that 'one of the major problems in determining the valuation of manufactured assets is the decision regarding which costs are relevant to future periods and thus should be included in asset valuation and which should be charged against current income'. That statement highlights the unresolved problem concerning direct costing and absorption costing. It should be noted also that both statements quoted really aim at income measurement, and its use both in financial reporting and in evaluating the outcome of a manager's decisions.

11.2 Requirements of decision-maker

Decisionmaking can be viewed as a threefold activity involving: (i) identifying a problem; (ii) analysing the data; (iii) choosing a suitable decision rule. These three activities collectively have an important bearing on accounting reports, which are used internally by management as well as by external users. Any report which fails to stress the key variables relating to a decision is useless to the decisionmaker. Rational decisionmaking thus requires that accounting reports be presented with relevant information in a clear form. For accounting purposes, the costs and revenue data must be classified and assigned to the individual divisions of the firm. Such assignments to products, processes or divisions within the firm promote a reporting format that will make the data relevant to the user.

11.3 Report format

The 'report format' means the physical arrangement and presentation of accounting data. Accounting reports are generally quantitative presentations. Such presentations can be shown in many ways; a particular format emphasises some aspect of the data, and draws the user's attention to particular items or to a special characteristic of an item.

Accounting reports generally group costs according to some classification, such as cost behaviour, control responsibility, time span or relation to product. Each classification is designed to serve a different purpose. If the costs on an income statement are classified as fixed or variable, the user can make use of the data for planning purposes. The contribution model facilitates this approach.

11.4 Contribution model

The contribution model combines allocation and format considerations to draw management's attention to the tactical decisionmaking process within the firm. It emphasises C–V–P relationships, which are important to many short-run managerial decisions. The contribution approach to reporting facilitates C–V–P presentations which are relevant to the decisionmaker. This necessitates an examination of the report structures of the traditional and contribution statements to show their differences. The two formats are illustrated and compared in Figure 11.1.

TRADITIONAL		CONTRIBUTION	
Sales revenue	$	Sales revenue	$
Cost of goods sold		Variable cost	
Gross margin		Contribution margin	
Selling & admin. cost		Fixed cost	
Net income	$	Net income	$

Figure 11.1 **Traditional and contribution statement compared**

11.5 Report structures

The contribution format identifies the relationship between product revenues and variable cost for the segments of a firm. The model can be contrasted with the traditional income model.

The traditional income model stresses the firm's activities – production, selling, administra-

Direct Costing and Absorption Costing 189

tion. Cost is also associated with these activities. In contrast, the contribution model emphasises cost behaviour in relation to volume; variable and fixed cost is the main classifications. Other features of the contribution model for a division of a large firm are shown in Figure 11.2.

```
            Net sales
            Variable cost

            Manufacturing
            Administration           _____
            Contribution margin           $

            Controllable fixed cost

            Marketing
            Research                 _____
            Short-run performance margin

            Traceable fixed cost (Committed)

            Depreciation
            Insurance                _____
            Segment margin

            Assigned cost

            Maintenance
            Executive salaries       _____
            Net income before tax         $____
```

Figure 11.2 **Contribution model for division of a firm**

COMMENT

(i) The first classification is to identify the cost categories as variable; this distinction is used to calculate a contribution margin
(ii) The second classification is to identify the fixed costs as controllable (and, by implication, non-controllable by divisional management); this distinction emphasises responsibility; it also helps to guage the effectiveness of managerial action
(iii) Some fixed cost is classified as committed; this aspect identifies for the decisionmaker cost data that are subject to periodic change, and cost data which reflect on the long-term commitments of the firm
   The point to note, however, is that these costs are incurred by central management on the division's behalf – so are not its manager's responsibility
(iv) Assigned cost implies that some cost has been assigned to a division of the firm; the traceability of the cost items to that division is thus indicated; obviously, a distinction can be made between traceable fixed costs and non-traceable fixed costs that have been allocated to the segment.

11.6 Further insights into contribution models

The contribution margin, when converted to money or cash, covers the fixed costs and also contributes to the profits of the firm. A division that does not make a positive contribution should be discontinued, unless it is vital to other parts of the firm. Note that an accounting model should not ignore interactions; to ignore interactions can lead to faulty decisions.

Managerial short-run decisions generally involve revenue and variable cost. Since the contribution margin is concerned with those relationships, the data is useful for making decisions on the division of a firm. Control, therefore, can be more effective if top management analyse and compare the results of the various divisions of the firm.

The short-run performance margin help top management to evaluate the effectiveness of divisional managers. This is so because included in the computations are revenue, variable cost, and controllable fixed cost, which are traceable to heads of departments.

The segment margin also captures such elements of traceable fixed cost which has a bearing on the long-term commitments of the firm. The committed fixed cost arises from decisions which are related to capacity. These decisions are made by the higher echelons of management.

The purpose of presenting accounting information is to facilitate the understanding of users. It also has an educational role. The presentation of accounting data in a suitable form to employees at the operating level enables them to understand the firm's long-term commitments. Similarly, presentation to the executives of the firm enables them to form reasonable judgements about the firm's activities. The segment margin in Fig. 11.2 can be used by the top executives of the firm to review previous decisions concerning committed cost levels in relation to current divisional performance.

Many contribution statements end with the segment margin, because non-traceable cost is not assigned to divisions. Another reason is that individual managers should not be held responsible for reported activities which include a high percentage of subjective cost assignments.

The assignment of cost is central to accounting. Thus a logical primitive of the contribution model is its link with inventory valuation.

11.7 Inventory valuation

An inventory valuation is used to determine the cost of goods sold. The cost of goods sold is associated with the firm's income statement. The traditional full cost method, i.e. absorption costing, requires that direct labour, direct materials, variable and fixed overheads be aggregated to form the cost of the units produced.

The solution to Example 11.1 draws attention to the characteristics of the absorption costing model.

EXAMPLE 11.1

The Hinkson firm incurred $10000 of committed fixed cost and variable cost of $1 per unit during an accounting period in which 10000 units were produced.

REQUIRED

(a) Show the absorption income statement if the units were priced at $3 each, and all the units were sold
(b) Show (i) the absorption income statement if only 4000 units were sold, and (ii) determine the ending inventory and its value

SOLUTION

(a) Determine the cost per unit:

Direct Costing and Absorption Costing

	$
Fixed cost	10000
Variable cost ($1 ×10000)	10000
Total cost	20000 ÷
Units produced	10000
Cost per unit	2

The absorption income statement is:

	$
Revenue ($3 ×10000)	30000
Cost of goods sold ($2 ×10000)	20000
Net income	$10000

(b)
(i) If only 4000 units were sold, the absorption income statement is:

	$
Revenue ($3 ×4000)	12000
Cost of goods sold ($2 ×4000)	8000
Net income	$4000

(ii) The ending inventory of 6000 units would be valued at $2 ×6000 = $12000.

COMMENT

Note that the net income figure in (a) differs from that in (b). In (a), however, no problem arises because all the units were sold.

In isolation, the income figire in (b) appears to be reasonable. But 'reasonableness' in accounting must be judged against another model which is just as useful. For analytical comparison, the break-even concept is resurrected:

$$B_r = \frac{FK}{SP - vc} = \frac{\$10000}{2} = 5000 \text{ units}$$

The break-even locus of 5000 units represents a sales volume which generates 0 profit. Yet at a sales level of 4000 units the traditional model shows a profit of $4000. The reason for the difference lies in the treatment of the fixed overhead expense. The traditional income model included only part of the overhead, that part assigned to units sold during the period, ie. $1 ×4000 units. The remaining $6000 of the overhead expense will be taken to the inventory account, and would be shown on the balance sheet.

11.8 Inventory valuation problems

The problem with inventory valuation, centres around the selection of the model that is most useful to decisionmakers. The absorption costing model is used in all published accounts; it stresses a functional classification of costs. Opponents of this method contend that full cost inventory and cost of sales information can be manipulated, and is thus, misleading.

Under absorption costing altering the production volume with sales held constant can affect the reported incomes. The solution to the Example 11.2 shows this clearly.

EXAMPLE 11.2

The Hinkson firm has a cost structure as follows. Fixed cost of $10000, variable cost of $1. The selling price of its sole product is $3. The sales volume is 4000 units and production volume for periods (i), (ii) and (iii) respectively 10000, 5000 and 4000 units.

REQUIRED

Show the absorption costing statement.

ABSORPTION COSTING STATEMENT

Period	(i) Units	(ii) Units	(iii) Units
Production volume	10000	5000	4000
	$	$	$
Fixed cost	10000	10000	10000
Variable cost	10000	5000	4000
Total cost	$20000	$15000	$14000
Units produced	10000	5000	4000
Cost per unit	$2.00	$3.00	$3.50
Sales volume	Units 4000	Units 4000	Units 4000
	$	$	$
Revenue	12000	12000	12000
Cost of goods sold	8000	12000	14000
Net income (Loss)	$ 4000	0	$(2000)

COMMENT

The net income figures range from $4000 to 0 profit, to a $2000 loss. Each net income figure depends on the production volume, which is determined by the firm's management—which is thus free to manipulate annual profit by making output and not selling it. This seems a most unreasonable way to measure income.

Many authorities advocate the use of direct costing for inventory valuation, so that the profit from the production system will become a function of the sales volume.

11.9 Direct costing model

The direct costing model uses cost behaviour as a basis for valuation and statement construction. The cost of production is classified as product-related or period-related. The product cost includes the manufacturing materials, labour, and the variable overheads that are

Direct Costing and Absorption Costing

directly associated with the product. Such cost varies with production. Period cost, however, includes those elements that are directly associated with the product.

The costing model utilises product cost in inventory valuation. This cost is assigned to the units produced, and consequently is used in the income calculation in proportion to the number of units sold during the period. What is the appearance of the direct costing income statement for Example 11.2? For each production volume, the statement is:

	$
Revenue ($3 × 4000)	12000
Variable production cost ($1 × 4000)	4000
Gross profit = Contribution margin	8000
Fixed period costs	10000
Net profit (Loss)	$(2000)

The format shows that the direct costing statement approximates the structure of the contribution model. It also reveals similar information to that found in conventional C–V–P analysis. But a distinction exists between the direct and absorption costing system.

11.10 Direct and absorption costing

The fundamental difference between the two systems is one of timing. The direct costing model takes all the fixed cost to the income statement immediately. The absorption costing model assigns the fixed cost to units produced during the period. The two costing systems can produce different periodic income numbers if production and sales volume fluctuate, i.e. differ from each other. The solution to Example 11.3 makes that point clear.

EXAMPLE 11.3

The manager of the Hinkson firm now tells you that for Year 1 and Year 2 the production and sales units of his firm were:

Units	YEAR 1	YEAR 2
Produced	6000	4000
Sold	5000	5000

REQUIRED

Show the direct and absorption costing statements for the two periods.

SOLUTION

	Direct costing Year 1 statement	Absorption costing Year 1 statement	Direct costing Year 2 statement	Absorption costing Year 2 statement
	$	$	$	$
Fixed cost	—	10000	—	10000
Variable cost	6000	6000	4000	4000
Total cost	6000	16000	4000	14000
Units produced	6000	6000	4000	4000
	$	$	$	$
Cost per unit	1.00	2.667	1.00	3.50
Revenue ($3 ×5000)	15000	15000	15000	15000
Cost of goods sold	5000	13333	5000	16667
Period cost	10000	0	10000	0
Net income (Loss)	$ 0	$ 1667	$ 0	$(1667)
Inventory values	$ 1 ×1000 $1000	$ 2.667 ×1000 $2667	0	0

COMMENT

In the absorption costing method, the fixed cost is assigned to the units produced. In Year 1 $1667 of the fixed cost of the unsold units is placed in the ending inventory. In Year 2, the fixed cost of $(3.50 ×40000— $2667) = $16667 is taken to the income statement.

In contrast, the direct costing model treats all the fixed cost as a period charge, and assigns them directly to the income statement.

From the calculations, it is clear that when production exceeds sales, the absorption model shows a higher profit than direct costing. When sales exceeds production, the absorption costing model shows a lower profit than the direct costing model. However, Ijiri et al. (1965) shows that this 'although often correct, it is not universally valid: for a given sales level, the management of the firm can record whatever profit it likes by choosing an appropriate output level.'

11.11 Use of direct costing

Direct costing is used for internal reporting purposes. From its format, variable cost data are readily obtained to aid contribution analysis. its statement shows that profitability does not fluctuate in response to adjustments in the production volume. Profits can thus be used as a basis for evaluation of the economic units of the firm. Of importance is the fact that direct costing emphasises the current effects of fixed cost on the divisions of the firm.

Direct Costing and Absorption Costing

11.12 Summary

The requirements of the decisionmaker are associated with the report format. The contribution format aids C–V–P analysis. The traditional model would have to be recast to accommodate such analysis. The contribution model can be linked with inventory valuation.

Differences exist between the income determination of the absorption and direct costing models. With the absorption model, net income is a function of both product and sales volume. With direct costing, the fixed cost is taken to the income statement immediately. The inventory values of both methods also differ.

The advocates of direct costing contend that it approximates economic reality, which makes it useful for managerial decisionmaking. Opponents of direct costing argue that it opposes the conventional reporting procedures. Direct costing is used for internal reporting (i.e., managerial assessment) while absorption costing is used for external reporting.

Bibliography

Hendriksen, E. S. (1970) *Accounting Theory* (R. D. Irwin) p. 270.
Horngren, C. T. (1977) *Cost Accounting: A Managerial Emphasis*, 4th edn (Prentice-Hall) p. 294.
Ijiri, Y. *et al.* (1965) 'The Effect of Inventory Costing Methods on Full and Direct Costing', in H. R. Anton and P. A. Firmin (eds), *Contemporary Issues in Cost Accounting* (Houghton Mifflin) pp. 441–52.
Weber, C. (1966) *The Evolution of Direct Costing*, Monograph 3 (Centre for International Education and Research in Accounting).
Yamey, B. S. (1978) 'Common Costs and Business Decisions: an Historical Note', *Accounting Historian*, vol. 2, no. 1, Winter, p. 1.

Problems

11.1 The budget of S Ltd provides for the manufacture and sale of 10000 spodgets per month, the unit standard cost being $6, made up:

	$
Direct material	3.5
Direct labour	0.5
Fixed overhead	2.0

The selling price of the spodget being $8.0
Production and sales quantities for period 1 and 2 were:

	PERIOD	
	1	*2*
Production	10000	10000
Sales	8000	12000

REQUIRED

(a) Prepare operating statements for each of the two periods, assuming:
  (i) the company uses marginal costing
  (ii) absorption costing is used

(b) Comment on the differences of the two system as regards:
  (ii) stock valuation
  (ii) periodic profit

ACCA, FE, Part B, Paper 6, Accounting 2, Costing, December, 1975.

REQUIRED

11.2

(a) From the information given below, prepare profit statements for the year based on:
   (i) marginal costing
   (ii) absorption costing

Comment on the difference in the profit figures you report for (i) and (ii) above

JB Ltd produces a single product, which is bottled and sold in cases. The normal annual level of operations, on which the production fixed overhead absorption is based, is 36000 cases.
Data for the last financial year were, for cases:

Production		40000
Sales		32000

	Per case	
	$	$
Selling price 60		
Cost:		
Production:		
Direct labour 12		
Direct materials	14	
Variable overhead	8	
Fixed overhead (budgeted and incurred)		216000
Selling and administrative cost:		
Fixed		50000
Variable	15% of sales revenue	

There was no opening stock of finished goods, and the work-in-progress stock may be assumed to be the same at the end of year as it was at the beginning.

(b) For making decisions based on cost data, the distinction between fixed and variable costs is important.

REQUIRED

(i) Explain why the above statement is true
(ii) Give brief details of two problems associated with the determination of fixed and variable cost
(iii) List three types of decision where the division between fixed and variable cost is important

ICMA, FS, Section A, Cost Accounting, May 1982.

11.3 Rumbles Ltd manufactures a single product, with a variable manufacturing cost of $12 per unit and a selling price of $20 per unit. Fixed production overhead is $90000 per period. The company operates a full absorption costing system, and the fixed overhead is absorbed into the cost of production on the basis of a normal activity of 15600 units per period, at a rate of $6 per unit. Any under or over absorbed overheads are written off to the profit and loss account at the end of each period. It may be assumed that no other expenses are incurred.

Summarised below are the company's manufacturing and trading results (showing quantities only) for periods 2 and 3.

Direct Costing and Absorption Costing

	PERIOD	
	2	3
	Units	Units
Opening stock	5000	11000
Production	17000	13000
	22000	24000
Less closing stock	11000	6000
Sales	11000	18000

The managing director of Rumbles Ltd, who has recently returned from a course on marginal costing, has calculated that as sales have increased by 7000 units in period 3, the company's profits should increase by $56000. However, the results produce by the accountant show that profits in period 2 were $34000 and in period 3 $24000. The managing director is somewhat surprised!

REQUIRED

(a) Produce columnar revenue accounts for both periods, showing how the profits of $24000 and $34000 were obtained
(b) Carefully explains, with supporting calculations:

  (i) the reasons for the reduction in reported profits between the two periods
  (ii) how the managing director has calculated that profits should increase by $56000 in period 3
  (iii) why profits have not increased by $56000 in period 3

ACCA, FE, Part B, Paper 6, Accounting 2, Costing, December 1980.

Chapter 12
Budgetary Planning

The advocates of budgeting maintain that the process of preparing the budget forces executives to become better administrators. Budgeting puts planning where it belongs – in the forefront of the manager's mind.　　　　(Horngren, 1977)

12.1 Introduction

One of the most important functions in an instrumental organisation[1] is the budgetary planning process. Budgetary planning is important because it tries first to capture, and secondly to co-ordinate all the heterogeneous activities – both human and physical – of the firm into a homogeneous plan of action. The management accountant plays an important role in that process.

What are the concepts of budgetary planning?

12.2 The budget

A firm's budget is a plan, in quantitative terms, showing its employees how its resources will be acquired and used over a specified time interval. A firm's budget can be split into two states: the current period and the long period.[2]

---

[1] A firm, unlike a church or prison, is an instrumental organisation. In the church, the organisation exists because the members share common objectives. In a prison, the objectives of the authorities are imposed upon the prisoners. An instrumental organisation exists because it satisfies the objectives of its members, even though its members may have differing (and even conflicting) objectives. It can be classified as a reward/punishment type of organisation *both* offering rewards *and* requiring sacrifices from its collaborators. Seen in this light, budgetary planning in firms can offer a bargaining mechanism in which the various objectives can compete to produce a consensus. The annual budgeting cycle will usually mean that the consensus between the divisions of a firm and its management is achieved for a year.

[2] Budgets for the long period are formed in the face of much greater uncertainty than those for the current period. As a result, long-period budgets tend to be prepared in a very general way, containing limited detail.

Budgetary Planning

12.3 Reasons for budgets

The rationale for budgets has five aspects

 (i) Authorisation – the budget is used to authorise the expenditure and activities contained in it
 (ii) Evaluation of performance – the planned activities and expenditures contained in the budget provide a standard against which the actual achievement of the firm can be measured and evaluated
 (iii) Co-ordination of activities – the piecemeal budgets of the sub-units of the firm are so framed that each sub-unit is made to contribute to the achievement of the overall budget
 (vi) Control – the setting up of organisational machinery to direct efforts towards the planned (or desired) aims
 The budget sets out the planned activity; subsequent deviations between achievement and plan will indicate the need for investigation and corrective action
 (v) Motivation – the budget is so constructed as to move employees from one target goal to another; indeed, this is bound up with the reward/punishment type of organisation environment and bureaucratic decision processes, where employees are given incentives to work towards the achievement of the firm's targets

12.4 Preparation of budgets

Budget preparation is a Management as well as an accounting task. If it is recognised that a firm will continue only because its members are prepared to maintain the coalition then the members of the firm should have a say in the budget preparation. Seen in this light, budgeting has behavioural implications.[1] The management accountant, however, will be responsible for the technical aspect of the cost data. Budgeting cost plans will always be constrained by a 'principal factor'.

12.5 Principal budget factor

An economic factor, which constrains the planning activities of the firm can be dubbed the principal budget factor. If 2000 units of a product can be made with the equipment and employees available, but only 1000 units can be sold, the principal budget factor is the quantity of units demanded by customers.[2] For ease of exposition, in the building of the budgets which follow customers' demand – i.e. the estimated sales – is deemed to be the limiting factor. It is thus imperative for the management accountant to ascertain the forecasted sales.

---

[1] See Ronen (1975) and Tosi (1975).
[2] If there is more than one limiting factor, linear programming can be used to determine the optimal plan.

12.6 Sales forecast

The sales forecast[1] will contain expectations about the demand for the firm's products, in quantitative terms at various prices. From feasible sales estimates which harmonise[2] with the production activities of the firm, the sales budget is prepared.

12.7 Sales budget

The sales budget contains data which relate to the planned sales for each product (or product group) of the firm.

12.8 Selling and distribution cost budget

This budget will contain the appropriate selling and distribution costs and certain promotional expenditure which are set by top management. The expenditures are constrained by the cash resources of the firm. An estimate of the available resources should also be made at the time of the sales forecast preparation, so that adequate consideration is given to such expenditures.

12.9 Production budget

This budget shows the quantity of each product to be made. It also shows the total cost of production of each product. In firms where standard items are produced, output is expressed in terms of the units produced. In firms where 'jobbing' predominates, production is expressed in terms of work hours.

Production capacity and sales quantities are unlikely to coincide exactly when established independently. When differences show up, the two budgets are reconciled with each other. From the data provided by the production budget, other budgets emerge. These are:

(i) Raw material purchasing budget
(ii) Labour budget
(iii) Factory expense budget
(iv) Inventory budgets
(v) Capital expenditure budget

---

[1] Budgets incorporate uncertainty. Forecasting, by quantifying the future in the budget, attempts to resolve some of the uncertainty. Some of the factors which should be taken into account in sales forecasting are: (i) past sales volume; (ii) pricing policies; (iii) competition; (iv) seasonal variances; (v) macro-economic indicators.

[2] An important role of budgeting is examining the interrelationship between various aspects of the firm's activities. In achieving harmony, the implications for production and other functions of particular, sales plans can be established and considered from the point of view of feasibility and utilisation of capacity. Other functions of concern might include marketing and promotion, transportation and administration.

12.10 Raw material purchasing budget

This budget indicates the quantities to be purchased, and the stock to be held. Where standard products are made, this budget indicates the standard estimates of raw material for production.

12.11 Labour budget

This budget contains data on standard labour hours for each production unit.

12.12 Factory expense budget

This budget contains expense data according to its fixed and variable elements. In very large organisations, there exists a number of budgets, one for each element of administration which can be identified as a separate budget centre. Each of these budgets indicates the costs to be incurred, differentiating between fixed, variable and semi-variable cost elements.

12.13 Inventory budgets

These budgets contain data for internal stocks. These are made up of:

(i) Finished goods inventory budget
(ii) Work-in-progress budget
(iii) Raw material stock budget

The finished goods inventory budget is coupled with the production and the sales budget. The work-in-progress budget provides for the unfinished production included in the production product. A link is also established with the raw material stock budget and the production budget.

12.14 Capital expenditure budgets

These budgets are generally prepared for a period longer than the other budgets – in large organisations, the time period can run from 5–20 years. However, for short-period analysis, the capital expenditure budgets are disaggregated into yearly budgets. Such budgets are geared to the current cash and production budgets, the future level of output, and the long-term development of the firm.

Capital expenditure budgets deal with investment proposals. The administration of the capital budget is generally separated from the operating budget; modern-day practice in some large firms allows project committees to be responsible for the authorising and monitoring of major capital projects, and the preparation of the capital budget.

12.15 Cash budget

This budget contains data which show the effects of the firm's budgeted activities on the movement of liquid resources.

A cash budget is important because it draws management's attention to the short-run aspect of financial decisions. It helps the financial manager to ensure that sufficient funds are available to finance the budgeted level of activities; it also indicates the period in which the cash resources are likely to be wanted. When the cash budget is constructed, and it shows a cash deficit, the financial manager can arrange short-term, additional finance via bank loans. If the cash budget shows a surplus, arrangements can be made for lucrative short-term deposits.

The cash budget is an important analytical tool. It has implications for relationships within the firm, and between the firm and its external environment. That, of course, depends on whether the firm's cash resources are managed well; indeed, if the cash budget shows a deficiency which is unacceptable to management then the other components of the master budget (see 12.16) will require revision until management finds an acceptable figure.

12.16 Master budget

The master budget is the final plan which summarises and integrates all the functional budgets and the resulting planned financial statements. It is an instrument which shows the detailed analysis and feasibility of forecasted decisions which are generated from the various units of the firm. As an instrument, it seeks to co-ordinate the various plans of the firm's units. In this way, the master budget serves to guide the firm's units towards its objectives.

The solution to Example 12.1 shows how the master budget is prepared.

EXAMPLE 12.1

The Horace firm desires a minimum ending cash balance each month of $100. The firm produces coral ashtrays, which are forecasted to sell for $10 each. The recent and forecasted sales (in units) are:

	Actual
Jan	200
Feb	240
Mar	280
	Forecasted
Apr	350
May	450
Jun	600
July	650

The ending inventories are supposed to equal 80 per cent of the next month's sales in units. The coral cost the firm $5 per piece. The firm pays its creditors as follows: 50 per cent in the month of purchase, the remaining 50 per cent in the following month.

The sales are on credit, and are payable within 15 days. No discounts are given. The sales department has discovered, however, that 25 per cent of a month's sales are collected by the month end. An additional 50 per cent is collected in the month following, and the remaining 25 per cent is collected in the second month following. Bad debts are negligible.

Budgetary Planning

The firm's monthly operating expenses are:

Variable:	$
Sales commision	0.5 per unit

Fixed:	
Wages and salaries	300
Utilities	100
Insurance expired	20
Depreciation	300
Miscellaneous	25

The operating expenses are paid during the month in cash, with the exception of depreciation and insurance expired.

New fixed assets will be purchased during May for $1000. The director plans to pay dividends of $700 each quarter, payable in the first month of the following quarter.

The firm's Balance Sheet at March 31, 19x1 was:

BALANCE SHEET

	$		$
Share capital	5 000	Fixed assets (Net)	2 700
P & L A/c	620	Current assets:	
		Debtors ($600	
Current liabilities:		February sales &	
Creditors (Purchases)	840	$2100 March sales)	2700
Dividends payable	700	Inventory (0.80 ×	
		350 units × $5)	1400
		Unexpired insurance	160
		Cash	200
	$7160		$7160

Short-term cash requirements can be obtained by borrowing at 15 per cent interest per year.

REQUIRED

Prepare

(i) a master budget for the three months period, ended 30 June 19X1
(ii) a sales budget, by month and in total
(iii) a schedule of budgeted cash collection for sales and debtors, by month and in total
(iv) purchase budget, in units and in dollars, by month and in total
(v) schedule of budgeted cash payments
(vi) cash budget, a budgeted income statement, and a budgeted balance sheet.

SOLUTION

SALES BUDGET SCHEDULE 1

	Apr	May	June	Quarter
Budgeted sales (units)	350	450	600	1400
	×	×	×	×
Budgeted selling price	$10	$10	$10	$10
Budgeted salses ($)	$3500	$4500	$6000	$14000

BUDGETED CASH COLLECTION SCHEDULE 2

	$	$	$	$
Feb	600			600
Mar	1400	700		2100
Apr	875	1750	875	3500
May		1125	2250	3375
Jun			1500	1500
Total cash collection	$2875	$3575	$4625	$11075

BUDGETED PURCHASES SCHEDULE 3

Budgeted sales (units)	350	450	600	1400
Add budgeted ending inventory[a]	360	480	520	520
Total requirements	710	930	1120	1920
Less beginning inventory	280	360	480	280
Required purchases (units)	430	570	640	1640
Unit cost	× $5	× $5	× $5	× $5
Required purchases	$2150	$2850	$3200	$8200

[a] 0.80 of the next month's sales in units

BUDGETED CASH PAYMENTS FOR PURCHASES SCHEDULE 4

	$	$	$	$
Mar	840			840
Apr	1075	1075		2150
May		1425	1425	2850
Jun			1600	1600
	$1915	$2500	$3025	$7440

CASH BUDGET SCHEDULE 5

	Apr	May	June	Quarter
	$	$	$	$
Cash balance beginning	200	100	100	200
Add receipts from				
customers Schedule 2	2875	3575	4625	11075
Total cash from trading available to meet disbursements	3075	3675	4725	11275
Less disbursements:				
Purchases of inventory Schedule 4	1915	2500	3025	7440
Sales commision $0.50 per unit	175	225	300	700
Salaries wages and	300	300	300	900
Utilities	100	100	100	300
Miscellaneous	25	25	25	75
Dividend paid	700	—	—	700
Purchase of equipment	—	1000	—	1000
Total	$3215	$4150	$3750	$11115
Excess (deficiency) of cash available over disbursements	(140)	(475)	975	160
Financing:				
Borrowing	240	575		815
Repayments			(815)	(815)
Interest[a]			30.56	(30.56)
Total	$240	$575	$(845.56)	$ 30.56
Cash, ending	$100	$100	$129.44	$129.44

[a] A815 × 0.15 × 3/12 = $30.56
$240 × 0.15 × 3/12 = 9.00
$575 × 0.15 × 1/6 = 14.38

Total interest expense $53.94

$(9.00 + 14.38) = $23.38 is the accrued interest which is a balance sheet item.

BUDGETED INCOME STATEMENT

	$	$
Sales revenue Schedule 1		
Less variable expense:		
Commission	700	7700.00
Contribution margin		6300.00
Wages and salaries	900	
Utilities	300	
Insurance expired	60	
Depreciation	900	
Miscellaneous	75	
Interest	53.94	2288.94
Income for quarter ended 30 June 19X1		$4011.06

BUDGETED BALANCE SHEET 30 JUNE 19X1

	$		$
Share capital	5000.00	$(2700+1000)$	3700.00
P & L A/C[a]	3931.06	Less depreciation	900.00
Current liabilities:		Total fixed assets	2800.00
Creditors (50% × $3200)	1600.00	Current assets:	
Accrued interest	23.38	Debtors (0.25 × $4500 + 0.75 $ × 6000)	5625.00
		Inventory (520 units × $5)	2600.00
		Cash Schedule 5	129.44
		Insurance unexpired $(160-60)$	100.00
	$11254.44		$11254.44

[a]
```
P & L A/C at 30 June
Balance, 31 March          620.00
      Add net income      4011.06
                          --------
                          4631.06
Less dividend declared     700.00
                          --------
              Balance $3931.06
```

COMMENTS

Observe that the master budget contains not only, e.g. the budgeted cash collection, but the projected income and balance statements as well.

12.17 Summary

Budgetary planning means the preparation of individual budgets by the divisions of the firm. A budget is constrained by a principal budget factor. The sales forecast plays a crucial role in the budget preparation.

Budgetary Planning

The various budgets of a firm may be: (i) sales budget; (ii) production budget; (iii) raw material budget; (iv) labour budget; (v) factory expense budget; (vi) inventory budget; (vii) capital expenditure budget; and (viii) cash budget. These budgets are interrelated, and when co-ordinated lead to the master budget.

The master budget is an 'anchor instrument'—it can be used as a reference for goal determination by the various units of the firm.

Bibliography

Davidson, S. et al. (1978) *Managerial Accounting: An Introduction to Concepts. Methods and Uses* (Dryden Press) ch. 9.
Horngren, C. T. (1977) *Introduction to Management Accounting*, 4th edn, ch. 6, p. 147.
Moore, C. L. and Jaedicke, R. J. (1976) *Managerial Accounting*, (South-Western Publishing Co.) ch. 17.
Ronen, J. (1975) 'Budgets as Tools of Control and Motivation', in J. L. Livingstone (ed.), *Managerial Accounting: The Behavioural Foundations* (GRID) pp. 157–65.
Tosi, H. (1975) 'The Human Effects of Managerial Budgeting Systems', in J. L. Livingstone (ed.), *Managerial Accounting: The Behavioural Foundations* (GRID) pp. 139–56.

Problems

12.1 Kerry-Blue Ltd is a company manufacturing two products using one type of material and one grade of labour. Shown below is an extract from the company's working papers for the next period's budget:

Product	R	B
Budgeted sales (units)	3000	4500
Budgeted material consumption per product (Wg)	6	2
Budgeted material cost ($3 per kg)		
Standard hours allowed per product (hr)	5	5

The budgeted wage rate for the direct workers is $4 per hour for a 44-hour week, overtime premium is 50 per cent and there are 65 direct operatives. The target productivity ratio (or efficiency ratio) for the productive hours worked by the direct operatives in actually manufacturing the product is 90 per cent; in addition, the amount of non-productive downtime is budgeted at 20 per cent of the productive hours worked.

There are 12 5-day weeks in the budget period, and it is anticipated that sales and production will occur evenly throughout the whole period. At the beginning of the period it is anticipated that the stocks will be:

Product	Units
K	1050
B	1200
Raw material	3700 kg

The target closing stocks, expressed in terms of the anticipated activity during the budget period, are:

Product	Days' sales
K	15 days
B	20 days
Raw material	10 days' consumption

REQUIRED

(a) Calculate the material purchase budget and the wage budget for the direct workers, showing both quantities and values for the next period
(b) Describe the additional information required in order to calculate the weekly cash disbursements for materials and wages during the above budget period

ACCA, PE, Accounting 2 costing, June 1981.

12.2 ABC Ltd manufactures three products from three basic raw materials in three departments. The company operates a budgetary control system, and values its stocks of finished goods on a marginal cost basis. From the data given below, you are required to produce for the month of June 19X9:

(a) Production budget
(b) Material usage budget
(c) Purchases budget
(d) Profit and loss account for each product and in total.

Budgeted data for June 19X9:

Product	A	B	C
	$	$	$
Sales	1500000	1080000	1680000
Stock of finished products at 1st June 19X9 (units)	3000	2000	2500
Department:	1	2	3
	$	$	$
Fixed production overhead	239000	201300	391200
Direct labour hr	47800	67100	65200
Direct materials [TYPE]	DM 11	DM 21	DM 31
Stock at 1 Jun 19X9 (units)	24500	20500	17500

The company is introducing a new system of inventory control which should reduce stocks. The forecast is that stocks at 30 June 19X9 will be reduced as follows: raw material by 10 per cent, finished products by 20 per cent.

Fixed production overhead is absorbed on a direct labour hour basis. It is expected that there will be no work-in-progress at the beginning or end of the month.

Administration cost is absorbed by products at a rate of 20 per cent of production cost, and selling and distribution cost is absorbed by products at a rate of 40 per cent of production cost.

Profit is budgeted as a percentage of total cost

Product	%
A	25
B	12½
C	16⅔

Budgetary Planning

Standard cost data, per unit of product:

Product per unit		A	B	C
	$			
Direct material				
DM 11	2.00	5	–	12
DM 21	4.00	–	10	9
DM 31	1.00	5	5	–

	Rate Per hr	hr	hr	hr
Direct wages Department:				
1	2.50	4	2	2
2	2.00	6	2	3
3	1.50	2	4	6
		$	$	$
Other variable cost		10	20	15

ICMA, PS, Part 1, Cost Accounting 2, May 1979.

12.3 At the Purcell Co. Ltd a proposed expansion, which would entail the setting up of a separate department to produce a new product, had previously been rejected on various (non-financial) grounds. However, the project was being re-examined. Details of the proposed expansion are as follows:

(i) A new department would be set up
(ii) Planned sales and production quantities are shown in following table:

PLANNED SALES AND PRODUCTION QUANTITIES

000 UNITS

Month	Sales quantity	Production quantity	Month	Sales quantity	Production quantity
Jan	Nil	6	Apr	10	21
Feb	4	8	May	14	22
Mar	6	14	Jun	18	21
			July onward	20	20

(iii) Standard labour costs are $5 per unit produced, but there is a guaranteed minimum wage payment per month of $75000; any production in excess of 20000 units in any one month will cause additional labour costs of 50 per cent per unit on the excess production only; all wage payments will be made in the month during which production takes place

(iv) Raw materials will usually be purchased, on 1 month's credit, in the month preceding manufacture, but the raw materials for the production of both January and February will be obtained early in January; raw materials cost will be $7 per unit

(v) Delivery cost will be $1000 per month plus $2 per unit sold, paid for in the month of sale; the $2 charge per unit relates to the amount to be paid to an external carrier for delivery to customers of the goods from Purcell's various central warehouses; the $10000 is a standing charge made by

Purcell's transport department for delivering the goods to warehouses – the transport department will, however, have to incur additional costs of only $2000 per month as a result of the proposed expansion; all delivery costs commence in February

(vi) Overhead cost directly incurred by the new department will be:

    (a) variable production overhead – $2 per unit produced, paid for in the month of production
    (b) fixed production overhead – $12000 per month, including $2000 depreciation; cash expenditure is being paid monthly from January onward

(vii) Overhead costs allocated to the new department will be:

    (a) fixed production overhead – $28000 per month
    (b) administration cost – $25000 per month

This allocated overhead is apportionment of general overhead, none of which will alter as a result of the expansion

(viii) Sales price per unit will be $20; the standard cost of production, based on the long-term monthly production, is $16:

	$	$
Direct labour		5
Direct materials		7
Variable overhead		2
Fixed production overhead:		
directly incurred	0.6	
allocated	1.4	
		2
		$16

This standard cost is to be used for stock valuation purposes

(ix) Sales are to be made on 2 months' credit, however, it is felt that the following sales payment pattern will be operative:

% of sales
60   paid for in accordance with credit terms
30   paid 1 month late
10   paid 2 months late

There are no settlement discounts.

Purcell's managing director states 'The main reason for reconsidering this expansion is liquidity. Purcell Ltd is expected to have a low cash balance at the end of July, when we were committed to pay for substantial capital commitments already entered into. This expansion should help to provide the needed funds. However, profit is also important, and so I need to know by how much Purcell Ltd will be better off as a result of this expansion. Just how much profit will appear in the accounts of the new department?'

REQUIRED

(a) For the period January–July, ascertain:

    (i) the profit which will appear in the management accounts as relating to the new department
    (ii) the incremental benefit to Purcell Ltd as a result of the expansion.

(b) Using an appropriate cash forecast, calculate the effect the expansion will have on Purcell Ltd's cash balance as at the end of July.

ACCA, PE, Section 2, Paper 14, Accounting 5, Management Accounting, December 1981.

Budgetary Planning

12.4

REQUIRED

For a company making one product, produce:

(a) budgeted production requirement (in units) for each of the months March, April and May
(b) budgeted purchase requirements of raw material (in units) for each of the months March and April
(c) budgeted profit and loss statement for April
(d) cash forecast for April

The following data are available as at 1 March:

1. Budgeted sales:

Mar	180000
Apr	240000
May	250000
Jun	230000

    The selling price is $2 per unit

    Sales are invoiced twice per month, in the middle of the month and on the last day of the month; terms are 2 per cent for 10 days and net 30 days
    Sales are made evenly through the month, and 50 per cent of sales are paid within the discount period; the remaining amounts are paid within the 30-day period, except for bad debts which average $\frac{1}{2}$ per cent of gross sales
    Estimated cash discounts and bad debts are treated as deductions from sales in the company's profit and loss statements

2. Stocks of finished goods were 36000 units on 1st March; the company's rule is that stocks of finished goods at the end of each month should represent 20 per cent of their budgeted sales for the following month
    No work-in-progress is held

3. Stocks of raw materials were 45600 kg on 1 March; the company's rule is that at the end of each month a minimum of 40 per cent of the following month's production requirements of raw materials should be in stock
    Payments for raw materials are to be made in the month following purchase, and materials can be bought only in lots of 40000 kg, or multiples thereof

4. The standard production cost of the product, based on a normal monthly production of 230000 units, is:

	Cost $per unit
Direct materials ($\frac{1}{2}$ kg per unit)	0.50
Direct wages	0.40
Variable overhead	0.20
Fixed overhead	0.10
Total	$1.20

    Fixed overhead includes $8000 per month depreciation on production plant and machinery; any volume variance is included in cost of sales

5. Production salaries and wages are paid during the month in which they are incurred

6. Selling expenses are estimated at 10 per cent of gross sales; administration expenses are $60000 per month, of which $800 per month relates to depreciation of office equipment; selling and administration expenses and all production overhead are paid in the month following that in which they are incurred

7. The cash balance is expected to be $12000 on 1 April

ICMA, PS, Part III, Management Accounting 1, November 1980.

12.5 Dyer Ltd manufactures a variety of products using a standardised process which takes 1 month to complete. Each production batch is started at the beginning of a month and is transferred to finished goods at the beginning of the next month. The cost structure, based on current selling prices, is

	%	%
Sales price		100
Variable cost		
Raw materials	30	
Other variable cost	40	
Total variable cost—used for stock valuation		70
Contribution		30

Activity levels are constant throughout the year and annual sales, all of which are made on credit, are 2.4 million. Dyer is now planning to increase sales volume by 50 per cent and unit sales price by 10 per cent. Such expansion would not alter the fixed cost of 50000 per month, which includes monthly depreciation of plant of 10000. Similarly raw material and other variable cost per unit will not alter as a result of the price rise.

In order to facilitate the envisaged increases, several changes would be required in the long term. The relevant points are:

(i) Average credit period allowed to customers will increase to 70 days
(ii) Suppliers will continue to be paid on strictly monthly terms
(iii) Raw material stocks held will continue to be sufficient for 1 month's production
(iv) Stocks of finished goods held will increase to 1 month's output or sales volume
(v) There will be no change in the production period and 'other variable cost' will continue to be paid for in the month of production
(vi) The current end of month working capital position is:

	$000	$000
Raw materials	60	
WIP	140	
Finished goods	70	270
Debtors		200
		470
Creditors		60
Net working capital—excluding cash		$410

Compliance with the long-term changes required by the expansion will be spread over several months. The relevant points concerning the transitional arrangements are:

(i) Cash balance anticipated for the end of May is $80000
(ii) up to and including June all sales will be made on 1 month's credit; from July, all sales will be on the transitional credit terms:

%
of sales

60 will take 2 months' credit
40 will take 3 months' credit

Budgetary Planning

(iii) sales price increase will occur with effect from August's sales
(iv) production will increase by 50 per cent with effect from July's production; raw material purchases made in June will reflect this
(v) sales volume will increase by 50 per cent from October's sales

REQUIRED

(a) Show the long-term increase in annual profit and long-term working capital requirements as a result of the plans for expansion and a price increase (costs of financing the extra working capital requirements may be ignored)
(b) Produce a monthly cash forecast for June–December, the first 7 months of the transitional period.
(c) Using your findings from (a) and (b) above make brief comments to the management of Dyer Ltd on the major factors concerning the financial aspects of the expansion which should be brought to their attention

Assume that there are 360 days in a year, and that each month contains 30 days

ACA, PE, Section 2, Paper 14, Accounting 5, Management Accounting, June 1981.

12.6 ABC plc is experiencing cash flow problems. The managing director asks you to devise a system to improve the company's ability to budget its cash position for one month ahead.
   An examination of past data products the following information:

Cash expenditure

(i) The company maintains a strict policy of payment for raw material supplies 1 calendar month after receipt of the goods
(ii) It has certain fixed monthly cash payments for all other expenditures than wages and salaries amounting to 30000 per month
(iii) Wages and salaries are in the main a fixed monthly cash expense, but there is an element which varies directly with the actual invoiced sales for each month
   The fixed component of the wages and salaries bill amounts to 30000 per month, with the variable element averaging 15 per cent of actual invoiced sales

After analysing this relationship further it is determined that it has:

> coefficient of determination value of 0.81
> standard error of the estimate value of 5000
> standard error of the regression coefficient value of 0.0009

Cash revenue

On average 60 per cent of customers pay their invoices one calendar month after their receipt and the remaining 40 per cent pay the invoices 2 calendar months after their receipt.

Data for the last 3 months reveals:

	Actual (invoiced) sales $000	Raw material purchases $000
Feb	150	60
Mar	165	70
Apr	140	55

REQUIRED

(a) Estimate the change in the company's cash position in May
(b) Estimate the limits on the change in the cash balance based on establishing the 95 per cent confidence intervals for cash expenses (the t-statistic for the 95 per cent confidence interval = 2.074 for the expense estimate)

(c) Explain the meaning of the terms 'coefficient of determination' and 'standard error of the regression coefficient' in the context of the above example

ICMA, PS, Part I, Qualitative Techniques, May 1981.

12.7 You have taken up at 1 November 19X7 an appointment as the managing accountant with a company manufacturing mainly for export. You arrive to find there is a cash crisis. The company had promised to repay a 1 October bank overdraft of $50000 by the year end. This had been agreed on the basis of expected profits of $164000 for the last quarter, as shown in section A below. The overdraft, however, had actually increased substantially at the end of October.

REQUIRED

Using the additional data provided in section B:

(a) prepare a cash budget separately for October, November and December 19X7
(b) explain briefly why the bank overdraft increased in October
(c) calculate whether or not the overdraft can be cleared by the year end

SECTION A

PRODUCT COST SHEET

	$ per unit
Up to 22000 units per month	
Direct materials	8
Direct wages	2
Direct expenses	1
	11

Over 22000 units per month

Direct wages and expenses increase by 50% on incremental quantities

Sales 10X7–8:

	Actual 000 units		Forecast 000 units
Jul	20	Nov	30
Aug	20	Dec	26
Sept	20	Jan	30
Oct	30	Feb	34

Profit forecast 4th quarter 19X7:

			$		$000	$000
Sales revenue	86000	@	15.00			1290
Direct cost	66000	@	11.00		726	
	20000	@	12.50		250	
						976
Contribution						314
Overhead cost:						
Production					90	
General administration					24	
Marketing					36	
						150
						164

Budgetary Planning 215

SECTION B

Work-in-progress takes one month to complete, direct materials are received at the commencement of each month, and the labour is spread evenly throughout the period

Finished goods are held in warehouse for 1 month for export packaging and delivered the following month

Customers' payments are received 10 per cent at the end of the month following despatch, 80 per cent at the end of the next subsequent, and the balance 1 further month later

Direct materials are paid for at the end of the month following their receipt

Direct and indirect expenses payments are made during the month they are incurred, except as indicated below

Production overhead includes:

(i) 60000 per year for rent which is paid twice a year in advance on 15 May and 15 November
(ii) 120000 per year for depreciation

Both of these are spread in equal monthly segments

Marketing overhead includes $36000 per year for sales commission, which is charged out monthly, but paid in arrears on 20 December

Direct wages are paid weekly in arrear, and it can be assumed that at each month end one-quarter of that month's cost is unpaid

There have been no changes in selling prices since July 19X7

Taxation should be ignored

ICMA, PS, Part III, Management Accounting 2, November 1977.

12.8 At the end of April 19–8, CD Ltd, which supplies a component to leading manufacturers in a segment of the engineering industry, fears that its largest customer EF Ltd is likely to be subject to a strike. This strike is expected to last from 1 May–31 July 19X8, during which time EF Ltd will be unable to purchase any components from CD Ltd.

CD Ltd is considering two possible plans for dealing with this situation:

PLAN A

To continue producing at its normal (effectively maximum) level of $100000 worth per month of the component, putting the unsold production into stock

If this is done, it will have enough stock to enable it to meet the higher demand from EF Ltd during August

PLAN B

To produce at the normal level during May, to stop production during June and July, and to re-start at the normal level in August

If this is done, it will be able to meet the higher level of demand from EF Ltd during August only

The following additional information is available:

1. Profit and loss statements for the year 31 January 19X8 and the 3 months to 30 April 19X8 (Appendix 1)

2. Balance sheets as at 31 January 19X8 and 30 April 19X8 (Appendix 2)

3. Budgeted monthly income statement for period May–August, if normal production is maintained (Appendix 3)

4. It is the company's practice to absorb fixed production costs into finished goods
   If, however, no goods are produced, fixed production costs for that month would be charged to profit and loss account
   Selling and administration costs can be regarded as fixed and charged to profit and loss account

5. Direct wages are paid in the months in which they are incurred
   Overhead is paid 1 month after it is incurred
6. Assume that selling prices remain constant over the period, and that tax is chargeable at 50 per cent

REQUIRED

(a) Prepare a cash forecast for the total 4 month period 1 May 19X8–31 August 19X8 for the company, if:

   (i) plan A were adopted
   (ii) plan B were adopted

(b) Prepare a balance sheet for the company as at 31 August 19X8, assuming that plan B were adopted
(c) Briefly identify the factors that are likely to influence the company's decision in favour of plan A or plan B

ICMA, PS, Part I, Management Accounting 1, May 1978.

APPENDIX 1

PROFIT AND LOSS STATEMENTS

	Year ended 31 Jan 19X8		3 months ended 30 Apr 19X8	
	$000	$000	$000	$000
Sales		1058.4		297.1
Cost of sales:				
Direct materials	236.7		66.1	
Direct wages	205.2		61.8	
Other expense	158.1		38.0	
		600.0		165.9
Selling and administration expense		252.4		69.4
Total		852.4		235.3
Profit before tax		$206.0		$61.8

APPENDIX 2

BALANCE SHEETS

	As at 31 Jan 19X8		As on 30 Apr 19X8	
	$000	$000	$000	$000
Fixed assets:				
Plant and machinery	637.3		637.3	
Less: Accumulated depreciation	140.1		158.1	
		497.2		479.2
Current assets:				
Stocks:				
Raw materials	19.2		22.0	
Finished goods	19.3		21.4	
	38.5		43.4	
Debtors	92.1		106.2	
Cash	111.2		99.2	
		241.8		248.8
		739.0		728.0
Issued capital	450.0		450.0	
Profit and loss account	140.6		158.7	
		590.6		608.7
Current liabilities:				
Trade creditors	62.2		64.4	
Other current liabilities	30.3		30.0	
Tax due	55.9		24.9	
		148.4		119.3
		739.0		728.0

APPENDIX 3

BUDGETED MONTHLY INCOME STATEMENT MAY–AUGUST 19X8 IF NORMAL PRODUCTION MAINTAINED

	$000	$000
Sales		100
Cost of sales:		
Direct materials	22	
Direct wages	20	
Fixed production cost	12	
		54
Selling and administration cost[a]		24
Total		78
Profit before tax		22

[a] includes depreciation $6000

Chapter 13
Budgetary Control

Control is a central and inescapable feature of all human organisation.
(Tannenbaum, 1968)

13.1 Introduction

The firm's budgetary plans, though not comprehensively self-contained, encompass search procedures for specific goal attainments by management, and thus are the reference base for budgetary control. Budgetary control results from the calculation and evaluation of variances which are derived from the comparison of the actual with the budgeted activities of the firm. Budgetary control thus implies that managers are responsible for mistakes or deviations from the budgetary plans; this is its corrective function. Within that context, budgetary control also means the application of rules for monitoring and harmonising production, administration and the general business and non-business activities of the firm in accordance with the firm's objectives.

The budgetary control system of the firm relies on (i) feedback information; (ii) variance analysis; (iii) a report format which shows the variances that should be brought to the attention of a particular manager.

13.2 Feedback information

Feedback information is best understood from a comparison with engineering systems. Central heating and temperature regulators are examples. The automatic control system of the human body also provides an example of a negative feedback system. These systems are homeostatic, i.e. they return to their preset condition.

A common feedback model is the thermostat, where the differences between the actual and the desired warmth are used as a signal for automatically changing the boiler activity (see Figure 13.1).

Figure 13.1 shows that the controller picks up the error signal or variance from the

Budgetary Control

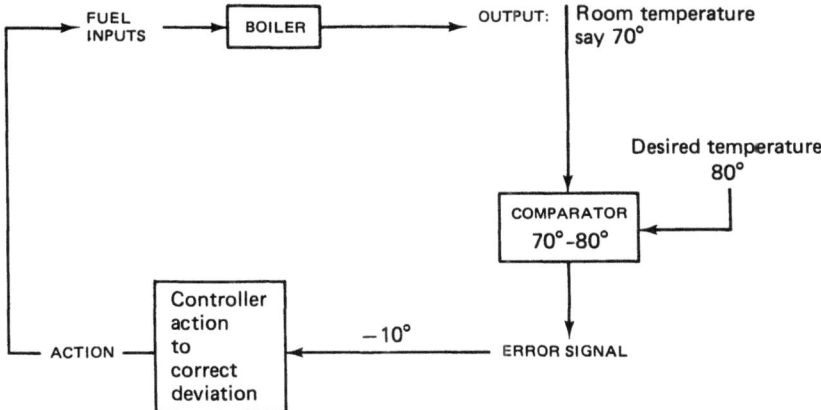

Figure 13.1 Thermostat model

comparator, which compares the actual and desired temperature and automatically alters the fuel inputs. By the use of feedback (the output of the system) the actual temperature thus causes changes in the inputs to the system.

Assume that the output of the system is a report of actual material prices, then the error signal is a price variance and the responsible manager becomes the controller. Observe, too, that this also illustrates that past performance is monitored in an automatic manner. In a similar way, if a standard costing system were in operation, it is obvious that it could be used to guide future action if past mistakes (once identified) can be avoided in the future.

13.3 Usefulness of feedback data

Feedback data can change the future plans of the firm given the model, change the model itself, or change the prediction method that provides input to the model. No corrective action is possible without feedback. Feedback, in an accounting sense, provides management with information about the way the system is operating, so that the variances between the actual performance and the desired level of performance can be assessed.

13.4 Usefulness of variance analysis

Variance analysis is useful to management in three ways.

(i) The calculation of variances at intervals within the budget period will give warning signals of the divergencies from the budgeted plan; appropriate action can then be taken by management to correct the situation

(ii) The calculation of variances at the end of a period generally indicates that the plans were inappropriate in various ways. This information is useful to management in the formulation of future plans

(iii) The calculation of variances enable management to evaluate the performances of individuals, and thus is useful in the determination of individual rewards and screening.

13.5 Report format of variance analysis

Just as the contribution format facilitates intelligent appraisal of the firm, so the report format of variance analysis can show the variances which are under the control of a particular manager. The procedure can be accomplished by distinguishing between the causes which are within the control of management, and those which are not. This leads to the concepts of controllable and uncontrollable cost, and management by exception.

13.6 Controllable and uncontrollable cost

The managers of the firm do influence cost. Controllable cost is a cost items that is directly influenced by a manager within a given time period. In practice, this idea is less clearcut. A cost item can, however, be charged to a manager where such a person has control over the acquisition and use of the resource. The purchase manager is for example responsible for the price at which the materials are bought; the production manager is responsible for the quantity used.

The cost items which are caused by factors outside the sphere of a particular manager are called uncontrollable costs. A composite wage rate, for example, is not under the control of the production manager. A variance caused by a change in the wage rate should thus be shown as uncontrollable variance in his variance report, but as a controllable variance in the report for the production unit.

13.7 Management by exception

This is a principle which focusses attention on any significant deviation from the budgeted plan. The logic of the idea is that the managers of the firm should not waste time on those activity areas that are proceeding according to plan; it is those activities that are not proceeding according to plan that are shown up by variance analysis.

13.8 Variance analysis

Variance analysis involves simple, arithmetical calculations which show the divergence of the actual from the planned results. The purpose behind the calculations is to find out the cause of each divergence. Where the actual cost incurred is greater than the budgeted cost, the variance is called unfavourable (U). Where the actual cost incurred is less than the budgeted cost, the variance is favourable (F). Where there is equality between budgeted and actual cost, no variance results.

The variance which occurs, for example, from the budgeted and actual profit is a total or global variance. It is the objective of variance analysis, however, to separate out and distinguish the separate elements which cause the global variance.

For the single input case, a general model exists which aids variance analysis. The model which shows the calculation of the quantity and price variance, for example, is shown in Figure 13.2. It applies to direct cost only.

Observe that the model can also be adjusted to accommodate other kinds of headings, and hence is adaptable to other forms of variance calculation.

Budgetary Control

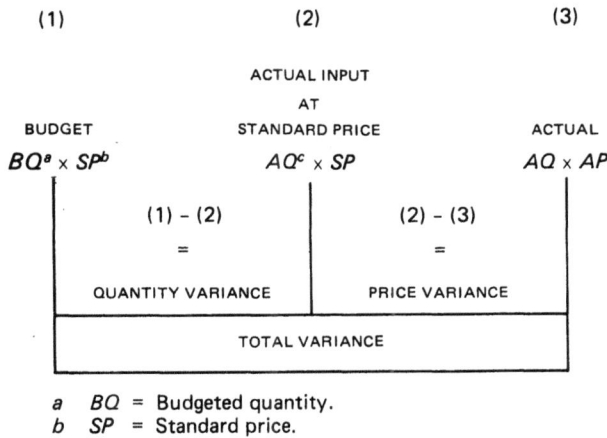

Figure 13.2 Quantity and price variance model

EXAMPLE 13.1

The budget of the Ivor firm, for the month of January, was as follows:

	Units
Production	500
Cost:	$
Materials 500 lb × $10	5000
Labour 500 hr × $1.25	625
Expense	250
Budgeted cost	$5875

The budgeted production was achieved, but the actual cost results for January were:

	$
Materials 500 lb × $12	6000
Labour 400 hr × $1.25	500
Expenses	350
	$6850

REQUIRED

Show via variance analysis and comments why the budgeted cost was exceeded.

SOLUTION

(i) Total variance is $975 unfavourable (U), i.e. $ (6850−$5875)
(ii) Actual cost of materials was $12 per lb, whereas the budgeted cost was $10
(iii) Labour hr used amounted to 400, whereas 500 hr were budgeted for
(iv) Firm's expenses amounted to $350; the budget provided for $250
(v) Total variance $975 U can be decomposed:

(a) Material variance $= AQ - BQ$
$= \$(5000 - 6000) = 1000\,U$

(b) Labour variance = Ahr $-$ Bhr
    = $(625 - 500) = 125 F
(c) Expense variance = $AE - BE$
    = $(250 - 350) = 100U

                    9750 U

Note that in terms of the previous model, the material variance is entirely due to price changes (500 lb × $2) and the labour variance is entirely due to usage (100 h × $1.25).

13.9 Price and quantity variance

The managers of firms make two types of decision which are important for cost control – the price and quantity decision. An important factor in variance analysis of this nature is the distinction made between price and quantity or usage variance. The solution to Example 13.2 below shows how the price and quantity variances are calculated, while the solution to Example 13.3 shows both variance calculation and the variance report.

EXAMPLE 13.2

The budgeted production of dept D1 of the Ivor firm for an accounting period was 2500 units of a standard product. The budget for the period required 2 lb of material (m) which was priced for the budget purposes at $3 per lb.
 The results at the end of the accounting period showed that the production of the 2500 units utilised 5050 lb of (m) which had cost $3.50 per lb.

REQUIRED

Calculate the price and quantity variances.

SOLUTION

The model is shown in Figure 13.3.

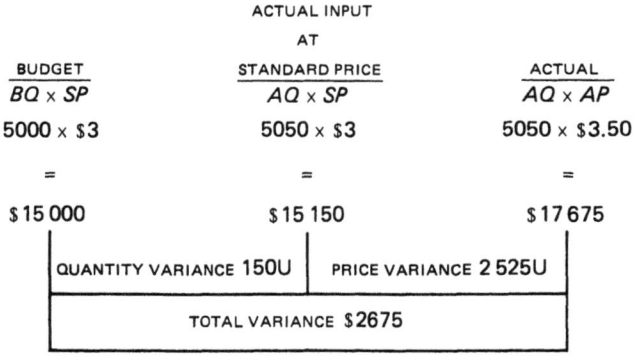

Figure 13.3 Ivor firm – Quantity and price variance model

Budgetary Control

EXAMPLE 13.3

A single product is processed in dept D2, which is a cost centre of the Ivor firm. The department's budget for February was:

	Units
Production	2500
	$
Components 2500 × $2	5000
Labour 4000 × $1.25	5000
Variable expense	250
Budgeted cost	$10250

During that month, half of the working days were lost because of a strike. The strike was settled by a wage increase of $0.50 per hour.

The actual cost of D2 for February was:

	Units
Production	1280
	$
Components	
1300 × $2.10	2730
Labour 1800 hr × $1.75	3150
Variable expense	125
Actual cost	$6005

REQUIRED

Calculate the relevant variances, and show the variance report.

SOLUTION

First, calculate the effect of the strike on budgeted cost:

	ORIGINAL BUDGET	BUDGET REVISION
	Units	Units
Production	2500	1250
Cost:	$	$
Components	5000	2500
Labour	5000	3500ª
Variable expense	250	125
	$10 250	$6125

ª 2000 hr × $1.75 = $3500.

The variance due to the strike action is:
$(10250 − 6125) = $4125

The other variances are now calculated:

(i) Labour usage variance = $(BQ - AQ) \times AR$
$= (2000 - 1800) \times \$1.75 = \$350$ F

(ii) Material variance = $(BQ - AQ) \times SP$
  $= (1250 - 1300) \times \$2 = \$100U$
(iii) Material price variance = $(SP - AP) \times AQ$
  $= \$(2.00 - 2.10) \times 1300 = \$130U$
(iv) Total variance = Revised budget cost – actual cost
  $= \$(6125 - 6005) = 120 F$

Based on the above analysis, the variance report will be:

DEPT D1 – VARIANCE REPORT FOR FEBRUARY

	$
Budgeted cost	10250
Less: Uncontrollable cost of strike	4125
	6125
Favourable controllable labour usage	350
	5775
Add controllable variances	
Material usage	100
Material price	130
Actual cost	$6005

COMMENT

The $4125 which we showed as uncontrollable above could have been avoided by paying the increase earlier. Examined in that way, the cost would be a 'controllable' one.

The direct cost variances examined above are not the only variances that require managerial attention and control. The other variances are interwoven with the general activities of the firm, and are given attention below.

13.10 Nature of overhead variance

Overhead variance occurs when the actual level of activity differs from the budgeted level, and when the actual overhead expenditure differs from the expenditure budgeted for that level of activity. Like everything else in cost accounting, the variance procedure is simply to separate the overhead into a fixed and variable element, and then to analyse each separately.

13.11 Variable overhead variance

Although the variable overhead varies directly with the level of production, the expected cost for the budgeted output can still be calculated, with the associated standard rate of variable cost per unit of output. If the actual variable cost proves to be more (or less) than the standard cost, the difference is termed a variable overhead expenditure variance. If the variable overhead varies with labour hours, an efficiency variance arises. This occurs when a given input of labour produces more (or less) than the budgeted output.

Budgetary Control

13.12 Absorption of fixed overhead

The fixed overhead absorption rate (FOHAR) is based on the formula:

$$\text{FOHAR} = \frac{\text{Budgeted fixed overhead}}{\text{Budgeted level of activity}}$$

As was shown in Ch. 3, the budgeted level of activity can be calculated from many bases.[1] If, however, the actual level of activity varies from the budget, the overhead will be over or under absorbed.

13.13 Fixed overhead variance

The difference between the actual and the budgeted amount of overhead is an expenditure variance. The variation in the level of activity does not cause any difference in the amount of expenditure, since the fixed overhead, by definition, is independent of the level of activity. A variation, however, will give rise to an under or over recovery of overheads if the absorption model is used. The calculated figure from the fixed overhead recovered by actual production and the budgeted overhead will give rise to a volume variance.

The volume variance can be analysed into its various elements: (i) efficiency; (ii) idle time; (iii) capacity. Examples, and the calculation of those variances are shown in Ch. 14.

13.14 Variance calculation by adjusting the budget

This is best shown by an example and comment.

EXAMPLE 13.4

The data below is the budgeted and actual cost of Department D3 for March, for the Ivor firm

	Budget	Actual
Production	Units 8000	Units 10000
Cost:	$	$
Material	40000	45000
Labour	32000	40000
Overhead:		
Fixed	10000	12000
Variable	15000	17300
	$97000	$114300

---

[1] This is examined again in Ch. 14, where reasons are given for the choice of a sensible base rate.

COMMENT

The budgeted cost can be expressed as an amount per unit of output, as follows:

	Budgeted cost per unit $
Materials	5.000[a]
Labour	4.000
Overhead:	
Fixed	1.250
Variable	1.875
	$12.125

[a] $40 000/8000 units = $5.00.

The unit cost is now used to calculate the revised budget, e.g. for the production of 10 000 units. This enables the variances to be simply calculated:
 (i) VO expenditure variance = $VO - AO$
    $(18750 - 17300) = \$1450\,F$
 (ii) FO expenditure variance = $BFO - AFO$
    $(10\,000 - 12\,000) = \$2000\,U$
 (iii) FO volume variance = $FO - BFO$
    $(12\,500 - 10\,000) = \$2500\,F$

Assume that all the variances fall within the manager of the department's sphere. The variance report for his attention is

DEPT D3-VARIANCE REPORT (ABSORPTION APPROACH) FOR MARCH

	$
Budgeted Cost	97000
Add: Budget revision variance $(97\,000 - 121\,250)$[a]	24250
	121250
FOh expenditure variance (U)	2000
	123250
Less: FOh volume variance (F)	(2500)
VOh volume variance (F)	(1450)
Material variance (F)	(5000)
	$114 300

[a] 10 000 units × $12.125 = $121 250.

13.15 Marginal or direct costing method

This method, as Ch. 11 showed, makes use of the contribution model. The fixed overhead and the variable cost is thus shown separately. If the actual activity is more (or less) than the budget, the budget is revised, and no change is made to the amount of the fixed overhead. In fact, only the expenditure variance is calculated for fixed overhead when the marginal or direct costing method is used.

Budgetary Control

The data from Example 13.4 is used to illustrate the direct costing method. The budget per unit information can be restated as follows:

		Units
Production		8000
Cost per unit		Total cost
Variable:	$	$
Material	5.00	40000
Labour	4.00	32000
Overhead	1.875	15000
	$10.875	87000
Fixed cost		10000
		$97000

COMMENT

Since the actual activity is 10 000 units, the budget is readjusted by revising the variable cost. The variances are calculated as follows:

(i) VO expenditure variance = $STVO - AVO$
 = $(18750 - 17300) = \$1450F$
(ii) FO expenditure variance = $BFO - AFO$
 = $(10000 - 12000) = \$2000U$

The variance report using direct costing is:

DEPT D3 – VARIANCE REPORT (DIRECT COSTING) FOR MARCH

Budgeted cost	97000
Add: Budget revision variance	
(8000–10 000) × $10.875	21750
Allowed Expenditure	118750
FO expenditure variance (U)	2000
	120750
Less: VO expenditure variance (F)	1450
	119300
Material price variance (F)	5000
Actual cost	$114300

13.16 Rationale of variance calculation

The calculation of variances is only a part of the control procedures of cost control. As part of a firm's control system, it has benefit and cost associated with it. The calculation and investigation of variances is deisgned to capture (via the feedback mechanism) the desired quality and quantity of the output at the desired cost level. In this way, it attempts to create co-ordination between the different sectors of the firm. The data bank that accrues to the firm provides management with insights on production operations, which facilitate the formulation of intelligent guidelines on management's part. This then permits management by exception.

The investigation of variances also reveals to management whether (i) actual cost is different from the planned cost; (ii) the level of activity has deviated from the plan; (iii) the plan is unrealistic in the light of the current environmental or sociopolitical situation.

13.17 Causes of variance

Variances in the firm generally stem from:
- (i) implementation deviations – the plans are at times unintelligently implemented
- (ii) prediction deviations – mistakes are made in predicting parameter values
- (iii) measurement deviations – mistakes are made in deriving cost items
- (iv) model deviations – failure of the piecemeal models to capture the relevant, economic reality of the firm's environment
- (v) human deviations – inability of the firm's personnel to perform according to the mathematical rigour and solution of the models, even if they replicate economic conditions
- (vi) random deviations – caused by chance events

The calculation of variances and their investigation leads to performance evaluation.

13.18 Evaluation of performance

The achievement of the budget is used as a basis of assessing the performance of managers in highly competitive economies. In such economies, the greater the competition the greater the need to control cost via the budget: such competition forces managers to avoid unfavourable variances.[1] The managers in turn push pressure down the organisation via a modified form of the legalistic, 'master–servant' relationship if unfavourable variances occur.[2]

Evaluations of performance, however, must be measured against the cause of variances. It follows that success in achieving the budget is not an ideal way for the assessment of managers, since the analysis examines activities only for short budget periods. The budget also does not take the off-period behaviour of the firm's employees into account. However, if the negative variances which result from the budget are evaluated intelligently by top managerment, managers' abilities can be gauged.

13.19 Human problems of budgetary control

Becker and Green (1962) emphasised the need for real participation (as opposed to pseudo-participation) for employees in the budgetary planning process. They state that if the budget is planned solely by top management, and is imposed on the lower levels of management, the latter's attitude towards such a budget may be antagonistic. Stedry (1960) also emphasised thus: 'Depending on the conditions under which a budget is drawn the budget can act as a motivating force and can induce better performance from the members of the organisation'. Such analyses

---

[1] Managers should also examine favourable variances (see 11.7 above).
[2] Responsibility and the investigation of variances are examined in ch. 14.

show that participation is conducive to motivation. In spite of that, however, there is the problem of what Cyert and March (1963) termed, 'organisation slack'.

When a manager has participated in the formulation of his budget, his performance will be evaluated in the context of that same budget. Given human behaviour, it can be expected that the manager will introduce bias into his targets to ensure that they are attainable. Gambling (1975) observed that organisation slack 'permits smoother personal relations within the cost centre, to the extent that the supervisor is not compelled to take adverse notice of every infringement of economy, and the worker may trade off more congenial discipline and surroundings against specific demands for improved conditions and rewards.

In spite of Gambling's insight into the matter, the following question can still be posed, since accounting, like theology, seeks after truth. How can budget biases be overcome in the budgetary process? Schiff and Lewin (1970) argued the case for the budget co-ordinator, and Phyrr (1970) argued the case for zero-based budgeting. Skinner (1973) highlighted some pointers which the author believes will eliminate this all-pervading accounting problem. It is important to note, however, that until a science of man has been created and tested empirically, the problem of managerial and employee's biases in the budget preparation will continue.

13.20 Summary

The logic of budgetary control is to harmonise the activities of the firm in accordance with the budget. Feedback data are necessary to do this. Variances emerge from the budgetary system; calculated from simple arithmetical manipulations.

The report format of variance analysis aids managerial decisionmaking. The format presented to managers can be either in the absorption costing or the direct costing format.

Budget variances lead to investigation, and consequently to the evaluation of managerial performance in competitive economies. Success in achieving the budget, however, is not an ideal way for assessing managerial performances, because of its short time span.

There are human problems with budgetary planning. It is generally believed that the budget acts as a motivating force, if the members of the organisation are really involved in its preparation.

'Organisation slack' is real in economic organisations; it can lead to biassed measurements. The control mechanism of management must always consider it when evaluating performance.

Bibliography

Becker, S. and Green, D., Jr (1962) 'Budgeting and Employee Behaviour', *Journal of Business*, 35, no. 4, October, pp. 392–402.
Becker, S. and Green, D., Jr (1964) 'Budgeting and Employee Behaviour: A Rejoinder to a Reply', *Journal of Business*, 37, no. 2, April, pp. 203–5.
Cyert, R. M. and March, J. G. (1963) *A Behavioural Theory of the Firm* (Prentice-Hall).
Gambling, T. E. (1975) *Modern Accounting: Accounting as the Information System for Technological Change* (Macmillan) p. 105.
Phyrr, P. A. (1970) 'Zero-Base Budgeting', *Harvard Business Review*, November–December, pp. 111–21.
Schiff, M. and Lewin, A. Y. (1970) 'The Impact of People on Budgets', *Accounting Review*, 45, no. 2, April, pp. 259–68.
Skinner, F. (1973) *Beyond Freedom and Dignity* (Pelican Books).
Stedry, A. C. (1964) 'Budgeting and Employee Behaviour: A Reply', *Journal of Business*, 37, no. 2, April, pp. 195–202.
Tannenbaum, A. S. (1968) *Control in Organisations* (McGraw-Hill).

Discussion questions

13.1 What role is played by budgetary control in management planning?

13.2 What is flexible budgeting?

13.3 Of what use is variance analysis to management?

13.4 Explain the concepts of 'controllable' and 'uncontrollable' cost.

13.5 Explain the principle of management by exception.

13.6 What are the causes of variances in the firm?

Problems

13.1 'If the budget is to be used as a control device (in the sense of prohibiting excessive expenditures) as well as a motivating device, then it clearly should be tied to the level of aspiration cycle rather than to a time schedule' (Becker and Green, 1962).

REQUIRED

(a) An explanation of this statement
(b) A discussion of the advantages and disadvantages likely to be found if the budgets are related to people's 'aspirations'

ACCA, PE, Section 2, Paper 14, Accounting 5, Management Accounting, December 1976.

13.2 Shown below is the previous month's overhead expenditure and activity, both budget and actual, for one department in a manufacturing company.

	Budget	Actual
Activity:		
Standard hr	8 000	8 400
Fixed overhead:	$	$
Salaries	6 750	6 400
Maintenance	3 250	3 315
Variable overhead:		
Power	17 600	20 140
Consumable materials	6 000	5 960
Indirect labour	4 400	4 480
Total overheads	$38 000	$40 295

The budgeted overhead shown above is based upon the anticipated activity of 8000 standard hours, and it should be assumed that the department's budgeted overhead expenditure and activity occur evenly throughout the year. Variable overheads vary with standard hours produced.

The company operates a standard costing system, and the department's total overheads are absorbed into production using a standard hour rate.

REQUIRED

(a) Calculate the following variances incurred by the department during the previous month:

Fixed overhead volume
Fixed overhead expenditure
Variable overhead expenditure

(b) Draft a suitable operating statement which will assist management in controlling the department's overhead
(c) Explain why the difference between budgeted and actual activity will cause a change in the anticipated profit by the amount of the volume variance calculated in (a) above

ACCA, FE, Part B, Paper 6, Accounting 2, Costing, June 1981.

13.3 The Super Efficient Co. Ltd decided to install and operate a new system of flexible budgetary control and, having studied its cost, ascertained that at an operating level of 1.4 million units, its standard cost amounted to $0.34 per unit, made up as follows:

Materials 30 g @ $0.005 per g	0.15
Labour 12 m @ $0.60 per hr	0.12
Variable expense	0.01
Fixed expense	0.06
	0.34

The company decided also to set a standard selling price per unit of $0.40 (to give a standard profit of $0.60 per unit), and to prepare the budget for its next accounting year on this basis. However, in the course of the year, the directors realised that sales would amount only to 1.2 million units, and so they asked the chief accountant to flex the original budget to take account of this fact, and to give them a new budgeted profit for the year. The eventual outturn for the year was an actual profit of $37000, made up as follows:

	$	$
Sales (1.2 million × $0.45)		540 000
Materials 40 million g @ $0.006 per g	240 000	
Labour 240 000 hr @ $0.70 per hr	168 000	
Variable expense	15 000	
Fixed Expense	80 000	503 000
		37 000

REQUIRED

Prepare a statement showing:

(a) original budget for the year
(b) flexed budget for the year
(c) analysis of the variance between the original budget and the actual results
(d) a short explanation of the meaning of each variance shown

ICA Final, Advanced Accounting III, May 1971.

13.4 Processors Ltd, a manufacturing company in a process industry, prepares an annual budget which it updates after the first 6 months of each financial year. You are given the following information, from which the later budget will be prepared:

Manufacturing cost:
Variable (according to quantity produced)

	Kg	per Ng
Materials	23 000	1 000
Labour	3 60 000	0.80
		per cent
Power	24 00 000	0.01

	Months	$ per month
Fixed		
Works overhead	12	@ 20 000

Distribution cost:
Variable (according to quantity sold)

	Kg	%
Carriage	20 000	2.40
Fixed		$
	Months	per month
Transport office	12	@ 1000
Selling cost		
Fixed	12	@ 7500
Administrative costs:		
Fixed	12	@ 14 000

	Kg	
output and sales	20 000	
selling price		Calculated to show a 20% profit margin on total budgeted cost

The financial year commences on 1 January. During the course of the year to which the above figures relate, prices rise rapidly. It is decided to re-budget for the year, on the assumption that as from 1 July all variable costs are increased by 5, per cent and all fixed costs by 1 per cent.

During the first half of the year, the volume of output and sales is 2½ per cent above budget, and it is estimated that this higher rate will be maintained for the rest of the year if there is no change in selling price. However, if the selling price is raised, it is anticipated that every $0.20 increase in price per kg will result in a decrease of 20.5 kg in the quantity sold in the half year. It is decided to increase price from 1 July by $2.40 per kg.

Assume that stock levels remain constant, and are not affected by changes in output or sales.

REQUIRED

(a) Calculate the initial selling price per kg based on the budget as first prepared (i.e. ignoring events occurring after 1 January)
(b) Prepare a statement showing the revised budgeted profit for the year, taking into account all the above decisions and events

ICA, Final, Advanced Accounting III, May 1971

Chapter 14
Standard Costing

For which of you, intending to build a tower, sitteth not down first and counteth the cost, whether he hath sufficient to finish it? (LUKE 14: 18)

14.1 Introduction

The epigraph quotation highlights the fact that standard costing was in vogue from the time man first began to think of his welfare. The dictionary defines the word 'standard' as 'a definite level of excellence, attainment, or a definite degree of any quality, viewed as a prescribed object of endeavour or as a measure of what is adequate for some purpose'. An accounting definition[1] is 'A predetermined cost calculated in relation to a prescribed set of working conditions, correlating technical specifications and scientific measurement of materials and labour to the prices and wage rates expected to apply during the period to which the standard cost is intended to relate, with an addition of an appropriate share of budgeted overhead' (ICMA, 1974).

Standard cost is a 'should be' cost. Standard cost includes material, labour and overhead cost that is loaded on to a product as it takes shape; standard cost is necessary for planning purposes. This chapter shows the reasons for standards, how they are set, and how variances are calculated and interpreted.

14.2 Types of standard cost

Standard cost can be classified into three main categories: (i) basic standards, (ii) ideal standards, and (iii) attainable standards.

---

[1] From the quotation, it is clear that standard costing adopts the application of engineering concepts to the determination of cost. The statement also implies that by carefully measuring the required physical and human inputs of the firm's production processes, the consumption of production can be measured for a given output. When those consumption factors are multiplied by standard price, the result is a seemingly scientific engineered money cost which serves as a reference measurement against which the actual money cost of the firm is evaluated.

Basic standards are standards held unchanged for long periods of time. They are established for use within the firm for long-term evaluations. They provide an unchanging base for the comparison of actual cost over time with the same standard. As an information tool, basic standards are unimportant in terms of variance analysis, because they are not kept up to date in response to the influence of changing price and changing productivity. From basic standards, however, current standards can be developed.

An ideal standard is one which can be attained under favourable conditions. An ideal standard is applied when management believes that it will enhance motivation; the setting of an ideal standard for labour draws on ergometrics.

Attainable standards for labour show the costs to be incurred under normal production operating conditions. Attainable standards make allowances for normal wastage of materials, machine breakdown and employees' fatigue. Attainable standards are used by most firms as targets for employees. Attainable standards also encompass motivational features.

14.3 Mechanics of standard costing

(i) Standard costs are built up for each major component or product. The costs are recorded on standard cost cards, which itemise the separate elements for direct material, direct labour and factory overhead
(ii) Accounting records are maintained for the collection and analysis of both standard and actual cost
(iii) The variance between actual and standard cost is isolated and evaluated in money terms
(iv) From this, the accounting variance report is prepared; standard costing also employs the concept of the standard hour

14.4 The standard hour

In everyday life, there exist standards of behaviour which are qualitative. In marketing, qualitative standards exist in the form of customer satisfaction. In assessing a purchase possibility, customers are helped if the quality of products from different suppliers are of comparable standard. The accountant needs to make his standards more explicit by quantifying them. He wants to measure output, and be able to compare and aggregate the activities connected with different products; he needs a common standard. In cost accounting there is therefore the standard hour. The standard hour relates to the output of the firm – that is to say, the quantity of output which should be produced in one hour. A standard hour does not measure time; it measures the 'work content of an hour', assuming a constant level of effort, so that we can compare and aggregate different products on the basis of a standard work content.

14.5 Reason for standard costing

Standard costs provide a rationale for the evaluation of actual costs. By its very nature, standard costing is associated with forward planning, hence the setting of standards and their revision calls for detailed studies of the function of the firm. Such analyses create enhanced awareness on

Standard Costing

management's part. The use of standard costing is a means of control, whereby management can delegate responsibility for cost — an established costing system within a firm, enables relevant, low cost data to be obtained by management. Because standard costing is linked with sensible planning, management need not concern itself with those activities that are proceeding in a 'normal' way.

14.6 Setting of standard cost

Standard cost setting requires the establishment of a standard cost for each major component or product produced by the firm. Each product is broken down into its various elements of cost, and standards in dollar units are established.

Table 14.1 shows the build-up of the variable production cost items (in unit dollars) that are required in standard cost planning for the making of a product.

Table 14.1 Variable production cost

Standard direct material cost	$
Standard direct labour cost	
Standard variable overhead cost	
Total variable production cost per unit	$

The elements of Table 14.1 require individual derivation.

14.7 Standard direct material cost

There are three factors which determine the standard cost of materials: (i) specification; (ii) quantity; (iii) price. These items are determined respectively by the design, production and buying departments.

The direct material price standard should reflect the delivered cost of materials, net of discounts. The standard price of 1 lb of the material (m), for example, might be determined:

	$
Purchase price, grade A, in 500 lb quantities	5.48
Freight, by truck, from the supplier's plant	0.25
Receiving and handling	0.07
Less: purchase discount	(0.40)
Standard price per lb	5.40

Observe that the standard price shows a particular grade of the material, which was purchased in a specific lot size and delivered by a particular truck. Allowances also have been taken into account for handling and discounts. The standard price of 1 lb of the material (m) should therefore be $5.40.

The direct quantity standard shows the amount of the material going into each unit of the finished product, as well as an allowance for waste and spoilage. The standard quantity of the material (m) going into a unit of a product may be found by adding suitable allowances to the ideal quantity needed to meet the technical requirements of the product. Technically, a regular table will require four legs, and this may be the quantity called for in the bill of materials provided by the engineer, but the standard quantity may add further allowances to this. A typical calculation may appear as follows:

	lb
Ideal quantity per bill of materials	3.0
Allowance for waste and spoilage	0.2
Allowance for rejects	0.3
Standard quantity per unit of product	3.5

The rejects are those units which are rejected at the final inspection. Once the price and the quantity standard has been established, the cost of the material (m) per unit of the finished product is calculated as follows:

3.5 lb × $5.40 = $18.90 per unit

That figure will appear as one item on the standard cost card of the product.

14.8 Standard direct labour cost

The factors involved in setting a standard direct labour cost for a product are: (i) standard grade of labour; (ii) standard time for a particular operation; and (iii) standard rate of pay, which includes an allowance for fringe benefits and other related costs.

The standard grade of labour is determined by the personnel department, in association with the production department. The standard time is determined by the production department, in conjunction with the work study personnel.

The caclulation might be as follows:

	$
Basic wage rate per hr for grade C labour	10.0
Employment taxes, at 15% of the basic rate	1.5
Fringe benefits, at 20% of the basic rate	2.0
Standard rate per direct hour	$13.50

The work study personnel play an important part in establishing the standard direct labour time required to complete a unit of a product. The work study personnel also take the demands of the unions, who are concerned about employees' welfare, into account. The standard time developed thus includes allowances for refreshments, the personnel needs of employees, clean

Standard Costing

up and machine downtime. The resulting standard time might appear as follows:

	hr
Basic labour time *per* unit	2.5
Allowances for breaks and needs	0.2
Allowances for clean up and machine downtime	0.1
Allowances for rejects	0.2
Standard hr *per* unit of product	3.0 hr

Once the rate and standard time has been set, the standard labour cost per unit of the product can be calculated:

3.0 hr × $13.50 = $40.50 per unit

The figure of $40.50 will be shown with direct materials as one item on the standard cost card of the product.

14.9 Standard variable overhead cost

The standard variable overhead rate is calculated from the formula:

$$\frac{\text{Budgeted variable overhead}}{\text{Budgeted activity}}$$

= Standard variable overhead (VO) absorption rate

The variable overhead may be absorbed on a unit or on an hourly basis. If a unit basis is used, the standard variable cost is equal to the absorption rate. If an hourly basis is used, the absorption rate is multiplied by the standard time for the production of one unit.

From the formula, it is obvious that the standard variable overhead cost is a figure which represents the variable portion of the predetermined overhead rate. If the variable portion of the predetermined overhead rate was $6, and the overhead was applied to units of product on a basis of direct labour hours, the standard variable overhead cost per unit of the product would be:

3.0 hr × $6 = $18 per unit.

Figure 14.1, which represents a standard cost card, summarises the details of the examples.

	(1) STANDARD QUANTITY OF HOURS	(2) STANDARD PRICE $	(3) STANDARD COST (1) × (2) $
Direct materials	lb 3.5	5.40	18.90
Direct labour	hr		
Direct labour	3.0	13.50	40.50
Variable overhead	3.0	6.00	18.00
Total standard cost per unit			$77.40

Figure 14.1 **Standard cost card**

Having established the basics, the general model examined in 13.8 above is used to show how the variances from standards are calculated for the one-product case.

EXAMPLE 14.1

The John-Hill Co. makes a single product. The direct material and the direct labour standard for the product are:

Direct	Standard quantity	Price $	Standard cost $
Materials	8 lb	2	16
Labour	0.5 hr	6 per hr	3

During an accounting period, the following activity took place:

(i) 12000 lb of material were purchased at a cost of $1.50 per lb
(ii) All the material purchased was used to produce 1800 units of the product
(iii) 800 hours of direct labour time were recorded during the period, at a total labour cost of $5000

REQUIRED

Calculate:

(i) material price and quantity variance for the period
(ii) labour rate and efficiency variance for the period

SOLUTION

(i) Figure 14.2 shows the model.

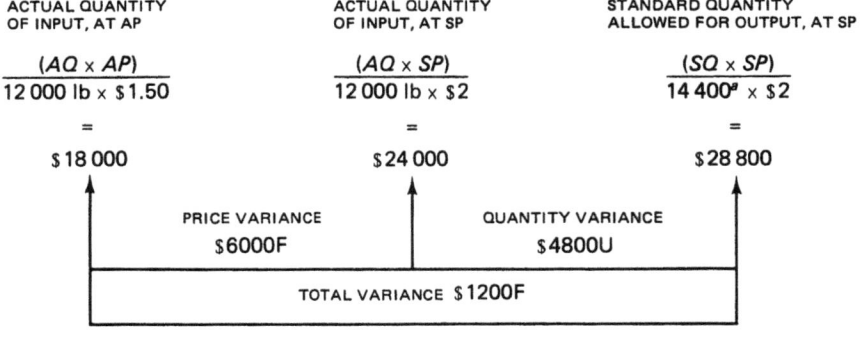

a 1800 units × 8lb = 14400 units.

Figure 14.2 **John-Hill Co.–material price and quantity variance model**

Alternative solution is:

Material price variance
= $(1.50 − 2.00) × 12000 lb   = $6000 F
Material quantity variance
= lb(1200 − 14400) × $2   = $4800 O

(ii) Figure 14.3 shows the model.

Standard Costing

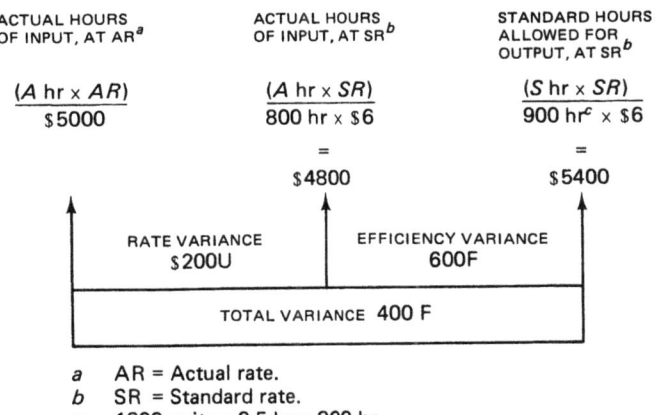

Figure 14.3 John-Hill Co. – labour rate and efficiency variance model

Alternative solution is:

Labour rate variance
= $(6.25^a − 6.00) \times 800$ hr × $200 U
^{a} $5000/800$ hr = $6.25.

Labour efficiency variance
= hr $(800 − 900) \times \$6$ = $600 F

COMMENT

Observe that variance analysis has features of input–output analysis. The input represents the actual quantity and actual prices of direct materials, direct labour and the variable manufacturing overhead used. The output represents the good production of the period, expressed as the standard quantity of the inputs allowed valued at their standard price. By 'standard quantity' is meant the amount of the direct material, direct labour, or variable manufacturing overhead that should have been used to produce what was produced during the period. The standard quantity might be more (or less) than what was actually used; this, of course, depends on the effectiveness or ineffectiveness of the firm's operations, which points inevitably to the causes of the variance(s).

14.10 Causes of variance from standard

The cause of the material price variance can be attributed to (i) a general increase in the market price of the material; (ii) a change in the quality caused by the usual standard quality not being available to the firm; (iii) buying in small quantities, which results in a loss of discount; (iv) inadequate information on supply sources, which results in a price increase for the material.

The quantity variance can occur because of (i) deviation from the planned level caused by a change in handling or loading arrangements; (ii) inability of the management function to measure the actual usage in a precise way.

The rate variance can be caused by (i) a wage agreement, the details of which were not anticipated by management; (ii) wrong grade of labour used; (iii) change in operating conditions; (iv) unscheduled productivity scheme, where employees receive higher wages per hour for producing more output units per hour.

The efficiency variance can happen for several reasons: (i) operations were not performed in accordance with the standard procedures; (ii) amount of output which can be achieved in an hour may have been misjudged when the standard of performance was evaluated; (iii) bottlenecks in the departments, which result in idle-time; (iv) machine breakdown; (v) deviation from planned material quality, which causes a change in the speed of handling and a lag in machine throughput.

Standard cost variances can be associated with managerial responsibility (that aspect was examined in ch. 13). There are, however, other sensitive areas in the standard costing system of the firm, which require managements' attention. An examination of the management – flexible budget nexus is therefore necessary.

14.11 Nature of a flexible budget

A flexible budget is geared towards a range of activity. It is seemingly dynamic. It helps the management function to determine what cost should have been at a particular level of activity. The preparatory steps in drawing up a flexible budget are; (i) Select a suitable measure of activity (eg. units of output); (ii) determine the relevant range over which the activity of the firm is expected to fluctuate during a cost accounting period; (iii) collect data giving the costs which will be incurred over the relevant range; and (iv) analyse the costs into its behavioural cost components, i.e. variable or fixed utilising the appropriate method of analysis selected from those outlined in ch. 8.

14.12 Mechanics of the flexible budget

This is best shown by an example.

EXAMPLE 14.2

Assume that the production of the John-Hill firm normally fluctuates between 9000 and 12000 units each month. Assume also that a study of cost behaviour patterns over the relevant range of the firm shows the variable portion of overhead as:

Cost	Variable cost formula per unit $
Indirect materials	0.20
Power	0.05

Standard Costing

The budget based on the variable cost formula is:

JOHN-HILL FIRM–FLEXIBLE BUDGET FOR . . .[a]

Budgeted production		Units		
	Cost formula	Examples of possible production		
		units 9000	units 10 000	units 12 000
Variable overhead cost:	$	$	$	$
Indirect materials	0.20	1800	2000	2400
Lubricants	0.06	540	600	720
Power	0.05	450	500	600
Total	$0.31	$2790	$3100	$3720

COMMENT

This flexible budget enables the management function to compare actual results for the period against the comparable budget level anywhere within the relevant range. Observe, too, that the management function is not stuck with a single budget, as with the traditional static model format.

14.13 Measurement of activity

In ch. 3, we showed the general nature of the calculation of overhead, but did not specify what was the best base for the firm to use. What is the best base will be viewed differently by each firm; an activity base, however, should be based on the existence of a causal relationship between the activity base and the overhead costs. Why? Because common sense indicates that variable (but not fixed) overhead cost does vary as a result of changes in the activity base. In a machine shop, for example, electricity usage and lubrication need would vary according to the number of machine hours worked. Machine hours, in this case, is the correct base to use in the flexible budget. The activity base should be expressed in units rather than in dollars. Why units? Simply because the dollar is a liar, and because units as a measure of activity are value free, i.e. subject to few distorting influences. The activity base should be simple, and should be understood by the management function who is evaluated by it.

14.14 Fixed overhead analysis

The analysis of fixed overhead differs from that of variable overhead because of the nature of fixed cost. A problem is created in product costing with fixed overhead cost since a given level of fixed overhead cost spread over a small number of units produced will give a higher cost per unit than if the same amount of cost is spread over a larger amount of units. Consider this data:

Month	Fixed overhead (1)	Units produced (2)	Unit cost (3)
	$		
1	10000	5000	2.0
2	10000	2500	4.0
3	10000	1500	6.7

Notice the fluctuating nature of the unit cost. For product costing purposes, the management function must stabilise the fixed portion of the unit cost so that a single unit cost figure can be used for an accounting period, without regard to the month-by-month change in the activity levels. The necessary stability is accomplished through the use of the predetermined overhead rate, which is calculated from:

$$\frac{\text{Estimated total manufacturing overhead cost}}{\text{Denominator activity}}$$

The estimated data come from the flexible budget. The denominator activity is the budgeted activity level for the coming period. Consider the flexible budget for the John-Hill firm shown below:

John-Hill Firm–Machine Dept.

Budgeted machine hr				6000
	Cost formula	Machine hr		
		2000	4000	6000
	Per machine hr			
	$	$	$	$
Variable overhead cost:				
Indirect labour	0.30	600	1200	1800
Lubricants	0.20	400	800	1200
Total	$0.50	1000	$2000	$3000
Fixed overhead cost:				
Depreciation		200	200	200
Supervisory salaries		1000	1000	1000
Insurance		100	100	100
		$1300	$1300	$1300
Total overhead cost variable and fixed		$2000	$3300	$4300

Standard Costing

Assume that the budgeted activity level for the coming period is 6000 hours. This 6000 hours is the denominator activity in the formula. The numerator in the formula is either the variable or fixed cost. From the model, the total predetermined overhead rate is:

$$\frac{\$4300}{6000 \text{ hr}} = \$0.7167 \text{ per machine hr}$$

The variable part is:

$$\frac{\$3000}{6000 \text{ hr}} = \$0.5 \text{ per machine hr}$$

The fixed part is:

$$\frac{\$1300}{6000 \text{ hr}} = \$0.2167 \text{ per machine hr}$$

For every standard machine hour of operations the work-in-process will be charged with $0.7167 of overhead, of which $0.5 will be variable cost, and $0.2167 fixed cost. If a unit of a product is expected to take 2 machine hours to make at standard levels of performance, its cost will contain $0.5 × 2 hr = $1 variable overhead and $0.2167 × 2 hr = $0.433 fixed overhead, a total of $1.433 (or 2 × $0.7167).

There is no doubt that the flexible budget provides the management function with the data needed for calculating the amount of overhead cost that will be charged to the production units, together with the denominator activity figure which is used as a stabiliser of the fixed overhead element of unit cost.

14.15 Application of overhead in standard costing

When standards are in operation in a firm, overhead is applied to work-in-process on the basis of the standard hour allowed for the output of the period, rather than on a basis of the actual number of hours worked. The manufacturing overhead account, for the standard costing system is illustrated in Figure 14.4.

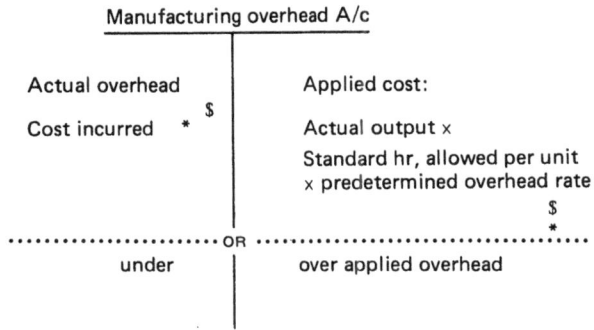

Figure 14.4 Manufacturing overhead A/c – standard costing

The use of standard hours in the calculation of applied cost ensures that every production unit which passes through the manufacturing process bears the same overhead cost, regardless of the time variation that may be expended in its manufacture.

14.16 Fixed overhead variance analysis

The general model again provides the format for the calculation of the fixed overhead variances. It introduces a new term, the 'denominator' volume or activity. This refers to the budgeted activity level for the period. The model is shown in figure 14.5, with the appropriate headings.

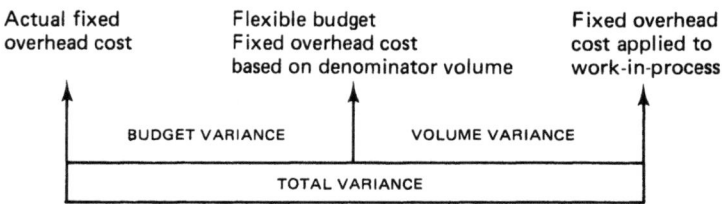

Figure 14.5 Denominator volume/activity model

The budget variance shows the difference between the actual fixed overhead cost and the budgeted fixed overhead cost, as shown in the flexible budget. The budget variance conveys information about changes in price factors, rather than managerial performance.

The volume variance is a measure of the utilisation of plant facilities. It is calculated by comparing the denominator activity figure with the standard hours allowed for the output of the period, and multiplying any difference by the fixed portion of the predetermined overhead rate. It is calculated as follows:

$$\text{Fixed portion of predetermined overhead rate} \times \left(\frac{\text{Denominator}}{\text{hr}} - \frac{\text{Standard}}{\text{hr}} \right) = \frac{\text{Volume}}{\text{variance}}$$

Note that this variance arises when the budgeted activity level is not achieved exactly. Variances examined in earlier sections did not arise directly from a difference in total volume, but were differences that could be defined at the 'per unit' level. Fixed cost, by its fixed nature, does not fit well with a per unit concept.

'Fixed costs per unit' is really a contradiction in terms, and this gives rise to many problems for the cost accountant. The step of establishing standard fixed costs per unit relies on the assumption that the budgeted activity level will be achieved. To the extent that it is not achieved, the volume variance will occur. Therefore (i) if the denominator activity and the standard hours allowed for the output of the period are the same, there is no variance; (ii) if the denominator activity is greater than the standard hours allowed for the output of the period, the volume variance is unfavourable, which points to an underutilisation of the firm's available facilities; (iii) if the denominator activity is less than the standard hours allowed for the output of the period, the volume variance is favourable, which points to an overutilisation of the firm's available facilities.

The solution to Example 14.3 illustrates the salient points of this analysis.

Standard Costing 245

EXAMPLE 14.3

The John-Hill firm operates a standard costing system. The firm manufactures a single product. Information from the flexible budget for a period is:

	hr
Budgeted DLH	1600[a]
	$
Budgeted VO	30 000
Budgeted FO	50 000

[a] Denomination activity level.

During the period, actual results recorded were:

	hr
Actual DLH	13 800
	Standard hr
Standard DLH allowed	14 000
	$
Actual VO	29 000
Actual FO	49 500

The overhead rates are based on standard DLH. At the end of the acounting period, the manufacturing overhead account showed the data in Figure 14.6.

```
          Manufacturing overhead A/c
              $         |         $
  Actual   78 500       | Applied   70 000
           ........     | .....................
            8 500       |
```

Figure 14.6 John-Hill Co. – Manufacturing overhead A/c

REQUIRED

(i) Compute the predetermined overhead rate used during the period
(ii) Show how the $70 000 figure in the manufacturing overhead account was calculated
(iii) Analyse the $8500 under applied overhead figure in terms of variable overhead spending and efficiency variance, and fixed overhead budget and volume variance

SOLUTION

(i) $\dfrac{\$(30\,000 + 50\,000)}{16\,000 \text{ DLH}} = \$5$ per DLH

Variable element $= \dfrac{\$30\,000}{16\,000 \text{ DLH}} = \$1.875$ per standard DLH

Fixed element $= \dfrac{\$50\,000}{16\,000 \text{ DLH}} = \$3.125$ per standard DLH

(ii) 14 000 standard hr × $5 DLH = $70 000

(iii) Variable overhead and fixed overhead variance models are shown in Figures 14.7A and 14.7B

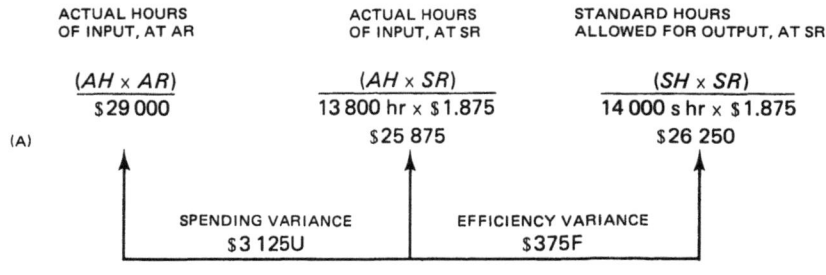

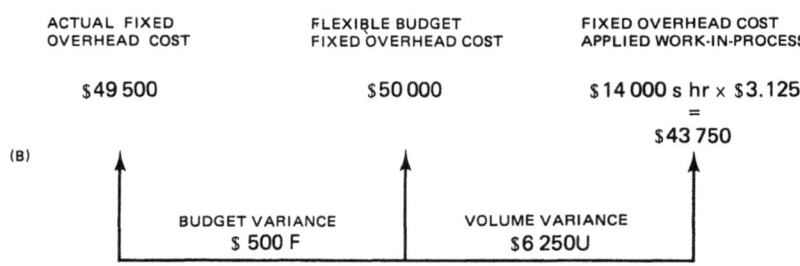

Figure 14.7 Models of (A) variable and (B) fixed overhead variance

An alternative calculation of the fixed overhead variances is:

	$
Budgeted FO	50 000
Actual FO	49 500
	$ 500 F
FO volume variance	
Hr (16 000 – 14 000) × $3.125	= 6250 U

VERIFICATION

	$
VO spending	3125 U
VO efficiency variance	375 F
FO budget variance	500 F
FO volume variance	6250 U
	$8500 U

We turn now to an examination of control ratios.

14.17 Control ratios

Control ratios indicate to the management function how labour and the fixed resources of the firm have effectively (or ineffectively) been used. The control ratios are:

Standard Costing   247

(i) *Activity ratio*, which compares the actual levels of production with the planned level of production. It is expressed as:

$$\frac{\text{Standard hours equivalent of actual production}}{\text{Budgeted output in standard DLH}} \times 100$$

The ratio shows the extent to which actual output corresponds to budgeted output.

(ii) *Efficiency ratio*, which measures the rate of efficiency of the production operations. The actual time taken to achieve the actual production is compared with the time such production should have taken. The ratio is expressed as:

$$\frac{\text{Standard hours equivalent of actual production}}{\text{Actual hours worked}} \times 100$$

(iii) *Capacity ratio*, which gauges the utilisation of the available capacity by comparing the actual hours worked with the budgeted hours. The formula is:

$$\frac{\text{Actual hours worked}}{\text{Budgeted hours}} \times 100$$

The solution to Example 14.4 shows how these ratios are calculated.

EXAMPLE 14.4

A department of the John-Hill firm produces two products X_1 and X_2. The standard time for the production of the two products is respectively 20 and 25 minutes. The budget for a particular month is 12 000 units of X_1 and 14 100 units of X_2.

Durng the particular month, 8600 labour hours were worked and 12 600 units of X_1 and 14 700 units of X_2 were produced.

REQUIRED

Compute the ratios, and comment on them.

SOLUTION

The standard hours equivalent of actual production for the particular month is calculated as follows:
Standard hr:

$$12\,600 \times \frac{20}{60} = 4200\ (X_1)$$

$$14\,700 \times \frac{25}{60} = \underline{6125}\ (X_2)$$

$$\underline{10\,325}$$

The budget in terms of the standard hours is

$$12\,000 \times \frac{20}{60} = 4000\ (X_1)$$

$$14\,100 \times \frac{25}{60} = \underline{5875}$$

$$\underline{9875}$$

$$\text{Activity ratio} = \frac{10\,325}{9875} \times 100 = 105\%$$

The activity ratio shows that the actual level of production exceeded the budget level by 5 per cent.

$$\text{Efficiency ratio} = \frac{10\,325 \times 100}{8600} = 120\%$$

The efficiency ratio implies that the actual hours worked were less than the budgeted hours by 13 per cent.

$$\text{Capacity ratio} = \frac{8600}{9875} = 87\%$$

14.18 Variance analysis in technical firms

In some technical manufacturing firms, various combinations of materials by the management function can be adopted in order to obtain a unit of the finished product. Fabrics, lumber, plastics and some chemicals can be mixed in various ways without affecting the quality of the finished product. This implies that, to some extent, the materials which are put into the process can be substituted in certain proportions for each other.

When a standard costing system is instituted in such firms, the 'standard mix' becomes the tool of managerial evaluation. The standard mix will be the cheapest way of producing a level of output of the correct quality; the standard mix will give rise to a quantity variance, which can be decomposed into a mix and a yield variance.

An important condition for the calculation and evaluation of mix and yield variance is the establishment of a base unit of measurement of the different quantities of the input factors.

The mix variance requires a notional calculation. To arrive at this; we need to ask what the standard cost of the inputs would be if the inputs put into the manufacturing process had been combined in some standard proportion. In setting these proportions, we need to compare directly the quantities of different input materials. An assumption must be made to establish common weights to apply to each type of material. In general, these weightings are based on physical properties (e.g., lb) rather than an economic factor.

A mix variance arises because a greater or lesser proportion of more expensive material was used in the output than was called for by the standard specification.

A yield variance depends on the total amount of input that was used to achieve the given output, and not upon proportions. If a greater (or lesser) total quantity of material inputs was used than was called for by the standard specification, a yield variance arises.

The solution to Example 14.5 shows the necessary steps which are needed to calculate these variances.

EXAMPLE 14.5

A standard batch of products in a chemical process requires inputs in the proportions shown below (the proportions being established in terms of lb of material).

Chemical	Standard proportion	Standard price
	%	$
1	70	5
2	10	12
3	20	26

Standard Costing

A standard production loss of 10 per cent is planned for by management. The actual input quantities and the prices, to produce 950 lb of the output were:

Chemical	Actual input	Actual price	Total cost
	lb	$	$
1	670	6	4020
2	125	10	1250
3	205	25	5125
	1000 lb		$10395

REQUIRED

Calculate the mix and yield variance.

SOLUTION

Step 1 Calculate the data which would appear on the standard cost sheet:

Chemical				
1	0.70×100 =	$70 \times \$5$	=	$350
2	0.10×100 =	$10 \times \$12$	=	120
3	0.20×100 =	20×26	=	520
		100		990
	Normal loss	10		
	Expected output	90 lb		990

Standard cost of 90 lb is: $\dfrac{\$990}{91 \text{ lb}} = \$11$ per lb

Step 2 Calculate the total material cost variance:

	$
Actual cost of 950 lb	10395
Standard cost of 950 lb × $11	10450
	$55 F

Note that the sum of individual variances calculated below will equal $55 F.

Step 3 Determine (i) whether the inputs were purchased at their standard cost, (ii) whether the inputs were used in their standard proportion and (iii) whether the yield from the processes is at the expected level. The insights which result aid the variance calculation. The procedures are as follows:

Material price variance

Actual inputs × $Ap\text{-}Sp$

$$\begin{bmatrix} 670 \\ 125 \\ 205 \end{bmatrix} \times \begin{bmatrix} 1 \\ 2 \\ 1 \end{bmatrix} = \begin{matrix} \$ \\ 670 \text{ U} \\ 250 \text{ F} \\ 205 \text{ F} \end{matrix}$$

Total material price variance $215 U

Mix variance

$$\begin{matrix}\text{Standard}\\\text{quantities}\end{matrix} - \begin{matrix}\text{Actual}\\\text{quantities}\end{matrix} \times SP$$

$$\begin{bmatrix} 700 \\ 100 \\ 200 \end{bmatrix} - \begin{bmatrix} 670 \\ 125 \\ 205 \end{bmatrix} = \begin{bmatrix} 5 \\ 12 \\ 26 \end{bmatrix} \quad \begin{matrix}\$\\ 150\text{ F}\\ 300\text{ U}\\ 130\text{ U}\end{matrix}$$

Total mix variance $280 U

The assumption that proportions are determined in terms of lb of materials means that these variances are simply the quantity of wage variances.[1]

YIELD VARIANCE

The calculations below are also necessary:

Total input	1000 lb
Normal loss	100
Expected output	900
Actual output	950
Yield variance	50 lb F

50 lb × $11 per lb = $550 F

VERIFICATION

	$
Material price variance	215 U
Mix variance	280 U
Yield variance	550 F
	$ 55 F

The application of the general model to the analysis of variances, where many interrelated production activities of the firm are considered, is cumbersome. Matrix methods, however, can be used which simplify the calculation. An application of matrix methods to a large problem is illustrated in Werner and Manes (1967).

We must, however, now examine the investigatory nature of variance analysis and its 'blame laying' philosophy.

14.19 Variance analysis and 'blame laying'

The typical standard cost model of most firms attempts to capture significant economic events which are future oriented into a current production situation. The model also incorporates

---

[1] Little work has been done in showing how more sophisticated bases for setting proportions can be utilised. Bromwich (1969) is critical of the traditional approach and suggests that calculations should be made with reference to suitable mix proportions that correspond to actual prices. He does not demonstrate how this might be done, particularly for inputs measured in entirely different units (e.g. gal, lb and ft). A modelling approach with potential for this kind of problem has been developed by Pichler (1954).

Standard Costing

standard of work performance (based on expectations) for production workers which are formulated by the management function. A feature of the standard cost model is that unfavourable variances, which connote 'wrongdoings' are attached to a manager of a department, who in turn attributes blame to the employees of his department.

It is clear from what has been said from ch. 13 onwards that management's perception of economic reality is imperfect. It follows that the budgeting and standard cost models based thereon are faulty. That statement begs the question. Should unfavourable variances which result from prediction be laid on the shoulders of a manager? To the extent that the future is unknowable (and, at times, unmanageable), a manager should not be blamed for an unfavourable variance which occurred as a result of a wrong parameter prediction. Similarly, the employees of a department should not be blamed if their work activities fail to comply with the standards simply because work standards are imperfectly set. 'Blame laying' leads to dysfunctional behaviour. Would this lack of blame laying, (which is a part of the philosophy of western cultures) enable the managers and employees of firms to 'fiddle the system' better? No, since the standard cost model and the budget would still be operated by management to keep each department of the firm within a dynamic, feasible region. It follows that the investigation of variances should be undertaken when they are persistent, and result in a department shifting away from its feasible region. In sum, we are saying that the questions which should concern management when examining unfavourable variances are 'what is wrong?', and 'what should be done to correct them if they are persistent and are shifting the firm away from its feasibility region?'[1]

14.20 Summary

Standard cost is a 'should be' cost. Standard cost can be classified into three categories: basic, ideal and attainable. Attainable standards are usually set for employees in the production process.

Standard costing means the establishment of standard cost for each product made by the firm. The setting of standards takes allowances into account. This is so in the case of standard direct material and standard direct labour cost – the design, production, and purchasing departments determine the standard quantity of the former; the personnel and the production departments establish the grade, time and the standard rate of pay of the latter. Standards, however, are imperfect.

Variances are calculated from standards. The causes of variances from standard can be attributed to many factors.

The flexible budget helps management to determine what costs should have been at a particular level of activity. The activity base should be expressed in units, rather than in dollars. The flexible budget plays an important role in fixed overhead analysis. Fixed overhead variance analysis shows the importance of the denominator volume or activity. The budget variance informs management about changes in price factors, rather than managerial performance. The volume variance informs management about the utilisation of plant facilities.

The control ratios which help management to monitor the production system are: (i) activity ratio; (ii) efficiency ratio; (iii) capacity ratio.

It was stated that management's perception of economic reality is imperfect, and that their budgeting and standard data based on such information was faulty. It was argued that the unfavourable variances which occurred as a result of using such data should not be attributed to management ineffectiveness or employees' waywardness, since 'blame laying' leads to dysfunctional behaviour. It was pointed out that unfavourable variance investigation should be undertaken when variances are persistent and would result in a department shifting away from its feasibility region.

---

[1] The reader should note that statistical quality control techniques can be used to establish whether or not unfavourable variances are sufficiently statistically significant to justify management's attention (see Amicucci (1965), Dopuch (1974), and Noble (1968)).

Bibliography

Amey, L. and Eggington D. A. (1973) *Management Accounting: A Conceptual Approach* (Longman) ch. 15.
Amicucci, D. J. (1965) 'Budget Trend Variance Reports', *Bulletin of the National Accounting Association*, 46, pp. 9–14.
Bromwich, M. (1969) 'Standard Costing for Planning and Control', *Accountant*, April, pp. 585–6.
Dopuch, N. *et al.* (1974) Cost Accounting, 2nd edn, (Harcourt, Brace Jovanovich) ch. 12.
ICMA (1974) *Terminology of Management and Financial Accountancy* (ICMA) p. 26.
Noble, C. E. (1968) 'Calculation Control Limits for Cost Control Data', in D. Solomons (ed.) *Studies in Cost Analysis*, 2nd edn (Sweet & Maxwell) pp. 444–51.
Pichler, O. (1954) 'Probleme der Planrechtung in Der Chemischen Industrié', in *Chemische Technik*, Bd 6, ss. 293–300; 316; 392–405.
Solomons, D. (1961) 'Flexible Budgets and the Analysis of Overhead Variances', in H. R. Anton and P. A. Firmin (eds), *Contemporary Issues in Cost Accounting* (Houghton Mifflin) pp. 359–69. St Luke, ch. 14, v. 28.
Werner, F. and Manes, R. (1967) 'A Standard Cost Application of Matrix Algebra', *Accounting Review*, July, pp. 516–27.
Zeff, S. A. (1959) 'Standard Cost in Financial Statements – Theory and Practice', in H. R. Anton and P. A. Firmin (eds), *Contemporary Issues in Cost Accounting* (Houghton Mifflin) pp. 348–58.

Problems

14.1 Compound XYZ is manufactured in batches of 100 cylinders, the standard input material per batch being 250 gal of ABC of $1.20 per gal.

During November 30 batches of XYZ were produced from an input of 7450 gal of ABC which cost $9076.

REQUIRED

(a) Calculate the material price and usage variance, and show the relevant entries in the work-in-progress account, assuming the materials are debited thereto at actual cost price
(b) Discuss the limitations of material price and usage variances as instruments of management control, making reference to the variances you have calculated in (a).

ACCA, FE, Part B, Paper 6, Accounting 2, Costing, December 1975.

14.2 Nit-faster are importers of domestic knitting machines. Currently, they import and distribute two models, the super NF-PC and the family NF. 12 months ago, using the sales forecast produced by the general sales manager, the managing director compiled the following table of information of contribution margins for each model and the total contribution for the firm.

BUDGETED SALES AND CONTRIBUTION FOR 12 MONTHS COMMENCING 1 JULY 19x5

	SUPER NF-PC			FAMILY NF			TOTAL		
	Units	Price	Total	Units	Price	Total	Units	Price	Total
		$	$000		$	$000		$	$000
Sales	10000	210	2100	6000	100	600	16000	168·75	2700
Variable cost	10000	140	1400	6000	70	420	16000	113·75	1820
Contribution		70	700		30	180		55·00	880

The managing director has just received details of the actual performance for the 12 months concerned. These show that the unit prices and cost were as forecast, making the unit contribution for

Standard Costing

each of the models as budgeted. However, a closer examination of the figures, which are provided below, shows that although total unit sales have fallen short of the estimates, the total contribution is greater than the forecast.

ACTUAL SALES AND CONTRIBUTION FOR 12 MONTHS ENDED 30 JUNE 19x6

	SUPER NF-PC			FAMILY NF			TOTAL		
		Price	Total		Price	Total		Price	Total
	Units	$	$000	Units	$	$000	Units	$	$000
Sales	12000	210	2520	2000	100	200	14000	194·29	2720
Variable cost	12000	140	1680	2000	70	140	14000	130·00	1820
Contribution		70	840		30	60		64·29	900

REQUIRED

Prepare a report to the managing director, which analyses the favourable contribution variance in a way which:

(i) differentiates between the quantity and mix variance
(ii) shows the physical volume variance for the individual models

ACCA, PE, Section 2, Paper 14, Accounting 5, Management Accounting, December 1976.

14.3 The Britten Co. Ltd manufactures a variety of products of basically similar composition. Production is carried out by subjecting the various raw materials to a number of standard operations, each major series of operations being carried out in a different department. All products are subjected to the same initial processing which is carried out in depts A, B, and C; the order and extent of further processing then depends upon the type of end product to be produced.

It has been decided that a standard costing system could be usefully employed within Britten Ltd, and a pilot scheme is to be operated for 6 months, based initially only on dept B, the second department in the initial common series of operations. If the pilot scheme produces useful results, then a management accountant will be employed and the system would be incorporated as appropriate throughout the whole firm.

The standard cost per unit of dept B is:

		$
Direct labour (14 hr at $2 per hr)		28
Direct materials:		
(i) Output of dept A (3 kg at $9 per kg)		27
(ii) Acquired by and directly input to dept B		
Material x (4 kg at $5 per kg)	20	47
Variable overhead (at $1 per DLH worked)		14
Fixed production overhead:		
(i) Directly incurred by dept B[a]		
Manufacturing overhead (per unit)	3	
(ii) Allocated to dept B		
General factory overhead (per unit)	8	11
Standard cost per unit		100

[a] Based on normal production of 400 units.

In the first month of operation of the pilot study (Month 7 of the financial year), dept B had no work-in-progress at the beginning and the end of the month. The actual costs allocated to dept B in the first month of operation were:

	$	$
Direct labour (6500 hr)		14000
Direct materials:		
(i) Output of dept A (1400 kg)[a]	21000	
(ii) Material × (1900 kg)	11500	32500
Variable overhead		8000
Fixed overhead:		
(i) Directly incurred manufacturing overhead	1600	
(ii) Allocated to dept B[b]	2900	4500
		$59000

[a] Actual cost of output of dept A.
[b] Based on actual expenditure on joint manufacturing overheads and allocated to depts in accordance with labour hours worked

The production manager feels that the actual cost of $59000 for production of 500 units indicates considerable inefficiency on the part of dept B. He says, 'I was right to request that the pilot standard costing system be carried out in dept B as I have suspected that they are inefficient and careless – the overspending of $9000 proves I am right'.

REQUIRED

Prepare a brief statement which clearly indicates the reasons for the performance of dept B, and the extent to which that performance is attributable to dept B. The statement should utilise variance analysis to the extent it is applicable and relevant.

ACCA, PE, Section 2, Paper 14, Accounting 5, Management Accounting, December 1981.

14.4 Summarised below are the actual results and cost variances for period 10 for Toanna-Lee PLC, which manufactures two products:

	PRODUCT A	PRODUCT B	
	Units	Units	$
	5000	6200	
Production			285600
Actual direct wages paid			204000
Variable overhead incurred			31500
Fixed overhead incurred			240000
Variances from standard cost were:			
Direct material usage			7200 F[a]
Direct material price			13600 A
Direct wages efficiency			5600 A
Direct wages rate			6000 A
Variable overhead expenditure			2300 A
Variable overhead volume			11600 F
Fixed overhead expenditure			18000 A

[a] F indicates a favourable variance, A an adverse variance.

Standard Costing

The total cost variances for each element of cost are the only variances omitted from the above schedule

The company uses only one grade of direct material and, throughout period 10, the actual price paid was $0.40 per kg above standard price; the standard material cost of product A is $36 per unit

The company employs only one grade of direct labour; during period 10, the actual wage rate paid was $3.40 per hour; 3 standard hours are required to produce one unit of product A

Fixed and variable overhead absorption rate is based upon standard hours produced

There were no stocks of materials, work-in-progress or finished goods held at either the beginning or end of the period

REQUIRED

(a) Calculate for period 10:

    (i) Actual quantity of direct material consumed, in kg
    (ii) Actual price, per kg, paid for the material
    (iii) Actual DLH worked
    (iv) Actual DLH worked in excess of standard

(b) Construct the total standard cost per unit for each product

ACCA, FE, Paper 6, Accounting 2, Costing, December 1981.

14.5 A company has contracted to machine 20000 castings in the year 19X1. The machine shop budget which includes this work is based on operating for 50 weeks of 40 hours each. The normal standard for the company is set to allow a 90 per cent labour utilisation. This particular job was estimated to need 4 ideal standard hours of labour at $3 per hour.

As the work involves new technology, the expected standard used in the estimate was based on normal standard, but allowed additionally for 5 per cent of finished castings to be rejected on final inspection. Of these, 3 per cent could be reworked in an average 20 per cent of original machine time and would then be useable. The balance would be scrapped, incurring a penalty of $6 per casting. Sufficient manpower was allowed to complete 400 castings per week on the basis of the expected standard.

The company operates a time recording system and the paid hours are obtained from time clock records. In addition, the machinists record the direct time spent on the machining operations on job cards. In the period since 1 January the paid hours have averaged 44 per week. The extra 4 hours are paid at a premium rate of time and a half. The job cards showed an average of 32 hours per week on the direct machine operations. Of the initial output, 7 per cent have been rejected with 4 per cent subsequently reworked, using an average 25 per cent of original machine time each. No analysis is maintained of the time paid but not utilised on direct machining.

REQUIRED

From the information given:

A. Calculate:

    (a) average manpower in the 19X1 budget for this contract
    (b) for each good machined casting produced, the number of direct labour hours needed and the cost incurred based on:

        (i) normal standard
        (ii) expected standard
        (iii) current actual rate

    (c) no. of good machined castings which will be completed in the first 25 weeks, if the current actual rate continues throughout
    (d) average manpower needed in the second 25 weeks to complete the contract, if the expected standard was achieved throughout that period
    (e) additional cost incurred in 19X1 on the contract, over that originally estimated, assuming that the first 25 weeks continue at the current actual rate, and that in the second 25 weeks the expected standard is achieved, but the hourly rate increases to $3.20

B. Outline briefly a procedure you would advocate to analyse and control the difference between the paid hours and the DLH utilised

ICMA, PS, Part III, Management Accounting, May 1981.

14.6 Blythe Valley Canners Inc. operate a fruit canning plant. The business is seasonal but the management have become adept at producing business plans and utilise flexible budgeting procedures for controlling overhead expenditure.

The budget for the maintenance dept based on 60 000 machine hours for 19X9 is shown below together with the results for the quarter ended 31 March 19X9:

	$	Budget $	$	First quarter $
Variable costs:				
Labour		120000		38500
Supplies (mechanical)		32000		10500
Power		16500		6200
		168500		55200
Fixed costs:				
Supervision	24000		6300	
Supplies (sundry)	7500		1800	
Rent and depreciation	12000		2800	
Other	4500		1500	
		48000		12400
Total		$206500		$67600

All fixed cost is expected to accrue evenly throughout the year. During the first quarter 18 000 machine hr were worked. Blythe Valley's management had based their plans on the expectation that in the first quarter, one-third of the annual output would be achieved; this was consistent with the seasonal behaviour in previous years.

REQUIRED

(a) Compute the fixed overhead spending variance and the variable overhead spending variance attributable to the maintenance department
(b) Prepare a report analysing the variances found in (a) above by type of expenditure
(c) Calculate the planned under or over applied overhead attributable to *fixed* costs of the maintenance dept for the quarter ended 31 March, assuming output is measured on a machine hour basis

Indicate the treatment of the resulting value in the reported interim accounts for Blythe Valley

Chapter 15
Linear Programming and Cost Accounting

The phrase 'opportunity cost' ... is now somewhat out of fashion. But I believe that there is a very good reason for this. The analysis of optimal decisions in terms of costs and benefits has, to some extent, been superseded. Nowadays, even those who, like myself, are not mathematicians are inclined to think and speak in terms of maximising an objective function subject to constraints. And this new jargon is not used solely to 'snow' the uninitiated; for it offers a more elaborate and more refined apparatus for structuring decision problems.   (Gould, 1974)

15.1 Introduction

Linear programming is a mathematical tool which helps (via its quantification and solution processes) the management function to gain insight into complex, economic cases. Some complex cases which have a bearing on cost accounting and can be solved by linear programming are:

(i) product mix
(ii) sequencing of the firm's machines
(iii) the transfer pricing problems between the divisions of a firm

The adjective 'linear' describes the measurement phenomenon of two or more variables which represent some aspect of economic reality in a mathematical model. The word 'programming' simply means an iterative procedure which works away at a problem until a final, optimal result is achieved.

The explicit features of cost accounting are planning, control, and profitability. These can be associated with the constant planning that is required by the management function, to mix employees, machines, materials and money in some proportion in order to achieve substantial benefit for the firm. Linear programming is not only an effective planning tool in such matters, but also gives better decisions than some accepted cost accounting techniques.

15.2 Assumptions of linear programming

These assumptions are: (i) additivity; (ii) divisibility; (iii) deterministic model; and (iv) proportionality. (i) means that the activities of the model must be additive in the objective function and the constraints. (ii) means that fractions of the model, decision variables, are acceptable in the solution. (iii) means that all the model coefficients are known, and hence constant. (iv) means that the objective function, constraints and relationships must be linear[1] with the added implication that the resource utilisation must be proportional to the level of each activity.

For linear programming to be an effective decision tool, four conditions must exist:

(i) well-defined objective function
(ii) alternative courses of action
(iii) variables must be interrelated
(iv) resources must be finite and economically quantifiable

15.3 General form of linear programming model

Linear programming can be used when a problem under consideration by the management function can be expressed by a linear objective function. The objective function can either be one of maximisation or minimisation. The constraints can be expressed as equalities, or inequalities, or in a combination of the two. The maximisation model can be expressed as

$$\text{Maximise } Z = c_1 x_1 + c_2 x_2 + c_n x_n \quad \text{(objective function)}$$

Subject to
$$a_{11} x_1 + a_{12} x_2 + \ldots + a_{1n} x_n \leq b_1$$
$$a_{21} x_1 + a_{22} x_2 + \ldots + a_{2n} x_n \leq b_2$$
$$\vdots$$
$$a_{m1} x_1 + a_{m2} x_2 + \ldots + a_{mn} X_n \leq b_m$$

explicit constraints

$$x_1, x_2 \ldots x_n \geq 0$$

implicit non-negativity constraints

COMMENT

For a_{ij}, b_i and c_j, numbers can be substituted. The variables (x_{j_s}) are to be determined in such a way that the constraints will be satisfied, and the objective maximised. The objective function's value is Z.

Line 1 indicates, for example, the contribution of products. C_1 is the contribution to be realised in producing a unit of product 1. The variable x_1 represents the number of units of product 1 to be produced. The value of x_1 will be determined via the solution process. The m inequalities are the explicit constraints. They state that a maximum amount of each resource, such as resource i, is available. That amount is b_i. Each product, for example, the jth product,

---

[1] Some of the firm's constraints will be non-linear. The non-linearities will be approximated to linear form by management, so as to avoid the difficulties of working with cumbersome and at times inefficient, non-linear algorithms.

Linear Programming and Cost Accounting

requires a_{ij} units of resource i to produce a unit of product j. Each constraint thus states that the amount of resources used in production cannot exceed that which is available. The implicit non-negativity constraints state that the variables must be non-negative. Obviously, if an economic combination is engaged in production, positive quantities must by definition be produced.

The standard form of the minimisation model is:

$$\begin{aligned}
\text{Minimise} \quad & Z = c_1 x_1 + c_2 x_2 + \ldots + c_n x_n \\
\text{Subject to} \quad & a_{11} x_1 + a_{12} x_2 + \ldots + a_{1n} x_n \geq b_1 \\
& a_{21} x_1 + a_{22} x_2 + \ldots + a_{2n} x_n \geq b_2 \\
& \quad \vdots \qquad \vdots \qquad \ldots \qquad \vdots \\
& a_{m1} x_1 + a_{m2} x_2 + \ldots + a_{mn} x_n \geq b_m \\
& x_1 \ldots \quad x_2 \ldots \quad \ldots \quad x_n \geq 0
\end{aligned}$$

A similar interpretation holds for the above, except that the objective function represents the minimisation of costs.

EXAMPLE 15.1

Assume that a manufacturing firm produces and sells two products respectively called x_1 and x_2. The consultant to the organisation advises that a linear programming model should be utilised to determine the optimum product mix, since it gives a better solution than 'the rule of thumb method' formerly used by the decisionmakers. Table 15.1 contains the relevant cost data.

Table 15.1 Price and cost data per unit

	$	$
Selling price	32	29
Direct labour	20	10
Direct materials	4	10
Variable overhead	5	5
Fixed overhead	50	50
Products	x_1	x_2

The cost of the materials of the two products is $2 per lb; direct labour is paid at the rate of $5 per hr; there are 800 DLH and 120 lb of direct materials available per week

The formulation of the product requires:

variable definition
contribution per product calculation
calculation of labour rate
calculation of direct material rate

Variable Definition

Let x_1 and x_2 respectively represent the production of the contribution per product.
The contribution per product calculations are:

	$	$
Selling price	32	29
Less variable cost:		
Direct labour	20	10
Direct materials	4	10
Variable overhead	5	5
Contribution (z)	$3	$4

The objective function of the problem is therefore:

Maximise $Z = 3x_1 + 4x_2$

Labour rate calculations:

Direct labour ($)	= 20 (x_1)	10 (x_2)
Divided by hr rate ($5)	= $4x_1$	$2x_2$

Incorporating the DLH available, the inequality constraint is:

$4x_1 + 2x_2 \leqslant 80$

The direct material rate calculations are:

Direct material ($)	4(x_1)	10(x_2)
Divided by cost per lb ($2)	$2x_1$	$5x_2$

Incorporating the direct material available, the inequality constraint is:

$2x_1 + 5x_2 \leqslant 120$

Since the number of products to be produced cannot be negative, x_1 and x_2 must be no less than 0, i.e. $x_1 \geqslant 0$, $x_2 \geqslant 0$.

The linear programming model is:

Maximise $Z = 3x_1 + 4x_2$ (Contribution per product)
Subject to $4x_1 + 2x_2 \leqslant 80$ (Labour hour constraint)
$2x_1 + 5x_2 \geqslant 120$ (Material constraint)
$x_1 \geqslant 0, x_2 \geqslant 0$ (Non-negative constraints)

15.4 Observations on linear programming solution

Any solution to the problem that is found must be feasible. A feasible solution satisfies all the constraints, but need not maximise the objective functions. Some feasible solutions are:

$x_1 = 0, x_2 = 0$; $x_1 = 10, x_2 = 20$; $x_1 = 0, x_2 = 24$.

On the other hand,

$x_1 = 24, x_2 = 10$

is infeasible, because all the constraints are not satisfied. If it is not possible to find a feasible solution, this indicates one of two things – (i) the model has been incorrectly formulated, (ii) inconsistencies have been built into the model. However, of all the feasible solutions to the problem, only a sub-set exists which will satisfy the constraints. The required solution is called an optimal feasible solution. The simplex algorithm ensures this.

15.5 Simplex format

Table 15.2 shows a formation for setting up a linear programming problem.

Table 15.2 Simplex format

Basic variables	Value	x_1	x_2	...	X_n	X_{n+1}	X_{n+2}	...	X_{n+m}	Check row
X_{n+1}	b_1	a_{11}	a_{12}		a_{1n}	1	0		0	
$\vdots$	b_j	a_{22}	a_{22}		a_{2n}	0	1		0	
X_{n+m}	b_n	a_{m1}	a_{m2}		a_{mn}	0	0		1	
$z_j - c_j$	0	$-c_1$	$-c_2$		$-c_n$	0	0		0	

The table is explicit. The check row column is the sum of the rows of the matrix. In the optimising process, the same operations are performed upon the checksum as upon the corresponding equation, so that the sum of the transformed coefficients and constant will equal the transformed checksum for every equation, otherewise an error must have been made. In this way, the checksum provides an easy check of manual calculations.

The model formulation of Example 15.1 needs modification to comply with the structure of Table 15.2. The modification is simply the additions of the slack variables (i.e. X_{n+j}s) to the respective constraints of the model. The modified model is:

Maximize $z = 3x_1 + 4x_2 + 0x_3 + 0x_4$
Subject to $\quad 4x_1 + 2x_2 + x_3 \quad\quad = 80$
$\quad\quad\quad\quad\quad 2x_1 + 5x_2 \quad\quad + x_4 = 120$
$\quad\quad\quad\quad\quad x_1 \geq 0;\ x_2 \geq 0.$

The x_{n+j}s are termed slack variables. In a minimisation problem, they are called surplus variables. Note that the x_{n+j}s are given a unit matrix in the initial linear programming model, and are called basic variables. All other variables are termed non-basic variables. Further, the basic variables in a linear programming optimum solution always have their corresponding unit matrix.

15.6 Procedures of simplex method

(i) Set up the initial tableau as shown in Table 15.2 with numerical data
(ii) Scan the $z_j - c_j$ row
   If all the coefficients of the $z_j - c_j$ row are ≥ 0, stop; the current basis is optimal
   Read off the solutions from the matrix
   Substitute the solutions into the original linear system to determine whether the system is satisfied; if it is not, a mistake has occurred
   If any of the coefficients of the $z_j - c_j$ rows are ≤ 0, select the largest as indicator of the pivot column and go to (iii)
(iii) Determine the leaving basic variable (i.e. the pivot row) (a) by picking out each coefficient of the pivot column that is positive, i.e. $a_{ij} \geq 0$; (b) divide each basic variable coefficient by the a_{ij}s; (c) select the minimum
   Call the minimum $\lambda j = v_j/a_{ij}$
   Go to (iv).
(iv) Circle the a_{ij} which gives the minimum value; call it the pivot element
   In the case of two a_{ij}s having minimum ties, choose one arbitrarily

(v) Use the mechanics embodied in the Gauss–Jordan method of matrix inversion to transform the matrix
Go to (ii)

Applying these procedures to the model, we obtain Tableau (i):

Tableau (i)

Basic	Value	X_1	X_2	X_3	X_4	CK	Workings
X_3	80	4	2	1	0	87	LE (1)
X_4	120	2	⑤	0	1	128	→LE (2)
$zj - cj$	0	−3	−4	0	0	−7	LE (3)

x_2 is the pivot column, x_4 the pivot row

The arrows show the entering and leaving variable; LE is the linear equation. The minimum

$$\lambda_1 = \left(\frac{120}{5}, \frac{80}{2}\right)$$
$$= 24$$

Tableau (ii)

X_3	32	$\left(\dfrac{16}{5}\right)$	0	1	$\dfrac{-2}{5}$	$\dfrac{179}{5}$	→ LE5 = $\overline{LE}$ 1 − 2LE
X_2	24	$\dfrac{2}{5}$	1	0	$\dfrac{1}{5}$	$\dfrac{128}{5}$	LE4 = LE 2 ÷ 5
$zj - cj$	96	$\dfrac{-7}{6}$	0	0	$\dfrac{4}{5}$	$\dfrac{477}{5}$	LE6 = LE 3 + 4LE (4)

$$\text{Minimum } \lambda_2 = \frac{\frac{32}{16/5}}{\frac{24}{2/5}} = 10$$

Tableau (iii)

X_1	10	1	0	$\dfrac{5}{16}$	$\dfrac{-1}{8}$	$\dfrac{179}{16}$	LE7 = LE 5 ÷ $\dfrac{16}{5}$
X_2	20	0	1	$\dfrac{-1}{8}$	$\dfrac{1}{4}$	$\dfrac{169}{8}$	LE8 = LE 4 − $\dfrac{2}{5}$ LE 7
$zj - cj$	110	0	0	$\dfrac{7}{16}$	$\dfrac{5}{8}$	$\dfrac{1777}{8}$	LE9 = LE 6 + $\dfrac{7}{5}$ LE (7)

All the $z_j - c_j$ values are ≥ 0. The problem is optimal, with solutions $(X_1, X_2, z) = (10, 20, 110)$.

Linear Programming and Cost Accounting 263

15.7 Insights into solution process

The simplex method converges to a finite optimal solution if one exists, or it will show that no optimal solution exists. If at any optimal solution a non-basic variable has a 0 value in the $z_j - c_j$ row, an iteration can be undertaken (provided that the pivot ratio is positive) to bring that variable into the basis. The result of such an iteration is called an 'alternative optima'. It should be noted that in such cases a non-basic variable becomes basic, but the objective function's value (z) does not change.

15.8 Algebraic method

A linear programming model can be written as:

Maximise $Z = Cx$
Subject to $Ax = b$
$x \geqslant 0$

Where c and x = matrices of the order n by 1

$b = m$ by 1
$A = m$ by n

A solution to the system, if one exists, is:

$X = A^{-1}b.$

A^{-1} is a ready reckoner, which can be used to give, quick, decision variable solutions. Applying the technique to Example 15.1, we have:

$$x = A^{-1}b = \begin{bmatrix} \frac{5}{16} & \frac{-1}{8} \\ \frac{-1}{8} & \frac{1}{4} \end{bmatrix} \begin{bmatrix} 80 \\ 120 \end{bmatrix}$$

Hence, $x_1, x_2 = [10, 20]$. Substituting $x = A^{-1}b$ into the objective function, we have:

Maximise $Z = cA^{-1}b$

$$= [3, 4] \begin{bmatrix} \frac{5}{16} & \frac{-1}{8} \\ \frac{-1}{8} & \frac{1}{4} \end{bmatrix} \begin{bmatrix} 80 \\ 120 \end{bmatrix}$$

$$= \begin{bmatrix} \frac{7}{16} & \frac{5}{8} \end{bmatrix} \begin{bmatrix} 80 \\ 120 \end{bmatrix} = 110$$

COMMENT

The reader may infer from the above that all that is required is the algebraic method or the utilisation of the reverse matrix for solving larger, linear programming problems. An algebraic solution to many real world costing problems is cumbersome. One the other hand, the reverse matrix for many costing problems may not lend itself to easy manipulation, since the number of

15.9 The dual

To every linear programming model, a dual exists. The dual of a linear programming problem is its opposite. A matrix representation of a primal and dual problem using only one matrix is shown below.

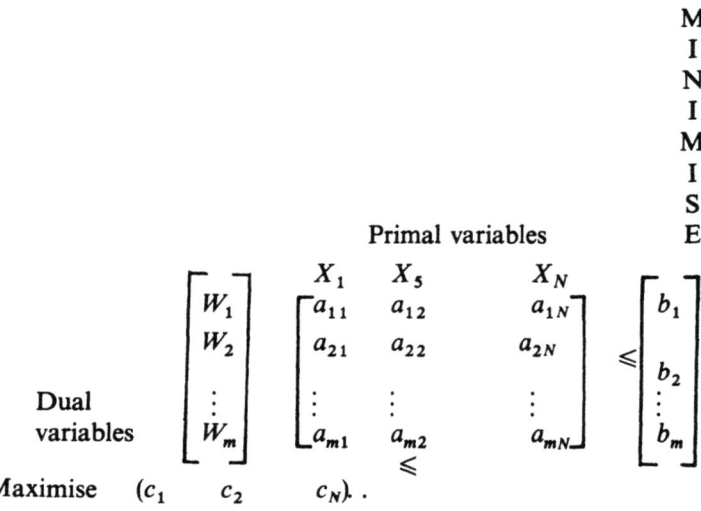

The dual of Example 15.1 is:

Minimise $T = 80\ W_1 + 120\ W_2$
Subject to $\quad 4\ W_1 + 2\ W_2 \geq 3$
$\quad\quad\quad\quad\quad 2\ W_1 + 5\ W_2 \geq 4$
$\quad\quad\quad\quad W_1 \geq 0,\ W_2 \geq 0$

The dual problem can be solved via the simplex method by adding artificial and surplus variables to the respective constraints, together with another objective function which is a summation of the 'greater than or equal to' constraints. In the tableau below, it is written as $Cj^* - zj$.

Tableaux (i)–(iii) respectively show the solution procedures.

Tableau (i)

Basis	Value	W_1	W_2	s_1	s_2	Check
a_1	3	4	2	−1	0	8
a_2	4	2	⑤	0	−1	10
$cj - zj$	0	80	120	0	0	200
$cj^* - zj$	−7	−6	−7	1	1	−18

Linear Programming and Cost Accounting

Tableau (ii)

Basis	Value	W_1	W_2	s_1	s_2	Check
a_1	$\frac{7}{5}$	$\boxed{\frac{16}{5}}$	0	-1	$\frac{2}{5}$	4
w_2	$\frac{4}{5}$	$\frac{2}{5}$	1	0	$\frac{-1}{5}$	2
$c_j - z_j$	-96	32	0	0	24	-40
$c_j^* - z_j$	$\frac{-7}{5}$	$-\frac{16}{5}$	0	1	$\frac{-2}{5}$	-4

Tableau (iii)

Basis	Value	W_1	W_2	s_1	s_2	Check
w_1	$\frac{7}{16}$	1	0	$\frac{-5}{16}$	$\frac{1}{8}$	$\frac{5}{4}$
w_2	$\frac{5}{8}$	0	1	$\frac{1}{8}$	$\frac{-1}{4}$	$\frac{3}{2}$
$c_j - z_j$	110	0	0	10	32	152

COMMENT

(i) There is no need to work with the artificial unit matrix in the tableau
(ii) The artificial variables, like the $c_j^* - z_j$ row, are driven to 0, and are eliminated from the solution
(iii) The $c_j^* - z_j$ row is a necessary condition for obtaining a solution to such a system
(iv) The optimal z and T values are the same
(v) The procedures would be cumbersome if they were applied to a larger problem with mixed constraints

Incidentally, an algorithm exists for solving minimisation problems. In 15.10 below, the algorithm which was developed by Lemke (1954) is explained.

15.10 The dual algorithm

In tableaux format, the solution processes with explanation appended are as follows:

Tableau (i)

Basis	Value	W_1	W_2	s_1	s_2	Check
s_1	-3	-4	-2	1	0	-8
s_2	-4	-2	$\boxed{-5}$	0	1	-10
$c_j - z_j$	0	80	120	0	0	200

(a) Scan the value vector[1], and select the most negative value, (i.e., -4)

Determine

$$\frac{c_k - z_k}{w_{ik}}, w_{ik} < 0 = \underset{j}{\text{Max}}$$

$$= \left[\frac{-80}{2}, \frac{-120}{5}\right] = -24$$

Circle the pivot and transform the matrix

Tableau (ii)

s_1	$-\frac{7}{5}$	$\left(-\frac{16}{5}\right)$	0	1	$-\frac{2}{5}$	-4
w_2	$\frac{4}{5}$	$\frac{2}{5}$	1	0	$-\frac{1}{5}$	2
cj – zj	-96	32	0	0	24	-40

(b) Repeat (a)

Tableau (iii)

w_1	$\frac{7}{16}$	1	0	$-\frac{5}{16}$	$\frac{1}{8}$	$\frac{5}{4}$
w_2	$\frac{5}{8}$	0	1	$\frac{1}{8}$	$-\frac{1}{4}$	$\frac{2}{2}$
cj – zj	-110	0	0	10	20	-80

(c) Repeat (a)
As can be seen, primal feasibility, as well as dual feasibility, has been maintained
The problem is optimal with solutions

$$w_1, w_2, z = [\tfrac{7}{16}, \tfrac{5}{8}, 110]$$

$-z_1$ is of course multiplied by -1

COMMENT

The rationale for the use of the dual algorithm lies in its application to:

(i) mixed problems, where there are $\leqslant$ or $\geqslant$ constraints
(ii) for some linear programming problems, the dual is easier to solve than the primal
(iii) its mechanics aid in the determination of integer solutions, in integer programming, where certain variables are restricted to 0 or 1–for example, in certain capital budgetary cases. In fact, the dual algorithm is applicable to the class of bounded problems where certain variables are restricted to lie within certain limits.

It should be obvious to the reader that there is also an economic aspect to the dual and its solutions. The economic significance of the dual in relation to Example 15.1 is now examined.

---

[1] Ch. 2* introduces the reader to matrices.

Linear Programming and Cost Accounting

15.11 Economic significance of the dual

The dual problem of Example 15.1 can be stated as finding a set of measures for the firm's resources, such that the total cost of the firm's resources is minimised subject to the constraints which specify that the cost of the firm be set in a manner which is consistent with the alternative uses for the resources.

The objective function indicates that the total cost of the firm is made up of 80 hours at wage rate $W_1 + 120$ material units at cost price W_2. The constraints imply that the imputed cost of the x_is now rewritten in terms of W_is should be greater or equal to the contribution.

The dual optimum solution indicates the value of the scarce resources. The statement implies that if at an optimal dual solution, the mix of resources required to produce a unit of product exceeds the contribution, the firm should produce 0 units of that product. Conversely, the statement also implies that the imputed cost should equal the contribution earned from producing a product.

Incidentally, it is those 'shadow prices' which are so valuable to managerial decisions. It can be seen that if the firm were negotiating an outside price per unit for its materials, the minimum price at which it would sell the materials per unit is given by $W_2 = \$0.625$.

A linear programming optimal model also contains valuable information for management decisions. These decisions areas are examined below in relation to Example 15.1

15.12 Sensitivity analysis

Sensitivity analysis is concerned with analysing the effect of changes[1] in the objective function coefficients, i.e. the c_js and the right hand side constants, i.e. the b_js. The optimum tableau of the linear programming model aids the analysis. Sensitivity analysis is useful to the management function for the following reasons:

(i) it helps to determine which decision variables are critical
(ii) for control purposes
(iii) it determines the range of values which certain decision variables can take on without effecting a change in the optimum solution

It should be noted that sensitivity analysis examines the changes in one variable at a time, while holding other factors constant. To demonstrate the mechanics of sensitivity analysis, the model of Example 15.1, together with its optimum solution, are reproduced below for convenience.

Model

Maximise $z = 3x_1 + 4x_2$ (Contribution per product)

Subject to $4x_1 + 2x_2$ 80 (Labour hr)
            $2x_1 + 5x_2$ 120 (Material)

$x_1 \geq 0, x_2 \geq 0.$

Optimum tableau

Basis	Value	x_1	x_2	x_3	x_4
x_1	10	1	0	$\frac{5}{16}$	$\frac{-1}{8}$
x_2	20	0	1	$\frac{-1}{8}$	$\frac{1}{4}$
$z_j - c_j$	110	0	0	$\frac{7}{16}$	$\frac{5}{8}$

[1] The reader would gain great insight into the solution processes of the simplex and the dual procedures if their methods were now compared.

For explanatory purposes Table 15.3 below shows in algebraic notations the special features of the optimum tableau.

Table 15.3 The optimum tableau

V_{xb} = Value of basic variables = $A^{-1}b$ $Z = c_{xb}$ coefficients of the basic variables	I = Unit matrix of basic variables 0 = zero vector of basic variables	$A^{-1}n$ = coefficients of non-basic vectors $c x_b A^{-1} n - c_{xn}$ = vector of reduced cost, i.e. dual values of non-basic variables

To examine the effects of changes in the objective function, a parameter θ must be added to each objective function coefficient, one at a time. The value of θ for each coefficient is also subject to the optimality conditions. In relation to Table 15.3, the above statement can be expressed as:

$$c_{xb} A^{-1} n + \theta U A^{-1} n - c_n \geq 0 \tag{15.1}$$

Where c_{xb}, c_n = As defined above u = Vector which contains a 1 and 0s elsewhere, and which is updated each time a sensitivity analysis is performed.

Let us see how equation (15.1) can be used by management of test the changes in the objective function coefficients. Suppose that the contributon to profits and overheads in Example 15.1 were changed from c_1 to $c_1 + \theta$. The management may want to know the range in costs for which the original optimal solution holds.

Substituting the relevant values into the Equation (15.1), the answer can be found as follows:

$$[3 \ 4]\begin{bmatrix} \frac{5}{16} & \frac{-1}{8} \\ \frac{-1}{8} & \frac{1}{4} \end{bmatrix}\begin{bmatrix} 1 & 0 \\ 0 & 1 \end{bmatrix} + \theta[1 \ 0]\begin{bmatrix} \frac{5}{16} & \frac{-1}{8} \\ \frac{-1}{8} & \frac{1}{4} \end{bmatrix}\begin{bmatrix} 1 & 0 \\ 0 & 1 \end{bmatrix} - [0 \cdot 0] \geq 0$$

or reading from the optimum tableau (which is easier), we get:

$\frac{7}{16}\frac{5}{8} + \theta[\frac{5}{16} - \frac{1}{8}] \leq 0$ which gives:[1]

$\frac{7}{16} + \frac{5}{16}\theta \geq 0 \to \theta \geq \frac{-7}{5}$ (Lower range)

$\frac{5}{8} - \frac{1}{8}\theta \geq 0 \to \theta \leq 5$ (Upper range)

The lower and upper ranges imply that the coefficient of x_1 in the objective function can decrease to 8/5 i.e. $(3 - 7/5)$ or increase t 8, i.e. $(3 + 5)$ without a change in the optimum basis.

In a similar way, if c_2 increases from c_2 to $c_2 + \theta$, its range can also be found from the optimum tableau as follows:

$[\frac{7}{16} \ \frac{5}{16}] + \theta[-\frac{1}{8} \ \frac{1}{4}] \geq 0$ which gives:

$\frac{5}{16} + \frac{1}{4}\theta \geq 0 \to \theta \geq \frac{-5}{4}$ (Lower range)

$\frac{7}{16} - \frac{1}{8}\theta \geq 0 \to \theta \leq \frac{7}{2}$ (Upper range)

The cost ranges imply that the coefficient of x_2 can decrease to 11/4, i.e. $(4 - 5/4)$ or increase to 15/2, i.e. $(4 + 7/2)$ without a change in the optimum basis.

We turn now to the right hand side constants. In order to calculate the changes on the requirement vector, the parameter is added to each constant, one at a time.

Algebraically, we have:

$A^{-1}(b + \theta u^t) \geq 0$, or

$A^{-1}b + \theta A^{-1}u \geq 0$

---

[1] Sensitivity analysis can also be applied to the matrix of coefficients, i.e. the a_{ij}s, but this is not usually done in practice.

Assuming that management wants to know the range for the b_is over which the parameters in the optimum basis hold, substitute the relevant coefficients into one of the above equations, and solve for θ. The range for the available hours b_1 of our problem is calculated as follows:

$$\begin{bmatrix} \frac{5}{16} & \frac{-1}{8} \\ \frac{-1}{8} & \frac{1}{4} \end{bmatrix} \left[\begin{pmatrix} 80 \\ 120 \end{pmatrix} + \theta \begin{pmatrix} 1 \\ 0 \end{pmatrix} \right] \geq 0$$

Or reading again from the optimum tableau, we obtain

$[10 \quad 20] + \theta [\frac{5}{16} \quad \frac{-1}{8}] \geq 0$ which gives:
$10 + \frac{5}{16}\theta \geq 0 \to \theta \geq -32$ (Lower range)
$20 - \frac{1}{8}\theta \geq 0 \to \theta \leq 160$ (Upper range)
$\therefore \quad -32 \leq \theta \leq 160$

Thus b_1 can decrease to 48, or increase to 240, and the parameter X_1 would remain in the optimum solution. In a similar way, the change in b_2 is found to lie within the range of $-80 \leq \theta \leq 80$, which means that b_2 can decrease to 40, or increase to 200, and the parameter X_2 will still be in the optimum solution.

Sometimes, sensitivity analysis and range data will not answer all management questions. Management may wish to know how a solution changes when one, two or more objective function, right hand side and matrix coefficient parameters change over a particular range. Such questions are answered by parametric programming.[1]

15.13 Parametric programming

Parametric programming seeks to find all the possible solutions to a linear programming problem in which one or more coefficients are a linear function of some parameter. Parametric programming can be applied on any coefficient or combination of coefficients. In practice, parametric programming is undertaken on:

(i) making one or more requirement vector entries, a linear function of a parameter
(ii) making one or more objective function coefficients, a linear function of a parameter

Example 15.2 illustrates how a parametric coefficient is applied to a problem, and show via calculation and explanation how its ranges are determined in the optimising process.

EXAMPLE 15.2

Reconsider Example 15.1. Assume that management did not know the material availability, and wished to test the impact of changing the resource on the model within any range.[2]

REQUIRED

Construct the model, and solve it.

---

[1] The determination of the ranges or bounds here is a simple matter; where there are many inequalities, the most limiting factor is chosen.
[2] Mathematically, those questions can be answered by solving the problem for each of the questions. Parametric programming performs the calculations in one run. The reader should note, that parametric programming is an extension of sensitivity analysis.

SOLUTION

Call the unknown material availability K – the model now becomes:

Maximize $z = 3x_1 + 4x_2 + 0x_3 + 0x_4$
Subject to $\quad 4x_1 + 2x_2 + x_3 + 0x_4 \leq 80$
$\quad\quad\quad\quad 2x_1 + 5x_2 + 0x_3 + 1x_4 \leq k$
$\quad\quad\quad\quad x_1 \geq 0, x_2 \geq 0.$

Using our tableau presentation, we get:

Tableau (i)

Basis	Value	x_1	x_2	x_3	x_4	Check	Explanations
x_3	80	4	②	1	0	87	Bounds: $\infty > k \geq 0$
x_4	k	2	5	0	1	$8+k$	Set $k = \infty$
							Simplex algorithm is applicable
$zj - cj$	0	-3	-4	0	0	-7	↑↓ Entering variable and leaving variable
		↑	↓				

Tableau (ii)

Basis	Value	x_1	x_2	x_3	x_4	Check	Explanations
x_2	40	2	1	$\frac{1}{2}$	0	$\frac{87}{2}$	Conclusion (i):
							$\infty > k \geq 200$; $x_1 = 0$
							$x_2 = 40$; $x_3 = 0$
x_4	$k - 200$	$\widehat{-8}$	0	$\frac{-5}{2}$	1	$k - \frac{419}{2}$	$x_4 = k - 200$.
							$z = 160$
							Decrease k
							The dual algorithm is applicable
$zj - cj$	160	5	0	2	0	167	
		↑		↓			

Tableau (iii)

Basis	Value	x_1	x_2	x_3	x_4	Check	Explanations
x_2	$\frac{k}{4} - 10$	0	1	$\left(\frac{-1}{8}\right)$	$\frac{1}{4}$	$\frac{k}{4} - \frac{71}{8}$	Conclusion (ii):
							$200 \geq k \geq 40$
x_1	$25 - \frac{k}{8}$	1	0	$\frac{5}{16}$	$\frac{-1}{8}$	$\frac{418 - k}{16}$	$x_1 = 25 - \frac{k}{8}$; $x_2 = \frac{k}{4} - 10$,
							$x_3 = x_4 = 0$, $z = 35 + \frac{5k}{8}$,
$zj - cj$	$35 + \frac{5k}{8}$	0	0	$\frac{7}{16}$	$\frac{5}{8}$	$\frac{577}{16} + \frac{5k}{8}$	Decrease k
				↓	↑		

Tableau (iv)

								Conclusion (iii):
x_3	$80 - 2k$	0	-8	1	-2	$71 - 2k$		$40 \geqslant k \geqslant 0$
x_1	$\dfrac{k}{2}$	1	$\dfrac{5}{2}$	0	$\dfrac{1}{2}$	$4 + \dfrac{k}{2}$		$x_1 = \dfrac{k}{2}, x_2 = 0, x_3 = 80 - 2k,$ $x_4 = 0, z = \dfrac{3k}{2}$
$zj - cj$	$\dfrac{3k}{2}$	0	$\dfrac{7}{2}$	0	$\dfrac{3}{2}$	$5 + \dfrac{3k}{2}$		k cannot be decreased further Stop
	↓							

COMMENT

The first attempt at parametric programming may lead to some confusion, especially if the reader has not mastered the methods of the simplex and dual algorithms. The reader should always bear in mind that parametric programming tests *increments*. The increments (or range of increments) for the parameter can also be specified by the decisionmaker. The above model can also be solved by starting with the range $0 < k \leqslant \infty$.

15.14 Summary

Linear programming is a mathematical tool which works away at a problem until an optimum result is achieved. A linear programming solution which incorporates all of the activities of the firm can be used by management for intelligent, decisionmaking. Sensitivity analysis can be applied to the optimum solution of a linear programming problem. Sensitivity analysis is a practical way of taking uncertainties into account. However, it may be unrealistic to adopt linear techniques in non-linear situations, and a warning of the dangers of such action has been made by Baumol and Bushnell, (1967).

Bibliography

Baumol, W. J. and Bushnell, R. C. (1967) 'Error Produced by Linearization in Mathematical Programming', *Econometrica*, vol. 35, no. 3–4, July–October.
Dantzig, G. B. (1963) *Linear Programming and Extensions* (Princeton University Press) chs 5–9.
Gauss, S. I. (1969) *Linear Programming*, 3rd edn (McGraw-Hill) chs 4–5, 8.
Gould, J. R. (1974) 'Opportunity Cost: The London Tradition', in Harold Edey and B. S. Yamey (eds) *Debits, Credits, Finance and Profits* (Sweet & Maxwell).
Lemke, C. E. (1954) 'The Dual Method of Solving the Linear Programming Problem', *Naval Research Logistics Quarterly*, vol. 1, no. 1.
Wagner, H. M. (1975) *Principles of Operations Research*, 2nd edn (Prentice-Hall) chs 5–9.
Zionts, S. (1974) *Linear and Integer Programming* (Prentice-Hall) chs 2, 5.

Problems

15.1 The management accountant of Fenton Enterprises Ltd. has suggested that a linear programming model might be used for selecting the best mix of five possible products, A, B, C, D, E.

The following information is available:

(i)	PER UNIT OF PRODUCT				
	A	B	C	D	E
	$	$	$	$	$
Selling price	48	42	38	31	27
Costs:					
Materials	15	14	16	15	16
Direct labour	18	16	6	4	4
Fixed overhead[a]	9	8	3	2	2
Total cost	42	38	25	21	22
Net profit	$6	$4	$13	$10	$5

[a] Based on 50 per cent of direct labour cost.

(ii) Expected maximum unit demand per week for each product at the prices indicated:

A	B	C	D	E
1500	1200	900	600	600

(iii) Cost of materials includes a special component which is in short supply; it costs $3 a unit
Only 5800 units will be available to the company during the year
The number of units of the special component needed for a unit of each product is:

A	B	C	D	E
1	1	3	4	5

(iv) Labour is paid at a rate $1.50 per hr, and only 20000 hours will be available in a week
(v) The management of Fenton Enterprises Ltd has ruled that expenditure on materials must not exceed $30000
(vi) All other resources are freely available in sufficient quantities for planned needs

REQUIRED

(a) Formulate a linear programming model, stating clearly the criterion you use
(b) Describe the problems likely to be encountered in the application of linear programming to determine the 'best' product mix for Fenton Enterprises Ltd.

ACCA, PE, Section 2, Paper 12, Management Mathematics, December 1976.

15.2 Consider the following primal problem:

Minimise:
$$Z = 60a + 120b + 40c + 25d$$

Subject to:
$$1.5a + 4b + c \geq 15$$
$$2a + 2b + c + d \geq 12$$
$$a, b, c, d \geq 0$$

REQUIRED

(a) State the dual problem
(b) Why is it of some advantage to solve the dual instead of the primal problem?
(c) Solve the dual problem

Linear Programming and Cost Accounting

15.3 A pharmaceutical manufacturer wishes to produce a type of tablet which is to contain a minimum quantity of two nutrients, X and Y. Three ingredients, A, B, and C, which contain the nutrients, are being considered for use in the tablets. The amount of nutrient each contain and its price per unit are given in the following table:

	INGREDIENTS		
	A	B	C
Unit price	40	25	50
Nutrient			
X(No. of units)	1	1	2.5
Y(No. of units)	4	2	2

Each tablet is to contain at least five units of nutrient X and eight units of nutrient Y.

REQUIRED

(a) Formulate a linear programming model to determine the amount of A, B and C in each tablet for minimum cost
(b) Formulate the dual of the above, and solve the dual problem
(c) Explain (but do not solve) how you would obtain the solution to the original problem from the final tableau of the simplex solution to the dual problem

ACCA, PE, Section 2, Paper 12 (alternate paper used at the Birmingham Centre), Management Mathematics, December 1979.

15.4

REQUIRED

'In the context of a profit maximising linear programme:

(i) state how linearity in the data is to be determined
(ii) state how a management accountant would define the exact nature of the 'profit' determined by such a programme
(iii) observe that each linear programme designated as the 'primal' programme has a 'dual'; describe briefly with the help of an example what is meant by the term 'dual'
(iv) give two examples, other than that in (b) below, of the possible application of a linear programming analysis in the field of management accounting

(b) A company, Portland PLC, has five products in its range and is currently running the following sales/production programme:

	PRODUCTS				
Details	A	B	C	D	E
Sales in units	50 000	40 000	70 000	60 000	20 000
Per unit:					
Sales ($)	3.50	3.00	4.50	5.00	2.00
Variable cost ($)	1.50	1.26	2.00	2.34	0.88
Labour hr	2.00	1.50	3.00	2.80	1.00
Machine hr	1.00	0.80	1.50	1.20	0.40

This programme fully utilises the availability of labour and machine time.
A linear programme reveals that labour units have a shadow price of $1.00 per hour, and machine hours have a shadow price of $0.30 per hour.

REQUIRED

Determine the optimal production programme from the above information, and compare the contribution earned with that of the existing programme.

ICMA, PS, Part I, Quantitative Techniques, May 1982.

15.5 A livestock farmer may purchase one or more of three types of grain, each containing different amounts of four nutritional elements; the data are given in the table below. He specifies that any feed mix for his livestock must at least meet minimal nutritional requirements, and he seeks the least costly among all such mixes. Suppose his planning horizon is 1 month, and he purchases enough to fill his needs for this month.

Nutritional ingredients	NUTRITIONAL CONTENT OF 1 UNIT OF GRAIN			Minimum total requirement over planning horizon
	1	2	3	
A	2·0	3·0	7·0	1250
B	1·0	1·0	0	250
C	5·0	3·0	0	1000
D	0·5	0·25	1·0	200
Cost per unit	40	30	80	
Amount purchased	x_1	x_2	x_3	

Basis	Value	x_1	x_2	x_3	s_1	s_2	s_3	s_4	Check
x_2	$\frac{900}{11}$	0	1	0	$\frac{4}{11}$	$\frac{6}{11}$	0	$\frac{28}{11}$	$\frac{929}{11}$
s_3	$\frac{950}{11}$	0	0	0	$\frac{8}{11}$	$\frac{43}{11}$	1	$\frac{56}{11}$	$\frac{870}{11}$
x_1	$\frac{1850}{11}$	1	0	0	$\frac{4}{11}$	$\frac{5}{11}$	0	$\frac{28}{11}$	$\frac{1832}{11}$
x_3	$\frac{1050}{11}$	0	0	1	$\frac{1}{11}$	$\frac{4}{11}$	0	$\frac{4}{11}$	$\frac{1060}{11}$
$c_j - z_j$	$\frac{185\,000}{11}$	0	0	0	$\frac{40}{11}$	$\frac{60}{11}$	0	$\frac{600}{11}$	$\frac{184\,300}{11}$

REQUIRED

(a) How much would the farmer save by marginally reducing, one at a time, his minimal requirement of nutritional ingredients *A*, *B*, *C* and *D*?

(b) Carry out a sensitivity analysis on the requirement which, from (a), appears to have the greatest potential for saving him money (your analysis should assume that the given optimal basis remains the same in composition)

(c) By carrying out *separate* sensitivity analyses on *each* of the other three requirements, would you say that he can in fact do better (in terms of savings on the given optimal total cost) by reducing some requirement other than the one you consider in (b)?

Linear Programming and Cost Accounting

(d) Although the farmer now knows the above optimal plan, orders for grain had to be placed some months ago, and he ordered $x_1 = 200$, $x_2 = 100$. How much does it cost him (in terms of extra cost over and above the given optimal total cost) to use a plan which involves $x_1 = 200$, $x_2 = 100$, and what is the best value of x_3 to use with these given values of x_1 and x_2?

University of Birmingham, Degree of M.Soc.Sc., Graduate Programming for Economists, June 1972.

15.6 A manufacturing company has the option of using one or more of four different production processes. The first and second process yield product A, and the third and fourth product B. The inputs for each process are labour, measured in man weeks, tons of resource R, and crates of material S. The manufacturer, deciding on a week's production schedule, is limited in the range of possibilities by the available amounts of manpower and the two other inputs. The full technology and input restrictions, including output limits imposed by the availability of packaging materials, are given in the table:

	INPUTS FOR ONE ITEM OF PRODUCT				Total avail- abilities
	A		B		
	PROCESS				
	1	2	3	4	
Man weeks	1	1	1	1	16
Tons of resource R	6	4	2	1	100
Crates of material S	2	4	8	10	35
Unit profit	2	4	k	9	
Production level	x_1	x_2	x_3	x_4	
Production limits	30	20	10	5	

Investigate how total profit and the shadow price of labour varies for $6 \geqslant k \geqslant 10$. Illustrate the relationship graphically.

University of Birmingham, Degree of M.Soc.Sc., Graduate Programming for Economists, June 1972.

Chapter 16
Capital Budgeting

Capital budgeting involves the generation of investment proposals; the estimate of cash flows for the proposals; the evaluation of cash flows; the selection of projects based an acceptance criterion; and, finally, the continual reevaluation of investment projects after their acceptance.   (Van Horne, 1977)

16.1 Introduction

Capital budgeting techniques provide business managers with criteria for sinking scarce money into capital projects. Capital projects include buildings, land, vehicles or other socially desirable project. Such assets are important to the firm,[1] because the firm's profits (and its continuity in business) is derived from their use. The firm's future development also rests on (i) selection of capital projects; (ii) their replacement, when the projects are outdated through technology or obsolescence; (iii) discarding of previously accepted projects which are no longer attractive to the firm. When the firm's management invest in capital projects, it does so with the understanding that the service benefit to be obtained will last for a lengthy period of time.[2]

16.2 Timing of capital projects

The time element is of importance to capital budgeting, because the benefit arising therefrom is received over some future period. The management function must thus time the start of project to take any advantage of any favourable interest rates which exist in the market. Because of the time period, the cost estimates associated with the project must be discounted and the risk of the project gauged.

To perform the calculations associated with the evaluation of the capital expenditure decisions

---

[1] Governments also initiate capital projects, and the techniques here are equally applicable.
[2] Time is a relative concept: a blast furnace may be estimated by management to last 20 years, a motor vehicle to last 5 years.

Capital Budgeting 277

of the firm, standard mathematical formulae and discount tables[1] exist which facilitate the calculation. Below the methods are presented, together with examples and their solution.

16.3 Compound interest

Compound interest is calculated on the principal outstanding at periodic time intervals. The time interval could be the end of a month, quarter or at the year end. The compound sum after one period is:

$$S = P[1+i] \qquad (16.1)$$

Where S = Compound sum
P = Principal
i = Nominal annual interest rate, expressed as a decimal

If funds are invested with annual compounding, the compound sum after a period of n years is:

$$S_n = P[1+i]^n \qquad (16.2)$$

Where S_n = Compound sum after n years
n = No. of years

Interest is at time compounded continuously, daily and semi-annually. In such cases, the compound sum is derived from:

$$S_n = P\left[1 + \frac{i}{m}\right]^{mn} \qquad (16.3)$$

Where m = No. of times interest is compounded

EXAMPLE 16.1

Raymond puts $5000 in a city bank for 3 years. The bank's interest rate is 5 per cent.

REQUIRED

Compute the amount that will accrue to Raymond at the end of 3 years, if the initial amount was compounded annually.

SOLUTION

Use equation (16.2) as follows:

S_n = $5000 $(1 + 0.05)^3$
    = $5000 (1.157625)
    = $5788.13

At the end of 3 years, Raymond would have $5788.13.

EXAMPLE 16.2

Suppose Raymond placed the $5788.13 in another city bank for 5 years. The bank interest rate is 1¾ per cent per quarter, compounded quarterly.

---

[1] The discount tables are found in the Appendix, pp. 317–27.

REQUIRED

Determine the amount that will accrue to him at the end of 5 years.

SOLUTION

Use equation (16.3) as follows:

S_n = \$5788.13 $(1 + 0.0175)^{4 \times 5}$
   = \$5788.13 $(1.0175)^{20}$
   = \$5788.13 (1.41477820)
   = \$8188.92

At the end of 5 years, Raymond would have \$8188.92.

Note that $1\frac{3}{4}$ per cent per quarter compounded quarterly is equivalent to a 'true' annual rate of

$(1 + 0.0175)^4 - 1 = 0.07186$ or 7.186%.

This is larger than $(4 \times 1\frac{3}{4}$ per cent$)$, i.e. 7 per cent, although $1\frac{3}{4}$ per cent per quarter compounded quarterly is generally expressed as a rate of 7 per cent compounded quarterly. Here, 7 per cent is a nominal rate, and not the 'true' or effective rate.

Equation (16.3) can be adjusted if continuous compounding is required. In this case, equation (16.3) becomes:

$$S_n = P \left[\lim_{m \to \infty} 1 + \frac{i}{m} \right]^{mn} \qquad (16.4)$$

rearranging:

$$S_n = P \left[\lim_{m \to \infty} \left[1 + \frac{i}{m} \right]^{m/i} \right]^{in}$$

As $m \to \infty$, $\left(1 + \frac{i}{m}\right)^{m/i} \to e$, the base of the Naperian logarithms.

Equation (16.4) can be written as:

$$S_n = P e^{in} \qquad (16.5)$$

The values of e^x are shown in Table 16.10.

Table 16.1 Values of e^x

x	e^x
0.63	1.8776
0.64	1.8965
0.65	1.9155
0.66	1.9348

EXAMPLE 16.3

Roy puts \$6000 in a bank for 8 years. The bank interest rate is 8 per cent.

Capital Budgeting

REQUIRED

Determine the amount Roy will obtain at the end of 8 years.

SOLUTION

Use equation (16.5) and Table 16.1.

$$S_n = \$6000 \, e^{(0.08) \cdot 8}$$
$$= \$6000 \, e^{0.64}$$
$$= \$6000 \, (1.8965)$$
$$= \$11379$$

At the end of 8 years, Roy will obtain $11379.

16.4 Future value of annuity

A firm saves a certain sum each year in order to get a required amount within a given period of time. When a payment is made each year for n years at the interest rate i, the future value of an annuity is expressed as:

$$F = A_1(1+i)^{n-1} + \ldots + A_n(1+i)^0 \qquad (16.5)$$

Where F = Future value of annuity
$A_1 \ldots A_n$ = Amounts paid into annuity at end of year
i = Rate of return
n = No. of years

Assuming that the payments are equal each period, equation (16.5) can be expressed as:

$$F = A[(1+i)^{n-1} \ldots + \ldots + (1+i) + 1] \qquad (16.6)$$

Multiplying both sides of equation (16.6) by $(1+i)$:

$$F(1+i) = A[(1+i)^n \ldots + \ldots + (1+i)] \qquad (16.7)$$

Subtracting equation (18.6) from equation (18.7):

$$F_i = A[(1+i)^n - 1]$$

Solving for F:

$$F = A\left[\frac{(1+i)^n - 1}{i}\right] \qquad (16.8)$$

EXAMPLE 16.4

Ronald places $3000 per annum into an annuity at the end of each year for 9 years.

REQUIRED

Calculate the amount Ronald will obtain if the interest is compounded annually at 10 per cent.

SOLUTION

Use equation (16.8):

$$F = \$3000 \; \frac{(1+0.10)^9 - 1}{1.10}$$

$$= \$3000 \, (13.5795)$$
$$= \$40735.50$$

Ronald will have $40735.50 at the end of 9 years.

16.5 Sinking fund payments

A firm usually creates a sinking fund to pay off a debt or an obligation by setting aside a certain sum of money at periodic intervals. The sinking fund calculations can be determined from equation (16.8), reproduced here for convenience:

$$F = A\left[\frac{(1+i)^n - 1}{i}\right]$$

Solving for A,

$$A = F\left[\frac{i}{(1+i)^n - 1}\right] \tag{16.9}$$

EXAMPLE 16.5

Roree Ltd requires $30000 in 15 years to pay off a debenture issue. A sinking fund was established, and yearly payments were made thereto. Assume that the firm can earn 15 per cent on its money in the fund.

REQUIRED

How much money must it place into the fund for 15 years to accumulate the $30000?

SOLUTION

Use equation (16.9):

$$SFP = \$30000 \; \frac{0.15}{(1+0.15)^{15} - 1}$$

Where SFP = Sinking fund payments
$$= \$30000 \, (0.02101705)$$
$$= \$630.51$$

Roree Ltd must put $630.51 into the fund each year for 15 years to accumulate $30000.

16.6 Present value

Present value (PV) is a sum which is discounted and is to be received at some future time. In relation to capital budgeting, it implies that a project should be accepted if the difference

Capital Budgeting

between the values calculated after discounting the revenue and cost outflows of a project at the marginal cost of capital of the firm is positive.

The PV of a sum to be received in the future can be derived from equation (16.2):

$$S_n = P(1+i)^n$$

Solving for P gives:

$$PV = S_n \left[\frac{1}{(1+i)^n} \right] \qquad (16.10)$$

The firm, in undertaking a capital project, expects a series of cash inflows at periodic intervals for a period of n years. The cash series for analytical purposes can be expressed as the sum of the individual inflows. Hence equation (16.10) can be expressed as:

$$PV = \frac{S_1}{(1+i)} + \frac{S_2}{(1+i)^2} + \ldots + \frac{S_n}{(1+i)^n} \qquad (16.11)$$

If both the S_js and is are constant, equation (16.11) is reduced to:

$$PV = \sum_{t=1}^{n} \frac{S_n}{(1+i)^t} \qquad (16.12)$$

if $S_1 = S_2 = S_n = S$ this becomes

$$PV = S \sum_{t=1}^{n} \frac{1}{(1+i)^t} \qquad (16.13)$$

EXAMPLE 16.6

Roree Ltd expects to receive a cash inflow of $3500 each year for 10 years as a result of starting a new project.

REQUIRED

Determine the present value of the sum discounted at 9 per cent.

SOLUTION

Utilise[1] equation (16.13):

$PV = \$3500(6.14144569)$
$\quad = \$22461.80$

The PV of $3500 per annum for 10 years, discounted at 9 per cent, is $22461.80.

---

[1] When the cash flows are uniform as in the example, add the discount factors for the number of years and the given percentage and simply multiply the cash flow by the aggregated factor. The procedure is easier.

16.7 Capital recovery

An individual (like a firm) usually has to repay a mortgage or a debt to a bank. The capital recovery calculations can be determined from equations (16.10 and 16.9), reproduced below:

$$PV = S_n \left[\frac{1}{(1+i)^n} \right] \tag{16.10}$$

$$F = A \left[\frac{(1+i)^n - 1}{i} \right] \tag{16.9}$$

SOLUTION

Substitute equation (16.9) for S_n in equation (16.10):

$$PV = A \left[\frac{(1+i)^n - 1}{i} \right] \left[\frac{1}{(1+i)^n} \right]$$

$$F = A \left[\frac{(1+i)^n - 1}{i(1+i)^n} \right]$$

Solve for A:

$$A = PV \left[\frac{i(1+i)^n}{(1+i)^n - 1} \right] \tag{16.14}$$

EXAMPLE 16.7

Roree Ltd needs $117000. A city bank, after an examination of the balance sheet structure of the firm, agrees to provide a mortgage at 10 per cent for 20 years with equal annual year end payments

REQUIRED

Calculate the amount of the year end payments.

SOLUTION

Use equation (16.14):

$$\text{Mortgage payments} = \$117000 \; \frac{0.10(1.10)^{20}}{(1.10)^{20} - 1}$$

$$= \$117000 \; \frac{0.67275}{5.7275}$$

$$= \$13742.78$$

Roree Ltd would pay $13742.78 for 20 years to repay the $117000 mortgage.

16.8 Summary

This chapter has shown the mechanical, arithmetic calculations required for the discounting procedures which are an integral part of capital expenditure analysis.

Capital Budgeting

Bibliography

Hummel, P. M. and Seebeck, C. L. (1970) *Mathematics of Finance* 3rd edn (McGraw-Hill).
Van Horne, J. C. (1977) *Financial Management and Policy*, 4th. edn. (Prentice-Hall) chap. 4.

Problems

16.1

(a) A company borrows $100000 on the last day of the year and agrees to repay it by four equal amounts, the repayments being made at the end of each of the following 4 years. Compound interest at 12 per cent per annum is payable.

REQUIRED

What is the amount of each payment?

(b) $1000 is invested at 12 per cent per annum, with interest added every quarter end.

REQUIRED

How long will it take for the investment to amount to $3000?

ICMA, FS, Section B, Mathematics and Statistics, May 1982.

16.2 A loan of $10000 was borrowed at 10 per cent per annum to be paid back over 3 years. At the beginning of the second year, the interest rate dropped to 8 per cent per annum. Initially the loan repayments (paid at the end of each year in equal amounts to cover capital and interest) were calculated so that the loan would be repaid within 3 years. Subsequently, when the interest rate fell, the loan repayments were recalculated so that the loan could be repaid in the original time period of 3 years.

REQUIRED

(a) Calculate the annual loan repayments before and after the fall in interest, and show the amount outstanding at the end of each of the 3 years.
(b) ow the balace outstanding at the end of each year if the original loan repayments are continued throughout the period until the loan is repaid.
(c) If no repayments are made during the life of the loan, what lump sum would have to be repaid at the end of the 3 years?
(d) Assuming a discount rate of 10 per cent throughout the period of the loan, calculate the NPV of each of the three schemes as at the time the loan is taken
Explain briefly why your three answers differ, if they do

ACCA, PE, Section 2, Paper 12, Management Mathematics, June 1978.

Chapter 17
Project Financing and the Cost of Capital

> Discounting, as a means of legislating for uncertainty, has considerable practical merits.
> (Shackle, 1970)

17.1 Project financing

The financing of a capital project, whether from internal or external sources, necessitates the computation of the firm's cost of capital.[1] The cost of capital can be used by management as a measure to cut off certain projects if the return in percentage terms falls below it.

There are various types of capital expenditure which can be undertaken by management. Capital expenditure decisions are bound up with depreciation and taxation procedures; both of which affect profit, and hence have an impact on the cash in flows and out flows of the firm. Cash flows are central to capital expenditure decisions.

The tax laws of many countries permit the inclusion of depreciation as a tax deductible expense. From a capital budgeting view, the following points about depreciation should be noted: (i) it is an accounting expense; (ii) it is not an out flow of cash; (iii) the dollar values deducted for depreciation on the firm's revenue statement are added to any earnings after taxes to obtain the firm's cash flow from operations.

17.2 Cost of Capital

The cost of capital is a guide measure to the rates of return expected by those parties contributing to the financial structure of the firm – creditors, preferred and ordinary shareholders, unions, investment and government institutions.

The cost of capital represents the cost of funds used to acquire the total assets of the firm. It can

---

[1] The computation of the cost of capital is the subject of the subsequent sections of this chapter.

be calculated from historical data, using a weighted average of the cost associated with each type of capital included in the firm's financial structure.[1] This is the traditional method. However, since the financial, historical structure of the firm is made up of residual values and is not indicative of the dynamics of the firm, the marginal costing approach is used to determine the cost of capital. In project analysis, it is the earnings above that rate that add to the profit of the firm.

Of interest to the analysis which follows is the financial structure shown in Figure 17.1. Calculation of the marginal cost of capital requires further explanation.

```
                                                  $
        Ordinary shares    (Market value)
        Preference shares  (Market value)
        Retained earnings
        Long-term debt
        Current liabilities
                                              _____
                                                  $
                                              ==========
```

Figure 17.1 Firm's financial structure

17.3 The Cost of Equity

The firm's cost of equity can be linked with the price of the ordinary shares, its dividend and dividend growth rate, to give:

$$K_{os} = \frac{D_1}{P_c} + g \tag{17.1}$$

where K_{os} = Cost of ordinary shares
D_1 = Expected dividend in period 1
P_c = Current market price
g = Growth rate of dividend per year

Since the cost of capital represents the amount that the firm earns on the net proceeds derived from new issues, flotation costs come into the evaluation. For new issues, equation (17.1) is modified to:

$$K_{Nos} = \frac{D_1}{P_c(1-F)} + g \tag{17.2}$$

Where K_{Nos} = Cost of new equity
F = Flotation cost, expressed as percentage of market price

The cost of the firm's irredeemable preference shares can be derived in a similar way to equation (17.2). The equation is:

$$K_{Np} = \frac{D_{Np}}{P_{Np}(1-F)} \tag{17.3}$$

---

[1] The cost of capital to be used in project appraisal is the subject of some debate in the finance literature. Readers should consult Arditti (1973), Baumol and Burton (1967) and Keane (1977; 1978) for insights into the debate. Note, however, that regardless of the methods advocated, the cost of capital required is a future value and any measure will be an estimate.

Where K_{Np} = Cost of new preference issue
D_{Np} = Dividend on new preference issue
F = As defined above
P_{Np} = Sale price of new preference issue

17.4 Retained earnings

It is suggested in the literature that retained earnings are not relevant to the calculation of the cost of capital. Commonsense, however, points to the fact that individuals (like firms) do retain some part of their earnings for investment purposes. What is this portion that firms should include in the cost of capital calculation? That portion must be, from a shareholder's view, the dividend forgone. The dividend forgone is the opportunity cost of that portion of the retained earnings which should be distributed as dividend. It is therefore logical to suggest that the shareholders of the firm require a return on funds available for reinvestment at the same rate (or greater) than they are obtaining from the existing investments (K_{os}). There may be some savings associated with using retained earnings as a source of finance, rather than paying out dividends and raising new equity. The savings on retained earnings avoid the liability of shareholders to personal income tax that would have been payable on the distribution of a dividend. The brokerage and flotation costs associated with a new issue are also avoided. The cost of retained earnings for the cost of capital computations can thus be expressed as::

$$\pi_E = K_{os}(1 - t_m) \qquad (17.4)$$

Where π_E = Cost of retained profit
K_{os} = as defined above
t_m = Shareholders' tax rates payable on dividend but not on retention

17.5 The cost of debt

The debts which make up the firm's financial structure are classified as long-term and short-term debt. The total debt structure of the firm has a decisive interaction with its other parts. But why include current liabilities as a parameter in the determination of the firm's cost of capital? The reasons are: (i) firms do make use of trade credits; (ii) in practice, firms resort to commercial credit to finance current assets; (iii) many capital projects have an impact on working capital and also require short-term financing; (iv) short-term finance does have an interest cost of at least that interest that would have been earned if the amount provided was put on deposit at the bank; in many cases, the opportunity cost will be the cost of interest payable on the overdraft which is avoided. In calculating debt cost, allowance must be made for the effect of being able to charge interest expense against tax. When flotation costs are involved, the marginal cost of the components of debt can be derived from:

$$K_{di} = \frac{I(1 - t_{mr})}{P_d(1 - F)}$$

Project Financing and the Cost of Capital

Where K_{di} = After tax cost of specific component of debt
  I = Interest
  t_{mr} = Firm's marginal tax rate
  P_d = Price of debt
  F = As defined above

17.6 Calculating the marginal cost of capital

When a company has equity and debt sources, the overall cost of capital must be calculated by combining the cost of the elements of capital. In combining these costs a weighted average must be found. The appropriate weights to be used are the relative current market values. The Example 17.1 and its solution illustrate the calculation of the costs of the elements of capital and their combination in determining the overall cost of capital.

EXAMPLE 17.1

The Puma firm plans to raise $420000 of new capital:

Ordinary Shares

$200000–the current market price is $60 based on expectations of dividends of $2 next year growing at 12 per cent per annum thereafter; flotation cost, estimated at 15 per cent

Preference shares

$90000; flotation cost estimated at 4 per cent
Price $50 per share, with a stated dividend of $5 per share

Long-term debt

$80000 at 7 per cent – flotation cost 3/4 per cent

Current liabilities

$50 000 at 14 per cent – no flotation cost
The firm's marginal tax rate is 40 per cent

REQUIRED

Compute the cost of each component, and the marginal cost of capital.

SOLUTION

(i) *Cost of ordinary shares*

$$K_{os} = \frac{D_1}{P_c} + g = \frac{\$2}{\$60(1-0.15)} + 0.12$$

$$= \frac{\$2}{\$60(0.85)} + 0.12 = 0.1579$$

(ii) *Cost of preference shares*

$$K_{Np} = \frac{D_{Np}}{P_{Np}(1-F)} = \frac{\$5}{\$50(1-0.04)}$$

$$= \frac{\$5}{48} = 0.1042$$

(iii) *Cost of long-term debt*

$$K_{d_1} = \frac{I(1-T_{mr})}{P_{d_1}(1-F)} = \frac{\$5600(1-0.40)}{\$80000(1-0.0075)}$$

$$= \frac{3360}{79\,400} = 0.0423$$

(iv) *Cost of short-term debt*

$$K_{d_2} = \frac{I(1-T_{mr})}{K_{d_2}} = \frac{\$7000(1-0.40)}{\$50000}$$

$$= \frac{4200}{50000} = 0.0840$$

(v) *Marginal cost of capital*

	Market values	Market weights	After tax cost	Weighted after tax cost
	$			
Ordinary shares	200000	0.4762	0.1579	0.0752
Preference shares	90000	0.2143	0.1042	0.0223
Long-term debt	80000	0.1905	0.0423	0.0081
Current liabilities	50000	0.1190	0.0840	0.0100
	$420000	10000		

Marginal cost of capital	= 0.1156

The marginal cost of capital of the Puma firm is 11.56 per cent approx.

COMMENT

In computing a marginal cost of capital using market data, as above, it is assumed that the capital sources are available to meet the financing needs of the project. If this assumption is invalid because projects are being considered which require more funds than are available, then a capital rationing situation exists. As with other problems involving a limited availability of an input resource, this introduces opportunity cost considerations. The discussion in 15.11 of Linear programming indicates that a shadow price for capital may exist.

Bibliography

Anton, H. R. (1956) 'Depreciation, Cost Allocation and Investment Decisions', in T. F. Keller and S. A. Zeff (eds), *Financial Accounting Theory II, Issues and Controversies* (McGraw-Hill).

Arditti, F. D. (1973) 'The Weighted Average Cost of Capital: Some Questions on its Definition, Interpretation and Use', *Journal of Finance*, 28, September, pp. 1001–8.

Baumol, W. and Burton, G. M. (1967) 'The Firm's Optimal Debt Equity Combination and the Cost of Capital', *Quarterly Journal of Economics*, 81, November, pp. 547–78.

Keane, S. M. (1977) 'The Irrelevance of the Firm's Cost of Capital as an Investment Decision Tool', *Journal of Business Finance and Accounting*, Summer, pp. 201–16.

Keane, S. M. (1978) 'The Cost of Capital as a Financial Decision Tool', *Journal of Business Finance and Accounting*, Autumn, pp. 339–52.

Lent, G. E. (1967) 'Tax Incentives for Investment in Developing Countries', *IMF Staff Papers*, vol. xiv, no. 2, July, pp. 249–323.

Shackle, G. L. S. (1970) *Expectation, Enterprise and Profit* (George Allen & Unwin) p. 97.

Problems

17.1 Explain what is meant by capital budgeting.

17.2 The summarised balance sheet of Wareham PLC shows:

Capital employed	$000	Capital	$000
£1 shares	1000		
Reserves	5000		
Book value of equity	6000		
5% Irredeemable debentures	4000		
	$ 10000		
Employment of capital:			
Sundry Assets	$10000		

Wareham's debentures are currently selling at $62.50 per $100 nominal. Their shares sell at $1.25 per share, this price reflecting expectations that the next dividend, due in a year, will be 20p per share and will grow at an annual rate of 4 per cent therafter

REQUIRED

Calculate the weighted average cost of capital for Wareham Ltd.

Chapter 18
The Analysis of Capital Investment Decisions

Investment is the sacrifice of current financial advantage (such as purchasing power) in return for some future return; the decision to invest or not to do so involves a comparison of the current sacrifice with future expectations.   (Vatter, 1973)

18.1 Introduction

Money is a scarce commodity. In nearly all firms the amount of money available for capital investments is limited. Hence, the management function must have some criteria for the acceptance, rejection or postponement of investment proposals. It must also have some cardinal system by which investments can be ranked for acceptance by the firm.

Some of the methods used to evaluate capital investments by the management function are: (i) pay-back; (ii) accounting rate of return; (iii) net present value (NPV); (iv) profitability index (PI); and (v) internal rate of return (IRR). These methods are now defined, and examples shown.

18.2 Pay-back

The purpose of the pay-back method is to ascertain the time period in which the capital cost of the investment will be recovered from the cash generated by the investment. Pay-back measures the investment's liquidity and capital recovery, rather than its economic profitability.

Investments can be accepted, rejected and ranked via the pay-back method. In the latter case, the shorter the pay-back period, the higher the ranking.

EXAMPLE 18.1

The Rolston firm wants to invest in one of two projects, which have cash profits and estimated lives as shown below.

The Analysis of Capital Investment Decisions

REQUIRED

Determine the pay-back period.

	PROJECT	
	1	2
Capital cost ($)	$6000	$10000
Estimated (Life) (yr)	7	10
Annual cash flow ($)	$2000	$2500

SOLUTION

$$\text{Pay-back} = \frac{\text{Capital cost}}{\text{Annual cash flows}}$$

$$= \$\frac{6000}{2000} \qquad \$\frac{10000}{2500}$$

$$= 3 \text{ yr} \qquad 4 \text{ yr.}$$

The pay-back periods for projects 1 and 2 are respectively 3 and 4 years. Project 1 is preferred.

The pay-back method is a simple device which can be used by management to determine the capital recovery period. The method fails to highlight the expected revenues beyond the pay-back period. From Example 18.1 the total profitabilities of the projects are as follows:

	PROJECT		
Total cash flows:	7 × $14000	$14000	10 × $2500	$25000
Capital cost		6000		10000
		$8 000		$15 000

If the projects were mutually exclusive, project 1 would have been selected, although project 2 is in the long run more profitable. The concentration of capital expenditure on projects having short pay-back periods may thus result in the rejection of projects which are profitable to the firm in the long run. Merrett and Sykes (1963) state: 'It causes assessors to concentrate on unimportant and often irrelevant characteristics of an investment project to the detriment of its significant characteristics' Weingartner (1969), with the total liquidity position of the firm in mind, points out: The usually designated speculative and or precautionary motive of firms to hold liquid or near liquid funds in order to seize upon unexpected opportunities is a different motive from that which requires each new investment separately to recover its original cost within a short time'.

The method also fails to consider (i) all flows occurring after the end of the pay-back period; (ii) the time value of money; (iii) the cost of funds used to support the investment during the pay-back period. (iii) can, however, be incorporated into the pay-back method, as shown below.

EXAMPLE 18.2

Suppose the firm in Example 18.1 requires a rate of return of 10 per cent.

SOLUTION

This problem requires a schedule to be produced showing the effects of the cash inflows paying back the initial outlay and imputing an interest charge to the net amount outstanding.

	PROJECT	
	1	2
	$	$
Initial outlay	6000	10000
Interest at 10%	600	1000
	6600	11000
Cash inflow Year 1	2000	2500
Net amount outstanding	4600	8500
Interest at 10%	460	850
	5060	9350
Cash inflow Year 2	2000	2500
Net amount outstanding	3060	6850
Interest at 10%	306	685
	3366	7535
Cash in flow Year 3	2000	2500
	1366	5035
Interest at 10%	137	504
	1503	5539
Cash inflow Year 4	2000	2500
	(497)	3039
Fully paid back interest		304
		3343
Cash inflow year 5		2500
		843
Interest		84
		927
Cash inflow Year 6		2500
		—
Fully paid back		

COMMENT

Since project 1 is paid back in less than 4 years, whilst project 2 is not paid back until more than 5 years have elapsed, project 1 is preferred. The time value of money can be incorporated by the use of the 'discounted pay-back' method; discussion of this is postponed until discounting methods have been introduced.

Samuels and Wilkes (1977) state that 'pay-back is a safety first criterion'. From this statement, a set of working conditions for management can now be posited. If the management function feels uncertain about the expected cash flows to be received beyond a certain period; if liquidity is a problem within the firm, and management desires to finance other investments by internal financing becuase of high external interest rates; if the risk of the social product is great because of obsolescence, technological change and competition, then (and only then) pay-back should be used. In such cases, the pay-back method has advantages.

18.3 Accounting rate of return

The accounting rate of return method shows the yearly after tax or pre tax income expressed as a percentage of the investment outlay employed by the firm. The accounting rate of return can be calculated in a variety of ways, and the solution to Example 19.3 shows these methods.

EXAMPLE 18.3

The Rolston firm estimates that project 3 will have the projected cash flow statement shown below:

	Project 3
	$
Investment outlay	15000
Estimated life (yr)	5
	$
Annual profit before depreciation	5000
Annual depreciation (straight line)	3000
Annual net income	2000

REQUIRED

Determine the accounting rate of return for the project.

SOLUTION

We shall consider four methods:

(i) *Annual accounting return on investment*

$$\frac{\text{Annual income}}{\text{Investment outlay}} \times 100 = \frac{2000}{15000} \times 100 = 13.33\%$$

(ii) *Annual accounting average investment*

$$\frac{\text{Annual income}}{\frac{\text{Investment outlay}}{2}} \times 100 = \frac{2000}{7500} \times 100 = 26.67\%$$

(iii) *Average annual accounting rate of return on average investment*

$$\frac{\text{Total income} - \text{Investment outlay}}{\frac{\text{Investment outlay}}{2} \times \text{yr}} \times 100 = \frac{25000 - 15000}{37500} \times 100 = 26.67\%$$

It can be seen that the result of method (iii) is identical to that of method (ii), but method (iii) calculations are based on the whole life of the project while method (ii) considers the average for 1 year of the project only.

(iv) *Average book return on investment*

$$\frac{\text{Total income} - \text{Investment outlay}}{\text{Weighted average investment}^a}$$

$$= \frac{10000 \times 100}{\dfrac{15000 + 12500 + 9000 + 6000 + 3000}{2} \times 5 \text{ yr}} = 22.27\%$$

[a] The sum of the book values of the asset each year.

An advantage of the accounting rate of return is its simplicity of calculation. The disadvantages, however, outweigh the advantage since the accounting rate of return can be calculated in many ways. This tends to confuse issues. The accounting rate of return also does not consider the timing of the expected cash inflows. The accounting rate of return is misleading. It is misleading because the value of an asset to the firm is associated with the management function's ability to generate maximum service benefit from it. The firm's balance sheet (to which those figures would be affixed) is a mere listing of the acquired investments and the sources of capital used to obtain and maintain those investments. The listing reflects residual values, which differ to a marked degree from market and production values. In capital investment decisions, it is not the sunk costs, but the market values, which are relevant. The accounting return therefore does not indicate the real values or earning power of a project. It is also distorted by the accounting conventions used in the measurement of accounting profit in particular the methods used for calculating depreciation; these are generally based on historical cost, and ignore the time value of money.

18.4 Net present value (NPV)

The present value criterion is a simple procedure for evaluating proposed capital investments in the absence of capital rationing. The procedure involves summing the present values of the estimated cash out flows to support the investment with the present values of the estimated cash inflows which may result from the project's operations.

The cash inflows and outflows are discounted to a present value using the firm's cost of capital. The NPV is the difference in the present values of the inflows and outflows. Algebraically, the procedure is:

$$\text{NPV} = \sum_{t=0}^{n} \frac{S_t}{(1+k)t} - K_0 \gtreqless \qquad (18.1)$$

Three rules emerge from equation (18.1). These are: (i) if NPV is positive (>0), the project is expected to earn a return in excess of the required rate (k); if NPV is 0, the yield is expected to equal the required rate; if NPV is negative (< 0), the yield is expected to be less than the required rate. It follows that only those projects which have positive or 0 NPVs meet the NPV criterion for acceptance.

EXAMPLE 18.4

The Rice Co. have just purchased a machine for $15000. On the day it is delivered they discovered that a more modern machine is available costing $25000 which will reduce operating cost by $4000

The Analysis of Capital Investment Decisions

per annum. Both machines have a 10-year life, 0 salvage value at the end of 10 years and are identical in all other respects. The machine they have just purchased can be sold immediately, but will realise only $10000.

Assume (i) that the tax credit on this type of machine is 10 percent; (ii) that the firm has a 20 per cent marginal tax rate and a 15 per cent required rate of return; (iii) that it uses the straight line method of depreciation.

REQUIRED

Advise the Rice Co. whether the new machine should be purchased.

SOLUTION

The Rice Co. have two alternatives—either to continue to use the existing machine, or to sell it and buy the more modern one.

(i) Calculate the cash outflow required to acquire the modern machine:

	$
Purchase price of new machine	25000
Less sale price of old machine[a]	(10000)
Less investment tax credit 0.10 × 25000	(2500)
Add tax on sale of old machine 0.20 × 10000	2000
	$14500

a The original purchase price is a sunk cost, and not relevant here.

(ii) Calculate the increase in the annual cash inflow:

	Change in income	Change in cash flow
	$	$
Reduction in cost	4000	4000
Increase in depreciation $\dfrac{25000}{10} - \dfrac{15000}{10}$	(1000)	
Increase in earnings	3000	
Tax at 20 per cent	(600)	(600)
Increase in earnings after tax	$2400	—
Increase in cash flow		$3400

(iii) Calculate the NPV using the discount rate of 15 per cent:

Year	Amount	Discount factor	Present value
	$		$
0	(14500)	1	(14500)
1–10	3400	5.0188	17064
			$2564

COMMENT

Since the NPV is positive, the Rice Co. should be advised to change the machine. It is a pity that the old machine is to be sold. Had the company known the modern machine would be available, it would have been better never to have purchased the old machine. Nevertheless, it would be wrong to operate the old machine when the value of savings from replacement exceed the replacement cost.

18.5 Profitability index (PI)

PI is the ratio of the present value of the after tax cash inflows to the outflows. It can be expressed as:

$$PI = \frac{\sum_{t=1}^{n} \frac{S_t}{(1+k)t}}{K_0} \tag{18.2}$$

A ratio of 1 or greater shows that the investment under analysis has an expected return equal to or greater than the discount rate (K). PI is a measure of the investment's profitability in dollar terms. The profitability index must be used with caution, since it does not consider the size of projects.

EXAMPLE 18.5

Four projects have been put forward to top management by two foremen. The after tax cash flows for each is shown in Table 18.1. The firm's cost of capital is 15 per cent.

REQUIRED

Rank the projects in order of profitability.

Table 18.1 After tax cash flow

| | PROJECT | | | |
Time	1	2	3	4
Yr	$	$	$	$
0	−10000	−15000	−20000	−40000
1	3800	8000	10000	15000
2	4000	7000	10000	15000
3	5000	7000	10000	18000
4	5000	9000	10000	20000

SOLUTION

Calculate the present value of the cash inflows and outflows for each project. The present values of the inflows and outflows are:

PV	1	2	3	4
	$	$	$	$
Outflows	−10000	−15000	−20000	−40000
Inflows	12475	21998	28550	47657

The Analysis of Capital Investment Decisions

The profitability indexes are:

1. $\dfrac{\$12475}{10000} = 1.2475$

2. $\dfrac{\$21998}{15000} = 1.4665$

3. $\dfrac{\$28550}{20000} = 1.4275$

4. $\dfrac{\$47657}{40000} = 1.1914$

The projects would be ranked as follows: 2, 3, 1 and 4. Note, however, that projects 3 and 4 have higher NPVs than projects 1 and 2. It is important to note that every project is profitable, so ranking is needed only if capital is rationed (e.g., only $40000 available) or if projects are mutually exclusive.

18.6 Internal rate of return (IRR)

The National Association of Accountants[1] defines the internal rate of return to be 'the maximum rate of interest that could be paid for the capital employed over the life of an investment without loss on the project'. When a project IRR is (i), it is meant that if the firm were to place an amount equal to the investment into a fund earning a rate (i) each period, it could withdraw from the fund an amount equal to ΔS_t one period from now; an amount equal to ΔS_{t_2} two periods from now, and at the end of period t, withdraw ΔS_t and exhaust the fund. The IRR is thus that rate which must be earned on the unrecovered portion of the investment.

EXAMPLE 18.6

The manager of the Ronald firm asks you to determine the IRR of a project which has an after tax cost of $10000 and an after tax cash inflow of $180000 in Year 4.

SOLUTION

The IRR is that rate which discounts the project's cash flows to a NPV of 0:

∴ PV of $180000 − $100000 = 0

Recall equation (18.1)

$$NPV = \dfrac{S_t}{(1+K)^4} - K_o$$

$$= \dfrac{180000}{(1+K)^4} = 100000$$

Present value factor $= \dfrac{1}{(1+K)^4} = 0.5556$

Looking up the present value tables, the closest present value factor to 0.5556 when $t = 4$ is 0.5523. This corresponds to an interest rate of 16 per cent. 16 per cent is therefore the IRR of the project.

---

[1] See Horngren (1977).

18.7 Unequal net cash flows

When an initial investment generates unequal net cash flows, the IRR of the investment can be found by 'trial and error' and linear interpolation. The presentation which is outlined below consists in narrowing the possible values for IRR within a 5 per cent range. The formula

$$\text{IRR} = i_2 - (i_2 - i_1)\frac{NPV_2}{NPV_2 - NPV_1} \qquad (18.3)$$

is appropriate. i_1 and i_2 are the rates used respectively to obtain NPV_1 and NPV_2. If $i_2 > i_1$, NPV_2 is negative while NPV_1 is positive.

EXAMPLE 18.7
The management of the Ronald firm is considering the purchase of a $30000 machine which will generate operating benefits of $14000 in Year 1, $17000 in Year 2 and $9000 in Year 3. The appropriate capital cost rate is 30 per cent, and the tax rate is 40 per cent.

REQUIRED
Calculate the IRR of the investment.

SOLUTION

(i) Set up the NPV equation
Calculate the after tax operating benefits for Years 1, 2 and 3.
These are $8400, $10200, and $5400

$$NPV = -\$30000 + 30000\frac{0.4 \times 0.3}{i + 0.3} + \$8400\frac{1}{(1+i)} + \$10200\frac{1}{(1+i)^2} + \$5400\frac{1}{(1+i)^3}$$

Set $i = 0$
$NPV = \$(30000 - 36000) = \$6000$.

(ii) Compute a percentage of i
First, the i value can be approximated from the problem
Since the sum of the three cash inflows is known to be $30000, use the average cash inflows and find the discount factor:

Discount factor $= \dfrac{30000}{8000} = 3.75$, which corresponds to 26 per cent.

For i = 26%
NPV = −$7780

The IRR of the investment lies between 0 percent and 26 per cent.
Narrow the range:

$$\frac{0+26}{2}\% = 13\%$$

CONDITION

(i) if NPV is positve using the 13 per cent rate, the IRR lies between 13 per cent and 26 per cent
(ii) If NPV is negative, the IRR lies between 0 per cent and 13 per cent

For $i = 13\%$
NPV = −$2463

The Analysis of Capital Investment Decisions

(iii) Use the 5% range

For $i = 5$ per cent
NPV $= -\$2208$

So i is between 5 per cent and 13 per cent

For $i = 10$ per cent
NPV $= -\$878$

So i is between 5 per cent nd 10 per cent

At this point, there exists a range for which the difference between the extreme values is 5 per cent, with a positive NPV at one end, and a negative NPV at the other

(iv) Calculate the IRR by interpolation, using

$i_2 = 10\%$, $i_1 = 5\%$
$NPV_1 = 2208$, $NPV_2 = -878$

$$IRR = 10\% - (10\% - 5\%) \frac{-878}{-878 - 2208}$$

$= 10\% - 5\% \times 0.2845$
$= 8.5774\%$

(v) Check calculations[a]

$i = 8.5774\%$ gives:
NPV $= \$(30000 - 29939) = 0$

[a] This is approximately zero.

The difference of 61 is due to error in using linear interpolation. The IRR of the investment for the Ronald firm is 8.5774 percent.

The IRR of an investment can be compared with the required rate by management, to decide upon its acceptability or rejection. If the IRR of an investment is greater than the required rate and NPV is also > 0, the investment is acceptable. Where many investments are evaluated by management, they can be ranked according to their computed IRRs. The investment with the largest IRR is ranked first, and all others follow the numerical sequence 2, 3 ... N.

18.8 Multiple internal rates of return

The determination of an internal rate of return is not as straightforward as Example 18.7 implies when an investment has a sequence of changes in sign of each cash flow e.g. $+-+,-+-$. The conditions for multiple rates of return are highlighted by Longbottom and Wiper (1978). They showed that for multiple rates to occur the graph of NPV against the rate used must cut the axis twice (see Figure 18.1), which give rise to a minimum and a maximum point.

The determination of multiple IRRs in a 2-year investment is facilitated by the quadratic function.

$$X = \frac{-b \pm \sqrt{b^2 - 4ac}}{2a} \tag{18.4}$$

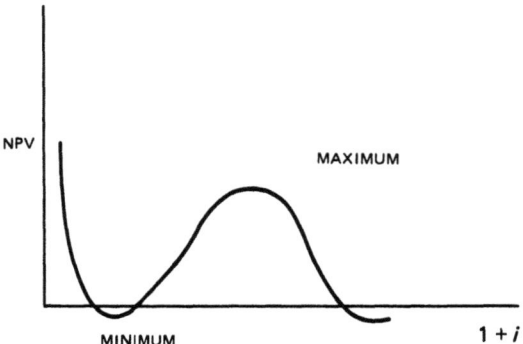

Figure 18.1 Graph of NPV against rate of return

EXAMPLE 18.8

The Robert firm wants to invest in a new project which has the following cash outflows and inflows:

Time	Cash flows
0	−210.7
1	460
2	−250

REQUIRED

Determine the IRRs of the project.

SOLUTION

Set up the problem using the quadratic formula:

$$\frac{-250}{(1+i)^2} + \frac{460}{(1+i)} - 210.7 = 0$$

Let $X = \frac{1}{(1+i)}$, then

$$\frac{1}{(1+i)} = \frac{-460 \pm \sqrt{211600 - 210700}}{-500}$$

$$= \frac{-460 \pm 430}{-500}$$

$$\frac{1}{(1+i)} = \frac{430}{500} \qquad (18.5)$$

$$\frac{1}{(1+i)} = \frac{490}{500} \qquad (18.6)$$

The Analysis of Capital Investment Decisions

From equation (18.5)

$i_1 = 16.3$ per cent

From equation (18.6)

$i_2 = 2$ per cent

The multiple rates of return are respectively 2 per cent and 16.3 per cent.

It is not possible simply to identify which of such rates is the relevant one without carrying out NPV calculations, and being aware of a known cut off rate.

18.9 Discounted pay-back

In 18.2 above, it was indicated that it was possible to adapt the pay-back method to allow for the time value of money. The method sets out to find the period required to generate cash inflows which have a NPV which is at least equal to the initial outlay, i.e. to find how long the project must continue before the NPV becomes positive.

EXAMPLE 18.9

Reconsider the case of the Rolston firm in Examples 18.1 and 18.2. The two alternative projects had capital costs respectively of $6000 and $10000, annual cash flows of $2000 and $2500 and lives of 7 and 10 years. The cost of capital is taken to be 10 per cent.

REQUIRED:

Calculate the pay-back period using the discounted pay-back method.

SOLUTION:

Discounted payback period = n yr,
 Where capital cost = annual cash flows × annuity factor for n years at appropriate cost of capital:

	PROJECT	
	1	2
Annuity factor =	$\dfrac{6000}{2000}$	$\dfrac{10000}{2500}$
	= 3	4

A reading from annuity tables for cost of capital of 10 per cent shows that for $n = 3$ the annuity factor $= 2.4869$, and for $n = 4$ the factor $= 3.1699$. Therefore for a factor of 3, n lies between 3 and 4 years. The approximated period can be found by interpolation; the result is 3.74 years. An annuity factor of 4 similarly corresponds to 5.34 years.

The discounted pay-back period for project 1 is less than that for project 2; project 1 is therefore preferred.

18.10 Summary

The methods used to evaluate capital investments are pay-back; accounting rate of return; net present value (NPV); profitability index (PI); and internal rate of return (IRR).

The pay-back method should be used with caution. The accounting rate of return method is misleading, partly because of distortions arising from accounting profit measurement. Both methods ignore the time value of money, although it has been shown that the pay-back method can be adapted to take account of this factor.

The NPV method, PI and IRR utilise discounting techniques in evaluating capital investments. The first two methods require a cost of capital as an input in the computation. The IRR method does not require such a rate. The rate has to be found, but must then be compared with the given cost of capital.

The methods are employed to rank and establish the acceptability of projects.

Bibliography

Horngren, C. T. (1977) *Cost Accounting: A Managerial Emphasis*, 4th edn (Prentice-Hall) p. 378–386.

Longbottom, D. and Wiper, L. (1978) 'Necessary Conditions for the existence of Multiple Rates in the Use of Infernal Rate of Return' *Journal of Business Finance and Accounting*, vol. 5, no. 4, Winter, pp. 295–304.

Merrett, A. J. and Sykes, A. (1973) *The Finance and Analysis of Capital Projects*, 2nd edn (Longman) pp. 120–142.

Samuels, J. M. and Wilkes, F. M. (1977) *Management of Company Finance* (Thomas Nelson) p. 159.

Vatter, W. J. (1973) 'Capital Budget Formulae', in W. E. Thomas (ed.) *Readings in Cost Accounting and Budgeting* (South-Western Publishing Co.) pp. 211–47.

Weingartner, H. M. (1969) 'Some Views on the Pay-Back Period and Capital Budgeting Decisions', *Management Science*, vol. 15, no. 12, August, pp. B594–B609.

Problems

18.1 The Carreton Co. is considering whether or not to replace an old machine that it has in use. The machine is completely depreciated, and has a salvage value of $5000. The company is considering two mutually exclusive alternatives. The one possible purchase is machine A which is similar in style to the old machine. It would cost $70000 and result in before tax cash inflows of $17600 per annum.

The other possible purchase is a new type, machine B, which has not up to now been tried out in the industry in which Carreton is engaged. It would cost $125000, and the expected before tax cash inflows resulting from use of the machine are $32500 per annum.

Both Machine A and Machine B have an expected life of 10 years. The machine at present in use could probably be kept going for another 10 years, but the high maintenance costs and low productivity would mean that the machine would only just about break even over the period.

It can be assumed that all three machines would have 0 scrap value in 10 years' time. The corporation tax rate is 50 per cent. Both possible acquisitions would qualify for a capital allowance of 100 per cent in the first year of operation. The firm's cost of capital is 12 per cent. You may assume that annual cash flows are paid (or are received) on the last day of the year.

REQUIRED

Should the firm replace the existing machine, and if so should replacement be with a similar type of machine (A), or with the new type of machine (B)?

ACCA, PE, Section 3, Accounting 6, Financial Management, December 1981.

18.2 Oxtel Co. Ltd has $2.5 million available to purchase a new factory. If Oxtel goes ahead with this venture, it is estimated that it will generate cash flows of $270000 in the first year, $360000 in the second year and $450000 each year thereafter. However, certain speculative members of the company have suggested that it might be financially better to purchase an area of land alongside its present site, which has just come onto the market at $2.5 million. They believe that, with the expected expansion of industry in the immediate area of their current plant, the value of the land in 10 years' time should be $6.5 million.

The Analysis of Capital Investment Decisions   303

The speculators argue that the new factory will have a life of 10 years only, and that the gain on the land speculation will leave the original $2.5 million plus a surplus of $3.8 million, while the factory investment will merely give a surplus of $4.23 million and a factory with a negligible scrap value.

REQUIRED

(a) Comment on the validity of the argument in respect of the surplus of $3.8 million and $4.23 million
(b) Using a discount rate of 10 per cent, compare the two investments and advise Oxtel on its investment policy
(c) If the required rate of return were 10 per cent, what is the minimum price at which you would sell the land in 10 years' time?

ACA, PE, Section 2, Paper 12, Management Mathematics, December 1976.

18.3 A company is considering investing in a project with the following characteristics:

(i) Equipment is to be purchased costing $70000, payable at once and having a life of 5 years with no residual value. The equipment is used to produce one type of product whose sales are budgeted as follows:

Year to 30 June	Units
1983	20
84	40
85	50
86	30
87	10
Total	150

(ii) The selling price of the units is to be $4000 each
(iii) Cost of units are:

Direct materials ($)	1200 each
	%
Variable production overhead	50 of direct wages
Variable selling and administration overhead	10 of selling price

(iv) Direct wages are paid at $3 per hour
The first unit to be produced is budgeted to take 1505.3 manhours of work, and an 80 per cent learning curve applies to direct wages
(v) Fixed overhead relating to this project is $12000 per annum
(vi) The company requires a 12 per cent DCF return on its investments

REQUIRED

(a) Calculate whether or not the project meets the company's investment criterion, based on:
  (i) the average direct wages rate for the whole quantity of units budgeted to be sold
  (ii) the direct labour times expected to be required in each individual year
(b) Comment briefly on the relative merits of bases (a)(i) and (a)(ii) above

Ignore the effects of tax and inflation.
Note that an 80 per cent learning curve on ordinary graph paper would show the following

relationship between the x axis (volume) and y axis (cumulative average cost of elements subject to the learning curve):

x	y	x	y
	%		%
1	100	70	25.48
2	80	80	24.40
10	47.65	90	23.50
20	38.13	100	22.71
30	33.46	110	22.03
40	30.50	120	21.41
50	28.39	130	20.86
60	26.77	140	20.38
		150	19.93

ICMA, PS, Part III, Management Accounting 1, May 1982.

18.4 A company engineer had considered investing $20000 in additional manufacturing facilities which would take 1 year to build. He calculated that profit, after depreciation charges would be:

Year	$ per yr
1, 2	62000
3, 4	32000
5, 6	17000
7–10	7000

The engineer assumed that the average profit of $25000 per year would be taxable at 50 per cent, giving a net profit of $12500 per year. On the $20000 investment this was an average return of 6¼ per cent per annum. As the project would have to be financed by loaned capital at 12 per cent per annum, he concluded it was not worth undertaking.

He has asked you, as the newly-appointed management accountant, to review the project. In doing so, you find he has used the following data:

Make-up of investment	T $000
Plant	120
Buildings	60
Working capital	20
	Yr (straight line)
Depreciation	
Plant	10
Buildings	15

He has not taken into account:

Residual values (end of project)

| Plant | 5% of original cost |
| Buildings | equal to written double value |

The Analysis of Capital Investment Decisions

Tax allowances
(on capital investment)

Plant	first year 100% of investment
Buildings	5% of straightline per year with balancing charge/allowance to equate with net cost in final year

Other relevant data are:

1. Scrap value and working capital would be recovered at end of Year 10
2. Corporation tax and tax allowances would be lagged by 1 year for payment/credit
   The company has sufficient profits overall to absorb any capital allowances as they arise
3. The $200000 loan would be made available by a merchant bank at the beginning of the project. Interest would be charged annually in advance on the amount outstanding at the beginning of each year; the interest would be paid gross to the bank, but would be an allowable expense in calculating the company's taxable profit
   All income from the project would be used to reduce the loan

REQUIRED

(a) Prepare an annual cash flow statement for the project
(b) Calculate the annual surplus/deficit cash flow expected to arise based on the loan arrangements outlined and assuming to reinvestment opportunities exist for any surplus
(c) State if you would recommend acceptance of the project, assuming that the data on which the project is based are reasonably reliable, giving brief reasons for your decision

ICMA, PS, Part III, Management Accounting 2, November 1979.

18.5 The following information is given relating to a proposed capital expenditure project:

	$
Cost of project	350000
Cash inflow per annum, prior to tax	80000
Scrap/residual value	nil
Working capital requirements:	
At commencement of project	10000
After 1 year, a further	10000
All released at end of the 7th year	20000

Taxation assumptions:
(i) corporation tax is at the rate of 50 per cent
(ii) the first year allowance is at the rate of 100 per cent, and there are sufficient corporate profits available from other activities to absorb the whole amount of this allowance in the first year
(iii) tax payments are made and allowances are received in the year following that to which they relate

Grants – 20 per cent tax-free regional development grant is available, and it is expected that this will be received 1 year after the purchase and installation of capital equipment

Expected life of equipment	6 yr
Company cut off rate	18 per cent after tax

REQUIRED

(a) Compile a discounted cash flow (DCF) statement to ascertain whether or not the project is acceptable
(b) Calculate the approximate DCF rate of return (IRR) for the project

ICMA, PS, Part III, Management Accounting 1, May 1976.

18.6 Gateway Ltd, a car hire firm, is considering its future cash flows. The directors of the company are interested in the period from the end of January 19X1 to the end 19X6. In particular, they wish to decide on the optimal replacement cycle for the fleet of 30 hire cars. On 1 January 19X1, the company purchased its existing fleet at a cost of $300000; the vehicles to be depreciated in the accounts over a 3-year life, on a straight line basis. The resale value of a 1-year old car of the type used in the fleet is at present $7000.

Inflation is at the rate of 10 per cent per annum, and it is thought that it will continue at this rate for the foreseeable future. New car prices will increase in line with inflation, but second hand values are expected to remain at the present levels for a number of years. The resale value of a 2-year old fleet car is at present $4000 and the scrap value of a 3-year old car is $500.

The revenue from operating the fleet is expected to be $250000 in 19X1. This annual revenue is expected to increase at a rate of 10 per cent per annum, irrespective of the age of the vehicles. The operating and maintenance costs for 19X1 are estimated to be:

$	Year of life
70000 for cars in	1st
100000	2nd
160000	3rd

Operating and maintenance costs are expected to increase at a rate of 10 per cent per annum in line with inflation. The cars are not worth keeping for longer than 3-years.

The company's cost of capital is 15 per cent.

REQUIRED

(a) You are asked to advise the company on the optimal replacement policy for its fleet of cars for the period 1 February 19X1 to 31 December 19X6
    Ignore taxation, and assume that the cash flows relating to revenue and operating costs arise on the last day of the respective years
(b) Comment in general terms on how taxation influences investment decisions

ACCA, PE, Section 3, Accounting 6, Financial Management, June 1981.

18.7 Hurdlevack Ltd relies on the pay-back method of project evaluation, requiring that investments repay capital within 3-years. The board are currently considering the four projects listed below:

Project	A	B	C	D
	$	$	$	$
Sales	40000	75000	60000	60000
Direct costs	16000	27000	15000	18000
Depreciation	8000	40000	30000	35000
Investment	12000	16000	9000	7000
Initial investment	120000	160000	90000	70000
Project life (yr)	15	4	3	2

The engineering department have asked the board to evaluate these opportunities by means of a DCF technique. The finance department have been unwilling to use a DCF technique because of difficulty in establishing an appropriate discount rate. They therefore propose to calculate each project's IRR and let the board determine appropriate hurdle rates.

[Note: The hurdle' rate is the minimum acceptable IRR]

REQUIRED

(a) Calculate each project's pay-back period and state which of the opportunities is acceptable by his criterion
(b) Calculate each project's IRR and using a hurdle rate of 15 per cent, state which of the opportunities is acceptable by this criterion
(c) Suggest why the above two project appraisal methods do not give answers which are consistent with each other for the accept/reject decision
    Which should the board employ?
(d) Briefly outline some of the elements which should be considered when determining the appropriate hurdle rate for an individual project

ACCA, Paper 3.2, Financial Management, 1982.

18.8 Consider two projects J and K with the following cash flows:

	Year	J	K
		$	$
Investment	0	(200000)	(200000)
	1	70000	—
	2	70000	—
	3	70000	—
	4	70000	—
	5	70000	—
Per year	6–9	—	200000
	10	—	—
	11	Scrapped no no salvage value	Scrapped no salvage value

REQUIRED

(a) Rate of return
(b) Pay-back periods, and their reciprocal
(c) Assuming a 10 per cent minimum required rate of return, the NPV
(d) Based on information from (a), (b) and (c), which project would you choose if J and K are mutually exclusive?
(e) What factors other than those considered in (a)–(d) would influence the choice of a managing director?

University of Birmingham, Degree of M.Com. Final Examination, Quantitative Methods II, May 1970.

Chapter 19
Risk and Uncertainty in Capital Budgeting[1]

For most projects, the expected value alone is not a sufficient basis for appraisal. Carsberg, 1974)

19.1 Introduction

In previous discussions, the data surrounding capital appraisals were treated as if they were known with certainty. Conjectures, however, are part of life and are embodied, (even if not explicitly stated) in nearly all accounting data.

In this chapter, the concepts of risk and uncertainty are clarified. Examples are also given to show how risk is evaluated in capital selection.

19.2 Definition of risk and uncertainty

'Risk' means (i) that the decisionmaker is aware of all the possible future states of the economy which may occur, and affect the relevant parameters of a decision model; (ii) the decisionmaker is able to place a probability on the value of the occurrence of each of those states of nature.

'Uncertainty' means (i) that the decisionmaker may or may not be aware of all the possible states that affect a decision; (ii) may or may not be able to place a probability distribution on the occurrence of each state of nature.

19.3 Expected value of probability distribution

Since risk is inherent in all investment decisions, the expected return associated with various decision alternatives must be considered. In order to do so, the probability distribution which

---

[1] This chapter treats the concept of risk and uncertainty in a very simple way. Readers should consult Bower and Lessard (1973), Hillier (1963), Nielson (1956), Phelps (1962) and Van Horne (1969) for further detail.

Risk and Uncertainty in Capital Budgeting

describes possible outcomes must be calculated, along with the mean or expected value of the cash flows, in order to evaluate alternative courses of action.

The expected value of a probability distribution can be expressed in equation form as:

$$\bar{R} = \sum_{i=1}^{n} R_i P_i \qquad (19.1)$$

Where $\bar{R}$ = Expected value
R_i = Return associated with ith outcome.
$\bar{P}_i$ = Probability of occurrence of ith outcome.
N = No. of possible outcomes.

EXAMPLE 19.1

The manager of the Stanley firm faces conditions of risk in terms of economic strength in the coming year. Three different states may occur: Strong economy with $P = 0.4$; moderate economy with $P = 0.5$; and weak economy, with $P = 0.1$.

The firm has a single investment which is supposed to offer returns as follows:

		$
Strong	0.4	9000
Moderate	0.5	8300
Weak	0.1	1000

REQUIRED
Determine the expected return for the investment.

SOLUTION

$\bar{R} = 0.4\ (\$9000) + 0.5\ (\$8300) + 0.1\ (\$1000) = \$7850$ The expected return for the Stanley Firm is $7850.

19.4 Absolute measures of dispersion

Statisticians speak of the absolute and relative measures of risk. They link the concept with the amount of variability or dispersion that is present in the probability distribution. The measures of dispersion include: (i) range; (ii) mean absolute dieviation; (iii) variance; (iv) standard deviation; (v) coefficient of variation, which is the relative measure of dispersion.

The equation forms are:

RANGE

$$R_g = H_v - L_v \qquad (19.2)$$

Where R_g = Range of distribution
R_v = Highest value in distribution
L_v = Lowest value in distribution

MEAN ABSOLUTE DEVIATION

$$MAD = \sum_{i=1}^{n} P_i(|R_i - \bar{R}|) \qquad (19.3)$$

Where P_i, R_i and $\bar{R}$ are as defined before, and figures shown between lines $||$ are absolute values.

VARIANCE

$$\sigma^2 = \sum_{i=1}^{n} P_i(R_i - \bar{R}) \tag{19.4}$$

STANDARD DEVIATION

$$\sigma = \sqrt{\sum_{i=1}^{n} P_i(R_i - \bar{R})^2} = \text{square root of variance}$$

Risk, in the financial literature, is associated with a decision-maker's utility function.

EXAMPLE 19.2

REQUIRED

From Example 19.1, determine the value for each measure of risk as defined above, and comment on each.

SOLUTION

$R_g = \$(9000 - 1000) = \$8000$

COMMENT

The value implies that there is an $8000 difference between the highest and the lowest return that could be earned with the investment:

$MAD = 0.4(|\$9000 - \$7850|) + 0.5(|\$8300 - \$7850|) +$
$\qquad + 0.1(|\$1000 - \$7850|)$
$\qquad = 0.4(\$1150) + 0.5(\$450) + 0.1(\$6850)$
$\qquad = \$1370$

COMMENT

MAD shows the average variability of the values of the distribution from the mean without regard to the sign of the deviation.

$\sigma^2 = 0.4(\$9000 - \$7850)^2 + 0.5(\$8300 - \$7850)^2 +$
$\qquad + 0.1(\$1000 - 7850)^2$
$\qquad = 0.4(\$1150)^2 + 0.5(\$450)^2 + 0.1(\$ - 6850)^2$
$\qquad = \$5322,500$

COMMENT

The use of σ is affected by the order of magnitude of the relevant variable. This is misleading. The coefficient of variation, which is σ/EV eliminates the problem:

$\sigma = \sqrt{\sigma^2}$
$\quad = \sqrt{5\,322\,500}$
$\quad = \$2307$

COMMENT

The standard deviation is a measure of how representative the expected return is of the entire distribution. Statisticians maintain that the larger the standard deviation, the less representative the mean is, because of the greater scatter around the mean.

$CV = \dfrac{\$2307}{\$7850}$

$\qquad = 0.2938$

Risk and Uncertainty in Capital Budgeting

COMMENT

The coefficient of variation shows the amount of risk as measured by the standard deviation per dollar of expected return. Note that the lower the coefficient of variation, the smaller the amount of relative risk that is envisaged. When evaluating alternative capital projects that have different expected returns, the coefficient of variation is required to compare in a meaningful way the 'riskiness' of the alternatives.

19.5 Decision-maker's utility function[1]

With respect to risk, decision-makers may be classified as (i) risk averse; (ii) risk indifferent; or (iii) risktakers.

Risk averse decision-makers have decreasing marginal utilities for increases in wealth.

Risk indifferent decision-makers have constant marginal utilities; their utility curves are linear.

Risktakers have increasing marginal utilities for larger increases in wealth. Figure 19.1 shows these various risk curves of decision-makers.

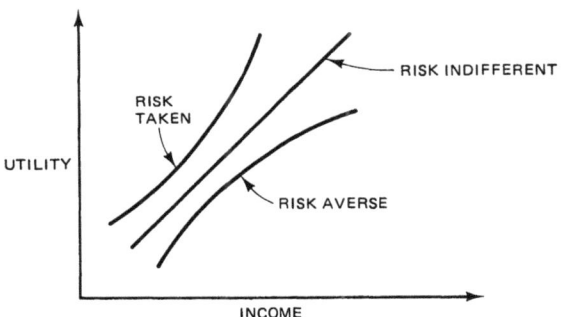

Figure 19.1 Decision-makers' risk curves

It is important to note that an individual may not always have the same attitude to risk. His attitude may change because of a number of factors. An individual with very low income may be prepared to risk a great deal, particularly if his current income is insufficient for his survival. The same person may become risk averse when he has an established reasonable income.

Having established the risk–return preferences of decisionmakers, we can show via the solution to example 19.3 a method for the evaluation of risk in the capital investment decision.

---

[1] A utility function is an attempt to quantify decision appraisal, where the preferences among alternatives are specified by a decisionmaker. Of importance to this function in investment analysis is what Winkler (1972) calls 'the axioms of coherence'.

EXAMPLE 19.3

Assume that the NPVs for the projects S_1 and S_2 of the Stardy firm are being estimated. Table 19.1[1] below contains the relevant information.

Table 19.1 Environmental data

State of economy	NPV		Chance of specific state of economy
	S_1	S_2	
	$000	$000	
High growth	3.5	6.0	3
Mid-growth	3.2	5.0	4
Normal	3.0	4.0	4
Stationary	2.9	3.0	5
Mild recession	1.9	2.0	3
Serious recession	1.5	−1.0	2
			21

REQUIRED

(i) Calculate the probabilities of occurrence
(ii) Calculate the expected values of the NPVs for the investments
(iii) Calculate σ^2, σ, and the coefficient of variation
(iv) Explain from the calculation which of the two investments are riskier

SOLUTION

(i) Probability of occurrence[2]
 = 0.14, 0.19, 1.19, 0.24, 0.14, 0.10

(ii)

S_1 value of outcome	Probability × value	S_2 value of outcome	Probability × value
$	$	$	$
3.5	0.49	6.0	0.84
3.2	0.61	5.0	0.95
3.0	0.57	4.0	0.76
2.9	0.70	3.0	0.72
1.9	0.27	2.0	0.28
1.5	0.15	−1.0	−0.10
Expected value	$\bar{R} = 2.79$		$\bar{R} = 3.45$

---

[1] The table can be interpreted as follows: the decisionmaker expects the NPV for the investments to range from e.g. $1.5–$3.5 (000) that out of 21 chances there are three chances that the economy will be in mild recession.

[2] Calculated from e.g. 3/21 = 0.14. Observe that the probabilities, sum to 1; they are called 'subjective probabilities'. Probabilities can also be calculated from historical data; they are termed objective probabilities.

Risk and Uncertainty in Capital Budgeting

The expected value of NPV for investment (S_1) is $2.79, for investment ($S_2$) $3.45

(iii) Calculation of σ^2 and σ

Investment (S_1)

Outcomes (1)	Deviation from expected value (2)	Square of deviation (3)	Probability of occurrence (4)	Probability × standard deviation (5)
3.5	0.71	0.5041	0.14	0.706
3.2	0.41	0.1681	0.19	0.0319
3.0	0.21	0.0441	0.19	0.0084
2.9	0.11	0.0121	0.24	0.0029
1.9	−0.89	0.7921	0.14	0.1109
1.5	−0.29	1.6641	0.10	0.1664

$$\Sigma = \sigma^2 = 0.3911$$
$$\sigma = 0.1974$$

Investment (S_2)

Outcomes (1)	Deviation from expected value (2)	Square of deviation (3)	Probability of occurrence (4)	Probability × standard deviation (5)
6.0	2.55	6.5025	0.14	0.9104
5.0	1.55	2.4025	0.19	0.4565
4.0	0.55	0.3025	0.19	0.0575
3.0	−0.45	0.2025	0.24	0.0486
2.0	−1.45	2.1025	0.14	0.2944
−1.0	−4.45	19.8025	0.10	1.9803

$$\Sigma = \sigma^2 = 3.7477$$
$$\sigma = 1.9235$$

(iv) Calculation of coefficient of variation

$$CV \text{ for } S_1 = \frac{0.1974}{2.79} = 0.0708$$

$$CV \text{ for } S_2 = \frac{1.9235}{3.45} = 0.5575$$

COMMENT

The coefficient of variation for S_2 is greater than S_1, therefore the conclusion is that S_2 is riskier than S_1. The choice of either S_1 or S_2, however, will depend on the decisionmaker's attitude to risk, and thus on his utility function.

19.6 Summary

This chapter introduced, in an elementary way, the concept of risk analysis in project selection. It showed that when the certainty assumptions are relaxed, the decisionmaker must employ statistical

Bibliography

Bower, R. S. and Lessard, D. R. (1973) 'An Operational Approach to Risk Screening', *Journal of Finance*, May, pp. 321–37.
Carsberg, B. (1974) *Analysis for Investment Decisions* (Accounting Age) p. 75.
Hillier F. S. (1963) 'The Derivation of Probabilistic Information for the Evaluation of Risky Investments', *Management Science*, April, pp. 443–57.
Hirschleifer, J. (1970) *Investment and Capital* (Prentice-Hall) ch. 8.
Nielson, N. C. (1956) 'The Investment Decision of the Firm Under Uncertainty and the Allocative Efficiency of Capital Markets', *Journal of Finance*, May, pp. 587–601.
Phelps, E. S. (1962) 'The Accumulation of Risk Capital: A Sequential Utility Analysis', *Econometrica*, no. 30, pp. 729–43.
Van Horne, J. C. 'The Analysis of Uncertainty Resolution in Capital Budgeting for New Projects', *Management Science*, April, pp. 576–86.
Winkler, R. L. (1972) *Introduction to Bayesian Inference and Decision* (Holt, Rinehart & Winston) pp. 260–64.

Problems

19.1 Electropoint Ltd is considering investing $12000 in a project which has the following probability distribution of cash flows in each of the next 3 years.

Cash flow x	Probability $P(x)$	Cash flow x	Probability $P(x)$	Cash flow x	Probability $P(x)$
$		$		$	
3000	0.3	6000	0.2	5000	0.3
5000	0.4	9000	0.3	13 000	0.6
6000	0.3	12 000	0.5	18 000	0.1

Assume that all cash flows are independent, and take place at the end of the year specified, and that there are no further cash flows after the end of Year 3. The company's cost of capital is 15 per cent per annum.

REQUIRED

(a) Calculate the expected NPV of the project
(b) Determine the variance V of the cash flows in each of the 3 years
(c) Determine the standard deviation of the NPV
(d) Comment on the analysis you have performed, and indicate how this might aid evaluation of the investment

ACCA, PE, Section 2, Paper 12, Management Mathematics, December 1981.

19.2 As plant manager of an engineering firm, you are required to choose between two types of equipment, A and B. The proposal has the following discrete probability distributions of cash flows in each of the next 4 years:

	PROPOSAL			
	A		B	
Probability	Net cash inflow	Probability	Net cash inflow
---	---	---	---
0.10	3000	0.10	1000
0.25	4000	0.25	2000
0.35	5000	0.35	3000
0.25	6000	0.25	4000
0.10	7000	0.10	5000

REQUIRED

(a) Compute for each proposal
 (i) expected value of cash inflows in each of next 3 years
 (ii) standard deviation
 (iii) coefficient of variation

(b) Write a short note explaining which proposal has the greatest degree of risk

University of Birmingham, Degree of B.Com.; B.Com (Accounting); B.Com (Russian Studies); B.Soc.Sc. Economics (Sessional Examinations); Accounting A & D, June 1976.

19.3
(a) Analyse, using graphical methods where appropriate, the conditions under which it is valid for firms to select two-period investment opportunities using discounting methods
(b) A firm which can normally raise all the finance it requires at 10 per cent has agreed with the government to limit investment to 1½ million in 19X3; the planning department have identified that the only feasible projects that could be adopted in 19X3 are:

Project	NPV 10%	IRR	Funds required
	$000	%	$000
A	40	18	200
B	64	14	500
C	60	20	400
D	200	22	800
E	96	15	600

The funds required must be invested at the start of each project. None of the projects will be available after 19X3

(i) Which projects should the firm select?
 Justify your method of selection
(ii) What is the cost of capital to the firm in 19X3?

19.4 The Nethan Co. is considering a proposal to acquire a new machine. Two reliable machines are available, and the following estimates have been produced by the company's forecasting department:

	MODEL	
	A	B
	$	$
Purchase price	5200	6500
Useful life (yr)	4	4
Scrap value	Nil	Nil
Annual operating cost	1200	850

In all other respects, the two machines are expected to perform identically. The finance department have been considering a number of ways to obtain the funds to enable one of the machines to be installed, knowing that one machine must be obtained if the company is to continue. Nethan's bankers have offered to make a loan, for which the machine will provide security, at 8 per cent. This appears appealing, since the cash flows associated with the machines are of similar risk to the company as a whole, which has a weighted average cost of capital of 12 per cent. In addition, attractive leasing contracts have been offered:

	MODEL	
	A	B
	$	$
Initial payment	1000	900
Annual payment, end of each year	1300	1600
Non-cancellable length of lease (yr)	4	4

REQUIRED

Identify which machine should be adopted, and how it should be financed, indicating your reasons for the discount rate(s) you have used in your calculations.

Appendix

Present Value Tables

Table 1 Amount of 1 at compound interest: $(1+r)^n$

Years (n)	Interest rates (f)														
	1	2	3	4	5	6	7	8	9	10	11	12	13	14	15
1	1.0100	1.0200	1.0300	1.0400	1.0500	1.0600	1.0700	1.0800	1.0900	1.1000	1.1100	1.1200	1.1300	1.1400	1.1500
2	1.0201	1.0404	1.0609	1.0816	1.1025	1.1236	1.1449	1.1664	1.1881	1.2100	1.2321	1.2544	1.2769	1.2996	1.3225
3	1.0303	1.0612	1.0927	1.1249	1.1576	1.1910	1.2250	1.2597	1.2950	1.3310	1.3676	1.4049	1.4429	1.4815	1.5209
4	1.0406	1.0824	1.1255	1.1699	1.2155	1.2625	1.3108	1.3605	1.4116	1.4641	1.5181	1.5735	1.6305	1.6890	1.7490
5	1.0510	1.1041	1.1593	1.2167	1.2763	1.3382	1.4026	1.4693	1.5386	1.6105	1.6851	1.7623	1.8424	1.9254	2.0114
6	1.0615	1.1262	1.1941	1.2653	1.3401	1.4185	1.5007	1.5869	1.6771	1.7716	1.8704	1.9738	2.0820	2.1950	2.3131
7	1.0721	1.1487	1.2299	1.3159	1.4071	1.5036	1.6058	1.7138	1.8280	1.9487	2.0762	2.2107	2.3526	2.5023	2.6600
8	1.0829	1.1717	1.2668	1.3686	1.4775	1.5938	1.7182	1.8509	1.9926	2.1436	2.3045	2.4760	2.6584	2.8526	3.0590
9	1.0937	1.1951	1.3048	1.4233	1.5513	1.6895	1.8385	1.9990	2.1719	2.3579	2.5580	2.7731	3.0040	3.2519	3.5179
10	1.1046	1.2190	1.3439	1.4802	1.6289	1.7908	1.9672	2.1589	2.3674	2.5937	2.8394	3.1058	3.3946	3.7072	4.0456
11	1.1157	1.2434	1.3842	1.5395	1.7103	1.8983	2.1049	2.3316	2.5804	2.8531	3.1518	3.4785	3.8359	4.2262	4.6524
12	1.1268	1.2682	1.4258	1.6010	1.7959	2.0122	2.2522	2.5182	2.8127	3.1384	3.4985	3.8960	4.3345	4.8179	5.3503
13	1.1381	1.2936	1.4685	1.6651	1.8856	2.1328	2.4098	2.7196	3.0658	3.4523	3.8833	4.3635	4.8980	5.4924	6.1528
14	1.1495	1.3195	1.5126	1.7317	1.9799	2.2609	2.5785	2.9372	3.3471	3.7975	4.3104	4.8871	5.5348	6.2613	7.0757
15	1.1610	1.3459	1.5580	1.8009	2.0789	2.3966	2.7690	3.1722	3.6425	4.1772	4.7846	5.4736	6.2543	7.1379	8.1371
16	1.1726	1.3728	1.6037	1.8730	2.1829	2.5404	2.9522	3.4259	3.9703	4.5950	5.3109	6.1304	7.0673	8.1372	9.3576
17	1.1843	1.4002	1.6528	1.9479	2.2920	2.6928	3.1588	3.7000	4.3276	5.0545	5.8951	6.8660	7.9861	9.2765	10.7613
18	1.1961	1.4282	1.7024	2.0258	2.4066	2.8543	3.3799	3.9960	4.7171	5.5599	6.5436	7.6900	9.0243	10.5752	12.3755
19	1.2081	1.4568	1.7535	2.1068	2.5270	3.0256	3.6165	4.3157	5.1417	6.1159	7.2633	8.6128	10.1974	12.0557	14.2318
20	1.2202	1.4859	1.8061	2.1911	2.6533	3.2071	3.8697	4.6610	5.6044	6.7275	8.0623	9.6463	11.5231	13.7435	16.3665
25	1.2824	1.6406	2.0938	2.6658	3.3864	4.2919	5.4274	6.8485	8.6231	10.8347	13.5855	17.0001	21.2305	26.4619	32.9190

Table 1 *(contd.)*

	16	17	18	19	20	21	22	23	24	25	26	27	28	29	30
1	1.1600	1.1700	1.1800	1.1900	1.2000	1.2100	1.2200	1.2300	1.2400	1.2500	1.2600	1.2700	1.2800	1.2900	1.3000
2	1.3456	1.3689	1.3924	1.4161	1.4400	1.4641	1.4884	1.5129	1.5376	1.5625	1.5876	1.6129	1.6384	1.6641	1.6900
3	1.5609	1.6016	1.6430	1.6852	1.7280	1.7716	1.8158	1.8609	1.9066	1.9531	2.0004	2.0484	2.0972	2.1467	2.1970
4	1.8106	1.8739	1.9388	2.0053	2.0736	2.1436	2.2153	2.2889	2.3642	2.4414	2.5205	2.6014	2.6844	2.7692	2.8561
5	2.1003	2.1924	2.2878	2.3864	2.4883	2.5937	2.7027	2.8153	2.9316	3.0518	3.1758	3.3038	3.4360	3.5723	3.7129
6	2.4364	2.5652	2.6996	2.8398	2.9860	3.1384	3.2973	3.4628	3.6352	3.8147	4.0015	4.1959	4.3980	4.6083	4.8268
7	2.8262	3.0012	3.1855	3.3793	3.5832	3.7975	4.0227	4.2593	4.5077	4.7684	5.0419	5.3288	5.6295	5.9447	6.2749
8	3.2784	3.5115	3.7589	4.0214	4.2998	4.5950	4.9077	5.2389	5.5895	5.9605	6.3528	6.7675	7.2058	7.6686	8.1573
9	3.8030	4.1084	4.4355	4.7854	5.1598	5.5599	5.9874	6.4439	6.9310	7.4506	8.0045	8.5948	9.2234	9.8925	10.6045
10	4.4114	4.8068	5.2338	5.6947	6.1917	6.7275	7.3046	7.9259	8.5944	9.3132	10.0857	10.9153	11.8059	12.7614	13.7858
11	5.1173	5.6240	6.1759	6.7767	7.4301	8.1403	8.9117	9.7489	10.6571	11.6415	12.7080	13.8625	15.1116	16.4622	17.9216
12	5.9360	6.5801	7.2876	8.0642	8.9161	9.8497	10.8722	11.9912	13.2148	14.5519	16.0120	17.6053	19.3428	21.2362	23.2981
13	6.8858	7.6987	8.5994	9.5964	10.6993	11.9182	13.2641	14.7491	16.3863	18.1899	20.1752	22.3588	24.7588	27.3947	30.2875
14	7.9875	9.0075	10.1472	11.4198	12.8392	14.4210	16.1822	18.1414	20.3191	22.7374	25.4207	28.3957	31.6913	35.3391	39.3738
15	9.2655	10.5387	11.9737	13.5895	15.4070	17.4494	19.7423	22.3140	25.1956	28.4217	32.0301	36.0625	40.5648	45.5875	51.1859
16	10.7480	12.3303	14.1290	16.1715	18.4884	21.1138	24.0856	27.4462	31.2426	35.5271	40.3579	45.7994	51.9230	58.8079	66.5417
17	12.4677	14.4265	16.6722	19.2441	22.1861	25.5477	29.3844	33.7588	38.7408	44.4089	50.8510	58.1652	66.4614	75.8621	86.5042
18	14.4625	16.8790	19.6733	22.9005	26.6233	30.9127	35.8490	41.5233	48.0386	55.5112	64.0722	73.8698	85.0706	97.8622	112.4554
19	16.7765	19.7484	23.2144	27.2516	31.9480	37.4043	43.7358	51.0737	59.5679	69.3889	80.7310	93.8147	108.8904	126.2423	146.1920
20	19.4608	23.1056	27.3930	32.4294	38.3376	45.2593	53.3576	62.8206	73.8641	86.7362	101.7211	119.1446	139.3797	162.8524	190.0496
25	40.8742	50.6578	62.6686	77.3881	95.3962	117.3909	144.2101	176.8593	216.5420	264.6978	323.0454	393.6344	478.9049	581.7588	705.6410

Table 2 Present value of 1 at compound interest: $(1+r)^{-n}$

Years (n)	Interest rates (r)														
	1	2	3	4	5	6	7	8	9	10	11	12	13	14	15
1	0.9901	0.9804	0.9709	0.9615	0.9524	0.9434	0.9346	0.9259	0.9174	0.9091	0.9009	0.8929	0.8850	0.8772	0.8696
2	0.9803	0.9612	0.9426	0.9246	0.9070	0.8900	0.8734	0.8573	0.8417	0.8264	0.8116	0.7972	0.7831	0.7695	0.7561
3	0.9706	0.9423	0.9151	0.8890	0.8638	0.8396	0.8163	0.7938	0.7722	0.7513	0.7312	0.7118	0.6931	0.6750	0.6575
4	0.9610	0.9238	0.8885	0.8548	0.8227	0.7921	0.7629	0.7350	0.7084	0.6830	0.6587	0.6355	0.6133	0.5921	0.5718
5	0.9515	0.9057	0.8626	0.8219	0.7835	0.7473	0.7130	0.6806	0.6499	0.6209	0.5935	0.5674	0.5428	0.5194	0.4972
6	0.9420	0.8880	0.8375	0.7903	0.7462	0.7050	0.6663	0.6302	0.5963	0.5645	0.5346	0.5066	0.4803	0.4556	0.4323
7	0.9327	0.8706	0.8131	0.7599	0.7107	0.6651	0.6227	0.5835	0.5470	0.5132	0.4817	0.4523	0.4251	0.3996	0.3759
8	0.9235	0.8535	0.7894	0.7307	0.6768	0.6274	0.5820	0.5403	0.5019	0.4665	0.4339	0.4039	0.3762	0.3506	0.3269
9	0.9143	0.8368	0.7664	0.7026	0.6446	0.5919	0.5439	0.5002	0.4604	0.4241	0.3909	0.3606	0.3329	0.3075	0.2843
10	0.9053	0.8203	0.7441	0.6756	0.6139	0.5584	0.5083	0.4632	0.4224	0.3855	0.3522	0.3220	0.2946	0.2697	0.2472
11	0.8963	0.8043	0.7224	0.6496	0.5847	0.5268	0.4751	0.4289	0.3875	0.3505	0.3173	0.2875	0.2607	0.2366	0.2149
12	0.8874	0.7885	0.7014	0.6246	0.5568	0.4970	0.4440	0.3971	0.3555	0.3188	0.2858	0.2567	0.2307	0.2076	0.1869
13	0.8787	0.7730	0.6810	0.6006	0.5303	0.4688	0.4150	0.3677	0.3262	0.2862	0.2575	0.2292	0.2042	0.1821	0.1625
14	0.8700	0.7579	0.6611	0.5775	0.5051	0.4423	0.3878	0.3405	0.2992	0.2633	0.2320	0.2046	0.1807	0.1597	0.1413
15	0.8613	0.7430	0.6419	0.5553	0.4810	0.4173	0.3624	0.3152	0.2745	0.2394	0.2090	0.1827	0.1599	0.1401	0.1229
16	0.8528	0.7284	0.6232	0.5339	0.4581	0.3936	0.3387	0.2919	0.2519	0.2176	0.1883	0.1631	0.1415	0.1229	0.1069
17	0.8444	0.7142	0.6050	0.5134	0.4363	0.3714	0.3168	0.2703	0.2311	0.1978	0.1696	0.1456	0.1252	0.1078	0.0929
18	0.8360	0.7002	0.5874	0.4936	0.4155	0.3503	0.2959	0.2502	0.2120	0.1799	0.1528	0.1300	0.1108	0.0946	0.0808
19	0.8277	0.6864	0.5703	0.4746	0.3957	0.3305	0.2765	0.2317	0.1945	0.1635	0.1377	0.1161	0.0981	0.0829	0.0703
20	0.8195	0.6730	0.5537	0.4564	0.3769	0.3118	0.2584	0.2145	0.1784	0.1486	0.1240	0.1037	0.0868	0.0728	0.0611
25	0.7795	0.6095	0.4776	0.3751	0.2953	0.2330	0.1842	0.1460	0.1160	0.0923	0.0736	0.0588	0.0471	0.0378	0.0304
30	0.7419	0.5521	0.4120	0.3083	0.2314	0.1741	0.1314	0.0994	0.0754	0.0573	0.0437	0.0334	0.0256	0.0196	0.0151
35	0.7059	0.5000	0.3554	0.2534	0.1813	0.1301	0.0937	0.0676	0.0490	0.0356	0.0259	0.0189	0.0139	0.0102	0.0075
40	0.6717	0.4529	0.3066	0.2083	0.1420	0.0972	0.0668	0.0460	0.0318	0.0221	0.0154	0.0107	0.0075	0.0053	0.0037
45	0.6391	0.4102	0.2644	0.1712	0.1113	0.0727	0.0476	0.0313	0.0207	0.0137	0.0091	0.0061	0.0041	0.0027	0.0019
50	0.6080	0.3715	0.2281	0.1407	0.0872	0.0543	0.0339	0.0213	0.0134	0.0085	0.0054	0.0035	0.0022	0.0014	0.0009

Table 2 (contd.)

	16	17	18	19	20	21	22	23	24	25	26	27	28	29	30
1	0.8621	0.8547	0.8475	0.8403	0.8333	0.8264	0.8197	0.8130	0.8065	0.8000	0.7937	0.7874	0.7812	0.7752	0.7692
2	0.7432	0.7305	0.7182	0.7062	0.6944	0.6830	0.6719	0.6610	0.6504	0.6400	0.6299	0.6200	0.6104	0.6009	0.5917
3	0.6407	0.6244	0.6086	0.5934	0.5787	0.5645	0.5507	0.5374	0.5245	0.5120	0.4999	0.4882	0.4768	0.4658	0.4552
4	0.5523	0.5337	0.5158	0.4987	0.4823	0.4665	0.4514	0.4369	0.4230	0.4096	0.3968	0.3844	0.3725	0.3611	0.3501
5	0.4761	0.4561	0.4371	0.4190	0.4019	0.3855	0.3700	0.3552	0.3411	0.3277	0.3149	0.3027	0.2910	0.2799	0.2693
6	0.4104	0.3898	0.3704	0.3521	0.3349	0.3186	0.3033	0.2888	0.2751	0.2621	0.2499	0.2383	0.2274	0.2170	0.2072
7	0.3538	0.3332	0.3139	0.2959	0.2791	0.2633	0.2486	0.2348	0.2218	0.2097	0.1983	0.1877	0.1776	0.1682	0.1594
8	0.3050	0.2848	0.2660	0.2487	0.2326	0.2176	0.2038	0.1909	0.1789	0.1678	0.1574	0.1478	0.1388	0.1304	0.1226
9	0.2630	0.2434	0.2255	0.2090	0.1938	0.1799	0.1670	0.1552	0.1443	0.1342	0.1249	0.1164	0.1084	0.1011	0.0943
10	0.2267	0.2080	0.1911	0.1756	0.1615	0.1486	0.1369	0.1262	0.1164	0.1074	0.0992	0.0916	0.0847	0.0784	0.0725
11	0.1954	0.1778	0.1619	0.1476	0.1346	0.1228	0.1122	0.1026	0.0938	0.0859	0.0787	0.0721	0.0662	0.0607	0.0558
12	0.1685	0.1520	0.1372	0.1240	0.1122	0.1015	0.0920	0.0834	0.0757	0.0687	0.0625	0.0568	0.0517	0.0471	0.0429
13	0.1452	0.1299	0.1163	0.1042	0.0935	0.0839	0.0754	0.0678	0.0610	0.0550	0.0496	0.0447	0.0404	0.0365	0.0330
14	0.1252	0.1110	0.0985	0.0876	0.0779	0.0693	0.0618	0.0551	0.0492	0.0440	0.0393	0.0352	0.0316	0.0283	0.0254
15	0.1079	0.0949	0.0835	0.0736	0.0649	0.0573	0.0506	0.0448	0.0397	0.0352	0.0312	0.0277	0.0247	0.0219	0.0195
16	0.0930	0.0811	0.0708	0.0618	0.0541	0.0474	0.0415	0.0364	0.0320	0.0281	0.0248	0.0218	0.0193	0.0170	0.0150
17	0.0802	0.0693	0.0600	0.0520	0.0451	0.0391	0.0340	0.0296	0.0258	0.0225	0.0197	0.0172	0.0150	0.0132	0.0116
18	0.0691	0.0592	0.0508	0.0437	0.0376	0.0323	0.0279	0.0241	0.0208	0.0180	0.0156	0.0135	0.0118	0.0102	0.0089
19	0.0596	0.0506	0.0431	0.0367	0.0313	0.0267	0.0229	0.0196	0.0168	0.0144	0.0124	0.0107	0.0092	0.0079	0.0068
20	0.0514	0.0433	0.0365	0.0308	0.0261	0.0221	0.0187	0.0159	0.0135	0.0115	0.0098	0.0084	0.0072	0.0061	0.0053
25	0.0245	0.0197	0.0160	0.0129	0.0105	0.0085	0.0069	0.0057	0.0046	0.0038	0.0031	0.0025	0.0021	0.0017	0.0014
30	0.0116	0.0090	0.0070	0.0054	0.0042	0.0033	0.0026	0.0020	0.0016	0.0012	0.0010	0.0008	0.0006	0.0005	0.0004
35	0.0055	0.0041	0.0030	0.0023	0.0017	0.0013	0.0009	0.0007	0.0005	0.0004	0.0003	0.0002	0.0002	0.0001	0.0001
40	0.0026	0.0019	0.0013	0.0010	0.0007	0.0005	0.0004	0.0003	0.0002	0.0001	0.0001	0.0001	0.0001	0.0000	0.0000
45	0.0013	0.0009	0.0006	0.0004	0.0003	0.0002	0.0001	0.0001	0.0001	0.0000	0.0000	0.0000	0.0000	0.0000	0.0000
50	0.0006	0.0004	0.0003	0.0002	0.0001	0.0001	0.0000	0.0000	0.0000	0.0000	0.0000	0.0000	0.0000	0.0000	0.0000

Table 3 Present value of an annuity of 1: $\dfrac{1-(1+r)^{-n}}{r}$

Years | Interest rates (r)

(n)	1	2	3	4	5	6	7	8	9	10	11	12	13	14	15
1	0.9901	0.9804	0.0709	0.9615	0.9524	0.9434	0.9346	0.9259	0.9174	0.9091	0.9009	0.8929	0.8850	0.8772	0.8696
2	1.9704	1.9416	1.9135	1.8861	1.8594	1.8334	1.8080	1.7833	1.7591	1.7355	1.7125	1.6901	1.6681	1.6467	1.6257
3	2.9410	2.8839	2.8286	2.7751	2.7232	2.6730	2.6243	2.5771	2.5313	2.4869	2.4437	2.4018	2.3612	2.3616	2.2832
4	3.9020	3.8077	3.7171	3.6299	3.5460	3.4651	3.3872	3.121	3.2397	3.1699	3.1024	3.0373	2.9745	2.9137	2.8550
5	4.8534	4.7135	4.5797	4.4518	4.3295	4.2124	4.1002	3.9927	3.8897	3.7908	3.6959	3.6048	3.5172	3.4331	3.3522
6	5.7955	5.6014	5.4172	5.2421	5.0757	4.9173	4.7665	4.6229	4.4859	4.3553	4.2305	4.1114	3.9975	3.8887	3.7845
7	6.7282	6.4720	6.2303	6.0021	5.7864	5.5824	5.3893	5.2064	5.0330	4.8684	4.7122	4.5638	4.4226	4.2883	4.1604
8	7.6517	7.3255	7.0197	6.7327	6.4632	6.2098	5.9713	5.7466	5.5348	5.3349	5.1661	4.9676	4.7988	4.6389	4.4873
9	8.5660	8.1622	7.7861	7.4353	7.1078	6.8017	6.5152	6.2469	5.9952	5.7590	5.5370	5.3282	5.1317	4.9464	4.7716
10	9.4713	8.9826	8.5302	8.1109	7.7217	7.3601	7.0236	6.7101	6.4177	6.1446	5.8892	5.6502	5.4262	5.2161	5.0188
11	10.3676	9.7868	9.2526	8.7605	8.3064	7.8869	7.4987	7.1390	6.8052	6.4951	6.2065	5.9377	5.6869	5.4527	5.2337
12	11.2551	10.5753	9.9540	9.3851	8.8633	8.3838	7.9427	7.5361	7.1607	6.8137	6.4924	6.1944	5.9176	5.6603	5.4206
13	12.1337	11.3484	10.6350	9.9856	9.3936	8.8527	8.3577	7.9038	7.4869	7.1034	6.7499	6.4235	6.1218	5.8424	5.5831
14	13.0037	12.1062	11.2961	10.5631	9.8986	9.2950	8.7455	8.2442	7.7862	7.3667	6.9819	6.6282	6.3025	6.0021	5.7245
15	13.8651	12.8493	11.9379	11.1184	10.3797	9.7122	9.1079	8.5595	8.0607	7.6061	7.1909	6.8109	6.4624	6.1422	5.8474
16	14.7179	13.5777	12.5611	11.6523	10.8378	10.1059	9.4466	8.8514	8.3126	7.8237	7.3792	6.9740	6.6039	6.2651	5.9542
17	15.5623	14.2919	13.1661	12.1657	11.2741	10.4773	9.7632	9.1216	8.5436	8.0216	7.5488	7.1196	6.7291	6.3729	6.0472
18	16.3983	14.9920	13.7535	12.6593	11.6896	10.8276	10.0591	9.3719	8.7556	8.2014	7.7016	7.2497	6.8399	6.4674	6.1280
19	17.2260	15.6785	14.3238	13.1339	12.0853	11.1581	10.3556	9.6036	8.9501	8.3649	7.8393	7.3658	6.9380	6.5504	6.1982
20	18.0456	16.3514	14.8775	13.5903	12.4622	11.4699	10.5940	9.8181	9.1285	8.5136	7.9633	7.4694	7.0248	6.6231	6.2593
25	22.0232	19.5235	17.4131	15.6221	14.0939	12.7834	11.6536	10.6748	9.8226	9.0770	8.4217	7.8431	7.3300	6.8729	6.4641
30	25.8077	22.3965	19.6004	17.2920	15.3725	13.7648	12.4090	11.2578	10.2737	9.4269	8.6938	8.0552	7.4957	7.0027	6.5660
35	29.4086	24.9986	21.4872	18.6646	16.3742	14.4982	12.9477	11.6546	10.5668	9.442	8.8552	8.1755	7.5856	7.0700	6.6166
40	32.8347	27.3555	23.1148	19.7928	17.1591	15.0463	13.3317	11.9246	10.7574	9.7791	8.9511	8.2438	7.6344	7.1050	6.6418
45	36.0945	29.4902	24.5187	20.7200	17.7741	15.4558	13.6055	12.1084	10.8812	9.8628	9.0079	8.2825	7.6609	7.1232	6.6543
50	39.1961	31.4236	25.7298	21.4822	18.2559	15.7619	13.8007	12.2335	10.9617	9.9148	9.0417	8.3045	7.6752	7.1327	6.6605

Table 3 *(contd.)*

	16	17	18	19	20	21	22	23	24	25	26	27	28	29	30
1	0.8621	0.8547	0.8475	0.8403	0.8333	0.8264	0.8197	0.8130	0.8065	0.8000	0.7937	0.7874	0.7812	0.7752	0.7692
2	1.6052	1.5852	1.5656	1.5465	1.5278	1.5095	1.4915	1.4740	1.4568	1.4400	1.4235	1.4074	1.3916	1.3761	1.3609
3	2.2459	2.2096	2.1743	2.1399	2.1065	2.0739	2.0422	2.0114	1.9813	1.9520	1.9234	1.8956	1.8684	1.8420	1.8161
4	2.7982	2.7432	2.6901	2.6386	2.5887	2.5404	2.4936	2.4483	2.4043	2.3616	2.3202	2.2800	2.2410	2.2031	2.1662
5	3.2743	3.1993	3.1272	3.0576	2.9906	2.9260	2.8636	2.8035	2.7454	2.6893	2.6351	2.5827	2.5320	2.4830	2.4356
6	3.6847	3.5892	3.4976	3.4098	3.3255	3.2446	3.1669	3.0923	3.0205	2.9514	2.8850	2.8210	2.7594	2.7000	2.6427
7	4.0386	3.9224	3.8115	3.7057	3.6046	3.5079	3.4155	3.3270	3.2423	3.1611	3.0833	3.0087	2.9370	2.8682	2.8021
8	4.3436	4.2072	4.0776	3.9544	3.8372	3.7256	3.6193	3.5179	3.4212	3.3289	3.2407	3.1564	3.0758	2.9986	2.9247
9	4.6065	4.4506	4.3030	4.1633	4.0310	3.9054	3.7853	3.6731	3.5655	3.4631	3.3657	3.2728	3.1842	3.0997	3.0190
10	4.8332	4.6586	4.4941	4.3389	4.1925	4.0541	3.9232	3.7993	3.6819	3.5705	3.4548	3.3644	3.2689	3.1781	3.0915
11	5.0286	4.8364	4.6560	4.4865	4.3271	4.1769	4.0354	3.9018	3.7757	3.6564	3.5435	3.4365	3.3351	3.2388	3.1473
12	5.1971	4.9884	4.7932	4.6105	4.4392	4.2784	4.1274	3.9852	3.8514	3.7251	3.6059	3.4933	3.3868	3.2859	3.1903
13	5.3423	5.1183	4.9095	4.7147	4.5327	4.3624	4.2028	4.0630	3.9124	3.7801	3.6555	3.5381	3.4272	3.3224	3.2233
14	5.4675	5.2293	5.0081	4.8023	4.6106	4.4317	4.2646	4.1082	3.9616	3.8241	3.6949	3.5733	3.4587	3.3507	3.2487
15	5.5755	5.3242	5.0916	4.8759	4.6755	4.4890	4.3152	4.1530	4.0013	3.8593	3.7261	3.6010	3.4834	3.3726	3.2682
16	5.6685	5.4063	5.1624	4.9377	4.7296	4.5364	4.3567	4.1794	4.0333	3.8874	3.7509	3.6228	3.5026	3.3896	3.2832
17	5.7487	5.4746	5.2223	4.9897	4.7746	4.5755	4.3908	4.2190	4.0591	3.9099	3.7705	3.6400	3.5177	3.4028	3.2948
18	5.8178	5.5339	5.2732	5.0333	4.8122	4.6079	4.4187	4.2431	4.0799	3.9279	3.7861	3.6536	3.5284	3.4130	3.3037
19	5.8775	5.5845	5.3162	5.0700	4.8435	4.6346	4.4415	4.2627	4.0967	3.924	3.7985	3.6642	3.5385	3.4210	3.3105
20	5.9288	5.6278	5.3527	5.1009	4.8696	4.6567	4.4603	4.2786	4.1103	3.9539	3.8083	3.6726	3.5458	3.4271	3.3158
25	6.0971	5.7662	5.4669	5.1951	4.9476	4.7213	4.5139	4.3232	4.1474	3.9849	3.8342	3.6943	3.5640	3.4423	3.3286
30	6.1772	5.8294	5.5168	5.2347	4.9789	4.7463	4.5338	4.3391	4.1601	3.9950	3.8424	3.7009	3.5693	3.4466	3.3321
35	6.2153	5.8582	5.5386	5.2512	4.9915	4.7559	4.5411	4.3447	4.1644	3.9984	3.8450	3.7028	3.5708	3.4478	3.3330
40	6.2335	5.8713	5.5482	5.2582	4.9966	4.7596	4.5439	4.3467	4.1659	3.9995	3.8458	3.7034	3.5712	3.4481	3.3332
45	6.2421	5.8773	5.5523	5.2611	4.9986	4.7610	4.5449	4.3474	4.1664	3.9998	3.8460	3.7036	3.5714	3.4482	3.3333
50	6.2463	5.8801	5.5541	5.2623	4.9995	4.7616	4.5452	4.3477	4.1666	3.9999	3.8461	3.7037	3.5714	3.4483	3.3333

Table 4 Terminal value of an annuity of 1: $\frac{(1+r)^n - 1}{r}$

Years (n)	Interest rates (r)														
	1	2	3	4	5	6	7	8	9	10	11	12	13	14	15
1	1.0000	1.0000	1.0000	1.0000	1.0000	1.0000	1.0000	1.0000	1.0000	1.0000	1.0000	1.0000	1.0000	1.0000	1.0000
2	2.0100	2.0200	2.0300	2.0400	2.0500	2.0600	2.0700	2.0800	2.0900	2.1000	2.1100	2.1200	2.1300	2.1400	2.1500
3	3.0301	3.0604	3.0908	3.1216	3.1525	3.1836	3.2149	3.2464	3.2781	3.3100	3.3421	3.3744	3.4069	3.4396	3.4725
4	4.0604	4.1216	4.1836	4.2464	4.3101	4.3746	4.4399	4.5061	4.5731	4.6410	4.7097	4.7793	4.8496	4.9211	4.9934
5	5.1010	5.2040	5.3091	5.4163	5.5256	5.6371	5.7507	5.8666	5.9847	6.1051	6.2278	6.3528	6.4803	6.6101	6.7424
6	6.1520	6.3081	6.4684	6.6330	6.8019	6.9753	7.1533	7.3359	7.5233	7.7156	7.9129	8.1152	8.3227	8.5355	8.7537
7	7.2135	7.4343	7.6625	7.8983	8.1420	8.3938	8.6540	8.9228	9.2004	9.4872	9.7833	10.0890	10.4047	10.7305	11.0668
8	8.2857	8.5830	8.8923	9.2142	9.5491	9.8975	10.2598	10.6366	11.0285	11.4359	11.8594	12.2997	12.7573	13.2328	13.7268
9	9.3685	9.7546	10.1591	10.5828	11.0266	11.4913	11.9780	12.4876	13.0210	13.5795	14.1640	14.7757	15.4157	16.0853	16.7858
10	10.4622	10.9497	11.4639	12.0061	12.5779	13.1808	13.8164	14.4866	15.1929	15.9374	16.7220	17.5487	18.4197	19.3373	20.3037
11	11.5668	12.1687	12.8078	13.4864	14.2068	14.9716	15.7836	16.6455	17.5603	18.5312	19.5614	20.6546	21.8143	23.0445	24.3493
12	12.6825	13.4121	14.1920	15.0258	15.9171	16.8699	17.8885	18.9771	20.1407	21.3843	22.7132	24.1331	25.6502	27.2707	29.0017
13	13.8093	14.6803	15.6178	16.6268	17.7130	18.8821	20.1406	21.4953	22.9634	24.5227	26.2116	28.0291	29.9847	32.0887	34.3519
14	14.9474	15.9739	17.0863	18.2919	19.5986	21.0151	22.5505	24.2149	26.0192	27.9750	30.0949	32.3926	34.8827	37.5811	40.5047
15	16.0969	17.2934	18.5989	20.0236	21.5786	23.2760	25.1290	27.1521	29.3609	31.7725	34.4054	37.2797	40.4175	43.8424	47.5804
16	17.2579	18.6393	20.1569	21.8245	23.6575	25.6725	27.8881	30.3243	33.0034	35.9497	39.1899	42.7533	46.5717	50.9804	55.7175
17	18.4304	20.0121	21.7616	23.6975	25.8404	28.2129	30.8402	33.7502	36.9737	40.5447	44.5008	48.8837	53.7391	59.1176	65.0751
18	19.6147	21.4123	23.4144	25.6454	28.1324	30.9057	33.9990	37.4502	41.3013	45.5992	50.3959	55.7497	61.7251	68.3941	75.8364
19	20.8109	22.8406	25.1169	27.6712	30.5390	33.7600	37.3790	41.4463	46.0185	51.1591	56.9395	63.4397	70.7494	78.9692	88.2118
20	22.0190	24.2974	26.8704	29.7781	33.0660	36.7856	40.9955	45.7620	51.1601	57.2750	64.2028	72.0524	80.9468	91.0249	102.4436
25	28.2432	32.0303	36.4593	41.6459	47.7271	54.8645	63.2490	73.1059	84.7009	98.3471	114.4133	133.3339	155.6196	181.8708	212.7930

Table 4 (contd.)

	16	17	18	19	20	21	22	23	24	25	26	27	28	29	30
1	1.0000	1.0000	1.0000	1.0000	1.0000	1.0000	1.0000	1.0000	1.0000	1.0000	1.0000	1.0000	1.0000	1.0000	1.0000
2	2.1600	2.1700	2.1800	2.1900	2.2000	2.2100	2.2100	2.2300	2.2400	2.2500	2.2600	2.2700	2.2800	2.2900	2.3000
3	3.5056	3.5389	3.5724	3.6061	3.6400	3.6741	3.7084	3.7429	3.7776	3.8125	3.8476	3.8829	3.9184	3.9541	3.9900
4	5.0665	5.1405	5.2154	5.2913	5.3680	5.4457	5.5242	5.6038	5.6842	5.7656	5.8480	5.9313	6.0156	6.1008	6.1870
5	6.8771	7.0144	7.1542	7.2966	7.4418	7.5892	7.7396	7.8926	8.0484	8.2070	8.3684	8.5327	8.6999	8.8700	9.0431
6	8.9775	9.2068	9.4420	9.6830	9.9299	10.1830	10.4423	10.7079	10.9801	11.2588	11.5442	11.8366	12.1359	12.4423	12.7560
7	11.4139	11.7720	12.1415	12.5227	12.9159	13.3214	13.7396	14.1708	14.6153	15.0735	15.5458	16.0324	16.5339	17.0506	17.5828
8	14.2401	14.7733	15.3270	15.9020	16.4991	17.1189	17.7623	18.4300	19.1228	19.8419	20.5876	21.3612	22.1634	22.9953	23.8577
9	17.5185	18.2847	19.0859	19.9234	20.7989	21.7139	22.6700	23.6690	24.7125	25.8023	26.9404	28.1287	29.3692	30.6639	32.0150
10	21.3215	22.3931	23.5213	24.7089	25.9587	27.2738	28.6574	30.1128	31.6434	33.2529	34.9449	36.7235	38.5926	40.5564	42.6195
11	25.7329	27.1999	28.7551	30.4035	32.1504	34.0013	35.9620	38.0388	40.2379	42.5661	45.0306	47.6388	50.3985	53.3178	56.4053
12	30.8502	32.8239	34.9311	37.1802	39.5805	42.1416	44.8737	47.7877	50.8950	54.2077	57.7386	61.5013	65.5100	69.7800	74.3270
13	36.7862	39.4040	42.2187	45.2445	48.4966	51.9913	55.7459	59.7788	64.1097	68.7596	73.7506	79.1066	84.8529	91.0161	97.6250
14	43.6720	47.1027	50.8180	54.8409	59.1959	63.9095	69.0100	74.5280	80.4961	86.9495	93.9258	101.4654	109.6117	118.4108	127.9125
15	51.6595	56.1101	60.9653	66.2607	72.0351	78.3305	85.1922	92.8694	100.8151	109.6868	119.3465	129.8611	141.3028	153.7500	167.2863
16	60.9250	66.6488	72.9390	79.8502	87.4421	95.7799	104.9345	114.9834	126.0108	138.1085	151.3766	165.9236	181.8677	199.3374	218.4722
17	71.6730	78.9792	87.0680	96.0218	105.9306	116.8937	129.0201	142.4295	157.2534	173.6357	191.7345	211.7230	233.7907	251.1453	285.0139
18	84.1407	93.4056	103.7403	115.2659	128.1167	142.4413	158.4045	176.1883	195.9942	218.0446	242.5855	289.8882	300.2521	335.0074	371.5180
19	96.6032	110.2846	123.4135	138.1664	154.7400	173.3540	194.2535	217.7116	244.0328	273.5558	306.6577	343.7580	385.3277	431.8695	493.9734
20	115.3797	130.0329	146.6280	165.4180	186.6880	210.7584	237.9893	268.7853	303.6008	342.9447	387.3887	437.5726	494.2131	558.1118	630.1655
25	249.2140	292.1048	342.6035	402.0425	471.9811	554.2422	650.9551	764.6054	898.0916	1054.7912	1236.6363	1454.2014	1706.8031	2002.6156	2348.8033

324

Table 5 Sinking Fund: $\dfrac{r}{(1+r)^n - 1}$

Year (n)	Interest rates (r)														
	0.01	0.02	0.03	0.04	0.05	0.06	0.07	0.08	0.09	0.10	0.11	0.12	0.13	0.14	0.15
1	1.0000	1.0000	1.0000	1.0000	1.0000	1.0000	1.0000	1.0000	1.0000	1.0000	1.0000	1.0000	1.0000	1.0000	1.0000
2	0.4975	0.4950	0.4926	0.4902	0.4878	0.4854	0.4831	0.4808	0.4785	0.4762	0.4739	0.4717	0.4695	0.4673	0.4651
3	0.3300	0.3268	0.3235	0.3203	0.3172	0.3141	0.3111	0.3080	0.3051	0.3021	0.2992	0.2963	0.2935	0.2907	0.2880
4	0.2463	0.2426	0.2390	0.2355	0.2320	0.2286	0.2252	0.2219	0.2187	0.2155	0.2123	0.2092	0.2062	0.2032	0.2003
5	0.1960	0.1922	0.1884	0.1846	0.1810	0.1774	0.1739	0.1705	0.1671	0.1638	0.1606	0.1574	0.1543	0.1513	0.1483
6	0.1625	0.1585	0.1546	0.1508	0.1470	0.1434	0.1398	0.1363	0.1329	0.1296	0.1264	0.1232	0.1202	0.1172	0.1142
7	0.1386	0.1345	0.1305	0.1266	0.1228	0.1191	0.1156	0.1121	0.1087	0.1054	0.1022	0.0991	0.0961	0.0932	0.0904
8	0.1207	0.1165	0.1125	0.1085	0.1047	0.1010	0.0975	0.0940	0.0907	0.0874	0.0843	0.0813	0.0784	0.0756	0.0729
9	0.1067	0.1025	0.0984	0.0945	0.0907	0.0870	0.0835	0.0801	0.0768	0.0736	0.0706	0.0677	0.0649	0.0622	0.0596
10	0.0956	0.0913	0.0872	0.0833	0.0795	0.0759	0.0724	0.0690	0.0658	0.0627	0.0598	0.0570	0.0543	0.0517	0.0403
11	0.0865	0.0822	0.0781	0.0741	0.0704	0.0668	0.0614	0.0601	0.0569	0.0540	0.0511	0.0484	0.0458	0.0434	0.0411
12	0.0788	0.0746	0.0705	0.0666	0.0628	0.0593	0.0569	0.0527	0.0497	0.0468	0.0440	0.0414	0.0390	0.0367	0.0345
13	0.0724	0.0681	0.0640	0.0601	0.0565	0.0530	0.0497	0.0465	0.0436	0.0408	0.0382	0.0357	0.0334	0.0312	0.0291
14	0.0669	0.0626	0.0585	0.0547	0.0510	0.0476	0.0443	0.0413	0.0384	0.0357	0.0332	0.0309	0.0287	0.0266	0.0247
15	0.0621	0.0578	0.0538	0.0499	0.0463	0.0430	0.0398	0.0368	0.0341	0.0315	0.0291	0.0268	0.0247	0.0228	0.0210
16	0.0579	0.0537	0.0496	0.0458	0.0423	0.0390	0.0359	0.0330	0.0303	0.0278	0.0255	0.0234	0.0214	0.0196	0.0179
17	0.0543	0.0500	0.0460	0.0422	0.0387	0.0354	0.0324	0.0296	0.0270	0.0247	0.0226	0.0205	0.0186	0.0169	0.0154
18	0.0510	0.0467	0.0427	0.0390	0.0355	0.0324	0.0294	0.0267	0.0242	0.0219	0.0198	0.0179	0.0162	0.0146	0.0132
19	0.0481	0.0438	0.0398	0.0361	0.0327	0.0296	0.0268	0.0241	0.0217	0.0196	0.0176	0.0158	0.0141	0.0127	0.0113
20	0.0454	0.0412	0.0372	0.0336	0.0302	0.0272	0.0244	0.0219	0.0195	0.0175	0.0156	0.0139	0.0124	0.0110	0.0098
21	0.0430	0.0388	0.0349	0.0313	0.0280	0.0250	0.0223	0.0198	0.0176	0.0156	0.0138	0.0122	0.0108	0.0095	0.0084
22	0.0409	0.0366	0.0327	0.0292	0.0260	0.0230	0.0204	0.0180	0.0159	0.0140	0.0123	0.0108	0.0095	0.0083	0.0073
23	0.0389	0.0347	0.0308	0.0273	0.0241	0.0213	0.0187	0.0164	0.0144	0.0126	0.0110	0.0096	0.0083	0.0072	0.0063
24	0.0371	0.0329	0.0290	0.0256	0.0225	0.0187	0.0172	0.0150	0.0130	0.0113	0.0096	0.0085	0.0073	0.0063	0.0054
25	0.0354	0.0312	0.0274	0.0240	0.0210	0.0182	0.0158	0.0137	0.0118	0.0102	0.0087	0.0075	0.0064	0.0055	0.0047

Table 5 (contd.)

	0.16	0.17	0.18	0.19	0.20	0.21	0.22	0.23	0.24	0.25	0.26	0.27	0.28	0.29	0.30
1	1.0000	1.0000	1.0000	1.0000	1.0000	1.0000	1.0000	1.0000	1.0000	1.0000	1.0000	1.0000	1.0000	1.0000	1.0000
2	0.4630	0.4608	0.4587	0.4566	0.4545	0.4525	0.4505	0.4484	0.4464	0.4444	0.4425	0.4405	0.4386	0.4367	0.4348
3	0.2853	0.2826	0.2799	0.2773	0.2747	0.2722	0.2697	0.2672	0.2647	0.2623	0.2599	0.2575	0.2552	0.2529	0.2506
4	0.1974	0.1945	0.1917	0.1890	0.1863	0.1836	0.1810	0.1785	0.1759	0.1734	0.1710	0.1686	0.1662	0.1639	0.1616
5	0.1454	0.1426	0.1398	0.1371	0.1344	0.1318	0.1292	0.1267	0.1242	0.1218	0.1195	0.1172	0.1149	0.1127	0.1106
6	0.1114	0.1086	0.1059	0.1033	0.1007	0.0982	0.0968	0.0934	0.0911	0.0888	0.0866	0.0845	0.0824	0.0804	0.0784
7	0.0876	0.0849	0.0824	0.0799	0.0774	0.0751	0.0728	0.0706	0.0684	0.0663	0.0643	0.0624	0.0605	0.0586	0.0569
8	0.0702	0.0677	0.0652	0.0629	0.0606	0.0584	0.0563	0.0543	0.0523	0.0504	0.0486	0.0468	0.0451	0.0435	0.0419
9	0.0571	0.0547	0.0524	0.0502	0.0481	0.0461	0.0441	0.0422	0.0405	0.0388	0.0371	0.0356	0.0340	0.0326	0.0312
10	0.0469	0.0447	0.0425	0.0405	0.0385	0.0367	0.0349	0.0332	0.0316	0.0301	0.0286	0.0272	0.0269	0.0247	0.0235
11	0.0389	0.0368	0.0348	0.0329	0.0311	0.0294	0.0278	0.0263	0.0249	0.0235	0.0222	0.0210	0.0198	0.0188	0.0177
12	0.0324	0.0305	0.0286	0.0269	0.0253	0.0237	0.0223	0.0209	0.0196	0.0184	0.0173	0.0163	0.0153	0.0143	0.0135
13	0.0272	0.0254	0.0237	0.0221	0.0206	0.0192	0.0179	0.0167	0.0156	0.0145	0.0136	0.0126	0.0118	0.0110	0.0102
14	0.0229	0.0212	0.0197	0.0182	0.0169	0.0156	0.0145	0.0134	0.0124	0.0115	0.0106	0.0099	0.0091	0.0084	0.0078
15	0.0194	0.0178	0.0164	0.0151	0.0139	0.0128	0.0117	0.0108	0.0099	0.0091	0.0084	0.0077	0.0071	0.0065	0.0060
16	0.0164	0.0150	0.0137	0.0125	0.0114	0.0104	0.0095	0.0087	0.0079	0.0072	0.0065	0.0060	0.0055	0.0050	0.0046
17	0.0140	0.0127	0.0115	0.0104	0.0094	0.0086	0.0078	0.0070	0.0064	0.0058	0.0052	0.0047	0.0043	0.0039	0.0035
18	0.0119	0.0107	0.0096	0.0087	0.0078	0.0070	0.0063	0.0057	0.0051	0.0046	0.0041	0.0037	0.0033	0.0030	0.0027
19	0.0101	0.0091	0.0081	0.0072	0.0065	0.0058	0.0051	0.0046	0.0041	0.0037	0.0033	0.0029	0.0026	0.0023	0.0021
20	0.0087	0.0077	0.0068	0.0060	0.0054	0.0047	0.0042	0.0037	0.0033	0.0029	0.0026	0.0023	0.0020	0.0018	0.0016
21	0.0074	0.0065	0.0057	0.0051	0.0044	0.0039	0.0034	0.0030	0.0026	0.0023	0.0020	0.0018	0.0016	0.0014	0.0012
22	0.0064	0.0056	0.0048	0.0042	0.0037	0.0032	0.0028	0.0024	0.0021	0.0019	0.0016	0.0014	0.0012	0.0011	0.0009
23	0.0054	0.0047	0.0041	0.0035	0.0031	0.0027	0.0023	0.0020	0.0017	0.0015	0.0013	0.0011	0.0010	0.0008	0.0007
24	0.0047	0.0040	0.0035	0.0030	0.0025	0.0022	0.0019	0.0016	0.0014	0.0012	0.0010	0.0009	0.0008	0.0006	0.0006
25	0.0040	0.0034	0.0029	0.0025	0.0021	0.0018	0.0015	0.0013	0.0011	0.0009	0.0008	0.0007	0.0006	0.0005	0.0004

Table 6 Annual Equivalent Annuity $\dfrac{r}{1-(1+r)^{-n}}$

Years (n)	Interest rates (r)														
	0.01	0.02	0.03	0.04	0.05	0.06	0.07	0.08	0.09	0.10	0.11	0.12	0.13	0.14	0.15
1	1.0100	1.0200	1.0300	1.0400	1.0500	1.0600	1.0700	1.0800	1.0900	1.1000	1.1100	1.1200	1.1300	1.1400	1.1500
2	0.5076	0.5150	0.5226	0.5302	0.5378	0.5454	0.5531	0.5608	0.5685	0.5762	0.5839	0.5917	0.5995	0.6073	0.6151
3	0.3400	0.3468	0.3535	0.3603	0.3672	0.3741	0.3811	0.3880	0.3951	0.4021	0.4092	0.4163	0.4235	0.4307	0.4380
4	0.2563	0.2626	0.2690	0.2755	0.2820	0.2886	0.2952	0.3019	0.3087	0.3155	0.3223	0.3292	0.3362	0.3432	0.3503
5	0.2060	0.2122	0.2184	0.2246	0.2310	0.2374	0.2439	0.2505	0.2571	0.2638	0.2706	0.2774	0.2843	0.2913	0.2983
6	0.1725	0.1785	0.1846	0.1908	0.1970	0.2034	0.2098	0.2163	0.2229	0.2296	0.2364	0.2432	0.2502	0.2572	0.2642
7	0.1486	0.1545	0.1605	0.1666	0.1728	0.1791	0.1856	0.1921	0.1987	0.2054	0.2122	0.2191	0.2261	0.2332	0.2404
8	0.1307	0.1365	0.1425	0.1485	0.1547	0.1610	0.1675	0.1740	0.1807	0.1874	0.1943	0.2013	0.2084	0.2156	0.2229
9	0.1167	0.1225	0.1284	0.1345	0.1407	0.1470	0.1535	0.1601	0.1668	0.1736	0.1806	0.1877	0.1949	0.2022	0.2090
10	0.1056	0.1113	0.1172	0.1233	0.1295	0.1359	0.1424	0.1490	0.1558	0.1627	0.1698	0.1770	0.1843	0.1917	0.1993
11	0.0965	0.1022	0.1081	0.1141	0.1204	0.1268	0.1334	0.1401	0.1469	0.1540	0.1611	0.1684	0.1758	0.1834	0.1911
12	0.0888	0.0946	0.1005	0.1066	0.1128	0.1193	0.1259	0.1327	0.1397	0.1468	0.1540	0.1614	0.1690	0.1767	0.1845
13	0.0824	0.0881	0.0940	0.1001	0.1065	0.1130	0.1197	0.1265	0.1336	0.1408	0.1482	0.1557	0.1634	0.1712	0.1791
14	0.0769	0.0826	0.0885	0.947	0.1010	0.1076	0.1143	0.1213	0.1284	0.1357	0.1432	0.1509	0.1587	0.1666	0.1747
15	0.0721	0.0778	0.0838	0.0899	0.0963	0.1030	0.1098	0.1168	0.1241	0.1315	0.1391	0.1468	0.1547	0.1628	0.1710
16	0.0679	0.0737	0.0796	0.0858	0.0923	0.0990	0.1059	0.1130	0.1203	0.1278	0.1355	0.1434	0.1514	0.1596	0.1678
17	0.0643	0.0700	0.0760	0.0822	0.0887	0.0954	0.1024	0.1096	0.1170	0.1247	0.1325	0.1405	0.1486	0.1569	0.1654
18	0.0610	0.0667	0.0727	0.0790	0.0855	0.0924	0.0994	0.1067	0.1142	0.1219	0.1298	0.1379	0.1462	0.1546	0.1632
19	0.0581	0.0638	0.0698	0.0761	0.0827	0.0896	0.0968	0.1041	0.1117	0.1195	0.1276	0.1358	0.1441	0.1527	0.1613
20	0.0554	0.0612	0.0672	0.0736	0.0802	0.0872	0.0944	0.1019	0.1095	0.1175	0.1256	0.1339	0.1424	0.1510	0.1598
21	0.0530	0.0588	0.0649	0.0713	0.0780	0.0850	0.0923	0.0998	0.1076	0.1156	0.1238	0.1322	0.1408	0.1495	0.1584
22	0.0509	0.0566	0.0627	0.0692	0.0760	0.0830	0.0904	0.0980	0.1059	0.1140	0.1223	0.1308	0.1395	0.1483	0.1573
23	0.0489	0.0547	0.0608	0.0673	0.0741	0.0813	0.0887	0.0964	0.1044	0.1126	0.1210	0.1296	0.1383	0.1472	0.1563
24	0.0471	0.0529	0.0590	0.0656	0.0725	0.0797	0.0872	0.0950	0.1030	0.1113	0.1198	0.1285	0.1373	0.1463	0.1554
25	0.0454	0.0512	0.0574	0.0640	0.0710	0.0782	0.0858	0.0937	0.1018	0.1102	0.1187	0.1275	0.1364	0.1455	0.1547

Table 6 (contd.)

	0.16	0.17	0.18	0.19	0.20	0.21	0.22	0.23	0.24	0.25	0.26	0.27	0.28	0.29	0.30
1	1.1600	1.1700	1.1800	1.1900	1.2000	1.2100	1.2200	1.2300	1.2400	1.2500	1.2600	1.2700	1.2800	1.2900	1.3000
2	0.6230	0.6308	0.6387	0.6466	0.6545	0.6625	0.6705	0.6784	0.6864	0.6944	0.7025	0.7105	0.7185	0.7267	0.7348
3	0.4453	0.4526	0.4599	0.4673	0.4747	0.4822	0.4897	0.4972	0.5047	0.5123	0.5199	0.5275	0.5352	0.5429	0.5506
4	0.3574	0.3645	0.3717	0.3790	0.3863	0.3936	0.4010	0.4085	0.4159	0.4234	0.4310	0.4386	0.4462	0.4539	0.4616
5	0.3054	0.3126	0.3198	0.3271	0.3344	0.3418	0.3492	0.3567	0.3642	0.3718	0.3795	0.3872	0.3949	0.4027	0.4106
6	0.2714	0.2786	0.2859	0.2933	0.3007	0.3082	0.3158	0.3234	0.3311	0.3388	0.3466	0.3545	0.3624	0.3704	0.3784
7	0.2476	0.2549	0.2624	0.2699	0.2774	0.2851	0.2928	0.3006	0.3084	0.3163	0.3243	0.3324	0.3405	0.3486	0.3569
8	0.2302	0.2377	0.2452	0.2529	0.2606	0.2684	0.2763	0.2843	0.2923	0.3004	0.3086	0.3168	0.3251	0.3335	0.3312
9	0.2171	0.2247	0.2324	0.2402	0.2481	0.2561	0.2641	0.2722	0.2805	0.2888	0.2971	0.3056	0.3140	0.3226	0.3419
10	0.2069	0.2147	0.225	0.2305	0.2385	0.2467	0.2549	0.2632	0.2716	0.2801	0.2886	0.2972	0.3059	0.3147	0.3235
11	0.1989	0.2068	0.2148	0.2229	0.2311	0.2394	0.2478	0.2563	0.2649	0.2736	0.2822	0.2910	0.2998	0.3088	0.3177
12	0.1924	0.2005	0.2086	0.2169	0.2263	0.2337	0.2423	0.2509	0.0596	0.2684	0.2773	0.2863	0.2963	0.3043	0.3135
13	0.1872	0.1954	0.2037	0.2121	0.2206	0.2292	0.2379	0.2467	0.2556	0.2645	0.2736	0.2826	0.2918	0.3010	0.3102
14	0.1829	0.1912	0.1997	0.2082	0.2169	0.2256	0.2345	0.2434	0.2524	0.2615	0.2706	0.2799	0.2891	0.2984	0.3078
15	0.1794	0.1878	0.1964	0.2051	0.2139	0.2228	0.2317	0.2408	0.2499	0.2591	0.2684	0.2777	0.2871	0.2965	0.3060
16	0.1764	0.1850	0.1937	0.2025	0.2114	0.2204	0.2295	0.2387	0.2479	0.2572	0.2666	0.2760	0.2855	0.2950	0.3046
17	0.1740	0.1827	0.1915	0.2004	0.2094	0.2186	0.2278	0.2370	0.2464	0.2558	0.2652	0.2747	0.2843	0.2939	0.3035
18	0.1719	0.1807	0.1896	0.1987	0.2078	0.2170	0.2263	0.2357	0.2451	0.2546	0.2641	0.2737	0.2833	0.2930	0.3027
19	0.1701	0.1791	0.1881	0.1972	0.2065	0.2158	0.2251	0.2346	0.2441	0.2537	0.2633	0.2729	0.2826	0.2923	0.3021
20	0.1687	0.1777	0.1868	0.1960	0.2054	0.2147	0.2242	0.2337	0.2433	0.2529	0.2626	0.2723	0.2820	0.2918	0.3016
21	0.1674	0.1765	0.1857	0.1961	0.2044	0.2139	0.2234	0.2330	0.2426	0.2523	0.2620	0.2718	0.2816	0.2914	0.3012
22	0.1664	0.1756	0.1848	0.1942	0.2037	0.2132	0.2228	0.2324	0.2421	0.2519	0.2616	0.2714	0.2812	0.2911	0.3009
23	0.1654	0.1747	0.1841	0.1935	0.2031	0.2127	0.2223	0.2320	0.2417	0.2519	0.2613	0.2711	0.2810	0.2908	0.3007
24	0.1647	0.1740	0.1835	0.1930	0.2025	0.2122	0.2219	0.2316	0.2414	0.2512	0.2610	0.2709	0.2808	0.2906	0.3006
25	0.1640	0.1734	0.1829	0.1925	0.2021	0.2118	0.2215	0.2313	0.2411	0.2509	0.2608	0.2707	0.2806	0.2905	0.3004

Index

absorption costing 7, 187
  compared with direct costing 52, 53, 193–4, 195
Alchian, A. A. 124
  and Demsetz, H. 2
  defines cost 1n
Amicucci, D. J. 251n
Arditti, F. D. 285n

Baumol, W. J. 5, 126n
  and Burton, G. M. 285n
  and Bushnell, R. C. 271
Becker, S. and Green, D., Jr 228, 230
Bierman, H. 38
Bower, R. S. and Lessard, D. R. 308n
budgetary control 218
  controllable and uncontrollable cost 220
  evaluation of performance and 228
  feedback information 218–19, 229
  human problems of 228–9
  management by exception 220, 227
  variance analysis 220–2, 229 (absorption of fixed overhead 225; causes of variance 228; fixed overhead variance 225; nature of overhead variance 224; price and quantity variance 222–3; rationale of variance calculation 227–8; report format 220, 229; usefulness 219; variable overhead variance 224; variance calculation by adjusting budget 225–7)
budgetary planning 198, 200n, 206
  principal budget factor 199
budgets 198
  capital expenditure budgets 201, 207
  cash budget 202, 207
  factory expense budget 201, 207
  flexibility and standard costing 240–1, 251
  inventory budgets 201, 207
  labour budget 201, 207
  master budget 202–6, 207
  preparation 199
  principal budget factor 199
  production budget 200, 207
  rationale 199
  raw material purchasing budget 201, 207
  role of sales forecasts 200, 206
  sales budget 200, 207
  selling and distribution cost budget 200
  uncertainty in 198n, 200n
by-products 83
  costing 84–5

capital budgeting 201, 276
  analysis of investment decisions 290 (accounting rate of return method 293–4, 301; determining multiple IRR 299–301; discounted pay-back method 301; internal rate of return (IRR) method 297, 301, 302; net present value (NPV) method 294–6, 301, 302; pay-back method 290–3, 301, 302; profitability index (PI) method 296–7, 301, 302; unequal net cash flows 298–9)
  capital recovery 282
  compound interest 277–9
  future value of annuity 279–80
  present value 280–1
  risk and uncertainty in 308, 313–14 (absolute measures of dispersion 309–11; decision-maker's utility function 311–13; expected value of probability distribution 308–9; risk defined 308; uncertainty defined 308)
  sinking fund payments 280
  timing of projects 276–7
Carsberg, B. 308
Charnes, A. et al. 157n
Coase, R. H. 2
Cocoran, A. W. 118n
cost accounting
  defined 1
  main features 257
  purpose of 3–4
  scope of 7
  tools of 7–8
cost allocation 46–7
  extension via linear programming 103–5
  purpose of 47
  service cost allocation to production departments 97

cost allocation – *continued*
    (by 'step method' 97, 99–103; to production departments only 97, 98–9)
cost behaviour 124
    fixed costs 126–7
    learning curve 129–32, 133
    patterns of typical cost functions 124–6, 133
    semi-variable cost 127–9
    step costs 126
cost estimation 136
    account analysis method 137, 147
    constructing total cost function of firm 136–7, 147
    derivation of accountant's cost function 138
    engineering approach 137, 147
    high–low method 138–9, 147
    regression analysis 140, 147 (analysis of variance and F test 147; derivation and use of variance/covariance matrix 146; multiple regression 140n; regression theory 145–6; simple regression 141–4; standard error 144–5)
    scatter charts 139–40, 147
cost–volume–profit (C–V–P) analysis 150–1, 162, 195
    break-even analysis 156–9
    break-even models 151–2, 155–6
    marginal contribution to sales ratio (MCSR) 152–3, 162
    multi-product case 153–5, 162
    short-period economic model 159–60
    similarities and dissimilarities of accountant's and economist's graph 160–2
    variable cost ratio (VCR) 153, 162
costs
    cost centres 5, 6
    cost units 5, 7, 42
    defined 1n
    differential 169–70
    direct 6, 42
    elements of 6
    fixed 5, 126–7, 180
    historical 7
    indirect 6
    overhead *see separate entry*
    standard 7–8
    variable 5
    see also relevant costs for decisions
Cyert, R. M. and March, J. G. 229

decision-makers
    attitudes to risks 311
    requirements of 187–8 (contribution model 188, 189–90; report format 188; report structures 188–9)
    utility function 310, 311–13
decisions
    decision accounting 3–4
    relevant costs for *see* relevant costs for decisions
direct costing 52, 53, 187
    compared with absorption costing 193–4, 195
    model 192–3
    use of 194
direct materials, accounting for 38–9, 53
Dopuch, N. *et al.* 138
    on learning curve 129, 251

Farag, S. M. 22n

firm, the
    budgetary planning in 198n
    defined 1
    importance of costing to 2
    instrumental nature of 198n
    objectives 4–5
    organisation chart 2–3, 4
    rationale for existence 2
Fisch, G. G. 2n
forecasting 200n
    sales 200

Gambling, Prof. T. E. 22n, 229
Gould, J. R. 257

Hendriksen, E. S. 1, 187
Hillier, F. S. 308n
Hohn, F. E. 21n
Horngren, C. T. 76, 109, 169, 187, 297n
    on budgeting 198

Ijiri, Y. 22n, 194
Institute of Cost and Management Accountants (ICMA) 89n, 233
    defines conversion cost 61n
inventory planning 109–10
    budgets 201
    costs of inventories 111
    Economic Order Quantity (EOQ) model 12, 110, 111, 119 (and quantity discounts 114–15; derivation of 111–14)
    inventory definitions 110–11
    model – fixed re-order level 110, 111
    production runs and 115–17
    ratios used as guides 109–10
    under probabilistic demand 117–19
inventory valuation 190–1
    problems of 191–2
issue pricing methods 13–17
    evaluation of 17–18
    FIFO 13, 14, 17–18, 19
    LIFO 13, 15, 18, 19
    standard price 13, 15–16, 18, 19
    weighted average cost 13, 16–17, 18, 19

Jaedicke, R. K. and Robichek, A. A. 157
job costing 57–8, 78, 85
    cost sheet 58
    mechanics of 58–61 (factory ledger entries 61, 62, 63)
    reports on completed jobs 64
    use of direct or absorption costing 61
    use of standard costing 61, 64
joint product costing 57, 78–9, 85
    methods 79–82
    reasons for 79
    unsuitable in management decision-making 82–3

Kant, Immanuel 21
Kaplan, R. and Thompson, G. L. 103
Keane, S. M. 285n
Knight, F. H. 2
Kohler, F. L. 57
Kosiol, E. E. 136

Index

labour
  accounting for direct 39–40, 53 (job cards 39, 40; job tickets 39; time booking 39; timekeeping 39; timesheets 39)
  budget 201
  remuneration 40–2
  setting standard cost 236–9 *passim*
learning curve 129–32, 133
Lemke, C. E. 265
Leontief, W. W. 22n
Lev, Baruch 110n
Lewis, J. P. 21n
linear programming 257, 271
  algebraic method 263–4
  assumptions 258
  conditions for effectiveness 258
  dual model 264–5 (algorithm 265–6; economic significance 267)
  extension of cost allocation via 103–5
  general form of model 258–60
  need for feasible solution 260
  parametric programming 269–71
  sensitivity analysis 267–9, 271
  simplex format 260–1, 264 (procedures 261–2; solution process 263)
Longbottom, D. and Wiper, L. 299

marginal costing 7, 287–8
Manes, R. 157n
Marple, R. P. 47, 47n
Marris, R. L. 5
material control 10–13
  accounting for direct 38–9
  issue to production 13
  purchasing 10–11
  reception 10, 11
  setting standard cost 235–9 *passim*
  stock control 10, 11–12
  storage 10, 11
matrices 21
  definition 21–2, 31
  determinant of 27
  equation and inverse systems compared 30–1
  identity matrix 27
  inverse of upper triangular input–output 32–4
  inversion 28–9
  multiplication of 24–6
  sub-matrices 22
  subtraction of 24
  transposition of 26
  vectors 23–4
Merrett, A. J. and Sykes, A. 291
Moore, C. L. and Jaedicke, R. K. 16n, 136
Morrison, T. A. and Kaczka, E. 157n
Morse, W. J. 132n
Most, K. S. 10

Nakanishi, A. 21n
National Association of Accountants, defines internal rate of return 297
Nielson, N. C. 308n
Noble, C. E. 251
Nurnberg, H. 139

opportunity cost 104n, 173, 257
  internal 175–6

organisation chart 2–3, 4
overheads 42, 53
  absorption of fixed 225
  absorption rate 48–50 (predetermined (POHR) 50, 51–2, 53)
  accumulation 43–4
  apportionment 44–6, 53
  arguments for and against absorption bases 50
  in standard costing 237–8, 239, 241–6
  purpose of overhead rates 42–3
  use of multiple rates 47–8
  variance of 224–5
Pacioli, Luca 21n
performance evaluation and review techniques (PERT) 64
Phelps, E. S. 308n
Phyrr, P. A. 229
Pichler, O. 250n
process costing 57, 65, 78, 85
  application of standards to 76–7
  concept of equivalent production 69–72
  concept of losses in production 73–6
  functions 65
  procedures 65–9 (abnormal spoilage 65–6, 86–9; factory ledger entries 68; normal spoilage 65)
profit, adequate 5n
project financing 284
  cost of capital 284–5, 287–8
  cost of debt 286–7
  cost of equity 285–6
  depreciation as tax deductible 284
  retained earnings 286

Qureshi, M. 189

relevant costs for decisions 169, 180
  and book values 176–80
  concepts impinging on decisions 169–70
  decisions with one scarce resource 173–5
  fixed cost 180
  internal opportunity cost 175–6
  types of decision (accept or reject 169; make or buy 170; ranking 170–3)
Rickwood C. P. 29
Ronen, J. 199n

St Luke, on standard costing 223
Samuels, J. M. and Wilkes, F. M. 292
Schiff, M. and Lewin, A. Y. 229
scrap 72–3n
Shackle, G. L. S. 284
shadow price 104n, 267
Simon, H. A. 5
Skinner, F. 229
Sprouse, R. T. and Moonitz, M., define cost 1n
standard costing 233
  control ratios and 246–8
  flexible budget and 251 (advantages 240; mechanics of 240–1; overheads and 241–3)
  mechanics of 234
  overheads (analysis of fixed 241–3; application of 243–4; base for measurement 241; fixed overheads variance analysis 244–6; setting variable 237–8, 239)
  rationale of 234–5

standard costing – *continued*
  setting of standard cost 235, 251 (direct labour 236–7, 238, 239; direct material 235–6, 237, 238, 239)
  types of standard cost 233–4 (attainable 235, 251; basic 235, 251; ideal 235, 251)
  use for job costing 61, 64
  variance analysis (and 'blame laying' 250–1; causes of variance 239–40; fixed overhead 244–6; technical firms' 248–50)
Stedry, A. C. 228

Taha, H. A. 109
Tannenbaum, A. S. 218
Theodore, C. A. 21n, 130n
  on learning-curve technique 124
Tosi, H. 199n

unit costing 57, 65, 67, 69

Van Horne, J. C. 308n
  on capital budgeting 276

variance analysis
  and 'blame laying' 250–1
  in budgetary control 219–29
  in overheads 224, 225, 244–6
  in standard costing 239–40, 244–6, 248–51
  in technical firms 248–50
Vatter, W. J., on investment 290
Vickers, D. 150

Walgenbach, P. H. *et al.* 57
Weingartner, H. M. 291
Werner, F. and Manes, R. 250
Williams, T. H. and Griffin, C. H. 97
Williamson, J. H. 5
Winkler, R. L. 311n
Wonnacott, R. J. and T. H. 141n

Yamey, B. S. 187

GPSR Compliance
The European Union's (EU) General Product Safety Regulation (GPSR) is a set of rules that requires consumer products to be safe and our obligations to ensure this.

If you have any concerns about our products, you can contact us on

ProductSafety@springernature.com

In case Publisher is established outside the EU, the EU authorized representative is:

Springer Nature Customer Service Center GmbH
Europaplatz 3
69115 Heidelberg, Germany

www.ingramcontent.com/pod-product-compliance
Ingram Content Group UK Ltd.
Pitfield, Milton Keynes, MK11 3LW, UK
UKHW051258180426
11947UKWH00020B/1783